ST ANNE'S ON THE SEA

St Anne's on the Sea

A history

PETER SHAKESHAFT

Other town and city histories available from Carnegie:

Graham Davis and Penny Bonsall, *A History of Bath: Image and Reality* (2006);
Derek Beattie, *Blackburn* (2007);   David Hey, *A History of Sheffield* (new edn,
2005);   Alan Kidd, *Manchester*;   John K. Walton, *Blackpool*;
Andrew White (ed.), A *History of Lancaster*;   John A. Hargreaves, *Halifax*

Forthcoming town and city histories:

Mark Freeman, *St Albans*;   Carl Chinn, *Birmingham*;   Andrew White, *Kendal*;
Trevor Rowley, *Oxford*;   Evelyn Lord, *Cambridge*;   John Doran, *Chester*;
W. Sheils, *York*;   Jeremy Black, *London*;   W. Maguire, *Belfast*;
John A. Hargreaves, *Huddersfield*;   Fred Gray, *Brighton*; Joan Dils, *Reading*;
Richard Rodger (ed.), *Leicester*;   Anthea Jones, *Cheltenham*;
Joan and Richard Allen, *Newcastle*;   David Hunt, *Preston*;   Andrew Walker, *Lincoln*

Of related interest:

Malcolm Greenhalgh: *The Ribble: a local and natural history* (2008)

Full details on www.carnegiepublishing.com

St Anne's on the Sea: A history

Copyright © Peter Shakeshaft 2008

First edition published in 2008 by
Carnegie Publishing Ltd
Carnegie House, Chatsworth Road,
Lancaster LA1 4SL
www.carnegiepublishing.com

ISBN 978-1-85936-159-7 (*hardback*)
ISBN 978-1-85936-182-5 (*softback*)

British Library Cataloguing-in-Publication data
A catalogue record for this book is available from the British Library

Designed, typeset and originated by Carnegie Publishing
Printed by Progress Press, Malta

Contents

Acknowledgements

In writing this history of Heyhouses and St Anne's on the Sea I have been helped by many people in different ways. I especially thank my wife Maureen who has assisted me throughout the research and writing of the book. For his constant encouragement, guidance, and advice I would like to thank Dr A. Crosby. I am most grateful to Mr J. A. Hilton, Lord of the Manor of Lytham, for allowing me unlimited access to former Clifton family papers, including previously uncatalogued material, now deposited at the Lancashire Record Office.

I thank Mrs M. Coupe for her support and enthusiasm. I also thank Mrs S. Allen, former archivist to Lytham Heritage Group, and her colleagues, for their efforts to locate relevant documents. I readily acknowledge the assistance of Mr B. Jackson, the County Archivist, and the staff of the Lancashire Record Office from where much of the material used has been drawn. The assistance of Mrs P. Virgo, and the staff of St Anne's Library has also been much appreciated.

Many of the photographs and illustrations have come from private collections. Ownership of each photograph/illustration is credited in the text and I am grateful for being allowed to reproduce them. I apologise if I have unknowingly infringed copyright in the use of any of these photographs.

I would like to thank the staff at Carnegie Publishing for an excellent production. With regard to the actual text, while every effort has been made to ensure that all the facts are correct any errors are entirely my own. Finally I hope you will have as much pleasure in reading this book about the town where I was born as I have had in writing it.

Pre-industrial Fylde: a section of Robert Morden's map of Lancashire which was surveyed and published in the 1720s. Neither Martin Mere nor Marton Mere had yet been drained; the Ribble estuary (the 'Aestuarium Bellisama') had not yet been improved for navigation; relatively few roads traversed the county (only the main road north to Scotland can be seen on this section of the map). Contiguous to the area that was later to become St Anne's the ancient settlements of Kirkham and Lytham are shown, as well as the smaller settlements at Freckleton, Bryning and Westby.
CARNEGIE COLLECTION

Glossary

amercement	A fine paid in a manorial court.
appurtenances	The rights and duties appended to an agreement over holding land attached to a house.
bloodwipe	A fine for bloodshed.
boon service	Seasonal manorial labour services performed by tenants such as harvesting or ploughing.
compoti	manorial accounts.
court baron	Assembly of the freehold tenants of a manor under the direction of the lord or his steward where in addition to manorial administration changes in tenancy were recorded.
court leet	Court held in the manor before the lord or his steward where the local bye-laws were enforced. Usually held at the same time as the court baron.
demesne	Belonging to the lord of the manor. A lord's demesne consisted of those manorial lands which were reserved for his personal benefit and on which the tenants gave free service.
depasture	To use for pasture.
distraint	Seizure of goods or animals for debt or other reason.
flat	A portion of the common field following its division.
headroom	A gutter or passage for water. The term 'headroom or gutter' occurs in the Lytham Manorial Court proceedings for 5 October 1709.
hey	An enclosure of land.
inmate	A person admitted to dwell for their money jointly with another person.
messuage	Dwelling House and its appurtenances.
moiety	Half share.

quitclaim	Disclaimer of rights, interest, and potential legal action from a grantor to a grantee.
rack rent	Practice by landowners of offering annual agreements rather than long term leases to their tenants.
recusant	A person who declined to attend his or her parish church. After 1570 the term usually applied to Roman Catholics but could apply to any non-conformist.
settlement	Not just the buildings but also the land which supported it.
stint	To regulate the number of livestock to graze on a common.
tithe	A tax of one tenth, specifically a tenth part of the annual produce of land or labour, formerly levied to support the clergy and the Church.
trammel	A long narrow fishing net, set vertically with floats and sinkers, consisting of two walls of large meshed netting between which is a net of fine mesh, loosely hung. The fish enters through the large mesh on one side, drives the fine netting through the large mesh on the other side and is thus trapped in a pocket or bag of the fine netting.
turbary	The right to dig turf (peat) for fuel, particularly important wherever there was a scarcity of timber.

Note on money

Old-style money is presented in the following manner: £6 6s. 6d. To convert to decimal currency, please note that there were 12 pence (d.) in each shilling (s.), and 20 shillings in each pound sterling (£).

For example:	1s. 0d.	=	£0.05
	10s. 0d.	=	£0.50
	£3 15s. 0d.	=	£3.75
	£6 6s. 6d.	=	£6.32½

Preface

This book is a history of the area that embraces the modern town of St Anne's on the Sea.* It therefore includes the now vanished farming community of Heyhouses which, until 1878, was an integral part of the manor, parish, and township of Lytham. In that year, when St Anne's and Lytham were created separate local government authorities, most of Heyhouses came within the boundaries of St Anne's. During the last one hundred and thirty years there have been numerous publications dealing with various aspects of the history of St Anne's, but relatively little that also encompasses the earlier history concerning Heyhouses. This new publication is an attempt to provide, for the first time, a picture of community life in this area of the Fylde stretching back almost one thousand years.

The detailed accounts of Lytham Priory provide an insight into farming activities from the fourteenth to sixteenth centuries. Although Heyhouses was first mentioned during the time of the Priory its development into a recognisable farming community followed the purchase of the Lytham estate by the Clifton family in 1606. From this time there is a growing written record, particularly the numerous leases and the detailed manorial court records. The principal source of this information is the Clifton family papers, most of which is now deposited at the Lancashire Record Office in Bow Lane, Preston.

Heyhouses has often been portrayed as a scattered farming community consisting of a few farms and cottages, whose insular inhabitants eked out a meagre living among the sand dunes. While it is probably true that for the majority 'their world' was contained within the parish of Lytham it was a well-ordered society and within two generations several families were relatively prosperous. A sense of community continued throughout the eighteenth and nineteenth centuries, with articulate men and women involved in all aspects of parish life.

The slow demise of Heyhouses began in the late nineteenth century with the development of St Anne's. In 1877 James Maxwell wrote several articles for the *St Anne's on the Sea Miscellany* in which he recorded the events that had

---

* Hereafter referred to as St Anne's.

taken place since the establishment of the new town just two years earlier. Since that time civic and community events have been reported in local newspapers, principally the former *Lytham Times*, and later the *St Anne's on the Sea Express/ Lytham St Anne's Express*. It is often from such sources that past historians have gleaned much of their information about the town.

The early days of St Anne's were, in fact, riven by dissent, with the St Anne's Land and Building Company, the Clifton estate, and the St Anne's Local Board rarely in agreement with each other. This situation was later recalled in an editorial in the *St Anne's Express*, in which James Bowman said 'St Anne's was born in argument'. By the beginning of the twentieth century the reputation of St Anne's as a high-class residential town had been established. One hundred years later its future direction is the focus of much debate, with attempts to preserve as much of its existing architectural heritage as possible while ensuring there are facilities necessary for a twenty-first-century community. These unfolding events will make interesting work for a future historian of the town.

Along Commonside, where the modern road leads into Central Drive, there were several cottages that had possibly been built as early as the late seventeenth century. In the 1940s the walls of one cottage were described as 'clay "clumped, stood, raddled and daubed" type', i.e. the clay was shaped into bricks (clumped), the bricks were then placed in position (stood), then they were cleaned off (raddled) and were finally daubed. On another cottage projecting cobbles below the roof were embedded into the walls so that, in times of storm, ropes could be held tight to keep the thatch from flying away.

The topography
of Heyhouses

Throughout this book, but particularly in Part I, there are numerous references to the highways, lanes, farms and cottages, which to generations of Heyhouses residents would have been the familiar places of their daily routines. The following is a summary of those now vanished places.

Black Leach

An extensive area of water, about half a mile long and a quarter of a mile wide, lying approximately north-east of Division Farm. Although reduced in size, the Black Leach was still marked on the Ordnance Survey map of 1840.

Commonside

Before the establishment of St Anne's, Commonside commenced at the site of Ansdell Baptist church and continued along the present Central Drive and Worsley Road. It turned left and continued as far as the site of St Anne's parish church (this stretch of the road was later referred to as Common Lane – now Church Road). It then turned right into what was to become Headroomgate Road. At this point it became a soft lane (track), overgrown with grass, and terminated at the junction with Leach Lane. This junction was probably always known as the 'gate [leading onto the common] by the headroom'.†

Crosslawnde

The Crosslawnde formed part of Lytham Hawes and was possibly the same land that was the subject of a dispute in 1351, between the Prior of Durham and others, concerning 100 acres of moor and marsh. It was presumably the same '100 acres more' referred to in the agreement made between Cuthbert Clifton and 32 tenants in 1608. The Crosslawnde is mentioned in 22 leases between 1616 and 1622 and, although it may be no more than coincidence, it is noteworthy that the acreage granted in those leases amounted to 112 acres, and that thereafter no subsequent lease makes mention of the Crosslawnde.

This photograph shows the surviving buildings of the hamlet of Cross Slack, as they appeared in 1928. The hamlet was situated on the site of, and adjacent to, the present St Anne's Old Links Golf Course. It name derives from the Crosslawnde, which formed part of Lytham Hawes. In seventeenth- and eighteenth-century leases and manorial records Cross Slack was usually mentioned by name to distinguish it from the area of Heyhouses.

A view of the
former hamlet of
Cross Slack taken
in 2007.

Although it is difficult to pinpoint its exact location it was almost certainly the
area which developed into the hamlet of Cross Slack.

Cross Slack

In addition to the farm of that name it was also the name of the small community
situated on the site of the present St Anne's Old Links Golf Course.

Dale Ends

The earliest reference to the Dale Ends in Heyhouses occurs in a lease granted
to Robert Cookson in 1613. The most precise indication of its location dates
from 1873 when, at a meeting of the Lytham ratepayers, it was agreed that 'the
Road – Dale Ends – and leading in a westerly direction from Northhouses Lane
be repaired with Gravel'.[1] It is therefore presumably the track which leads off
from North Houses Lane just south of the modern Radar Station.

Division Lane [West]

The part of Division Lane which originally formed the junction with Leach
Lane but now lies under, or a few yards to the north of, the main runway

of Blackpool Airport. The surviving part of the lane emerges near to South Shore cricket ground. Division Lane [East] still survives from the junction of Queensway to the junction with North Houses Lane.

(Lytham) Hawes
The large tract of land that lay across the present-day Ansdell and Heyhouses, and continued to the edge of Blackpool Airport. See also Crosslawnde.

Heyhouses Lane
Until c.1835, when Blackpool Road was made, Heyhouses Lane continued along the present Melling's Lane, named after the family of that name, to the junction with High Dam/Kilnhouse Lane.

High Dam Lane/ Kilnhouse Lane
The earliest mention of the name High Dam Lane occurs on a map of 1829. It appears to have been known by this name until renamed, sometime after the establishment of St Anne's, as Kilnhouse Lane after the farm of that name.

Hundred Acres
See Crosslawnde.

Leach Lane
There are several possible explanations for the original naming of the lane. The most probable is that it is the surviving part of Sunday Leach Lane. The Sunday Leach was a large shallow pool lying between present-day Watson Road and Highfield Road, Blackpool. The lane which passed this water then continued across (what became) Blackpool Airport until it linked to present-day Headroomgate Road (Commonside).

   Alternatively as it passed near to the Black Leach, and the Sandy Leach, it may always have been known as Leach Lane because it was indeed the lane which passed or led to both those waters.

Nineteen Acre Lane
This is the most difficult of the now vanished lanes to pinpoint. However, it almost certainly ran from the Lytham Hall gate, by present Regent Avenue, in a southerly direction to the junction of the present Worsley Road and Albany Road. It was the ancient link between Heyhouses and Commonside. There was no Smithy Lane until the 1850s.

North Houses [Lane]
The present North Houses Lane would appear to have been constructed in c.1853 when the 'dog-leg' leading from the moss to the gate at Lytham Hall

Nineteen Acre Lane. The ancient link between Heyhouses and Commonside. The lane ran in a southerly direction from the Lytham Hall gate by Regent Avenue to the junction of Worsley Raod and Albany Road. At the manorial court held in October 1639 an order was made that required 'all those w[hi]ch have any occupacion through the lane att the nynteene Acres Lane shall ... helpe to make a sufficient waye to passe on foot ...'

was straightened. The newly opened Lytham St Anne's Way (previously Moss Hall Lane) in effect follows the route of the original 'dog-leg'.

Sandy Leach

Reference to the Sandy Leach occurs in leases from 1610 until 1659. It does not, however, appear on any known map. In a lease granted to Robert Ball in 1616 it is described as 'two flatts lately improved from Lytham Hawes in the Crosslawnd', of which ten acres were at the north side towards the Black Leach and the others west from the Sandy Leach.[2] The principal clue to its location is in the lease granted in 1659 to George Salthouse 'of Lytham near the Sandy Latch'[3] but who (or his son of the same name), in another lease granted in 1678 is described as 'of Leatch Lane'.[4]

Twiggy Lane

The modern Highbury Road from Headroomgate Road to St David's Road, North.

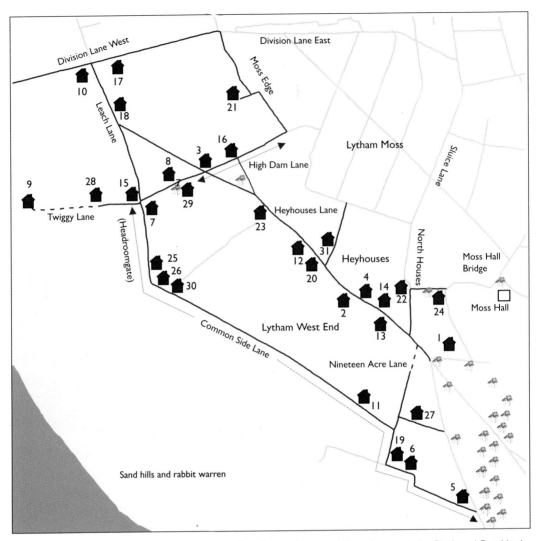

The location of farms and lanes in Heyhouses referred to in the text. Although present-day Blackpool Road had been constructed in the 1840s there was no Smithy Lane until a decade later, the link between Heyhouses and Commonside being Nineteen Acre Lane in the east and High Dam Lane (Kilnhouse Lane) in the west. Other than Smithy Lane replacing Nineteen Acre Lane, the scene remained little changed until the early twentieth century.

Former farms (the numbers in the list below relate to the plan; asterisks show extant farms)

1. Boardman's Farm*   Regent Ave.

2. Brook Farm   Heyhouses Lane – entrance to Pilling Avenue

3. Butcher's Farm   Junction of Kilnhouse Lane / Blackpool Road
                        (Shell Garage)

4. Cartmell's Farm   Heyhouses Lane – diagonally across to Brook
                        Farm

Church Farm House. Located on present-day Commonside, the building is of cobble construction, was previously thatched, and incorporates features dating back to c.1680s. It has been suggested that the farm may have had some connection with the early nineteenth-century Roman Catholic community. Unfortunately there is no documentary evidence to support this but, if true, the now demolished barn could possibly have been the tithe barn used for Roman Catholic worship.

Old cottages at Worsley Road, Ansdell

Maudsley's Farm. In addition to his pioneering work with contact lenses (see also the photograph p. 291) Frank Dickinson was a well-known local artist. His work includes this pen and ink drawing of Maudsley's Farm (demolished in 2005), but formerly located on Worsley Road (originally part of Commonside).

17.	Leach Farm	Division Lane – just east of junction with Leach Lane
18.	Leach Lodge Farm*	Leach Lane – junction of Blackpool Road.
19.	Maudsley's Farm	Worsley Road – facing Lytham St Anne's High School
20.	Model Farm	Heyhouses Lane – junction of Singleton Avenue
21.	Moss Edge Farm	Off Kilnhouse Lane to rear of Waste Disposal Centre
22.	North Houses Farm	North Houses Lane – facing down Lytham St Anne's Way
23.	'Old' School Farm	Heyhouses Lane – diagonally across from the 'Old' School
24.	Rawcliffe's Farm	Moss Hall Lane (Lytham St Anne's Way)
25.	Ryeheys Farm	Headroomgate Road – just north of former Vicarage
26.	Snape's Farm	Church Road – approximately entrance to Vicarage Close
27.	South Houses (Heys) Farm	Rufford Road – junction of Ollerton Road
28.	Twiggy Hill Farm	Highbury Road – junction of Grasmere Road
29.	West End Farm*	Ashley Road, but originally accessed from Kilnhouse Lane
30.	Whitesides Farm	Church Road – now site of Victoria Hotel
31.	Wilding's Farm	Wildings Lane

Part I

Heyhouses

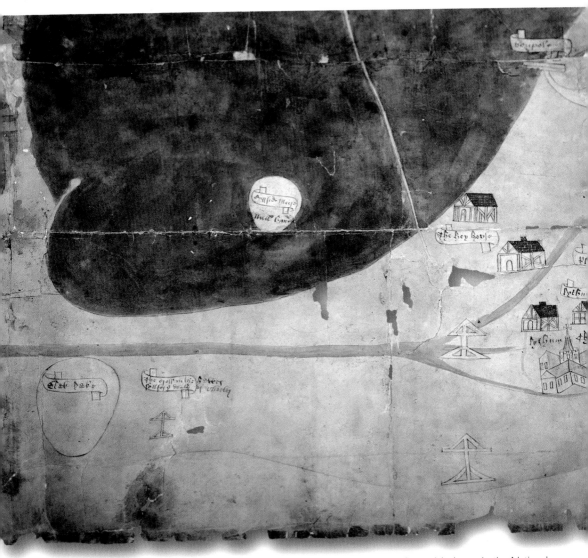

A map of south-west Fylde c.1530. This is a certified copy, drawn in 1700, of an original map in the National Archives. The original was prepared, in approximately 1530/32, as part of the evidence in a dispute between the Lytham Priory and the lord of the manor of Layton. It is the earliest known map to mark the site of 'the heyhouse'.

CHAPTER I

Early history

Almost nothing is known of the early human occupation of that part of the Fylde which, from the fourteenth century, developed into the farming community of Heyhouses, and is now the site of present-day St Anne's. However, this apparent scarcity of evidence does not necessarily mean that settlement was limited; future archaeological investigation may well help to extend the story.

Evidence of human presence in the Fylde around 10,000 BC was revealed in 1970 when the almost complete skeleton of an elk (*Alces alces*), a species whose European range is now restricted to Scandinavia, was unearthed 2½ feet below the surface of a site at Carleton, near Poulton. Beside the remains of the animal was a barbed spearhead that had been fashioned by the hand of one of the early Mesolithic hunters and food gatherers who had been directly or indirectly responsible for the death of the animal. Fieldwork carried out during the 1990s by Lancaster University Archaeological Unit, as part of the North West Wetlands Survey study of peatland archaeology, revealed evidence of human presence at nearby Peel and Ballam during the late Neolithic and early Bronze Ages, around 2500 BC. The publication on the survey records that 'it was noticeable that all of the fields surveyed in the Peel and Ballam area contained flints'.[1]

The publication also notes that 'prior to the survey there was little to suggest that there was any settlement associated with these finds'. The exception was the two sites from where W. Jackson collected flints in the 1920s. One was described as 'the Neolithic site', the other 'the valley in the sandhills at Lytham'. Unfortunately the exact locations of these finds are not known, but 'the Neolithic site' is thought to have been in the area of Starr Hills, Ansdell. In addition to these finds the *Lytham St Anne's Express* reported in 1986 that a flint arrow head had been found in garden soil in Durham Avenue, adding that in 1981 a flint cutting tool had been found in another garden in the same avenue.[2]

A century earlier, in 1893, workmen uncovered what appeared to be an old road, near the north end of Park Road, at a depth of over twelve feet below the surface.[3] At the time there was speculation that it may have led to the

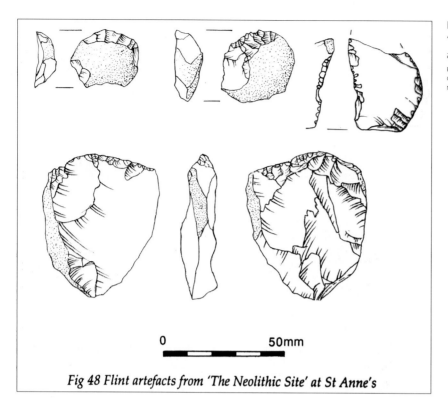

Flint artefacts from
'The Neolithic Site'
at St Anne's.
BY COURTESY OF
OXFORD ARCHAEOLOGY
NORTH

Fig 48 Flint artefacts from 'The Neolithic Site' at St Anne's

graveyard at Kilgrimol. Manwhile, in the same year the *Lytham Times* reported
the discovery of 'a prehistoric relic':

> A labourer, when excavating in St Annes sometime ago – at the end
> of January – came upon the stump of a tree ten feet below the surface.
> Underneath the tree and on a bed of peat he found what is supposed to
> be an ancient stone battle axe … The handle crumbled away at the touch,
> and the stone was sold for a very small sum to another labourer, and its
> whereabouts are not present known.[4]

By the time of the Roman occupation the district may have been settled by
a branch of the Celtic tribe of Brigantes called the Setantii, but again no direct
evidence of their presence in the area of present-day St Anne's has ever been
found. Nor has any evidence yet been found – in spite of the establishment of a
Roman fort at Kirkham during the first century AD – of any Roman settlement.
The nearest evidence to St Anne's was the discovery of Roman coins six feet
below the surface on the present Blackpool Pleasure Beach.[5]

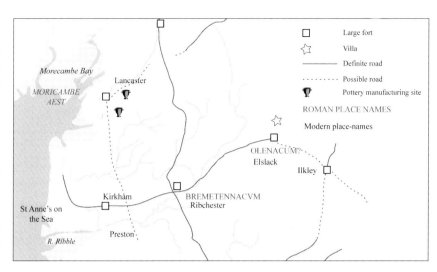

Part of north-west England in Roman times, noting the location of the modern town of St Anne's in relation to places of known Roman occupation. At nearby Kirkham, around AD 120, a small signal station/fortlet was replaced by a larger and more permanent fort which itself appears to have been abandoned around AD 150.

Angles and Scandinavians

After the final departure of the Romans from Britain in AD 410 the remaining Romano-British people in the Fylde probably formed part of a small British kingdom, with local populations surviving beyond the advance of the Northumbrian Angles in the early seventh century. It was possibly soon after the Anglian settlement that the parish of Lytham first acquired its present name. It should not be assumed, however, that because Lytham is an Anglo-Saxon place-name it was founded during that period, for it may have had a Celtic or even earlier name. The interpretation currently favoured by place-name scholars is that Lytham means 'at the slopes' – i.e. the dative plural (at) of the Anglo-Saxon word '*hlith*' (slope). The 'slopes' were presumably a description of the sandhills.

Until recently it was thought that it was settlers of Norwegian descent, from their settlements in Ireland, who had had the greatest Scandinavian impact on the North West, in the early tenth century, but, based on place-name evidence, it now seems that people of Danish or Anglo-Danish origin were also involved.[6] The area known as Amounderness, which encompassed the whole of the Fylde and beyond, incorporates the name of Agmund, a Scandinavian who must have had considerable authority. Evidence of the integration of the Scandinavian people with the existing Anglian population is again provided with the association of Anglian and Scandinavian place-names such as Newton with Scales, Bryning with Kellarmergh, and Clifton with Salwick, in which the first part is Anglian and the second part Scandinavian.

Although no Scandinavian name appears to have been added to that of Lytham it was almost certainly an Anglo-Scandinavian population that was working the land in Lytham at the time of the Norman Conquest.

CHAPTER TWO

Lytham Priory and the origins of Heyhouses

The Norman Conquest

The Norman Conquest of 1066 was a watershed in English history, and under the Normans the feudal system was refined into a new social order. The basis of Norman power was land, and ownership of land was held at the disposal of the king who divided out the country between his favoured barons. In the years following the Conquest the Hundred of Amounderness, which included Lytham, was granted to Roger of Poitou and was intermittently retained by him until his final expulsion from England in 1102.

The first surviving documentary reference to Lytham is the entry in the Domesday Book of 1086 when the township (spelt *Lidun* in the original) was said to contain two carucates of land. The carucate was the basic unit of taxation and originally was the amount of land that a team of eight oxen could plough each year. The actual acreage ploughed varied throughout the country and historically a Lancashire acre tended to be larger than in most other counties, even varying from township to township.

Assuming a figure of 120 acres per carucate then perhaps about 240 acres of land were being worked in the township of Lytham, although how much of this was in the area later to become known as Heyhouses is not known.

Nor do we know what events took place in Lytham during the hundred years following the Norman Conquest. Sometime during the reign of Richard I (1189–99) Richard FitzRoger, whose family appear to have been given the manorial rights, granted all his land of Lytham together with the church, to the Benedictine monks of the great Cathedral Priory of Durham, for the establishment of a daughter house of their order.

Cross Slack Farm situated at the west end of Highbury Road, near the junction of St David's Road, North. In 1869 the tenancy was taken by Thomas Gillett and was farmed by the family until the death of Bill Gillett in 1963. On the 1871 census the farm is described as Cross Slack Hall. It was demolished in c.1964

The establishment of Lytham Priory

Although Lytham Priory never achieved independence from Durham, it was the dominant economic and social force in the parish of Lytham for 350 years and, so far as is known, the only Lancashire monastic manor for which manorial court records survive.[1] When Richard FitzRoger granted his lands to Durham the bounds of Lytham Priory were described as being:

From the ditch on the western side of the burial yard of Kilgrimol, above which I [Richard FitzRoger] have erected a cross, westward unto the sea; and again from that ditch and cross, over towards the east along by the Curdismere over the great moss and the stream unto Balholm which said stream runs towards Swinebrigg, again from Balholm in a straight line over the moss, which lord John Count of Moretain (later to become King John) divided between himself and me, unto the northern side of Estholm-ker following eastwards unto the margin of the water which comes from Bircholm and separates Estholm-ker and Brining-ker following that division of water between us southward unto the ford[?] between Estholme and Couburgh, thence returning toward the west, and fetching a compass southward over the moss into the Pull beyond Snart's-alte where it falls upon the sea shore and so going towards the south across until the Ribill at the mid-stream following the mid-stream of that water westward unto the sea and so to the aforesaid ditch and cross ...[2]

Kilgrimol

The land conveyed by Richard FitzRoger thus comprised the whole area of the ancient parish of Lytham and therefore, apart from the addition of parts of Marton in 1878, included the boundaries of modern St Anne's. Although the exact location of Kilgrimol (the meaning of which continues to be the subject of debate, but possibly derives from the Celtic word 'kil', a chapel, and 'meols', sand dunes), has been the subject of speculation, it seems clear that the boundary eastwards followed the approximate line of the present Division Lane which, as we shall see later in this chapter, was the division between the manors of Lytham and Layton. It is also clear from the wording of the charter that although there was no evidence of a surviving church at Kilgrimol, there would appear to have been visible evidence of an ancient burial ground.

Probably because the area had few obvious landmarks, and may also have been affected by constantly shifting sands, there were regular disputes between the prior and monks as lords of the manor of Lytham, and the Butler family, as lords of the manor of Layton, over the boundary of Kilgrimol and Layton.

A declaration as to the boundary was made in 1272 by Ranulf de Dacre, the sheriff, and other arbitrators. The old cross on Cross How was the starting point; from it the boundary line went west to the sea, and east to another cross set up by the arbitrators on the road from Lytham to Layton and thence through the middle of the great moss between Marton and Lytham on the north side of Miggylund (Midgeland) as far as Swinebridge Brook. Kilgrimol and Northows (it is unclear whether this was the present North Houses Lane) however were to be common (inter-commoning) for both Lytham and Layton.[3]

The wording of this declaration makes no mention of the burial ground at Kilgrimol, but does refer to the 'old cross on Cross How' which was presumably the cross erected by Richard FitzRoger almost one hundred years previously. In view of all this conflicting evidence it is extremely difficult to say where Kilgrimol had been, though preserved folk memory may well have been the reason for the area continuing to be known by the later names of the Crosslawnde, Churchyard Slack, and Cross Slack.

Farming

It seems clear that the monks were engaged in demesne farming, running what might be described as a home farm. The earliest evidence of their farming practices is provided by the priory compoti which contain detailed accounts of the stock owned and crops grown from 1310 until shortly before the dissolution of the Priory in 1535. Land utilisation during this period has been described in the following terms:

> The cultivation of the land belonging to the cell required, it appears, over a score of oxen for the plough, and the corn, wheat, and other cereals grown was considerable, as was also the live stock reared. Some of the produce was sold, and the returns when the stock of grain was taken, simply state that there was enough left for next year's sowing, and for the maintenance of the house ... The monks evidently bred their own horses, cattle, sheep, pigs and poultry, and had little need to buy from their neighbours; they also brewed the beer required and baked their bread, and ground the corn, whilst the waters of the Ribble furnished abundance of fish, so that the larder was always well stocked, and if the the Prior and the 'fellows' did not live luxuriously they certainly fared well.[4]

Although it is not possible to determine the extent to which farming initially took place in the area later to be known as Heyhouses there are references, from 1391–92 onwards, to a meadow called Newhay, just to the north of the later Heyhouses, which suggests the enclosure of new land. This land was sometimes rented out, sometimes kept in hand, and it was recorded that tenants for it could not be found in 1439/40, a time of severe economic difficulty for landlords.[5]

In the early priory accounts there are references to both the North House and Kilgrimol. In 1460/61 the accounts record that 'nothing received from divers parishioners of the churches of Pulton [and] Byspham, for the moiety of the tithe of fish, calves, foals, and the fourth part of lambs and wool happening in Le Northouse and Kelgremell, namely between the cross and Le Mulpull (Mill Pool), which land is within the parish of Lythome.'

In 1503/04 the Priory did receive tithes from Poulton and Bispham but on this occasion there is the perhaps significant omission of a reference to Kilgrimol. There is no explanation for this but the same accounts also record that nothing was received for either the herbage of 'Le Greyn' between the manor and the town, or from 'the common oven', because of 'waste by sand storm'.

Although John Bochier (Butcher), when giving evidence in 1532 on behalf of the Butler family during the pleadings to be described later in this chapter, recalled that he had heard that 'Kelgrymoles Churchyard was worne into the see two or three miles'[6] we probably need to be sceptical of his claim and most evidence suggests that by the late fifteenth century the problem of blowing sand had increased, and was to continue for the greater part of the next century.

Heyhouses is never mentioned specifically in the accounts. The first known reference to the name is on a map made in connection with the disputes of the early 1530s between the Priory and the Butler family. A copy of the map, certified in 1700 as a true copy of the original, depicts a single building entitled 'the heyhouse' (part of the map is reproduced on page 2), but there is no indication to suggest for what purpose the building was being used.[7] However, another map, of apparently the same period, and also copied in 1700, depicts five buildings called 'Hyehowsses' adjacent to the already mentioned enclosure called 'New Hey'.[8] Two of these buildings are noted *tenement prioris* (tenement of the priory), while the other three are simply noted 'tenement'.

Either name would be appropriate: 'Heyhouse' by the fact that a dwelling was adjacent to the 'Newhey'; while 'Highhouses' would describe dwellings along a line of higher land between the moss and the common. However by the early to mid-sixteenth century it was Heyhouses that had become the recognised name for the area.

Inter-commoning disputes on the Hawes

Although the boundary between the manors of Lytham and Layton had been agreed in 1272, disputes, concerning separation of cattle from various townships that inter-commoned together on the Hawes, were still continuing in the early sixteenth century. At Michaelmas 1530 Edmund, prior of Lytham, exhibited a bill of complaint at the Duchy Court of Lancaster against Thomas Butler and his mother Dame Margaret Butler in which he stated that over 100 'riotous persons' had assembled at the boundary between Lytham and Layton (presumably Mad Nook corner at the junction of Queensway and Common Edge Road) and pulled down the house of Lawrence Billington.

They also pulled down the rails, and cast down the ditches belonging to the priory of Lytham 'by the space of 160 roods and more and laid them wide open so that cattle could come in'.[9] Although writs of subpoena were directed against Thomas Butler and Dame Margaret Butler, they never attended the court and no recompense was ever made for the damage.

The most serious incursions took place during May 1532. At midnight on 4 May 1532 two hundred tenants of the Butlers 'armed with all sorts of weapons' destroyed four hundred roods of ditches. On 7 May they returned and drove away 154 cattle belonging to the prior and his tenants. On 9 May three hundred 'riotous persons' pulled down an old cross called the 'Crosse of the hause'. This

Map of Lytham township and adjacent areas c.1530. A certified copy, drawn in 1700, of an original map in the National Archives. There is no indication as to the date of the original, but it must have been before 1536 as it too marks the site of 'Hyehowsses' during the time of the Priory. However, it is different from the map on p. 2 as the settlement is recorded in the plural with two of the five tenements noted 'tenement prioris'.

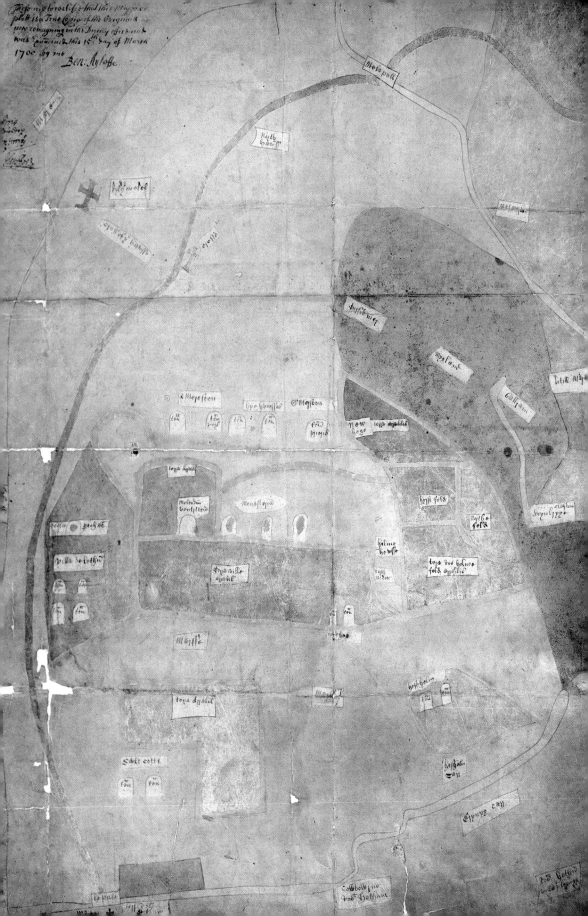

cross, it was claimed, had always been 'a sure bond of the division of the land' between the Priory of Lytham and those of the Butlers.

A house built by the prior was pulled down and there was also a threat to pull down the priory itself. According to the deposition presented at the later pleadings the prior was in such dread of his life that 'he left the county', presumably returning to the safety of the mother house at Durham. A warrant was issued against seventeen of the principal rioters, but when the court officers went to serve it they found such a number of persons assembled, who all said that 'they would keep no peace until they had their common', and were so threatening, that the sheriff's men 'dare not meddle with any of them'.

At the pleadings the chamber judges heard witnesses from both sides. Among those for the prior was George Noblet of Warton, aged sixty years or more, who said that when he was fourteen his father had been bailiff to the prior. He remembered that when tenants of the Butlers drove their cattle past the cross in the Hawes towards Lytham his father drove them back again until they had passed the said cross. He added that the cross in the Hawes had always been taken to be the boundary between the lordship of Lytham and the lordship of Layton.

John Butcher, on behalf of the Butlers, said that Thomas Butler and his ancestors, as lords of Layton were 'lords of the Hawes' and that they, and their tenants, 'have always use to have the common for themselves … from the Houndehill in Laton to the Cross pole towards Warton, without interruption of any man'.

In excess of fifty witnesses provided equally compelling evidence for and against the prior. The outcome of this complex case was that Dame Margaret Butler, Thomas Butler, and their tenants were ordered not to meddle with the said 'bowndes and devyses' towards Lytham until such time as they were able to provide further evidence in support of their claim.[10] It was at this time that a ditch, known as the Priors Ditch, was cut marking a clear division between the manors of Lytham and Layton.

These court proceedings provide one of the most detailed accounts of events in the lives of local people prior to the nineteenth century. The boundary was finally settled in 1609 when, as we shall see in Chapter 3, Cuthbert Clifton and others agreed to make a ditch – presumably an extension to the original Priors Ditch – along the present Division Lane.

Dissolution of the Priory

Lytham Priory was dissolved voluntarily by the parent house of Durham in 1535/36. On 4 March 1539, shortly before its own dissolution, Durham leased the priory house, church and manor at Lytham, for eighty years, to Sir Thomas Dannett, at a yearly rent of £48 19s. 6d. Following the dissolution of Durham it would appear that the crown confirmed the grant to the manor to Sir Thomas. In 1549 there was a complaint from Sir Thomas that he was unable to pay the rent in full due to loss of land and buildings caused by the blowing sands.

An inspection by the King's Chancellor and the General Surveyors of the Court of Augmentations & Revenues accepted that during the previous nine years Sir Thomas had incurred additional expenses of £55 15s. 0d. in an attempt to stay the sand from the land. They also found that 'the value of the following was lost and cannot be recovered, being wasted by the rage of sand there':[11]

99 Acres of arable land originally worth		16d.	per acre
5 Acres of pasture	"	20d.	"
4 Cottages & gardens	"	8s. 0d.	yearly
42 Acres of land re-let to tenants	"	16d.	per acre
410 Acres Common Pasture	"	6d.	"
28 Acres of marsh Land	"	3d.	"

There is no contemporary map of the area at this period of time, but on Saxton's map of 1577 the 'coastline' is shown to lie well to the east, directly against the mossland. It would therefore appear that the site of modern St Anne's was the area referred to in the complaint by Sir Thomas Dannett and that the blowing sand extended probably up to the district known as Blowing Sands (Common Edge Road, Marton).

Accordingly it was agreed that 'in consideration of the losses and damages that Thomas Dannett must sustain yearly in the profits of the said manor, the same Thomas Dannett shall be defaulted and have allowance yearly of £22 11s. 4d. of lawful money of England'.[12] This allowance reduced his annual rent to £26 8s. 2d. By 1555 Sir Thomas had either died or decided that it was uneconomical to continue working the land. The crown then granted the manor of Lytham to Sir Thomas Holcroft.

As a result of this purchase it would appear that a determined effort was made to stabilise the sand dunes by the planting of starr grass. By 1588 some measure of success must have been achieved as in that year a 'Rental of Lithum' names fifty-eight tenants, of whom sixteen were listed as being at Heyhouses. The Heyhouses rental amounted to 45s. 10d., with George Baggot paying the largest portion at 8s. 11d. Other surnames included in the rental were Cookson, Fisher, Harrison, and Salthouse.[13]

It is possible that throughout this period the former priory house had been occupied by the Rogerley family. In 1546 the name George Rogerley headed the Lay Subsidy (Tax) Roll for Lytham, and in 1572 there was a dispute between a Richard Cardwell and Elinor Rogerley who was described as 'ownce a farmer [lessee] of the manor'.[14]

In 1597 the son of Thomas Holcroft sold the estate to Sir Richard Molyneux.

The following year Sir Richard Molyneux leased the manor of Lytham to Ellen Rogerley (formerly Clifton), widow, and George Rogerley for £360. In contrast to the problems suffered by Sir Thomas Dannett this later lease, granted to Ellen and George Rogerley, refers to 'ten acres lately enclosed from the waste (Lytham Hawes)',[15] and, in the opinion of one writer, 'the juxtaposition of sand and moss and the likelihood of south-west winds blowing the sand over the mosslands thus giving it a rich yet warm light soil [was] a very important factor in the reclamation and land use'.[16]

CHAPTER THREE

Community life in the seventeenth century

The Clifton family and the enclosure of Lytham Hawes

At the beginning of the seventeenth century the Clifton family, whose principal residence was then at Westby, were looking to increase their Fylde landholdings. The Molyneux and Clifton families were related, and on 14 February 1606 Cuthbert Clifton negotiated the purchase of the Lytham estate from Sir Richard Molyneux, of Croxteth Hall, at a cost of £4,300. At the same time Molyneux lands north of the River Ribble were exchanged for Clifton lands south of the river. The subsequent story of the Clifton family will not form part of this book, but any reader wishing to know more about the family should refer to *The Clifton Chronicle*, published in 1990.[1]

Negotiations on behalf of Cuthbert Clifton were conducted by Lawrence Webster of Warton. And on 15 October 1607, 'in consideration of the good and Faithful Dealinge ... in Procuring a Purchaise of the lordshipps of Lithame and Little Marton from Sir Richard Molyneux his master' Cuthbert Clifton leased to Lawrence Webster thirty acres of land 'parcel of the common or waste land called Lythome Hawes, beginning near the fowlde of Lythome in the Hawes, and from there following near the moss edge towards Leton [Layton], sixty roods, and as long on the West side, and from the moss edge on either side in length towards the sea eighty roods ...'[2] As we shall see later in this chapter, this grant of land developed progressively into the farm known as Moss Edge Farm. It was clearly in the interests of Cuthbert Clifton to open up such wastes at the north-west end of the manor by enclosure and to create new farms. The subsequent land allocations created a landscape pattern which provided the framework that was the setting, almost three hundred years later, for the modern town of St Anne's. It was therefore a concerted policy – part of an overall business strategy – to exploit the new land and produce a growing rent income.

Saxton's map of Lancashire, showing the Fylde in 1577. This map was updated by Morden (see page vii) to include roads and sandbanks.

After the initial lease to Lawrence Webster no further leases were granted until 1610, the intervening three years being taken up with the enclosure, by private agreement, of Lytham Hawes and other wastes, and the ensuing disputes over the various rights of access to the Hawes. Sometime in 1607 there was a Bill of Complaint by Cuthbert Clifton that Edward Rigby, John Baille, William Bamber and Richard Hodgson 'pretendinge themselves to bee freehoulders of Layton and Marton' had unlawfully damaged the waste of Lytham.[3] In September the same year Cuthbert Clifton had himself to answer charges, brought by Edward Fleetwood of Rossall, concerning turbary rights on the Hawes, and the taking of wild cygnets from the Black Leach.[4]

The inhabitants within Lytham must also have expressed their concerns as to the future intentions of Cuthbert Clifton, and on 10 March 1608, following mediation by Thomas Tildesley, attorney for the County Palatine, it was agreed that Cuthbert Clifton 'shall leave so much of the common within the Hawes and other wastes in Lytham as the lands of the tenants shall amount to, and 100 acres more, and they shall be stinted by rent. The residue may be enclosed and let'.[5]

The dispute between Cuthbert Clifton and Edward Fleetwood, however, remained unresolved, and on 7 April 1608 further depositions were taken at Poulton on behalf of Cuthbert Clifton 'and other defendants against Edward Fleetwood'.[6] On 14 November 1608 the Duchy Court ordered that the enclosures made by Cuthbert Clifton were to remain.[7] However, as a result of new depositions taken at Lytham on 2 March 1609, the order of the Duchy Court was stayed on 22 June the same year until the matter could be tried at commom law.[8]

Finally on 26 September 1609, Cuthbert Clifton and nine men described as 'yeoman freeholders of Greate Layton, Greate Marton, and Bispham', having accepted that there had been 'Contentions between the inhabitants of Greate Layton, Greate Marton, and Bispham concerning the common of Pasture on Layton Hawes, Lythame Hawes, Marton Moss, and Lythame Moss' submitted to the decision of three independent arbitrators and agreed that Cuthbert Clifton should have the part of Lytham Hawes that he had lately enclosed 'lyinge from the cross in the Hawes and the Priors Ditch towards Lythame'. In addition Cuthbert Clifton was not 'to molest the uses of Layton Hawes and Marton Moss'. Also, a ditch was to be made as the boundary between Lytham and Layton.[9]

As will be recalled this northern boundary, between Lytham and Layton, had been a matter of several disputes going back to the thirteenth century. The agreement made in 1609 seems to have finally settled the matter and in a lease dated 17 March 1673, when the Priors Ditch is again mentioned, it is described as 'the Priers Ditch at Laton Hawes, lying in Lithom'.[10]

In a further lease, dated 13 May 1730, Henry Roe of Poulton and Peter

Leach Lodge Farm. The origin of the farm is rather obscure. It is possibly on the site of the messuage granted to George Salthouse 'of Litham near the Sandie Laiche [Leach]' in 1611. During the eighteenth century it was farmed by the Warbrick family, and later by the Moor family. In 1952, following the building of the main runway at Blackpool Airport, the then tenant, William Jameson, lost part of his farmland and shortly afterwards the Leach Lodge Farm was sold. The farmhouse survives, while the former outbuildings have been converted into modern dwellings.

Charnley of Lytham renounced any possible right (quitclaim) in a moiety of two acres of land described as on the 'south [side] of Priors Ditch at Marsh Side of Common called Layton Hawes'.[11] As Charnley's House was situated on the site of the later Division Farm, it suggests that the ditch is that which ran along Division Lane, part of which survives adjacent to South Shore Cricket Club

People of Heyhouses

Among those who readily accepted the opportunity to take out leases, and in effect to colonise the new land, were families already resident in the parish of Lytham, such as Bagot, Bennett, Carter, Cookson, Gaulter, Herdson, and Salthouse. In addition several families from Warton, in particular Elston and Webster, also took out leases at an early date.

The first leases, totalling thirty-five acres, were granted on 1 March 1610.[12] The first lease to refer specifically to Heyhouses was granted to Robert Walsh of Salt Coats (Lytham) on 26 October 1610 for 'three acres lately improved in Lytham Hawes, adjoining that of his brother at the Hey Howses'.[13] And in 1611 George Salthouse, 'of Litham near the Sandie Laiche', took a lease on a messuage near the Sandy Leach 'with certain improvements from Litham Hawes'.[14]

Sunday 10 June 1616 marked the culmination of the initial allocation when a further thirty-one leases were granted, totalling 162 acres.[15] Robert Walsh

took a lease on a further seven and a half acres of land. At some time during the preceding six years he had built a house on his previously acquired land, a fact noted in his new lease 'Robert Walsh of the Hey, husbandman: for £15 ... flatts of land, with a house built thereon, lately improved from Lytham Hawes'.[16]

Lawrence Webster of Warton, who in 1607 had been the first man to be granted land by Cuthbert Clifton, was, in 1611, granted a further lease on eight acres 'for service done and to be done'.[17] Other Warton men included Richard Elston whose descendants were to be responsible for the first attempts at education within the community; George Fletcher who in 1610 leased closes of ten acres near the Sandy Leach;[18] John Blevin who in 1611 leased a close of ten acres 'near the north Heyhouses, late in the tenure of William Harrison of Hestholme, gent';[19] and William Bonny, a carpenter, who in 1616 leased eleven acres 'on the Crosslawnde'.[20] From elsewhere in the Fylde Thomas Sanderson came from Great Marton, and Richard Hodgson, also a carpenter, came from Little Layton.

Throughout the seventeenth and eighteenth centuries the usual type of lease granted by the Clifton family was the three-life lease in which three people, often including at least one young child, were named in the lease. This remained valid until the deaths had occurred of all the three named people. However, the usual practice was to add another life whenever one of the named lessees died, so that the tenancy often continued on a more or less permanent basis.

A lease granted to John Salthouse on 10 June 1616, for a 'flatt lately improved

Heyhouses Farm photographed in 1963. The cops (see also the photograph on page 24) facing the farm have been removed preparatory to the making of Waddington Road. The farm and outbuildings were demolished in 1972.
BY COURTESY OF PETER FITTON

Heyhouses Farm was located on Heyhouses Lane facing down the modern Waddington Road, and was possibly on, or near to, the site of 'Elstons House' which was depicted on a late seventeenth-century map (see also the photograph on page 27).
PHOTOGRAPH: AUTHOR

from Lytham Hawes … two and a half acres … on the Crosslawnde',[21] was subsequently referred to in the lease dated 3 August 1657 concerning a cottage then in the tenure of Thomas Salthouse the elder, of the Heyhouses. This new lease granted to Thomas Salthouse the right to the 'said cottage or small messuage' for ninety-nine years 'if he the said Thomas Salthouse, John Salthouse his sonne, and John Cooban sonne of George Cooban … or any of

Coins from the St Anne's Hoard. On 28 June 1961, whilst uprooting an old sycamore tree in Beauclerk Gardens (part of the former site of Whitesides Farm), Douglas Jeffrey discovered a hoard of coins about thirty inches below the modern ground surface. There were 383 coins, of which 376 were of silver and seven of gold. In date the coins ranged from 1550 to 1643–44. They were most likely buried by a Royalist soldier during the unsettled times of the English Civil War.

them soe longe shall fortune to live'.[22] Unfortunately neither lease provides any clue as to where, in Heyhouses, the cottage was located.

In addition to fixing the rental, the lease also included details of the boon (manorial) services that the tenant was required to perform. In 1636 Trinity Salthouse of Cross Slack, in addition to other services, was required to provide one capon and six eggs at the Feast of St Andrew (1 December), and eight eggs at Easter, Midsummer, and 'the Feast of the Nativity of our blessed Lady' (8 September). In addition he was expected to spend a day and a half delving turf (i.e. cutting peat) and leading five loads of turf to the Hall, and a further two days shearing 'in the time of Corn Harvest'.[23]

In 1717 Robert Cowband, of North Houses, who leased a messuage and eighteen acres, was required, in addition to his rental of 18s. 10d., to provide annually an aughendale (seven quarts) of cockles and half a peck of mussels or 6d., thirty-six eggs, 6d. in lieu of turf delving, leading ten loads of turf to the Hall, 6d. in lieu of tithe hay, three days shearing, and three capons.[24]

The St Anne's Hoard

An account of the coins that comprised the discovery known as the St Anne's hoard was published in 1966.[25] The hoard was found on 28 June 1961 at Beauclerk Gardens, St Anne's, part of the former site of Whiteside's Farm, by Douglas Jeffrey a council employee, while he was uprooting a large old sycamore tree. It was about thirty inches below the modern ground surface, and contained within a small chamber pot. At an inquest held at St Anne's on 3 July 1961 the find was declared to be treasure trove and forfeit to the Queen as Duke of Lancaster.

In the hoard there were 383 coins, of which 376 were of silver and seven of gold. Three, including one of the gold coins, are Scottish, and one is Irish. The Scottish coins had a higher nominal value than their exchange value in terms of contemporary English money, so that the total face value of the hoard by English standards was £19 5s. 2d. In date the coins range from the reigns of Edward VI to Charles I, from 1550 to 1643–44.[26] A selection of the coins, and the small chamber pot, can be seen at the Harris Museum, Preston.

As none of the coins could have been struck after 1644 it is probable that the hoard had been accumulated by that date, and buried soon afterwards. During 1644 a substantial number of royalist forces had been present in the Lytham area and it is possible that the hoard had been buried by a soldier who was subsequently unable to retrieve it. Alternatively the unsettled times caused by the English civil war may have convinced a Heyhouses man or woman that it was prudent to conceal their savings until some form of stability was re-established. If this was indeed the case, we are left with the unanswered question of why the coins were not subsequently retrieved.

In his account of the hoard R. F. Taylor noted that 'one can surmise that he [the depositor] was not a small peasant'. He added that '[probate] inventories and wills of the period from the Fylde show that peasants, husbandmen and yeomen rarely possessed goods and property worth more than about £30'. Another author, picking up on the same theme, wrote 'I also know my sandgrown 'uns who in the seventeenth century were excruciatingly poor. No small peasant family would accumulate £19 5s. 2d., the face value of the coins, in one or three lifetimes.'[27]

In fact as early as 1617 the inventory of George Salthouse amounted to £62 2s. 4d., and in 1633 Richard Elston of Heyhouses left goods to the value of £40 10s. 6d. And, as we shall see, inventory amounts well in excess of £19 were not unusual in the second half of the seventeenth century. Admittedly these amounts represent the total of all goods and chattels, not just actual money, but nevertheless provide evidence that, in Heyhouses, there were men of some substance at the time that the hoard was buried.

Law and order

The manor of Lytham was a closed community in which everyone was a tenant of the squire. Outsiders could not readily move in and local people could not readily misbehave, as their tenancies (and reputation, livelihood and house) were entirely dependent upon good behaviour. The squire and his steward thus exercised tight social and moral control and this militated against petty crime and law-breaking.

As we shall see in Chapter 5 it was through the manorial court that this law and order was effectively maintained. However, matters outside the jurisdiction of the court were dealt with either at the quarter sessions held at Preston, or the assizes held at Lancaster. Quarter sessions were the meetings of the Justices of the Peace (magistrates), for each county, held at Easter, Midsummer, Michaelmas, and Epiphany to deal with cases, both judicial and administrative, that they were empowered to hear and determine.

Two late seventeenth-century cases heard at the quarter sessions involving Heyhouses people took place in 1670 and 1679. At the Michaelmas sessions held in 1670 a widow, Julian (always a female name at this time) Robinson, explained to the magistrates that on 30 July the same year she had taken a cottage, with two acres of ground, for a term of one year. She then resided there for six weeks 'without any molestation' until 13 September when:

> George Saultus of Cross Slack … and John Gauther of ye same came and violantly threw your petitioner and her said daughter forth of your petitioners house and did pull [down] all their close [of land] and since … your petitioner hath not beene att her house.[28]

The magistrates ordered that Julian and her daughter be allowed to stay. However it seems clear that, for some unknown reason, her neighbours at Cross Slack continued to object to her presence and, at the sessions held the following Easter, Julian had again to request the magistrates to allow her to continue to reside 'within the parish of Lytham'.

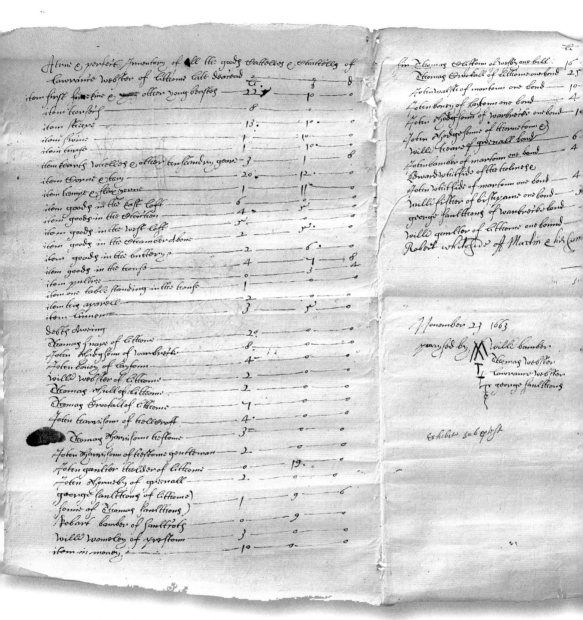

The probate inventory of Lawrence Webster, 1663. Following the purchase of the manor of Lytham by Cuthbert Clifton in 1606 families from outside the parish began to take up leases for land, including the Webster and Elston families from Warton. Within two generations both families had prospered and, on his death in 1663, 'the goods Cattells Chattels and Creditts' of Lawrence Webster were valued at £276 19s. 4d.

At Easter 1679 a petition, for what appears to have been a request for financial assistance, was presented by Robert Bamber on behalf of Richard Hornby, a tailor from Heyhouses. Entered on the document are two sets of figures, one for £1 7s. 4d. and another for £3 9s. 2d. The petition stated that:

> Robert Bamber Constable of Lytham can certify that Richard Hornby hee saw lyinge bloodinge & in a very sadd condition by a stroke of a horse upon his legg so sad a wound that hee is not able to stirr ride or stand which ye said Robert Bamber can certify that I saw the said Richard Hornby in that sad condition witnes my hands.[29]

Wealth and status in seventeenth-century Heyhouses

From the wills and probate inventories deposited at the Lancashire Record Office it is possible to study the wealth and status of some of the people who lived, worked, and died in Heyhouses during the seventeenth century.[30] An inventory was a central part of proving the will and was a list of personal goods, credits, and debts compiled under oath by friends and neighbours. Personal estate comprised both household goods and livestock and crops. It did not include property. The inventories also provide a picture of the farming practices carried on within the community, and this aspect will be looked at in more detail in Chapter 7.

Altogether fifty-two wills and inventories have been analysed and of the forty testators who gave their occupation or status only four considered themselves to be yeomen. A yeoman has been described 'as the status name of the most successful of those who worked the land', and 'the men who held it under the old order became farmers under the new'.[31] Nineteen other men called themselves husbandmen, an occupation described as 'an extremely common term of men in the old world, because it was the description of what so many of them were engaged in, tending the animals and tilling the soil'.[32]

A further twelve men did not name their occupation, but most if not all were almost certainly husbandmen. In total therefore thirty-one, or 59 per cent, of those making a will during the second half of the seventeenth century regarded themselves as husbandmen. As married women could not make wills at this time eight of the nine women were widows and one a spinster. In addition there was one bachelor, one blacksmith, one labourer, one sailor, one schoolmaster, one shoemaker, one tailor and one widower.

The valuations from the 52 inventories between 1658 and 1700 can be seen in the following table. As a measure of comparison a prosperous yeoman farmer might typically leave £100/£150 or even £200. A landowner or wealthy tradesman might leave as much as £750 or £1,000.

Total value of probate inventory	No. of persons
Up to £10	7
£11–£20	7
£21–£30	9
£31–£50	14
£51–£75	7
£76–£100	2
£101–£150	4
£151–£200	0
£201–£250	0
£251–£300	1

These provide interesting insight into a section of the community, but only tell us about the men and women who had money and possessions of some value to justify making a will. The day-to-day existence of many others working within the community can only be gleaned from alternative sources.

The values of the inventories of the four yeomen ranged from a high of £100 10s. 1d. for Lawrence Webster in 1691, to £32 5s. 8d. for William Norris in 1693. Lawrence Webster was almost certainly a descendant of his namesake who had acted as attorney for Cuthbert Clifton in the purchase of the Lytham estate, and who had died in 1613. In the burial register for Lytham parish church Lawrence (who died in 1691) is described as 'of Heyhouses' and it is possible that he was farming at Moss Edge. If so, his near neighbour was John Sanderson, another yeoman who was farming land at the Black Leach, and whose inventory was valued at £58 4s. 6d.

The highest inventory amount of all, however, was that of (another) Lawrence Webster who, when he died in 1663, left goods to the value of £276 19s. 4d., but described himself as a husbandman. In his will he made provision for all his children. This included a messuage in the parish of Lytham 'which was my mothers' to his daughter Elizabeth. Included among his minor bequests were two ewe lambs for his tenant Jane Bagot and one ewe lamb to Mathew Whiteside of Little Marton. His executors were his son James and his brother-in-law Nicholas Sanderson.

The most notable items in his inventory are the amounts of monies that he had both in his possession and owing to him, and this provides a glimpse of the means by which credit was obtained within the seventeenth-century Heyhouses community. As private country banks did not begin to develop until the mid-eighteenth century it was necessary for each community to organise its own credit system, and from the mid-seventeenth century inventories begin to record debts either 'owing by' or 'owing to'.

This practice would seem to have been in operation all over the country, and 'the provision of credit enabled people in the countryside to purchase more land, to erect new buildings and to survive bad harvests and misfortune on their farms. It attracted the men who lived in retirement, and the widows and spinsters who had money to spare, and who were able to live on the interest of their capital.'[33]

Lawrence Webster had £59 17s. 6d. owing to him by fifteen people. In addition, Sir Thomas Clifton owed him £16 19s. 2d. There was also a further £87 2s. 0d. in eleven bonds involving thirteen people. These amounts, together with £10 in money, totalled £173 18s. 8d., or 63 per cent of his personal estate.

In contrast, George Bennet also described himself as a husbandman. On his death in 1676, he left just £27 7s. 8d. In 1655 he had taken a lease on a messuage at Cross Slack, the contents of which were listed in his inventory. In 'the Chamber below the dwelling house' he had goods to the value of £2 3s. 1d.; in 'the loft above the Chamber that is above the dwelling house' there were goods valued at £1 2s. 6d.; in the Buttery goods valued at 4s. 0d.; and in the dwelling house goods valued at £2 13s. 6d.

In his will he stipulated that Margret, his wife was to have his 'dwelling house and Chamber and beast house now adjoining it and the eastmost bay in the barne' while his son Thomas was to have 'the west bay in the barne and the out share and the further beast house of my dwelling house'. Thomas was also instructed to take care of the 'writing and evidence belonging to the same [the lease]'.

Money-lending by widows was very typical and important. A comparison of the value of the inventories for the nine widows and one spinster reveals that in 1680 Ellin Crookall left £110 8s. 8d., an amount that included £50 in bills and bonds and £11 in debts desperate (overdue). Alice Hodgson, the only spinster, left £68 15s. 0d. that included £25 0s. 0d. in money. A further £38 0s. 0d. was in money owing from loans given to her neighbours and members of her family. The lowest amount for a widow was the £8 0s. 8d. left by Jennet Herdson in 1664.

Four inventories ranged between £21 and £31 including that of Margret Webster who left £25 11s. 2d. in 1674. The items that comprised her 'apparell', and which were valued at £1 6s. 8d., she bequeathed to various family members. To her daughters Ellinn and Margret 'either of them one hand Kerchief which of mine they will Choose'. To her daughters Elizabeth and Jane she gave 'all my Cloaths and to be devided betwixt them excepting one red peticoate which I give … unto Margret Singlton that I am grandmother unto and also I give … unto the said Margret one Coverlet blew and yelow at home.' In addition she gave Elizabeth an apron 'that is greene', and to Jane an apron 'that is white'.

Spinning and weaving

During the second half of the seventeenth century both flax and hemp were being grown in Heyhouses. Harvested in late July, flax was pulled up by its root and, in order to soften the tough outside of the stem, was first *retted* by being soaked in pools or slow-running water for up to two weeks. The rotted slimy outer surface was then removed by washing and cleaning, a process which could cause pollution of the watercourses, before the fibres were spread out to dry in the sun for four or five days. A similar process was also carried out with hemp, which was used in the production of coarser cloths, and in ropemaking, which again needed the fibres to be released from the hard woody stem.

When dry the flax was taken to be broken, or 'heckled', a process that involved beating the fibrous woody stem using various methods including 'scutching'. Finally, a heckle was used to separate and clean the fibres, before combing and carding them into alignment ready for the spinner, who drew and twisted the fibres using a spindle or spinning wheel. Only after washing and bleaching could the finished yarn be passed to the weaver.

Between the years 1655 and 1704 flax, hemp, linen, cloth, and spinning wheels are mentioned in eighteen wills or inventories. After this period there is no evidence to suggest that flax or hemp continued to be grown. In 1663 Lawrence Webster had hemp and flax yarn to the value of £1 11s. 0d. In 1680 Ellin Crookall had 'linnen' value £2 6s. 8d., 'linnen cloath' value 10s. 0d., 'hemp on yarne' value 5s. 0d., 'hemp and flax' value £2 6s. 0d., and 'wooll' value 4s. 6d. In 1685 John Webster had 'lyning' value 17s. 6d., 'hemp' value 10s. 0d., and 'hemp seed & other od Implaments' value 6s. 4d.

Only two inventories mention a spinning wheel. One was left by Robert Fletcher in 1675, and the other, in the same year, by William Waynewright who left goods to the value of £6 10s. 8d. including 'one cart & a pair of wheels & a spining wheele' valued at 9s. 2d.

On the evidence of these inventories it is unclear whether flax and hemp were being grown just for domestic use or as a commercial crop. Apart from three men who leased land early in the seventeenth century, no other reference has been found to anyone residing in Heyhouses who described themselves as a weaver (or webster). This is in contrast to the eastern Fylde, and the area south of the River Ribble, where flax/linen and hemp/canvas were substantial crops and products. It may be that weaving, as a principal occupation, was being carried out elsewhere in the parish, but it is only when a detailed analysis of all Lytham wills (not just Heyhouses) is carried out that a complete picture might emerge.

An undated map of the manor of Lytham, but probably dating from the late seventeenth century. Heyhouses is again (see the photograph on p. 11) referred to as 'the highe houses', but it is the specific mention of 'Elstons House' (see the photograph on p. 18) that is the more intriguing as it suggests that the family were of sufficient importance to have their property named on the map.

DDCL ACC 1108 NO 1. REPRODUCED BY PERMISSION OF THE COUNTY ARCHIVIST, LANCASHIRE RECORD OFFICE

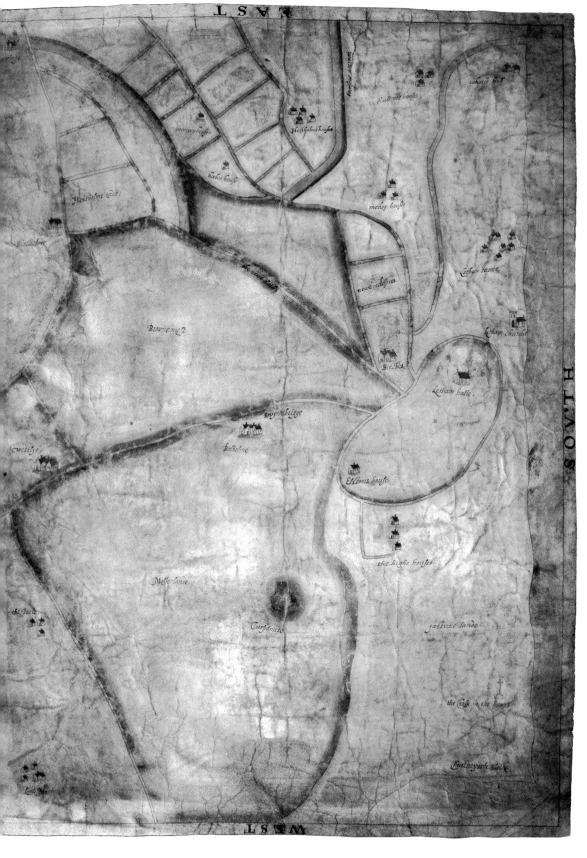

Community tradesmen

Due to a lack of sufficient information in their wills it is not possible to conclusively identify all the tradesmen who provided the necessary services for the late seventeenth-century community. However it would appear that Robert Fletcher was the shoemaker, Richard Carter the blacksmith, and the Hornby family the tailors.

In 1675 Robert Fletcher left £23 15s. 4d. Included with his spinning wheel were his 'toules and three pairs of shues and Lether and a pilsh [possibly a rug or pad laid over a saddle]' valued at 13s. 4d. In 1686 Richard Carter left £29 5s. 0d. including 'all the toyls belonginge to a blacksmith trayd' valued at £2 10s. 0d. And in 1694 Richard Hornby, who had obviously survived the fall from his horse fifteen years earlier, left £19 7s. 6d. Although there was no mention in his inventory of any item relating to his trade his son Lawrence was, in the same year, described as 'of Heyhouses, taylor'.

Thus by the end of the seventeenth century Heyhouses had become an established community within the parish and manor of Lytham, and although the dwellings were somewhat scattered they already covered most of the area that later became the town of St Anne's. In the next chapter we shall see how the community progressed until the commencement of its eventual slow demise that began in the late nineteenth century.

CHAPTER FOUR

The community in the eighteenth and nineteenth centuries

In the first half of the eighteenth century the Clifton estate began the practice of allocating an individual lease number to each farm and cottage on the estate. In 1812 a comprehensive survey of the estate was carried out, as part of which the same farms and cottages were recorded on a schedule which listed both their original and new lease numbers. The survey also named every field associated with the dwelling.[1] A similar procedure was carried with the production of the tithe map in 1839/40.[2] Thus by linking the numbers and/or names it becomes possible to identify many of the Heyhouses farms or cottages, and the name of the tenant, from the eighteenth century to the present day.

It is of course impossible to follow the story of every family who lived in Heyhouses during this period. Consequently the next part of the chapter will concentrate on the families associated with just three properties. They are in most respects representative of the many.

The Bagot family of Commonside

On 11 February 1702 Richard Bagot took out a lease on a cottage (Eaves' Farm) with two acres of land at Commonside. The fields he worked extended to the Nineteen Acre Lane. The annual rental was 2s. 3d. and the typical three-life lease was in the names of himself, his wife Ann, and his son John.[3] In June 1716 the lease was transferred to John Bagot but as a result of John's death, in July 1726, Richard found it necessary to take back the lease into his own name.[4] The transfer was completed on 10 June 1727.[5]

Three months later, on 1 September 1727, Richard Bagot made a will in which he named his wife Ann, his son Edward then aged twenty-one years,

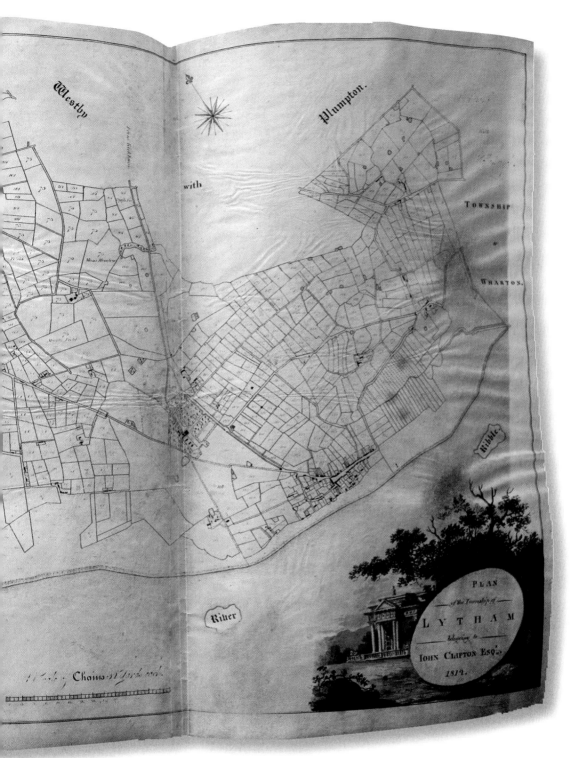

In 1812 a comprehensive survey of the Clifton estate was carried out. As part of the survey all farms and cottages, and all the fields associated with them, were allocated a number which was then entered onto the map drawn up as part of the survey. The map depicted here provides an overview of the manor but, in fact, is only a composite of several larger scale maps from which it is possible to study individual farms in detail.

his daughter Jennet Crookall, and his grandson John (the son of his late son John). When Richard himself died on 7 August 1728 his widow Ann was given the cottage and land which, on her own death, were to pass to their son Edward. In addition Edward was also to receive 'ye Table, Clock, fall-Chair, Cubbord, great Chist, fire-grate, tungs and all beds and bed-Clothes after my wife's decease'. All of these items were listed in the inventory to Richard's will together with 'three old beds, bedsteads and bedding' at £2 5s. 0d. Other household goods included 'Earthenware, two broken Kettles and other houshold goods in the buttery' at 4s. 0d.[6]

Edward, together with his mother, then took over the running of the farm. Ann appears to have died in 1744 (another Ann Bagot died in 1758) and in 1756 Edward renewed the lease on the same cottage and two acres of land at Commonside. In his will dated 17 March 1789 he gave his leasehold estate at Commonside 'wherein I now live' to his daughter Ann, who had married Thomas Webster, as 'I think my Son Richard not capable of manageing it to make a maintenance off it'.[7]

This decision appears to have ended the Bagot family connection with the farmstead which had given them their daily living throughout the eighteenth century. It did not, however, end the Bagot family farming connection with Heyhouses, as in 1771 another branch of the family took a lease on (what was to become known as) Butcher's Farm, but which as late as 1861 was still known as Bagot's House.

'Eaves' Farm. Located at the junction of Smithy Lane and Albany Road, the last occupants, prior to demolition, were the Eaves family. In the eighteenth century the land was farmed by the Bagot family. On 11 February 1702 Richard Bagot took out a lease on the cottage together with two acres of land. His annual rental was 2s. 3d. In 1756 Edward Bagot renewed the lease taken out by his father but in his own will he gave the lease to his daughter as 'I think my Son Richard not capable of manageing to make a maintenance off it'.

BY COURTESY OF THE FAMILY OF THE LATE FRANK DEAN

The Webster family at the Slated Barn

On 24 June 1737 Thomas Webster (but not the same Thomas who had married Ann Bagot) took a lease on the Slated Barn in Heyhouses Lane. Thomas Webster was then aged fifty-four and almost certainly a descendant of the Lawrence Webster who had negotiated the purchase of the Lytham estate for Cuthbert Clifton.[8] Apart from himself the other two 'lives' named in the lease were his sons James and Lawrence. When Thomas died in 1748 his son James inherited the Slated Barn. At this date the property comprised of 'the East Loft, the Chamber, the West Loft, Kitchin, and Buttery'.

Within three years James himself was dead and the original lease granted to his father consequently lapsed as all three 'lives' (including Lawrence, the youngest child) had died. In the inventory to James's will the appraisers valued 'Half the Houshold Goods given him by his Father not divided betwixt his Brother Thos Webster & him' at £8 10s. 6d.[9] On 26 February 1753 Thomas Webster (the brother) took out the lease on the Slated Barn.[10]

In addition to farming at the Slated Barn Thomas Webster was also an innkeeper in Lytham town and, on his death in 1776, his inventory listed the contents of both properties. By this date additions had been made to the Slated Barn and the property now comprised 'the Fire House (Living Room), the Buttery, the ground Chamber, the Room over the Buttery, the Kitchin, the Cart House, the Barn, the Shippen, and the Stable'.

The Elms (Elmhurst Farm). Located on Heyhouses Lane near the junction with Singleton Avenue, the present building was extensively rebuilt sometime during the late nineteenth century. It is, however, almost certainly another example of continuous occupation of a site from the early seventeenth century. In 1737 it was known as the Slated Barn – presumably because it had the first slated barn in the area. From that date until the mid-nineteenth century it was occupied by a branch of the Webster family.

Furniture in the Fire House included 'a Fire Grate, a Table, a Clock & Cup-board, a stool, nine chairs, three pewter dishes, a parcel of Bacon & other implements of Housewifery'. Contents in the room over the Buttery and Chamber were 'a pair of Bedstocks, a feather bed, Bolstard, Bed-clothes, a parcel of barley, & other Lumber'.[11]

The Slated Barn then passed to his son James Webster, who at some later date sub-let the property as in 1827, aged seventy-five, he was living at Freckleton. He must have died soon afterwards as the reverse of the 1753 lease notes that it 'Expired 1 Jan. 1831'.[12] In 1840 the tithe map apportionment names John Cookson and Mary Webster as joint occupiers of the Slated Barn. After this date, due to lack of documentary evidence, it is not possible to follow the pattern of ownership. By 1871 the property had been rebuilt and become known as Elmhurst Farm. The occupier was the Rev. Richard Thistlethwaite whose wife, Ellen, farmed seventy-seven acres.

Sometime during the late nineteenth and early twentieth centuries the property was divided into two and became known as 'the Elms'. The last tenant to farm the land was James Tomlinson who, as we shall see, was also the last foreman of the Lytham manorial court. Farming activity ceased at the Elms during the 1960s and in 1983 it was reconverted into one property.

Common Side House

On 8 March 1753 an indenture was made between Thomas Clifton and John Smith in which there is specific reference to an earlier lease made between the grandfather (also called Thomas) of Thomas Clifton and Ellen Smith, the mother of John Smith.[13] As Thomas Clifton (the grandfather) became squire in 1694 but did not die until 1720 this earlier lease must have been made between those years.

In the indenture of 1753 the property was described as 'All that one Messuage and Tenement Situate ... at or near the Head Room Gate in Lytham'. However, in his will, made in 1759, John Smith names the property as Common Side House. In addition to instructing that James, his son, was to inherit 'the House where I now dwell and Inhabit' John Smith also made provision for his wife and three daughters to continue to reside in the house 'whilst they keep themselves unmarried'.[14]

He also instructed his son 'to pay and discharge an Annuity of Three pounds fifteen shillings a year to Ann Yeat of Lancaster so long as she may happen to live'.[15] Ann Yeat was the sister of John Smith and who, in 1745, had married Francis Yeat. It would appear that prior to going to live at Lancaster, where Francis died in 1756, Ann and Francis Yeat had been the occupants of Common Side House.

In 1792 James Smith was living at Salwick and it is probable that Common

Common Side House. This is another surviving property from the now vanished Heyhouses farming community. In 1753 the then building was described as situated 'at or near the Head Room Gate in Lytham', but in his will six years later John Smith names the building as Common Side House. During the late nineteenth and early twentieth centuries it was occupied by the Greaves family. Following the demolition of the original Headroomgate Farm (see the photograph on p. 90) that name has now been applied to the property.

Side House had been let to a sub-tenant. Although the farm was not specifically named Robert Hall was at Common Side [House] by 1840 and continued to farm there until his death in 1863. In 1871 his widow, Ann, was still farming fourteen acres. By this date their eldest son, also called Robert, was the tenant at West End Farm where he farmed sixty-nine acres.

Living next to Ann Hall, in a cottage that then stood approximately at the entrance to the present-day Ashley Road, was Robert Greaves and his family. Robert was aged twenty-eight and described as a farm labourer. It would appear that Robert Greaves had taken over the daily running of the farm and by 1881 he was the new tenant. By this date, as a result of the early development of St Anne's, the location of the farm, together with all other properties on the road, is recorded as being on Headroomgate [Road].

The farm is clearly marked on the ordnance survey map of 1893, but is not specifically named. It would however continue for many years to be known as 'Greaves'' (or Headroomgate Road Farm) and as late as the 1930s the Clifton Estate made clear distinction between Headroomgate Farm and 'Greaves''

Farm.[16] However with the demolition of (the original) Headroomgate Farm in 1961 that name was subsequently applied to 'Greaves" Farm.

Wealth and status

Towards the end of the eighteenth century the practice of combining wills and inventories ceased, the last of 57 inventories analysed being dated 1776. These inventories provide a good indication of wealth during the eighteenth century, and allow us also to see if wealth had grown since the previous century:[17]

Total value of probate inventory	No. of persons
Up to £10	4
£11–£20	7
£21–£30	9
£31–50	16
£51–£75	9
£76–£100	2
£101–£150	5
£151–£200	4
£201–£250	1
£251–300	0

Due to a mixture of fashion and real change in describing their status, the clear distinction in wealth between a yeoman and a husbandman which had been quite evident in the seventeenth century became somewhat blurred a century later. During the eighteenth century many more Heyhouses men came to regard themselves as yeoman rather than as mere husbandmen. Of the fifty-seven testators twenty-four described themselves as yeomen, and only twenty-one considered themselves to be husbandmen. There were also three widows, one house carpenter, one sailor and one tailor.

The value of yeoman inventories ranged from £210 9s. 4d. for John Gaulter of Commonside (Whiteside's Farm) in 1719 to just £12 13s. 0d. for Christopher Hoole of Cross Slack in 1723. Although the three largest inventory amounts, all in excess of £100, related to yeomen, another thirteen had values lower than £71, an amount which was exceeded by two husbandmen.

The highest inventory value for a husbandman was that of Richard Cookson of the Pasture (within Heyhouses), whose inventory in 1758 was valued at £158 1s. 0d. In contrast eight others had inventory values of less than £30, including five with values under £20. The values for the three widows ranged from the £44 3s. 2d. for Margery Elston of Heyhouses in 1758 to the £5 6s. 2d. for Margaret Elston in 1718.

Among those who had loaned money to others was Lawrence Webster, senior. He probably resided at 'the Kiln' (Kilnhouse Farm) and in 1730 had £40 owing 'upon too Assignments', and £25 'upon too Bills'. In addition, Lawrence Webster makes the earliest reference to anyone in Heyhouses having money in a bank when, in his will, he instructed that 'and as for all my banck money yt Can begot into ye hands of my Executors Shall and may be reserved And Set out to use for ye best advantage'.

Although appraisers tended to give more detail for their own specialisms they usually recorded every item on the inventory. Sometimes each item was carefully noted while on other occasions the values of several less expensive items were listed together as one. When Roger Charnley, of Charnley's House (Division Farm), died in 1727 household items on the inventory included, in addition to furniture and bedding, 'eight plates and seven dishes of pewter' at 12s. 0d., 'seven sheets, two napkins and one towell' at 16s. 0d., and 'two iron potts' at 7s. 0d. By contrast, the inventory in 1754 of John Cowban comprised only three items, with a total value of £10 10s. 7d., including 'His great Chair' at just 1d.

Among the bequests made in 1727 by Margret Webster, a widow, were 'twenty shillings' to each of her grandchildren James Smith and Margaret Smith (presumably of Common Side House), and her 'Weaving Cloths' to her daughter Elizabeth. Included in her inventory was a 'Warming Pan' valued at 5s. 0d.; one bedstead and bedding at £1 5s. 0d.; one trunk at 3s. 0d.; and knives and forks at 4½d.; her 'wearing aparel' was valued at £1 15s. 0d.

In most cases it is only from the rooms listed in an inventory that we can gain any idea of the size or nature of the dwelling in which the deceased had lived and died. The lease granted to James Bennett in 1780 is exceptional in that it provides a detailed description of the cottage last known as 'Pey Bobs'. In 1730 this farmstead, which stood a few yards to the north-west of the present main entrance to the Government Buildings on Heyhouses Lane, was in the occupation of Thomas and Margaret Salthouse. When James Bennett took over the lease the premises were described as:

All that Messuage or Dwelling house consisting of ffive Bays of Building built chiefly of Stone and covered with Thatch containing a Housepart Chamber and Buttery and two Small Kitchins and one Lodging Room over the Buttery and Chamber aforesaid Together with the Outhousing thereunto belonging being a Barn of three bays built of Stone and covered with Thatch containing a cowhouse or Stable in one Bay and a Threshing and Corn Bay and also one small Cottage house with the said Messuage or dwelling house usually enjoyed built of Stone and covered with Thatch and containing a Housepart and a Lodging Room over it.[18]

On 30 January 1707 Thomas Clifton granted to John Gaulter 'All that messuage Tennemt Severll closes and pcells of land'. The 'pcells [parcels] of land' were seven fields, of varying acreage, including 'the great hey', 'the New hey', 'the Colliers hey [named after the Colly family]', and 'the nearer hooles hey [Hoole family]'. The cost of the lease was £111 and the annual rent agreed at 19s 10d. The messuage (now the site of the Victoria Hotel) remained in the tenancy of the Gaulter family until 1852 when it was taken over by the Whiteside family.

Hearth and Home

Items of household furniture are usually so well described that it is possible to gain a mental picture of the item concerned. However other entries such as 'all his apparrell' mean we must rely on alternative sources to understand how the yeomen and labourers, and the widows and the dairy maids, would have

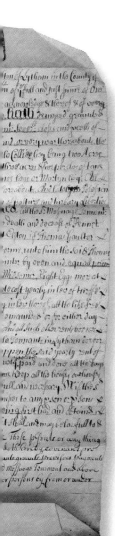

dressed. As we saw in the case of Margret Webster widows sometimes named specific items of clothing when making their wills. By contrast men rarely – if ever – did, and so the notes penned by 'Scrutator' in the *Lytham Times*, describing men's clothing of the 1820s, are therefore of particular interest:

> As a rule, artizans and labourers were clothed from neck to knee in fustian or barragan; the latter has been rechristened, and is now called moleskin ... Farmers require clothing as other people do, and to them a tailor is a necessity. In the days I speak of, a farmer made, in part or entirely, or he bought a web of cloth. But, instead of doing, as unthrifty people do, he did not send the cloth to the tailor, but he sent for the tailor to come to the cloth.[19]

Within the farmhouses of the yeomen and husbandmen, and the cottages of the labourers, the principal source of fuel was peat, otherwise known as turf. Extraction of turf was carried out on Lytham Moss by tenants of the Clifton estate who were allocated their own specific area known as a turf dale. As the manorial court regulated the extraction of the turf this, and other related aspects of life in Heyhouses, are explored in more detail in Chapter 5.

Law and order

As we saw in the previous chapter matters affecting law and order were dealt with at either the assizes, the quarter sessions, or the manorial court. The records for trials at Lancaster assizes are held at the National Archives (formerly the Public Record Office), at Kew. These records have not been researched for the purpose of this book but at least two cases are known concerning Lytham. One relates to an infanticide which took place at an unknown location within the parish in 1734.[20] The depositions of two of the people involved are reproduced in Appendix A, as is the evidence for the unfortunate loss of life of the mother.[21] The other case, concerning right of anchorage, is described in chapter 8.

At the quarter sessions, held at Preston on 1 January 1742, Jane Rimmer (possibly the same Jane Rimmer who was baptised at Lytham on 8 June 1718, the daughter of Robert Rimmer) pleaded not guilty to a charge of stealing 'half a pound of flax value four pence and one case knife value two pence belonging to Sarah Salthouse (the widow of Richard Salthouse of Heyhouses)'.[22]

At sometime during 1742 Jane Rimmer was named by the churchwardens of St Cuthberts in their visitation report, as having committed 'fornication' with Thomas Robinson.[23] Finally, at the quarter sessions held on 6 April the same year Jane Rimmer was further charged with stealing 'one muslin handkerchief value five pence and one white linnen apron value six pence belonging to

Margaret Miller', and was sentenced to be transported (presumably to the West Indies) for seven years.[24]

Poaching must always have been a problem and in the seventeenth century John Hall, a Lytham labourer, had, on 21 December 1641, been bound over by Edward Veale JP, of Layton, in the sum of ten pounds to:

... appear personally before the Justices of our Lord the King at the next sessions of the peace after the date of these presents to be held at Preston in Amounderness to receive whatever be imposed upon him by the said Court because he is verily suspected of coming by night into the warren of Thomas Clifton of Lytham esquire for rabbits.[25]

The problem, however, appears to have reached its zenith during the mid-nineteenth century, by which time the tight manorial control was beginning to break down. In August 1840 Josias Cartmell of Commonside wrote to the estate office to inform them that he had taken 'Lawrence Fenton of the Township of Great Marton':

in the verry Act of Poaching at A half Past 11 O'Clock Sunday Evening Pulling the Hare and Taking the Hare ought [out] of the Nets Togeather with all [h]is Nets for that Purpose.[26]

In September 1842 William Harrison, Robert Butcher, and Thomas Whiteside forwarded a petition to Thomas Clifton which

Sheweth That they are prisoners in the House of Correction, Preston, under a sentence of three months imprisonment for having illegally been in pursuit of Game upon your Liberties. That while here they have been served with summonses to appear before the Commissioners of Assessed Taxes to answer further complaints connected with the offence for which they are now suffering. That they now promise, in future to conduct themselves better, especially abstaining from such conduct as that which has led them hither. That they humbly crave for your kind interference when they shall appear before the Commissioners to answer a charge of offending the Laws of the Revenue.[27]

Apart from the possibility of being caught, brought before the magistrates, and sentenced to serve time in the house of correction, the poacher also risked being injured by the many traps set by the estate gamekeepers. An example of these traps was discovered during excavations for the laying out at St George's (Ashton) Gardens in February 1876. A workman struck his spade against a metal object which on being dug out:

proved to be an old spring trap of very large size, much corroded, and which had evidently been beneath the soil for very many years., it being discovered at a depth of eight feet from the surface. There have been many surprises as to what description of 'game' this trap was originally intended for, or whether it has not been used in long by gone years to trap poachers and intruders.[28]

Health

For many in eighteenth and nineteenth centuries Heyhouses daily life must have been a constant battle for survival. From the evidence provided by entries in the parish registers we know that from the middle months of 1726 to late December 1730 there was a significant increase in the number of deaths within the parish of Lytham, including many from Heyhouses.

The annual figures are quite startling. In 1725 there had been nine burials at St Cuthbert's. In 1726 this increased to fifteen, in 1727 to thirty-eight, and in 1728 to forty-seven. Burials then began to decrease from thirty-one in 1729, to thirty in 1730, and finally to just nine in 1731.[29] The causes of this high death rate is unknown but was probably due to ague, a malarial infection characterised by stages of chills, fever and sweating at regularly recurring times.

In the middle decades of the eighteenth century the people of the Fylde appear to have relied upon Dr Loxham of Poulton to minister to their needs. The foundation of his practice was midwifery, but in addition his account book shows he also dealt with amputations, dropsy, eyes, fever, hysterics, stomach and urinary, teeth and mouth, tumours and ulcers. From entries in his account book we know that he visited some twelve families in the Heyhouses area between the years 1756 and 1773. Among his patients was the wife of Alexander Moor of Heyhouses whom he assisted in the birth of a girl in 1760, and boys in 1761, 1763, and 1767. His fee on each occasion was 10s. 6d. In May 1759 he charged John Wolf of Commonside the sum of £4 0s. 0d. for 'setting his Doughters arm of a comp[oun]d fracture near ye cubit [elbow]'.

Payment was not always received, or perhaps even expected, on demand. On 18 November 1762 Dr Loxham came 'in ye night' (presumably on horseback from Poulton) to visit the wife of George Bagot of Heyhouses who was in labour. For this visit he charged £1 1s. 0d. Not until the following August did he receive 3s. 0d. 'in part' then nothing further until 1765 when he received a further 5s. 0d. An undated entry noted 'remains 13s. 0d.'.[30]

At some time during the first half of the nineteenth century friendly societies began to be formed, one of their objectives being to assist their members, who paid a weekly subscription, in time of sickness. Although there is no known documentary evidence that gives an indication as to the extent to which the

Richard Ansdell
R.A. (1815–85)
gave his name to
the area where
he lived, and in
1860 he built a
six-bedroom villa
which he named
Starr Hills. Several
of his paintings
were of local
scenes including
this, 'Rabbiting on
Lytham Common'.
In this painting an
estate gamekeeper
and his assistant
are seen with their
ferret and crop
of rabbits. Not all
such activity was
legal and, no doubt,
many rabbits ended
their days in the
cooking pots of the
poor.
BY COURTESY OF FYLDE
BOROUGH COUNCIL

residents of Heyhouses were involved with these societies, the will of George Westhead 'of Lytham' provides an insight into the practices of the time.

George Westhead died in 1849. When he had made his will three years earlier he instructed his executor William Smith, described as 'one of the people commonly called Quakers', to 'make Application and take possession of what Money may be allowed for Funeral Expences from the Lytham Union Sick Club whereof I am a Member ...'[31]

The churches, too, had their sick aid societies and in May 1876 John Peele was nominated by St Peter's (Lytham) Catholic Sick Aid Society to be 'steward for the Heyhouses'. At the same meeting the doctor's fee was increased from 2s. 6d. to 3s. 0d. 'per head'. And in 1887 and 1888 Edward Cross was made 'sick Visitor for the Heyhouses district'.[32]

Pastimes

In his *History of the Fylde* Porter noted that 'during the eighteenth and earlier part of the nineteenth centuries there was perhaps no pastime more popular amongst the adult members of all classes than the callous sport of cock-fighting; every village and hamlet in the Fylde had its pit, where mains were held at all times and seasons.'[33] In 1790 a notice appeared in Liverpool that 'the great main of cocks between John Clifton, Esq of Lytham, and Thomas Townley Parker, Esq of Cuerden, would be fought on Easter Monday, the 5th of April, and the three following days, at the new cockpit in Cockspur Street – to show forty-one cocks each'.[34]

Writing in 1880, 'Scrutator' attempted to justify the 'sport' (his word). He recorded that 'the late Rev Mr Robinson [vicar of Lytham, 1834–70] properly put down bull-baiting', but that 'cock-fighting was (and there is plenty of it yet) a very different thing'. 'Scrutator' considered that 'it would be a blind mistake to infer that inhabitants of Lytham were more immoral or cruel than they are now, for no better reason than some of them, then [the 1820s], occasionally sat or stood around a cockpit. There was a pit at Warton, and another at Heyhouses, and both were well attended in their day.'[35]

1871

The census of 1871 provides a description of Heyhouses just four years before the birth of St Anne's. The census enumerator had clearly been misled as to the distance he would have to walk in order to complete the return and, as a indication of his displeasure, noted the bounds of Heyhouses in some detail.

> The parish of Lytham known by the name of the 'West End' commencing at Whitesides Farm [Leach Farm] Cross Slack Lane, there to Leach Lane House to Cross Slack Farm, Twiggy Hills, Headroomgate to West End back to Headroomgate and down Commonside Lane, from this lane all built two houses cottages lighthouse cottages which are over a mile distant, returning to Commonside Lane thence to Singleton's Farm, back and round Common End to Shorrock Farm [on site of Ansdell Baptist Church] to Park Wall, thence by way of Woodlands to Heyhouses turning off to Shoemakers Row [Regent Avenue] and to Game Keeper in the Park, and then to Moss Hall and round to North Houses, returning to 'Trawl Boat Inn' Heyhouses, down Heyhouses Lane to 'West End' returning by way of Kiln House Farm Mellings Row and then to Heskeths Farm called Moss Edge – a distance of 11 miles above the limit mentioned.

A total of 647 men women and children were recorded as living within the 'West End'. Of these 362 (60 per cent) had been born within the parish of Lytham. A further seventy-three (11.3 per cent) had been born at Marton. Fifty-nine had been born elsewhere in the Fylde and an additional thirty-seven elsewhere in Lancashire. Of the remaining fourteen, eight came from other English counties, five from Ireland, and just one entry was left unrecorded. Just over half of the community was aged under twenty years, of whom almost two thirds were aged under eleven years. Only twelve individuals were aged over seventy.

Twiggy Hill
Farm. This farm
was located at
the junction of
Grasmere Road
and Highbury
Road (originally
Twiggy Lane), and
is another example
of an unexplained
name. The term
'hill' in Heyhouses
presumably refers
to a sandhill and,
for example, on
the 1871 census
Mellings Lane
is referred to
as Fish Hill, and
Regent Avenue
(Shoemakers Row)
as Rough Hill. In
the eighteenth
century an area
of Northhouses
was known as
Woostead Hill. In
1751 when Thomas
Salthouse took
a lease on four
acres of land he
was described as
Thomas Salthouse
of the Twiggy Hills.
DDEY ACC 5582 BOX
23. REPRODUCED BY
PERMISSION OF THE
COUNTY ARCHIVIST,
LANCASHIRE RECORD
OFFICE

Age	Number	
	Male	Female
0–10	100	108
11–20	71	65
21–30	54	44
31–40	40	36
41–50	26	27
51–60	20	20
61–70	12	12
71–80	5	5
81–90	–	2

Number of males = 328
Number of females = 319

Forty heads of household described themselves as farmers, fifteen as agricultural labourers, eight as farm labourers, and one as farm servant. In addition many wives and older children, including some of the 146 children described in the census return as scholars, would have been employed in farm work, together with hired labour such as cowmen, teamsmen, horsemen, ploughboys, and dairy maids, who themselves were often living at the farms.

An example of a family run farm was that of Richard Swarbrick at Model Farm. In 1871 Richard Swarbrick was a widower aged fifty-five farming 160 acres. Working the farm with him was his son Adam, aged thirty-three, and himself a widower, who is described as an agricultural labourer. His other sons were Thomas, the farm manager, John who was the teamsman, Richard, the cowman, and William who was described as a general worker. The only daughter, Isabella, was the dairy maid. There was one other son, James aged twelve, a scholar.

Sixteen heads of household described themselves as fishermen, and one other as a fish dealer. Altogether twenty-seven men name their occupation as fisherman. Five women, the daughters of fishermen, described themselves as fish sellers. Among other occupations were eight shoemakers, six dressmakers, but no tailor.

One of the shoemakers was Edward Cross who twenty years previously had served as a journeyman shoemaker to John Gillet, whose own ancestor had been recorded as a cordwainer (shoemaker) in the Lytham militia return of 1803. In 1871 Edward Cross was following his trade from his home in Regent Avenue, described on the census return as 'Shoemakers Row'. In order to meet the demands of the community he employed not only his own son but also a journeyman shoemaker from Preston.

Robert Franks and his son Richard, aged fourteen, were the community blacksmiths. John Nixon, who employed one man and one boy, was the wheelwright. And as we shall see, James Houseman was publican at the Trawl Boat. Although there were no shops in Heyhouses, James Atkinson aged seventy-nine described himself as a gardener and grocer.

The oldest person was Betty Ormond, a widow born in Lytham parish and then aged eighty-four. She was the mother in law of Alexander Moore with whom she lived, together with her daughter, at Leach Lodge Farm. The youngest person was William Simpson who had been born three days prior to the census and was the son of Edward and Elizabeth Simpson who farmed on Heyhouses Lane.

This, then, was Heyhouses in 1871. By the time of the next census of 1881 most of the area over which the exasperated census enumerator had walked, just ten years previously, had been included within the brand-new town of St Anne's. However before we reach that point in our story we shall look at certain aspects of the history of Heyhouses in more detail.

CHAPTER FIVE

The manorial court

The manorial court was a court of two parts. The court baron regulated matters relating to the manor; it was used to confirm the preservation of the rights of the manorial lord against the tenantry, and the rights of the tenantry against the lord; it also was the means of maintaining a record of changes in tenancy. The court leet dealt with civil matters such as punishing wrongdoers, hearing pleas, and making byelaws.

Lytham Priory retained its right, as lord of the manor of Lytham, to hold a manorial court until the priory was dissolved in 1536. The Clifton family likewise maintained law and order within their manor by the same means throughout the seventeenth and eighteenth centuries. Although a manorial court continued to be held until approximately 1947. its influence by the mid-nineteenth century was severely restricted and following the establishment of the Lancashire Constabulary in 1839 law and order, in theory, became the responsibility of the police.

The manorial court of 1611

The first court baron and court leet held by Cuthbert Clifton took place in 1611. It was probably held in April or May, as a second court was held on 25 October the same year.[1] In light of the role he had played in the acquisition of the manor it is reasonable to assume that Lawrence Webster of Moss Edge acted as steward to the court. As such, he would have announced the name of the manor, the type of court to be held, the name of the lord of the manor, where the court was being held, the date, and the name of the person who would preside over the court.

A call list of all those expected to attend the court would then have been read out, followed by the naming of the jury who corporately made decisions under oath on behalf of the community. This same formal introduction was still being used to open court proceedings in the 1940s.

At the first court of 1611 fifteen jurors, including Lawrence Webster, were appointed. Other jurors from Heyhouses were John Crookall, Richard Elston and Richard Walsh. The record of business transacted by the court followed

an established pattern. First there were the 'presentments', where the tenantry were indicted and often fined for breaches of byelaws and orders formerly made by the court. Three of the seven presentments in 1611 involved residents of Heyhouses. The fine for anyone found guilty of a 'bloodwipe' (a fine for causing bloodshed) was 3s. 4d., and it is intriguing to wonder whether the following example related to a dispute over the boundaries of land recently allocated on the Hawes:

> Alsoe we present a bloodwype beetween Richard Elston and William Hodgeson and both in the faulte savinge that William Hodgeson ye gyltie of the bloodwype and Richard Elston an affraye.

In such a low lying area as Heyhouses, with water threatening from inland and from the sea, it was absolutely fundamental to the security and survival of everyone, and to their continued wellbeing and livelihood, that the watercourses which criss-crossed the area were regularly cleaned out and properly maintained. Because of this, presentments relating to the watercourses were the predominant item at every manorial court.

After the presentments came the orders. In April/May 1611 twelve orders were made, relating to matters such as 'liberty of common' and 'payment to the herdsman'. The principle of seniority was strictly enforced, and for the tenants of Heyhouses the court made it clear what was expected of them.

In 1611 it was ordered that 'the newe Tenants they to paye halfe Boones and services and to have halfe libertie in ye Common', and from 1612 although new tenants were to have privileges of fishing and fowling existing tenants were to have priority.

After the orders had been made came the appointment of court officers. In 1611 the court retained the right to appoint the four churchwardens. In addition they also appointed two constables, four byelaw men, two foremen, two herdsmen, two affeerors (whose role was to fix and mitigate the penalties handed out by the jury) and an ale-founder.

The manorial court, 1611–1772

The court regulated events, and everyone was obliged to heed its rules. That does not mean to say, of course, that everyone readily accepted those rules, whether it was concerning the payment of taxes, or the obligation to serve as one of the court officials.

In 1615 the 'four sworn men' gathered together twenty-eight tenants 'unlawfully and without authoritie' and persuaded them to 'putt their hands to some wryting to drawe the Lord of Lithome to yeelde to some matters wherein they found themselves greeved'. Cuthbert Clifton however declined to 'yield' and the 'four sworn men' were each fined 5s. 0d.

In May 1646 George Saltus (Salthouse), son of Ralph Saltus, was fined 6s. 8d. for 'abusing the gauldlayers [tax collectors] and most parte of the parish'.[2] In April 1648 Jenet wife of Mark Salthus was fined 12d. for 'cursinge vehemently Thomas Webster [he] being a Juryman', and at the same court William Wainwright was fined 3s. 4d. for 'abusive speeches to Thomas Webster beinge a Juryman concerninge mendinge a head room which William Waynewright ought to bee hold and threateninge the said Thomas Webster with strockes [strokes?]'.

Sometimes it was the court officers themselves who were fined for not carrying out their duties. In October 1672 two 'barlemen' (byelaw men), John Webster and Thomas Salthouse, were each fined 1s. 0d. 'for not comeinge to view ye damage made by George Salthouse senior in George Salthouse ye younger his ground [probably Leach Lane] as they were desired by the said George and according to their oath in either of them'. Whatever the cause of this dispute, it was sufficient for George Salthouse the younger himself to be brought before the court in October 1675 'for speaking against the Lord of the Manor and the Jury this day many uncivil and opprobrious words callinge this Jury all names and many more uncivil language and words in the same nature as is informed to us upon oath.'

No doubt because of such unpleasant incidents there were occasions when men refused to accept an office of the court, in particular that of petty constable. It was not only in Lytham that the office, albeit for only a year, was regarded as a very disagreeable, thankless and time-consuming task. Within Lytham the appointment of the constable appears to have been made on the basis of rotation among those tenants with a landholding above a certain acreage. Those who refused to serve when their turn came round were fined. In October 1695, for example, the court ordered that William Bennett was to be fined 20s. 0d. 'if he take not ye oath for Constable in 10 days', and at the same court Christopher Hoole was to be fined 10s. 0d. 'if he do not next Tuesday take office upon him of one of ye preservers of ye Lord's Game'. A year later, in September 1696, John Gaulter was fined 20s. 0d. 'for refuseinge to take on him ye office of Constable in open Court beinge thereto appointed by ye Jury'. Even these relatively large fines were not always sufficient to deter someone refusing office, and in October 1700 James Smith 'for heyhouses' was fined 30s. 0d. for not accepting the office of constable.

Among other diverse offences George Carpinter (Carpenter) was fined 13s. 4d. in 1743 'for not keeping his housing in Tennantable repair'.[3] And in 1766 the jurors ordered that 'no Person or Persons within this Manor carry any fire from House to house or otherwise in the open high Way without being well Covered; any Person or Persons making any default we Amerce them in 13s. 4d. Each.'[4] Examples of the work of the court relating to the poor, the putting of livestock on the common, and concealing of wreck, can be found in other chapters of this book.

Highways

An Act of 1555 required the annual appointment of a surveyor of the highways for each township. The surveyor was empowered to raise local rates and was also responsible for the supervision of statute labour, whereby each able-bodied householder or tenant was required to give four days' statute labour a year, a requirement that was increased to six days a year from 1691.

Within the manor of Lytham responsibility for the maintenance of the lanes was undertaken by the manorial court. In 1639 the court ordered that 'all those which have any occupacion through the lane att the nynteene Acres Lane shall helpe to make a sufficient waye to passe on foot'. In 1754 the court ordered that 'every Person or Persons that passeth through the nineteen acre Lane either to Moss or Common that they repair the said nineteen acre Lane at such time as Thomas Salthouse Junr and Henry Hodgson shall order and direct in default thereof we amerce them in 6s. 8d. each.'[5] A similar order was also made in 1766.[6]

The present-day Heyhouses Lane was also an important thoroughfare and in 1679 the court made two orders concerning its maintenance:

> Wee order that Robert Cookeson and Robert Bennett shall amend and make sufficient way for horse and foot to passe through the lane by Robert Cookeson's house both towards the Mosse and the way through the heyhouses at or before the second of ffebruary next and soe to continue equall betwixt them either of them neglecting therein shall forfeit 3s. 4d.
>
> Wee further order that every Tenant within the Heyhouses shall amend the lane according as they have formerly done which leadeth through the same every one neglecting therein shall forfeit 3s. 4d.

The reality of seventeenth-century rural life in Heyhouses is brought into sharp focus by an order issued by the court in October 1686, when John Harrison 'of the heyhouses' was ordered to 'remove the middinge and clayhole which lyes in the lane before his housing beinge a great preyudice to all persons that travells in the said lane and make the passage good againe at or before ye 10th of December next or to forfeit 3s. 4d.'

The lane must also have been subject to flooding. In 1754 William Harrison and Thomas Winstanley were required to cleanse their ditches 'along the side of Heyhouses Lane from James Balls Ground and to where the water crosses the said Lane', presumably at the modern boundary between Pilling Avenue and the Government Buildings.[7]

No part of the manor escaped the attention of the officers of the manorial court, and in July 1759 the jurors ordered:

> Alexander Moor to mend repair and fill up one foul hole in a Gap betwixt his Closes of Ground in the By Way from William Warbrick's [Leach Lodge Farm] to the said Alexander Moor's house [Division Farm?] well and Sufficiently that Cart and horses may pass and give him time to the 14th of March next and in default we amerce him in £1 19s. od.[8]

The court records indicate that Alexander Moor made some attempt to comply with the court order and although they noted that the work was 'Not Done Sufficiently' the affeerors reduced his fine to 5*s*. 10*d*. However, at the manorial court the following June he was again charged with the same offence, for which he was fined 13*s*. 4*d*. On this occasion he complied with the order and the affeerors were able to note that the work was 'Done' and reduce his fine to 6*s*. 8*d*.⁹

Starr grass

As we saw in Chapter 3 the problem of 'rage of sand' had caused Thomas Dannett to request a reduction in his rental. Following the purchase of the estate by the Clifton family there appears to have been a determined effort to stabilise the sand dunes by the planting of starr grass. Starr grass was not to be

Starr grass. Following the purchase of the Lytham estate by the Clifton family there was a determined effort to stabilise the sand dunes by the planting of starr grass. Until the mid-nineteenth century the cutting of starr grass was forbidden. In 1667 the manorial court ordered that 'no person or persons shall Cutt or gett any Starr to give or sell within this Lordship … in the penaltie of five shillings and eight pence'.

collected for profit. The only recorded exception was in 1611 when permission was given for it to be sold to maintain a fatherless child.

In 1667 the manorial court ordered that 'no person or persons shall Cutt or gett any Starr either to give or sell within this Lordship to any person or persons whatsoever in the penaltie of five shillings and eight pence'. The order was enforced rigorously, and in October 1682 Thomas Cooban was fined the large sum of 13s. 4d. 'for permittinge and sufferinge his Wiffe to gett Starr in the Common contrary to a former order'.

At some time during the following half century the court appointed two 'star[r] lookers' and in 1739, ordered that:

> All People of this Township to whom notice shall be given by the Star[r] Lookers shall appear at a Day appointed to Plant Star[r] in Such Places as shall be judged Proper by the said Star[r] Lookers for the good of the Common upon Neglect of so doing Each person shall forfeit to the Lord of the Mannor 2 Shillings and Six Pence[10]

This order of 1739, together with measures taken to improve the state of the watercourses and strengthen the sea defences, were undoubtedly part of the efforts to protect the land from inundations of the sea such as occurred in the 'Great Flood' of December 1719. This was a disaster which, on the evidence of petitions presented to the magistrates at the quarter sessions, devastated not only Lytham but a number of other townships along the Lancashire coast (see Appendix B).[11] In addition, an Act of Parliament passed in 1741 entitled 'The Starr and Bent Act' made it an offence to cut, pull up, and carry away the starr. Those caught and convicted of the offence were to be fined twenty shillings by the magistrates, one half of which was to go to the informer and the other half to the lord of the manor. The introductory words to the Act provide an indication of the concern then prevailing among Lancashire coastal landowners, and their tenants.

> And whereas upon the north west coasts of this kingdom, and especially in the county palatine of Lancaster, the sea is bounded, and the adjacent lands are prevented from being overflowed by large sand hills, which are composed of such loose sand, that in dry weather when any violent strong west winds happen to blow, the same is carried away and thrown upon adjacent lands, not only to the damage thereof, but also to the great terror and danger of the inhabitants, who are thereby exposed to the inundation of the sea ...[12]

By the mid-nineteenth century it would appear that the law was not being enforced so strictly. When describing the violent storm of 8 January 1839,

John Melling, then aged nine and living in Mellings Lane, recalled that 'when we lay in bed we could see t'stars'. He added that so many farmhouses were stripped of their thatches that the cottagers could not get straw and they had to use starr grass.[13]

Turf dales

Turbary, the right to dig peat or turf for use as a fuel, almost certainly existed in the days of the priory, with each tenant allocated his own turf dale. The history of the drainage and reclamation of Lytham Moss is complex and was undertaken over a long period. By the time that Cuthbert Clifton purchased his Lytham estate in 1606, areas of turf on Lytham Moss, possibly from a line just north of the Dale Ends, had probably already been partially dug out.

In 1613 Robert Cookson took out a lease for five acres of land 'lately improved from Lytham Hawes in the Dayle Ends before the house of Robert Cookson'.[14] On the western side, the edge of the moss ran parallel to Moss Edge Farm which was being farmed by Lawrence Webster possibly as early as 1607.

Turf was dug with a 'feying spade'. First the digger, or delver, would mark out the cubes of turf to be cut using a T-shaped marker. Thus by crossing the lines cut by the markers points at right angles to one another a square grid was created on the ground. The delver would then use his feying spade. The blade of the spade was eighteen inches deep which ensured that an exact cube was removed.

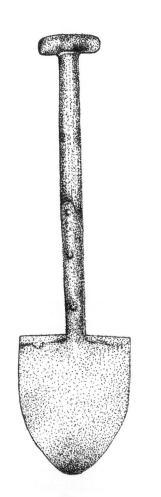

It was, however, the moss reeves, appointed by the manorial court, who regulated the extraction of the turf. In addition to cutting turf for their own use, most tenants also had to provide turf for Lytham Hall. In October 1664 William Noblet, Thomas Colly, Edward Smith, and John Dobson were each fined 6d. 'for loadinge turfe of ye mosse att a unlawful time', and in 1691 James Webster and John Gaulter, both of Cross Slack, were each fined 1d. 'for not leading boone turves to Lytham hall'.

There are also numerous references to turf or turves in seventeenth- and eighteenth-century inventories. In 1655, for example, William Cookson had turf to the value of £1 7s. 0d.; in 1727 Richard Bagot had turf to the value of 15s. 0d.; and in 1762 William Cowband had fuel (turf) to the value of £3 0s. 0d.

The cutting of the turf also affected the water levels on the moss. In 1709 the court was concerned that:

> there is severall tenants in this parish yt have more Moss than they need or make use of & by that means ye Moss is drowned and likewise Shall other tenants wants more mosse we therefore order that ye mosse reeves shall verie Stritly [sic] the said Mosse & if they find any peece of mosse that is not diged for turves before the first day of June every yeare that ye said mosse reeves shall set any tenant there that wants Mosse in that place & if any challenge then for so doing & bee fund [found] to have mosse enough besides shall forfeit for so doing 6s. 8d.

Following the construction of a new watercourse and new lanes across the moss, a series of orders was issued during the years 1760 to 1763. In August 1762 all 'Person or Persons' were required to 'fill up any Grip or Gutter along

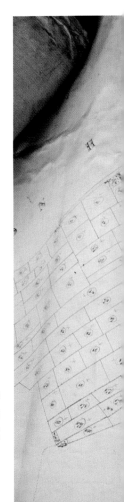

ST ANNE'S ON THE SEA

their shares of Moss in order to carry or Wheel Turves over the said Grips and in default we amerce them in 3s. 4d. Each'.[15]

Estate tenants continued to extract turf throughout the nineteenth century. In 1827 when Alice Greaves took a seven-year tenancy at the Trawl Boat she was permitted to 'delve and sell Turf without restriction upon condition that [she] do in the last year of the said term marl all the ground from which she shall have so delved Turf'.[16]

A particularly vivid account of delving for turf was recalled, in 1932, by Joseph Whiteside, who was born at Leach Farm in June 1871:

There was no coal at all used in the country around here in the [eighteen] seventies and early eighties. We dug peat, or turf as it was generally called, and every farm and cottage had its turf stack. The last turf was dug from land at the bottom of Kilnhouse Lane. I have walked from home to the Moss scores of times with other young fellows, and worked till dark at night turning turf for sixpence a night. The fires in the houses never went out in those days. A turf was placed in the 'asshole' at night,

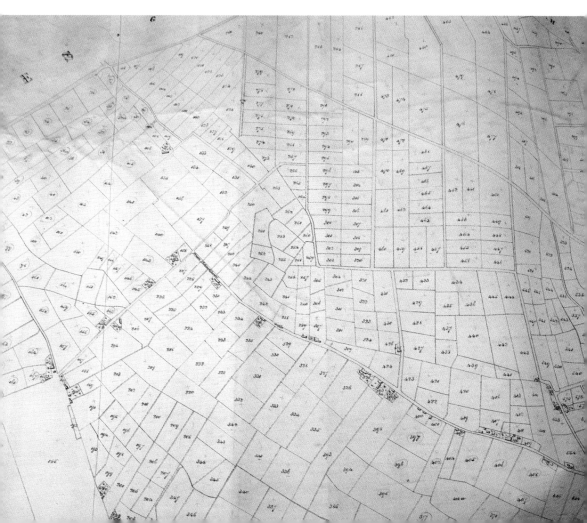

and the last one up would rake the ashes on the turf, and the turf would
be alight next morning ... Men used to cart these turves to Lytham and
sell them at ten a penny.[17]

Watercourses

As a result of this large-scale extraction of turf, it became absolutely imperative
to maintain the correct water levels in order to avoid the land being flooded.
In 1611 the court admonished Robert Carter, John Walsh 'of the heye', Edward
Hoole and William Cookson for 'lacke of makinge theyre part in the sea ditch';
at the same time ordering that 'for the makinge and repayreinge of the new
ditches in the hawes betweene Tenant and Tenant yt every one shall ditch hys
halfe on his own syde upon every one offendinge heerein 12d.' The same court
also ordered that:

> all water courses and headrooms be viewed by the fore men and they to
> appoint such convenient tyme as theye can and how every one shall bee
> doone, and for the watercourse within the Lordes demayne to bee drawne

After it had been
cut turf was
stacked in rows
and regularly
turned to allow it
to dry. Once dry
the turf blocks
were stacked in
overlapping circles
which curved
inwards to a
point. During the
winter turf was
used for fuel. In
this photograph,
of land between
Heyhouses Lane
and Church Road,
a turf stack can be
seen on the left.
BY COURTESY OF ST
ANNE'S LIBRARY

upon sufficient warninge by the whole Tenants ould and newe upon payne of every one offendinge hearin 6d.

Throughout the seventeenth and eighteenth centuries the court maintained a strict vigilance over the maintenance of the watercourses. At almost every court either a new order was issued, or an estate tenant was fined for not complying with a previous court order. In 1672 Margaret Fletcher and John Gaulter, both of Heyhouses Lane, were ordered to 'well and sufficiently bottome their ditches betweene their houses'. The power of the court was particularly in evidence in 1708 and 1709. An order of 5 October 1708 provides perhaps the most detailed description of the early eighteenth-century watercourses, and is reproduced in full as Appendix C.

At the same court Roger Charnley of Charnley's House (Division Farm), and John Warbrick of Leach Lodge were ordered to improve and maintain the watercourse between their two farms. It appears that Roger Charnley failed to comply with this order and on 5 October 1709 he was put, in the words of the manorial court book, 'on trial' at the manorial court. At least six witnesses were called, all of whom recalled the flow of the watercourse forty years previously. The outcome of the trial was that Roger Charnley was fined 'for not obeyinge an order made the last yeare for him'.

From 1712 to 1731 there are no known surviving records of the manorial court, even though it seems improbable that a court would not have been held. This is particularly disappointing as it means that, apart from the petition to the quarter sessions, there is no contemporary account of the 'Great Flood' of 1719. In the years following the flood, determined efforts were made to strengthen the defences against the sea. In 1732 it was decided to build a new sea wall from Lytham to Warton, and in 1736 there was an agreement to erect a new bridge and clow (floodgate) between Saltcoats, Lytham and the Lodge at Warton.

In 1760 all 'Person or Persons' were ordered to 'cut and open a sufficient Gutter or Watercourse along the new Lanes in the Moss'. At the same time a new watercourse – presumably the present-day 'Moss Sluice', which runs along the southern boundary of the Radar Station thence into Liggard Brook and out into the Ribble estuary at Dock Road, Lytham – was constructed. And in August 1765 the court ordered that

> All Person or Persons ... cleanse and scour their respective Share or Shares in the new Moss Sluice or Watercourse from the Division Lane to the Bow greave Bridge [in the grounds of Lytham Hall] and also their respective Watercourses at the Ends of their respective Share or Shares of Turbary well and sufficiently and give them to the 25th Instant and in default we amerce them in 6s. 8d. each. Affeered to 3s. 4d. each. Allowed time for performance of this order till Michaelmas.[18]

The court records from 1765 to 1772 confirm that the jurors remained ever watchful in order to ensure that not only the Main Sluice but all other watercourses and ditches were cleansed and scoured whenever necessary. Orders were regularly issued in respect of the watercourses at Marton Hey (Division Lane), Leach Lane, and North Houses. It was important work, without which farming within Heyhouses and on the moss would not have been able to function effectively.

The manorial court since the nineteenth century

After the court of 8 June 1772 no record of court proceedings has been located until those for the courts held at the beginning of the twentieth century. However, on the evidence of a range of various miscellaneous documents, there can be no doubt that the court continued to be held. And, in contrast to adjoining townships, the Clifton dominance in local affairs continued to hold sway.

In 1812 a printed notice headed 'Lytham Manor' was distributed throughout the manor concerning the taking of stones from the Double Stanner (the shore opposite what is now Riley Avenue). The notice pointed out that

> Mr Clifton having it in Contemplation to embank as much land as shall be deemed practicable near the Double Stanner, and to secure the same at the Star Hills adjoining, from the overflowing of the Sea, so as to bring the same to a State of Cultivation, and for the purpose of planting Timber and other Trees, is advised, that to effectuate such Measures the Stones thereabouts and extending to Cross Slack may be most advantageously used, and will save him an enormous Expence in the Scheme.

In the circumstances no owner of a sloop, flat or other craft was to be permitted to take away, presumably to use as ballast, any stones from Stanner End to Cross Slack. Those tenants who had leases were allowed – 'In the necessary Improvement and Repairs of their Tenements and the Highways within the Manor' – a proper quantity of both sand and stones from elsewhere on the estate provided they obtained a note in writing from the estate steward. However, if any tenant presumed to act to the contrary it was 'to be considered a Forfeiture of his Lease'.[19]

Even when law and order had become the responsibility of the Lancashire constabulary the estate was still able to maintain some control over the tenantry as is clearly demonstrated by its response to a disturbance that took place in Heyhouses on 'Sunday night' 25 January 1874.

On the evidence of census returns all the men involved resided in the area of Kilnhouse Lane/Leach Lane. They were aged between fifteen and twenty-

Main sluice, Lytham Moss. Maintenance of the many watercourses was of vital importance to avoid flooding and the subject dominated meetings of the manorial court until the 1945. In about 1760 a new Moss (Main) Sluice was constructed, into which all other watercourses flowed. This main sluice, which runs along the southern boundary of the Radar Station, itself then flows into Liggard Brook and out into the Ribble estuary.

two; one was a fisherman and the other six found employment on farms. In consideration of not being prosecuted for 'breaking down and destroying property in the Heyhouses belonging to John Talbot Clifton' seven men agreed to make payments, ranging from 5s. 0d. to 2s. 6d., 'towards the cost of making good the damage done'.[20]

By the late nineteenth century, however, the function of the manorial court was almost entirely given over to ensuring that the watercourses were properly scoured and cleaned. A notice dated 4 April 1872, signed by James Parkinson, foreman of the jurors, informed

> All Persons who have any Watercourses lying and being within the Parish of Lytham, are hereby required well and sufficiently to Scour and Cleanse the same betwixt [4 April] and Thursday 18 April. For every neglect they will be Fined without further notice.[21]

The court was therefore continuing to be an important factor in the efficient running of the estate, particularly for the farms in the Heyhouses area. Even the separation of Lytham and St Anne's into two local government authorities in 1878 made little difference to its role.

In June 1880 the court met at the Queen's Hotel, Lytham. Thirteen jurors were appointed, one of whom was also made constable. In addition, the court appointed two assessors, three ley leyers, three byelaw men, a searcher of weights and measures, three gamekeepers, two moss reeves, seven pinders, two wreck searchers, two overseers of moss lands, ten overseers of watercourses and sluices, three surveyors of brooks, four surveyors of waterfalls, and two overseers of the fishery.

These forty-six roles were shared among those required to attend the court, with several men undertaking six or more roles at the same time. The newspaper account of the court proceedings noted that 'Several were presented, and were fined in sums ranging from one shilling to one pound. The official gentlemen afterwards dined together ...'.[22]

At the beginning of the twentieth century, even though most of its decisions affected just the Heyhouses farming community, the court continued to meet in Lytham, rotating its venue between the Queen's Hotel, County and Commercial Hotel, Ship and Royal Hotel and the Talbot Hotel. All tenants on the estate were required to attend, though for some it was becoming something of an inconvenience. In 1904 John Swarbrick of Model Farm, although he attempted to justify his absence due to the fact he was making hay at the time, was still fined for non-attendance. In 1924 a similar fine was imposed on John Whiteside of South Heys Farm. He refused to pay the fine, commenting that he had been ill on the day the court had been held, and that he was aware that other tenants had been excused previously on account of illness. The concluding part of his letter, while accepting the function of the court, emphasised the need for the court to take account of prevailing farm practices:

> I quite agree with what you say in your letter with reference to keeping the watercourses clean, and have always done my duty as a member of the Jury in that respect, but I do think that for convenience of the Jury that the Meeting might be arranged some other time than in the midst of haytime, the farmer's busiest time of the year. I heard of above one farmer grumbling on Friday last for having to leave his hay to go to the meeting, the business of which a third of it in my opinion is a waste of time.[23]

During the twentieth century overseeing the cleaning of the watercourses involved regular contact with St Anne's Urban District Council, and subsequently with Lytham St Anne's Corporation. At the court held in 1918 St Anne's Council were presented for failure to have their length of Leach Lane watercourse sufficiently scoured and cleaned and also for tipping ashes, broken glass, nails, and papers along Kiln House Lane, one of the consequences of which was that two cows belonging to Robert Hall of Headroomgate Farm had been rendered lame.[24]

The differing attitudes about the relevance of the court between on the one hand the Clifton estate, and on the other by Lytham St Anne's corporation is clearly revealed in various correspondence written between 1928 and 1943.

In 1928 William Whinnerah, the estate manager, sent a letter of condolence to Mrs Violet Clifton on the death of John Talbot Clifton. In the letter he said he had been asked by the foremen of the Lytham, Westby with Plumptons and Little Marton manorial courts to convey their sympathy in her sad bereavement. He then continued by saying that:

> Although many of the old customs have fallen into desuetude these Manor Courts are still functioning and are of great practical use in seeing that all main watercourses within the Manors are cleansed twice a year and are kept in good condition which in a flat country such as this is of inestimable benefit.[25]

Mrs Clifton herself appears anxious to have retained the manorial traditions and in 1931 wrote asking for more information about the court. In reply William Whinnerah confirmed that the court was still held, adding that 'as a rule from fifteen to twenty people are in attendance, usually the principal tenants upon that part of the Estate'. He concluded, however:

> It seems doubtful whether outside their own bodies any powers accrue to them of enforcing their decisions, and such good as is undoubtedly done

rests entirely on a moral basis and the tenants pay cheerfully any small fine of half a crown or five shillings for any breaches they may be deemed to have made because they recognise it is for the common good.[26]

Lytham St Anne's corporation took a rather different view, and in reply to a fine imposed by the court in 1943, Walter Heap, the town clerk, observed:

I am afraid I am somewhat amused by the fining of the Corporation, or in fact, of anyone else in these days, but rather than make a serious point of the whole matter, I have suggested to the [Borough] Treasurer that we should pay the fine entirely without prejudice to the Corporation's position, and I will obtain a cheque for £2 and forward this in due course. Incidentally I think if we are to put up with this old fashioned nonsense, we had better in future take it seriously and ask to be allowed to appear whenever we are likely to be fined !! I think that is one of the privileges of a Britisher, is it not?[27]

The last court for which records have been found was held in 1945 at the Queens Hotel, Lytham. James Tomlinson, of the Elms, was re-appointed foreman of the jury, a post he had held since at least 1926; and Frank Sampson, of Model Farm, was appointed constable. Although there was a slight variation in responsibility other officers of the court undertook the same roles as had their predecessors of the previous three centuries.

Lytham St Anne's corporation were again fined, on this occasion 10s. 0d. for each of three offences of not cleaning watercourses. The same fine was imposed on Robert Bamber, of Butcher's Farm, for not cleaning Kilnhouse Lane Sluice, Robert Hesketh, of Moss Edge Farm, for not cleaning Destructor Brook, and John Dockeray, of Headroomgate Farm, for not cleaning Leach Lane Sluice. Arthur Watson of Leach Farm was fined 10s. 0d. for non-attendance.[28]

The final demise of the court came with the creation, in 1947, of the South Fylde Drainage Board, which took over responsibility for the watercourses. This was 236 years after the Clifton family had held their first manorial court. In April 1978 James Hilton

The Manor of Lytham embraces the whole of both Lytham and St Anne's. The present lord of the manor of Lytham is James Hilton, who purchased the title from the trustees of Harry Clifton in April 1978. A subsequent purchase of the extensive collection of Clifton family and estate papers has ensured that one of the most important historical collections in the county continues to be accessible.

BY COURTESY OF JAMES HILTON

of Lytham bought the title and manorial rights from Harry Clifton, and is the present lord of the manor of Lytham (a title that embraces both present-day Lytham and St Anne's).

CHAPTER SIX

The poor

Origins and administration of the Poor Law

Following the dissolution of the monasteries the responsibility for the maintenance of the poor passed to each parish or township. An Act of 1563 required that 'two able persons or more shall be appointed gatherers and collectors of the charitable alms of all the residue of people inhabiting in the parish', and in 1572 the parish office of overseer of the poor was created to supervise endowments and other charitable funds. The 1590s saw a catastrophic series of bad harvests and high food prices, and from 1597–98 onwards all parishes were allowed to levy a poor rate with a view to providing work for their paupers.

It was however, the Poor Law Act of 1601, amended by the act of Settlement in 1662, that was the basis of poor law administration until 1834. In accordance with the 1601 Act the poor rate collected by the overseers was to be spent in four ways: 'for setting to work the children of all such whose parents shall not be thought able to maintain them'; 'for setting to work all such persons, married or unmarried, having no means to maintain them, and who use no ordinary or daily trade of life to get their living by'; 'for providing a convenient stock of flax, hemp, wood, thread, and other ware and stuff to set the poor on work'; and 'for the necessary relief of the lame, impotent, old, blind, and other such among them being poor and not able to work'. The Act of 1662 amended the law by stating that everyone had a 'place of settlement'. Legitimate children inherited their father's place of settlement and married women took that of their husband. Illegitimate children were deemed to belong legally to their place of birth and, in order to avoid having to maintain them, the overseers of each parish took great pains to try and ensure that illegitimate children were not born within their township. The township constable, in addition to his responsibility for the maintenance of law and order, was also responsible for a wide range of other duties, including the apprenticing of pauper children, the supervision and removal of itinerant strangers and beggars, and the collection of child maintenance from the fathers of illegitimate children.

Our knowledge of how a particular township looked after its poor is largely dependent upon the survival of the overseers' or constables' accounts. Unfortunately no such records appear to have survived for the township of Lytham. However, the minutes of both the manorial court and the steward's account book, together with the papers among the quarter sessions records, provide some insight into the treatment of the poor of the area during the seventeenth century.

As already mentioned, there was always particular concern when an illegitimate birth was about to occur. In the case of Elizabeth Cookson the account of the birth of her child, and the means by which the overseers were able to determine the name of the father, is recorded in the certificate presented to the magistrates at the quarter sessions on 19 July 1637. All the women who witnessed the birth were the wives or widows of Heyhouses husbandmen:

> Isabell wife of William Crookoe [Crookall] of Lithame, Midwyfe
>> Elizabeth wyfe of John ffayre of the same
>> Alice the wyfe of Thomas Artwright
>> Anne the wyfe of Richard ffayre
>> Katherine relict John ffayre and
>> Katherine Cookson wid[ow] all of Lithame ...
> All the parties above named have testified upon their corporall oathes that Elizabeth Cookson of Lithame Spinster in the tyme of her most extremityes in labour did alwayes say and affirme that Willm Galter of Lithome aforesaid husb[andman] and no other was the ffather of that bastard Childe[1]

At the manorial court held on 28 May 1646 five women were each fined 6s. 8d. for bearing a child 'unlawfully begotten'. At the same court Hugh Snape, a Heyhouses man, was likewise fined 6s. 8d. for harbouring Margaret Snape who had also given birth to a child 'unlawfully begotten'.[2]

As these illegitimate births occurred during the English civil war it is perhaps noteworthy that in August 1644 about 2,700 soldiers, mostly cavalry, had been encamped about Lytham and Kirkham. Although there is no evidence to link this event to any of the births it must have been a time of general unrest in Heyhouses and, as we saw in Chapter 3, the coins known as the 'St Anne's Hoard' had been buried about this time. In the light of such disruptions the manorial court was no doubt particularly anxious to deter liaisons which might result in the parish being responsible for the upkeep of illegitimate children born as a result.

For an elderly person living on their own, life must have been particularly difficult. At Michaelmas 1656 Elizabeth Cookson (if she was the same Elizabeth Cookson, who twenty years earlier had given birth to an illegitimate child, her age had been somewhat 'increased') presented the following petition to the magistrates:

The petition of 'Christopher Whitehead of Lithom', 1656. 'A labouringe man for the space of eighteene yeares … and having a wife and six small children … and being destitute of an house or anie place of habitacon … but in danger to starve …' urged the magistrates 'by yo[u]r order releeve them …' by directing the 'churchwardens and overseers for the poore to make provision for an habitacon … and he shall endeavour by his handy labour to helpe towards the maintenance of them … as god may be pleased to enable him, beinge of himselfe in noe wyse able to maintaine them without the helpe of the Parish.' In the clerk's hand at the foot of the document can be discerned the verdict: 'Ch[urchardens] & Ov[erseers] of [the] poore to p[ro]vide.'

Sheweth that ye said petitioner beinge of the age of three score And three years & havinge Lived in the Parishe of Lytham … all the time of her life and nowe through age & hard laboure is growne very unable And canot earne money to pay for housinge as before But is att want of a place to lodge … the inhabitants of Lytham heyhouses are very willinge to build her a little house wheare in shee may live if that her Brother William Cooksonne would bee pleased they might build it upon the waste neare his house wheare the said Inhabitants of Lytham heyhouses did ffynd it most convenient …[3]

Just occasionally a series of documents survives which casts an unusual amount of light on the life of a particular individual. Thus, a series of events in the life of Christopher Whitehead, spanning almost thirty years, can be

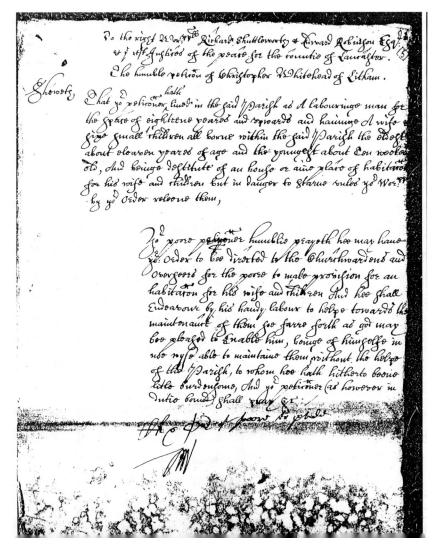

followed through information contained in various documents. At the manorial court held in April 1648 Richard Davie was fined 3s. 4d. 'for harbouringe Christopher Whitehead, an Inmate'.[4] In 1656 Christopher Whitehead presented a petition to the magistrates, at the Midsummer quarter sessions held at Preston, in which he requested them to order the churchwardens and overseers of the poor 'to make provision for an habitation for his wife and children'. He was described as having 'lived in the said Parish [Lytham] as a labouringe man for ... eighteen years ... and havinge a Wife & six small children all borne within the Parish the eldest about eleven years of age and the youngest about ten weeks old, And beinge destitute of an house or any place of habitation.'[5] Although the churchwardens and overseers of Lytham complied with the order the cottage was erected on ground within the parish of Kirkham. This brought an immediate response from the churchwardens and overseers of Kirkham who, at the quarter sessions held at Midsummer 1657, complained that, should Christopher Whitehead and his family became destitute, they could became responsible for their maintenance.[6]

In the end common sense prevailed and at Michaelmas the same year, Kirkham accepted that Christopher Whitehead could reside in their parish provided the magistrates were 'content to undertake to save the Parish of Kirkham harmless from the said Christopher Whitehead and his family'.[7]

It should not be assumed that all those seeking relief were feckless. In some instances they were suffering from genuine economic hardship and striving to maintain their dignity and independence. Christopher Whitehead would appear to have been such a man and, unusually for a seventeenth-century labourer, when he died in 1675 he left a will. His wife Anne was appointed sole executrix. By this date he had returned to reside within the parish of Lytham, but one of his six children had either died or left home. Of the surviving children one son and four daughters each received 2s. 6d. In addition his wife was instructed to pay all his outstanding debts, which amounted to £11 6s. 0d.[8]

The manorial court continued to set down regulations concerning the poor until at least the late seventeenth century. On 10 November 1678 it ordered:

> Wee order that no Tenant within this Lordshipp shall habor any poore person or Stranger longer that ye Statute provides in that case unlesse they bee not able to travaille & upon such necessity not above 4 nights at any time in paine of 20s except in Christmas[9]

The above order was further enforced on 4 November 1679 when:

> Wee order that no Tenant within this Lordship shall take in any tenant of any other townshipp except they have lycence from the Lord [of the Manor] & ye Jury then in office every defaulter shall forfeit 26s. 8d.[10]

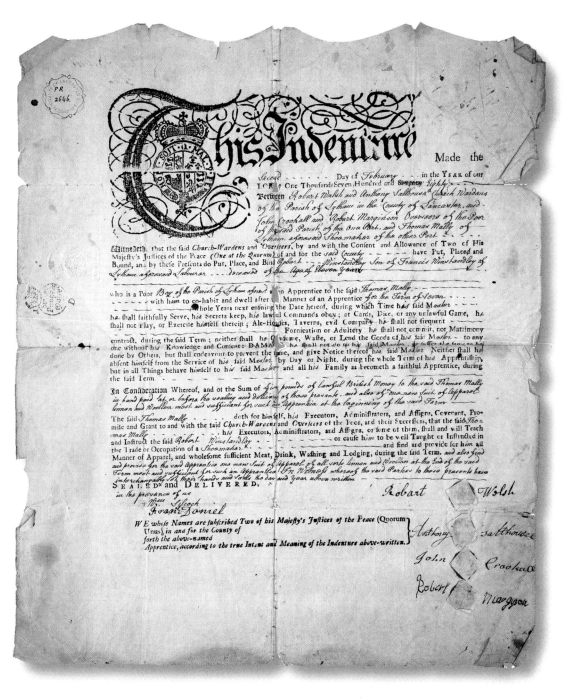

And on 5 October 1699 the court recorded that:

Wee order that if any inhabitant of this Township doe hyre any forrainer for a servant That such hyrer shal Indempnifie the Towne from Such Servants Settlement And in default hereof we present them for harbouring such Servant as an Inmate And fine them for such harbouring as the Law directs[11]

Because of the significant manorial control over the poor of the township the role of the overseer of the poor, in contrast to neighbouring townships such as Freckleton, appears to have been quite limited. It was quite an unusual circumstance and highlights the rather special case at Lytham. It may also be the reason for the apparent absence of township records which might, had they been kept (and survived), have told us much more of life in the community. Until at least the early eighteenth century it would appear that it was the steward at Lytham Hall who dealt with incidental payments to the poor, as suggested by the following entries from his account book:[12]

30 March 1697	To a poore man come out of Lancaster Castle by order 2s. 6d.
23 July 1697	To a poore woman at ye gates by your [the Lord of the Manor] order 2d.
16 May 1701	To a poore blind man by Master's order 2d.
7 April 1702	To two poore men by order 2d.

The absence of any township, as opposed to manorial, records makes it difficult to determine how the township raised the money to support its poor. In addition to the money given by the lord of the manor, perhaps those tenants whose property had a rental above a certain amount also had to contribute a particular yearly amount. We do know, however, that the poor also occasionally benefited from the bequests made by Heyhouses men. Thus, in 1685 Thomas Elston, a schoolmaster, gave £10 to 'the poore people in Lytham ... and to some other poore people of my relations'.[13] In 1710 William Sanderson requested that a 'penny Dole be given to ye poor on ye day of my funeral'.[14] Meanwhile, in 1743 John Herdson instructed his executors that the sum of £20 'shall be applyed from time to time to or for the use of the poor of the Township of Lytham ... Either for putting out Apprentices or otherwise as they [his Executors] shall think proper.'[15]

In 1745 Lawrence Webster 'of the Moss Edge within Lytham' instructed his executors that the monies raised from the sale of two closes of land be used 'to employ and distribute according to their discretion among such of my poor neighbours of this Parish of Lytham as they shall apprehend to want some assistance, but who do not receive alms, nor have any Allowance from the same.'[16] And in 1778 James Webster 'of the Kiln' likewise gave his executors 'the annual yearly sum of five pounds ... charged on my Leashold Estate' which the executors 'shall pay distribute and divide the same unto and amongst the poor inhabitants settled on the Township of Lytham who shall receive no Relief from the said Town'.[17]

Two examples of the putting out of apprentices took place in 1777 and 1780. Both orders were described as pauper apprenticeships. In 1777 Thomas

Melling, who with his mother Catherine and four of his siblings had been removed from Upholland to Lytham in 1771, was apprenticed as a groom & waiter to John Birley, a Kirkham merchant, for five years.[18] In 1780 Robert Winstanley, aged eleven, was apprenticed to Thomas Malley, a Kirkham shoemaker, for seven years.[19]

By the beginning of the nineteenth century the role of the manorial court, in so far as the poor were concerned, appears to have ceased, and at Easter 1803 a return, relating to the year 1802–03, was completed by the overseers. This provides a detailed account of how the poor law was then being administered in the township and is reproduced in full as Appendix D. Although it does not distinguish between Lytham town and Heyhouses it is almost certain that some of the monies mentioned will have been for the benefit of Heyhouses residents.

What the return does suggest is that the township of Lytham did not appear to have had a poor/work house and that all relief was provided 'out of house'. As far as is known Lytham never adopted the 1722 Workhouse Test Act, which allowed parishes to erect their own workhouse, and it is unclear if those requiring 'in house' relief were sent outside the parish – for example Freckleton occasionally sent those requiring in house relief to Brindle – or were cared for in their own homes.

The Poor Law Amendment Act passed in 1834 resulted in responsibility for the poor being taken away from the townships and parishes and placed in the hands of Poor Law Unions, controlled by Board of Guardians. The Act minimised the provision of outdoor relief and made confinement in the workhouse the central element of the new system, whilst at the same time discouraging all but the most desperate seeking admittance. Lytham became one of twenty-three townships in the Fylde Union and in 1844 a union workhouse was erected in Station Road, Kirkham, being replaced by a new workhouse at Wesham in 1907.

The absence of any contemporary records means that we only have a somewhat limited view of the lives and conditions of the poor in Heyhouses following the passing of the Act. On the 1841 census only one person in Heyhouses was described as a pauper; in 1851 there were four, in 1861 only one, and in 1871 three.

In 1851 Rebecca Melling aged 36, and already a widow, was described as a 'washerwoman & pauper'. Living with her were her three children Henry, a farm labourer aged 15, and Alice aged 9 and George aged 5, both of whom were 'scholars'. George Wade of Heyhouses, a widower aged 76, was living with his son Joseph who was an agricultural labourer. In 1871 Ellen Cartmell of Commonside Lane, a widow aged 81, was living with her son James, aged 45, who was a fisherman and a widower himself, together with Mary her great niece aged 8.

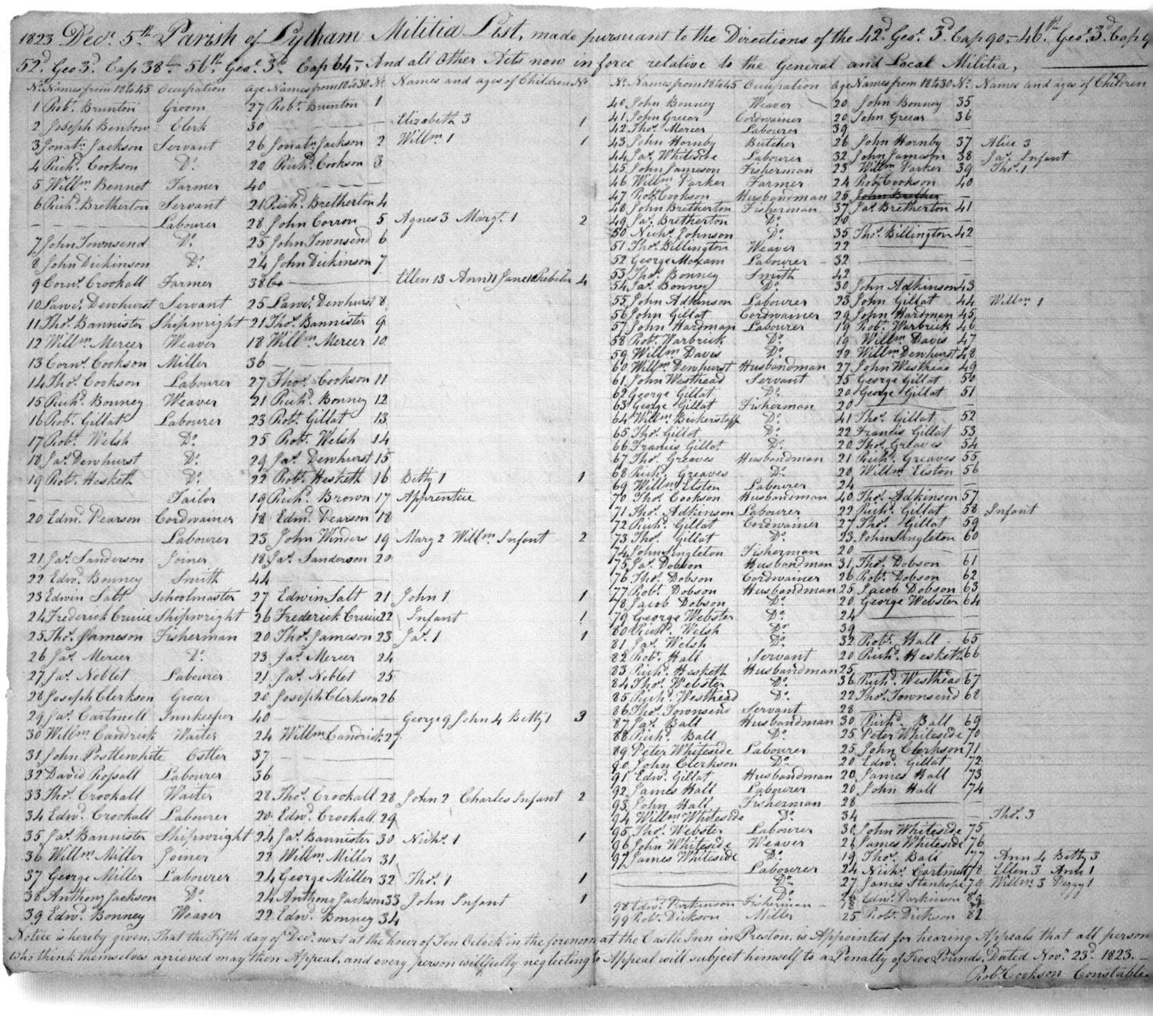
1823 Decr. 5th Parish of Lytham Militia List, made pursuant to the Directions of the 42d Geo. 3d. Cap. 90 – 46th Geo. 3d. Cap. 9 52d Geo 3d. Cap 38 – 56th Geo. 3d. Cap 64 – And all other Acts now in force relative to the General and Local Militia,

Notice is hereby given That the Fifth day of Decr. next at the hour of Ten O'clock in the forenoon at the Castle Inn in Preston, is Appointed for hearing Appeals that all persons who think themselves agrieved may then Appeal, and every person willfully neglecting to Appeal will subject himself to a Penalty of Five Pounds, Dated Novr. 23d. 1823. – Robt. Cookson Constable.

Without the survival of any overseer of the poor accounts, we do not know precisely how the poor of Lytham town and Heyhouses were treated. However, the militia return of 1823 for Lytham parish does provide a list of inhabitants by age, number of dependants and occupation (top of left-hand document). At the bottom of

In addition to any 'official' relief the Clifton family were also kept informed of day to day life on the estate and both Hetty, the wife of Thomas Joseph Clifton, and Lady Eleanor Cecily, the wife of John Talbot Clifton, were actively involved with the welfare of the tenants.

It was recalled that during the 1830s and 1840s Hetty Clifton, 'was better known to cottagers than even he [Thomas] was, her manner ("ways" the poor folks called it), her looks, her goodness, were much discussed. She was, when at Lytham, much amongst them and would, often and often, bring with her little presents for old and young … The estimation in which she was held by the tenantry … may be gathered from the language I heard used by a farmer soon after her death [1864]. He said – "You see, us Lytham farmers were proud of her, and when we were at Preston market we used to like to see her drive into the town."'[20]

The 1840s was a period when major improvements were being carried out on the Clifton family Lytham estate, and thereby a source of regular employment.

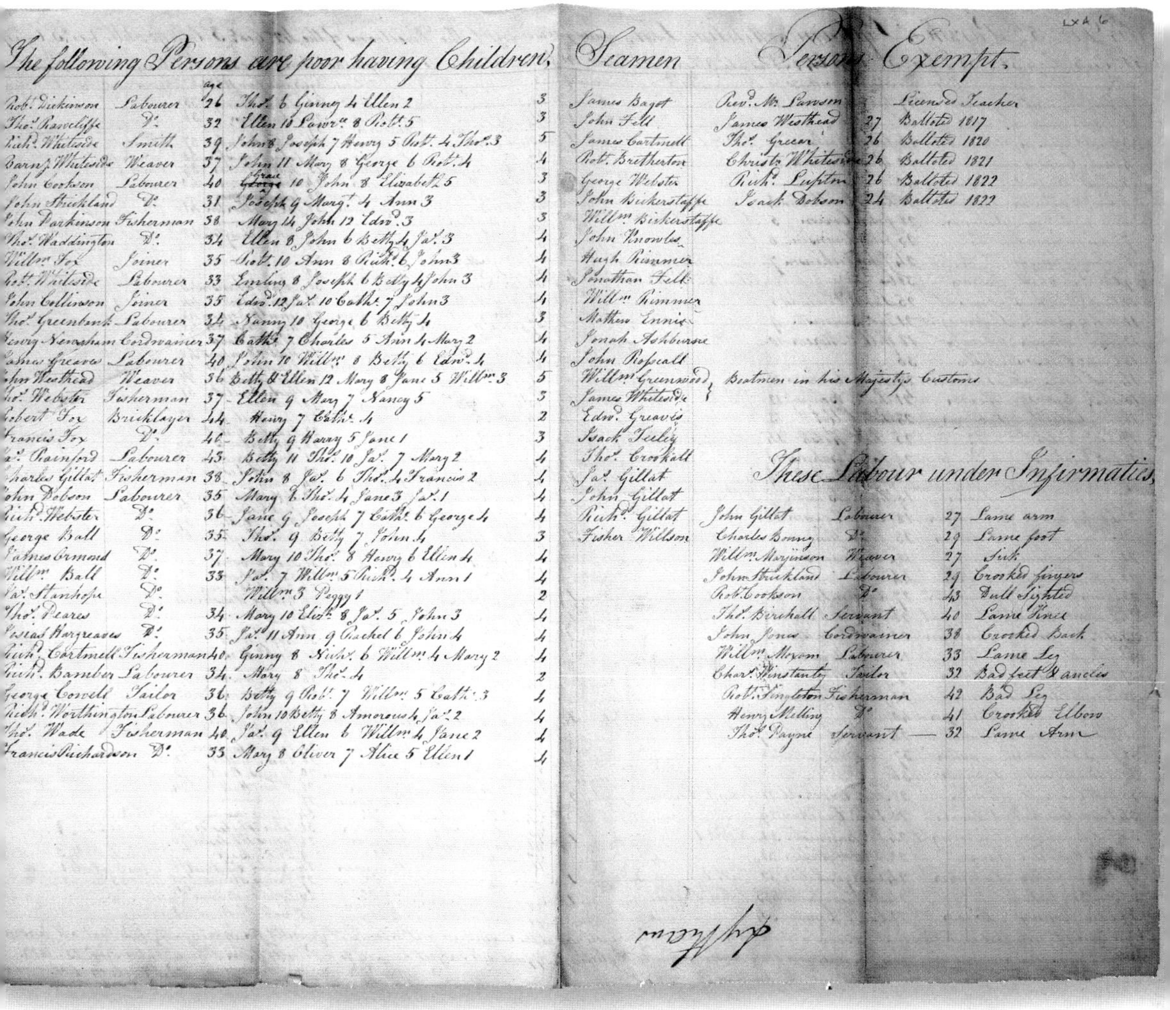

The following Persons are poor having Children

		age		
Robt. Dickinson	Labourer	26	Thos. 6 Ginny 4 Ellen 2	3
Thos. Rawcliffe	Do.	32	Ellen 10 Lawr. 8 Robt. 5	3
Richd. Whiteside	Smith	39	John 8 Joseph 7 Henry 5 Robt. 4 Thos. 3	5
Barny Whiteside	Weaver	37	John 11 Mary 8 George 6 Robt. 4	4
John Cookson	Labourer	40	Grace 10 John 8 Elizabeth 5	3
John Strickland	Do.	31	Joseph 9 Mary 4 Ann 3	3
John Parkinson	Fisherman	38	Mary 14 John 12 Edwd. 3	3
Thos. Waddington	Do.	34	Ellen 8 John 6 Betty 4 Jas. 3	4
Willm. Fox	Joiner	35	Robt. 10 Ann 8 Richd. 6 John 3	4
Robt. Whiteside	Labourer	33	Emily 8 Joseph 6 Betty 4 John 3	4
John Collinson	Joiner	35	Edwd. 12 Jas. 10 Cath. 7 John 3	4
Thos. Greenbank	Labourer	34	Nanny 10 George 6 Betty 4	3
Henry Newsham	Cordwainer	37	Cath. 7 Charles 5 Ann 4 Mary 2	4
James Greaves	Labourer	40	John 10 Willm. 8 Betty 6 Edwd. 4	4
John Westhead	Weaver	36	Betty & Ellen 12 Mary 8 Jane 5 Willm. 3	5
Thos. Webster	Fisherman	37	Ellen 9 Mary 7 Nancy 5	3
Robert Fox	Bricklayer	44	Henry 7 Cath. 4	2
Francis Fox	Do.	40	Betty 9 Harry 5 Jane 1	3
Jas. Rainford	Labourer	43	Betty 11 Thos. 10 Jas. 7 Mary 2	4
Charles Gillat	Fisherman	38	John 8 Jas. 6 Thos. 4 Francis 2	4
John Dobson	Labourer	35	Mary 8 Thos. 4 Jane 3 Jas. 1	4
Richd. Webster	Do.	36	Jane 9 Joseph 7 Cath. 6 George 4	4
George Ball	Do.	35	Thos. 9 Betty 7 John 4	3
James Ormond	Do.	37	Mary 10 Thos. 8 Henry 6 Ellen 4	4
Willm. Ball	Do.	33	Jas. 7 Willm. 5 Richd. 4 Ann 1	4
Jas. Stanhope	Do.		Willm. 3 Peggy 1	2
Thos. Peares	Do.	34	Mary 10 Eliz. 8 Jas. 5 John 3	4
Josias Hargreaves	Do.	35	Jas. 11 Ann 9 Rachel 6 John 4	4
Richd. Cartmell	Fisherman	40	Ginny 8 Richd. 6 Willm. 4 Mary 2	4
Richd. Bamber	Labourer	34	Mary 8 Thos. 4	2
George Corvell	Tailor	36	Betty 9 Robt. 7 Willm. 5 Cath. 3	4
Richd. Worthington	Labourer	36	John 10 Betty 8 Amorous 4 Jas. 2	4
Thos. Wade	Fisherman	40	Jas. 9 Ellen 6 Willm. 4 Jane 2	4
Francis Richardson	Do.	33	Mary 8 Oliver 7 Alice 5 Ellen 1	4

Seamen

James Bagot
John Fell
James Cartmell
Robt. Bretherton
George Webster
John Bickerstaffe
Willm. Bickerstaffe
John Knowles
Hugh Rimmer
Jonathan Fell
Willm. Rimmer
Mathew Ennis
Jonah Ashburne
John Roscall
Willm. Greenwood
James Whiteside
Edwd. Greaves
Isaac Seeley
Thos. Crookall
Jas. Gillat
John Gillat
Richd. Gillat
Fisher Willson

Willm. Greenwood, James Whiteside: Boatmen in his Majesty's Customs

Persons Exempt

Revd. Mr. Lawson		Licensed Teacher
James Westhead	27	Balloted 1817
Thos. Greear	26	Balloted 1820
Christr. Whiteside	26	Balloted 1821
Richd. Lupton	26	Balloted 1822
Isaac Dobson	24	Balloted 1822

These Labour under Infirmaties

John Gillat	Labourer	27	Lame arm
Charles Bonny	Do.	29	Lame foot
Willm. Marjinson	Weaver	27	Sick
John Strickland	Labourer	29	Crooked fingers
Robt. Cookson	Do.	43	Dull Sighted
Thos. Birchall	Servant	40	Lame Knee
John Jones	Cordwainer	38	Crooked Back
Willm. Moxom	Labourer	33	Lame Leg
Charl. Winstanley	Tailor	32	Bad feet & ancles
Robt. Singleton	Fisherman	42	Bad Leg
Henry Melling	Do.	41	Crooked Elbow
Thos. Payne	Servant	32	Lame Arm

the return (right), is a list of poor men with children, including those from Heyhouses, which also lists occupations. At bottom right is a list of a dozen men who 'Labour under Infirmities'. Around 13 per cent of families with young children were classed as poor at this date.

In 1851 it was noted that:

> On these and other operations one hundred and sixty labourers are employed, their wages being two shillings a day; the poor's rate are consequently diminished, being now only one shilling and fourpence in the pound, and none but the aged and infirm seek parish relief [21]

At Christmas 1847, in accordance with the directions of 'Mrs Clifton's Charity', beef was distributed to the poor. The names of those chosen to receive the beef were compiled by the parish clergy. The Rev. R. B. Robinson, vicar of St Cuthbert's, submitted the names of sixty-five individuals. Among those living in Heyhouses were James Melling, Harry Melling, Wil Melling, Widow Wilkin, Joseph Westhead, Mary Cartmell, and Robert Singleton. Ellen Webster, Nanny Johnson, and James Johnson resided at Commonside and James Bickerstaffe at North Houses. A further list of fifty-three 'Poor

Catholics' was compiled by the Rev. J. Walmsley; although he did not specify their place of residence, some, no doubt, were of Heyhouses.[22]

This tradition continued when John Talbot Clifton succeeded his father as lord of the manor in 1851. In November 1867, Lady Clifton, wrote two letters to James Fair from Guisborough Grange, Northampton.[23]

30 November 1867

Dear Mr Fair

I have returned you the list of game given away last year with a few scratchings & additions – There will be some Game I shd like given, but not sent, Floah [?] will know the people & therefore I will send the list to him & tell him to show it to you & you will give him the Game required – I have always thought the Clergy remiss about the poor, I think now it is a fashion for them to like to manage the poor themselves with no interference from the Owner of the Estate, Excepting as regards subscriptions for beautifying the Churches – This in my opinion is a mistake particularly for an Estate like the Colonels at Lytham.

16 December 1867

Dear Mr Fair

Yr letter of the 3rd Inst, I was unable to answer at that time, I think the selections you have made for the poor peoples Xmas clothing will do very well, Mrs Carter is very well able to tell you where it is most required, & if not already given I should like it done Early, …

Until her death in 1894 Lady Clifton made regular visits to the estate tenants, and the Clifton estate continued to fulfil a role until the social reforms of the twentieth century, such as the introduction of the old age pension in 1909, meant that the state gradually began to take over responsibility for the less fortunate in society.

CHAPTER SEVEN

Agriculture

Farming in the seventeenth century

As we have seen, the granting of leases for land on Lytham Hawes began during the first quarter of the seventeenth century. Once a lease had been granted it was the responsibility of each individual tenant to make a success of his own land. Some practices, however, such as control of access onto the Crosslawnde, required collective co-operation. Of the thirty-one leases, granted on 10 June 1616, sixteen make reference to the Crosslawnde. At the outset it became manorial policy that the new tenants took care to regulate access:

> William Galter of Lytham, sailor for £4: parcels of land lately improved from Lytham Hawes (12 acres) whereof 3 acres are exchanged with Richard Elston for land in the townfeild, 4½ acres lie on the Croslaunde, and 4 acres lie in the East on the common among his neighbours, occupiers of the Neinteine Acres ... Provided that the Sandy Laiche being now made several for the safety on the grounds on every side thereof shall be still at the lords will to dispose of and that there shall be a yate [gate] and stoops made and set at the head-room of the lane leading from the common at the charges of all occupiers of the hundred and two acres of land in the Crosslawndes yearly by them maintained, which yate shall be open every day in the summertime from 6 o'clock in the morning until 6 o'clock at night, for liberty of the tenants and inhabitants in Lytham to lead, drive, and fetch away their horses and cattle from the said Laiche so as they leave none behind. To join in provision of a keeper for the south side and half of the west side of the 102 acres, he being hired by the four having the greatest parts of the Crosslaunde.[1]

The four men who were required to hire a keeper were Lawrence Webster, Richard Fayer, Robert Ball, and Thomas Carter. They appointed John Maudsley:

LANCASHIRE COW.

John Maudsley of Lytham, blacksmith; for the yearly ditching and fencing
of the ditch on the north side of the Crosslawnde towards Pulton parish,
and keeping and watching on the said north side and half on the west side
of the 102 acres of land on the Crosslawnde, as a common servant to the
occupiers there ... of ... flatt lately improved from Lytham Hawes on the
North of the Crosslawnde and towards Pulton parish (8 acres).[2]

The analysis of the fifty-two inventories referred to in Chapter 3 provides
evidence of both pastoral and arable farming.[3] Forty-five inventories mention
cattle, and in 1663 Lawrence Webster had four kine and 'other young beasts'
with a value of £22 10s. 0d. Most farmers will have had beasts in various stages
of growth as for every beast slaughtered in the autumn it required five others
to maintain the breeding stock of the herd. Another example of this husbandry
is provided in the will of Thomas Webster who, in 1664, had 'All beasts young
and old' with a value of £21 10s. 0d.

Smaller herds included that of William Snape of Snape's Farm. When his
will was proved in 1687 he had beasts and cattle to the value of £12 3s. 4d. In
some instances beasts were shared between different family members, and in
1667 Richard Faire had a cow, a stirk, and two heifers valued at £7 0s. 0d. In
addition he had half of one stirk and half of one calf with a value to him of 15s.
0d. Widows too would keep at least one beast and in 1664 the cow of Jennet
Herdson was valued at £1 16s. 4d.

Not one inventory makes any mention of a bull, and it is almost certain that
this was provided by the estate. A requirement in the lease for the manor of

Lytham, granted to Ellen and George Rogerley in 1598, was that they had to keep 'a sufficient bull and boar for the use of the tenants'.[4] This requirement continued when the Clifton family acquired the estate and in 1699 and 1700 Gilbert Hayes, the then steward, noted in his account book:[5]

15 May 1699   A Bull   £5 6s. 6d.   Purchased at Inglewhite [Fair]
11 May 1700   A Bull   £3 19s. 6d.   Purchased at Inglewhite [Fair]

As might be expected thirty-seven inventories mention horses. In 1658 William Crookall had four nags and one mare with a value of £12 13s. 4d., and in 1699 Robert Sanderson had one gelding and two mares with a value of £7 10s. 0d. In addition to working the land, horses would also have been used for travel and in 1680 Ellin Gaulter, a widow, owned one mare with a value of £2 13s. 4d.

Thirty-five inventories mention sheep. Sheep were not suited to the wetter outlaying areas of the moss being prone to foot rot, and therefore not significant for farms without much common grazing. They were, however, better suited to the drier sandier soils of the common.

Although it is not until the mid-eighteenth century that there is documentary evidence of the regulations governing the number of sheep on the common, it is clear that sheep had been pastured there from at least the early to mid-seventeenth century. In 1644, during the civil wars, Cuthbert Clifton was said to have appropriated sheep from the adjacent Layton Hawes (part of which

A picture taken in 2007 of sheep on Lytham Moss, near the radar station. This scene would have been unimaginable to farmers in Heyhouses of the seventeenth to nineteenth centuries as sheep would not have been suited to the damp conditions of the mosslands. It was on the drier sandier soils of Lytham Common where sheep would have been pastured.
PHOTOGRAPH: AUTHOR

was owned by the Clifton family) and that 'for provision of his soldiers ... he caused many poor man's stock of sheep to be taken out of that Common belonging to Layton called the Hoos'.[6]

Although the majority of inventories simply state 'sheep', it would appear that during the last third of the seventeenth century the average value of an individual animal was around 2s. 6d. In 1663 Thomas Salthouse had four sheep with a value of 10s. 0d.; in 1667 Richard Faire had eight sheep with a value of £1 0s. 0d. and in 1693 William Norris had twenty-three sheep valued at £3 9s. 0d. The largest flock appears to have been that owned by Lawrence Webster, who in 1663 had sheep to the value of £13 10s. 0d. On the basis of 2s. 6d. for each animal he had a flock of around 108 sheep, and perhaps this fact alone provides the clue as to the reason for the value of his inventory being the largest of any farmer during this period.

Twelve inventories mention swine. In 1658 only William Crookall had more than one animal, his two swine being valued at £1 10s. 0d. Among those with just one animal were Lawrence Webster, whose hog was valued at 8s. 0d. in 1691, and George Elston whose swine was valued at 10s. 0d. in 1698. Poultry are mentioned in twenty-five inventories. Thomas Webster in 1664 had six hens and a cockerel valued at 2s. 4d., and in 1669 Ellin Salthouse, a widow, had poultry to the value of 1s. 4d. Even though they were probably present on most farms only the inventory of William Crookall refers specifically to geese, which together with his hens, were valued at 4s. 0d.

Nineteen inventories refer to range of different crops. Again, much of the Heyhouses area was unsuited to arable, so that such farming was limited to strip or drier ground between the moss and the sandhills. The two principal crops were barley and oats, which are each mentioned in thirteen inventories. Corn, presumably wheat, is mentioned in nine inventories; hemp is mentioned in thirteen; flax in eight; and rye, peas and beans are each mentioned once. Some of the barley was probably reduced to malt and used for brewing ale. Peas were also a field crop rather than a garden crop, as were beans, but which could also be used for fodder. Hemp and flax were probably grown for domestic use.

Once more it is the inventory of William Crookall that provides the most detail. At the time of his death he had 'Oats Barley Peas Beans – Sown/ Unsown' to the value of £6 3s. 4d. In 1680 Ellin Crookall, a widow and possibly the daughter in law of William, had oats and barley valued at £5. In addition she had 'Corn grown at Carters' valued at £2 1s. 6d. It is one of several examples of a widow continuing to farm following the death of a husband at a relatively young age. 'Carters' was presumably land rented from the Carter family on Heyhouses Lane.

Farming tools and equipment were bequeathed in wills and also listed in inventories. The appraisers compiling the inventory sometimes combined items together and, as in the case of William Salthouse in 1663, recorded 'all the husbandrie gear – £1 0s. 0d.'. A more detailed inventory was that of John Sanderson in 1687 whose 'Carts, wheels, plows, harrows, sweys, spades or pitchforks, & Husbandry geare' was valued at £1 16s. 8d. In 1680 the inventory of Ellin Crookall lists 'Carts, wheeles, plows, harrows, loose wood, & all other husbandrie geare' to the value of £1 16s. 8d. Among these items presumably were 'ye turfe Cart & New Wheeles With plow Arms for it, one payre of half trase & all other geare to fitt two horses to draw in ye Cart With Mucke cart & one harrow' already bequeathed in her will to her son, John Crookall.

Lytham Common

Before we begin to look at agriculture in Heyhouses during the eighteenth century it is perhaps necessary to have some understanding of the changes in the regulations governing the putting out of livestock onto Lytham Common.

The last two known occasions in which there is reference to the previously mentioned Crosslawnde occur in leases to Thomas Sanderson in 1620 for 'two flatts lately improved from the Crosse launde in Lytham Hawes – 8 acres',[7] and William Webster, a linen webster, in 1622, for a 'parcel of ground newly improved from the moss in Lytham Hawes – 4 acres ... of the Crosse Land'.[8] After 1622 the area is usually referred to as Lytham Common.

As we have seen there had always been manorial control concerning the number of livestock allowed onto the common. By the mid-eighteenth century evidence of increasingly intensive grazing occurs widely in Lancashire and this situation is reflected in several orders issued by the manorial court. On 7 May 1739 the court ordered that:

> That no Person Inhabitant of this Parish shall keep above two sheep upon the Common for an Acre of Inland Tenement in their Possession ... Lambs excepted. And that this order may be more effectively kept we order that Thomas Rowlandson, Shoemaker and Robert Windress of the Town shall view all the sheep in the said Parish twice a year that is to say about the twenty-fifth day of March and Martinmas and No Persons shall Put any sheep upon the said Common but only with one visible Wool Mark and if any Person or Persons shall keep above that number of 2 sheep for Every Acre in their possession as aforesaid Such Persons shall forfeit and Pay to the Lord of the Manor the Sum of 2 Shillings for Every sheep they shall keep there above that Number[9]

and on 23 June 1746:

> We order that no person or persons shall put or keep any Geese upon Lytham Common betwixt the Church and Laton-hays (Layton Hawes)

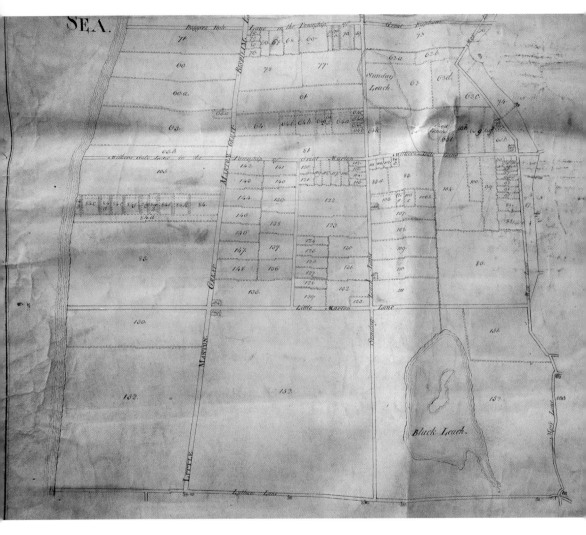

Layton Hawes Enclosure Award. The southern portion of a map showing the plots of land on Layton Hawes at the time the Hawes was enclosed in 1769. The Black Leach is marked, as also are some of the farms and cottages that were situated within the manor of Lytham. These farms and cottages were depicted as they appeared to the surveyor/artist. Thus Charnley's House (later Division Farm) is revealed as a more substantial dwelling than the nearby cottages.

after the 10th of July next in default thereof we Amerce all such person or persons in the Sum of one Shilling for every Goose so put or kept upon the said Common [10]

By 1752, possibly due to an increase in the number of cattle, it had become necessary to determine the number of cows each farmstead could pasture on the common. This was achieved by carrying out a survey, probably by Randolph

Penswick, the then steward to the Clifton family, entitled the 'Measure of Lytham Common'. Details of the survey, and its conclusions, were summarised in the Common Book of Lytham for the year 1755.[11]

The survey commenced at 'the broken brows' (Lytham Town?) thence to 'ye entrance on the Common by Church house ground' (near to St Cuthbert's Church) and continued along Commonside to 'Thos Gaulter's barn' (Whiteside's Farm). Somewhere between these two locations there was another entrance onto the common 'by Wm Winstanley's and James Crookall's' (possibly the junction of Commonside with Nineteen Acre Lane).

From Thos Gaulter's barn the surveyor turned right (Headroomgate Road) and continued 'from Thomas Booth's by the head room gate and [on]to John Wolf's barn' (Leach Lane/Division Lane). At this point he turned 'Westward ending at Wilkins fields' (Cross Slack), where he noted 'no more was Measured till I got passed Edwd Walmsley's house there being no pasture but all Starr [grass] etc'. The final entry in the survey notes 'from a litle behind Edwd Walmsleys to the Division ditch'. The total area surveyed was 416 acres 2 roods and 7 perches.

With the survey completed, the next stage was to allocate the number of cattle each tenant could pasture on the common. This practice of allocating what were known as cow/common gates was widespread in lowland/coastal townships on both sides of the River Ribble. Freckleton and Newton Marshgate Owners still operate this system today. In 1752 the Lytham surveyor computed that:

(i) the lease tenants and rack tenants, 'that have been free to the Common', together occupied 1240 acres of land on the estate;

(ii) 'the Common being 416 acres or upwards to Summer 200 Cows or thereabouts'.

From these two facts he determined that:

then it will be for every 7 acres of the above 1240 acres one Cow Gate and 23 Cow gates will remain in Mr Clifton's gift to be given part thereof to the Cottagers and the remainder to be disposed of to any industrious person as he shall think proper

Acres to one Cow   7   Acres 1240

So there will be 177 Cow Gates at One Cow for every seven acres of the above 1240 acres and 23 will remain my Masters gift as above mentioned.[12]

This survey would appear to reflect the increasing importance of the estate steward as a land agent, rather than merely an administrator, in that he

bypassed the manorial court procedures and dealt with the issues directly. The manorial court itself, however, continued to make the formal decisions:

> We order that no Person or Persons shall gather any Dung of the Common or Common of Pasture within the Parish of Lytham after the 22nd of August next and any Person or Persons so gathering any Dung as aforesaid we amerce them in 13*s*. 4*d*.   Each
>   (25 July 1757)[13]

> We order that no person or persons shall keep any bad or unsufficient Tup (a Ram) upon Lytham Common after the thirtieth of August that shall be judged to be unsufficient by the Tup Viewers and for every one making such default we amerce them in 6*s*. 8*d*.   Each
>   (9 July 1759)[14]

> We order that no person or persons shall put any Goods or Cattle upon Lytham Common without giving notice of such Cattle so put on the said Common unto the Tenter of the said Commons that is, or shall be appointed betwixt and the 5th instant and in default thereof we amerce them in 6*s*. 8*d*.   Each
>   (2 June 1760)[15]

The Lytham Lease Rents at Martinmas (11 November) 1762 show that the annual (?) price of one cowgate/common gate was 3*s*. 0*d*. James Smith of Common Side House had three common gates for which he paid 9*s*. 0*d*.; in

Brook Farm was situated on Heyhouses Lane at the entrance to the present-day Pilling Avenue. It was presumably so called because a major watercourse ran alongside its north-west boundary. At the manorial court held on 27 May 1754 there is mention of 'where the water crosses the said [Heyhouses] Lane'. Brook Farm was demolished in 1963.
BY COURTESY OF THE FAMILY OF THE LATE FRANK DEAN

addition he paid 6d. towards the tenter's wage for one common gate. Thomas Webster, who appears to have been farming at both the Slated Barn and Carters (Fancy Lodge), paid £1 1s. 0d. for seven common gates but nothing towards the tenter's wages. Ann Green, however, a cottager living next to Headroomgate Farm, was charged just 6d. for the 'tenters wages for one common gate'.[16]

These charges are explained in the summary associated with the 1784 Fylde Rental which stated that 'Mr Clifton stints his warren ground and permits his Tenants ... to turn their cattle to graze thereon in proportion to the quantity of land they hold under him paying a small consideration for the said priviledge ...' Tenants holding 'new' leases were charged 3s. 0d. per cow gate, while tenants holding 'old' leases were charged only 6d. In addition, tenants paying rack rent were likewise charged only 6d. 'per Cow gate for Summer Grass'.[17]

Due to an absence of documentary evidence it is not known when the practice of allocating common gates ceased, but the pasturing of cattle was still being carried out as late as 1853. Under the terms of a lease granted to William Swarbrick, of 'West End', it was agreed that his 'Cattle may be turned to pasture into the Sand Hills by being properly attended to, except in the Months of March, April, May and till the 20th June in each year'.[18]

Farming in the eighteenth century

On the evidence of the fifty-seven inventories for the years 1701 to 1773 it would appear that there had been a change in agricultural practices. Only eight inventories make reference to corn, barley or oats, and there is a much greater emphasis on pastoral farming.[19] As there is no obvious explanation for these changes it may have been that Lytham was typical of other areas in the Fylde where the poor quality of corn was almost certainly due to the farming practices which were described and criticised by John Holt in 1795. In his agricultural survey of Lancashire he remarked that 'in the Fylde which, from its fertility, has been called the Granary of the county, the soil has been still worse abused. Certain fields have been kept under cultivation, it is asserted, for more than a century, without intermission.'[20]

There was one notable addition to the traditional crops. Lancashire was the first English county in which the potato was grown, and in the Lytham steward's accounts for 19 June 1703 Francis Winstanley was paid 4s. 8d. 'for seven bushels pottetows to set at 8d. per bushel'.[21] In his will, made in 1729, Thomas Bamber gave to Richard Crookall 'ye Potatoes money that James Winstanley oweth me'. The first specific mention of the crop being grown in Heyhouses is in the 1746 inventory of James Colly, who had potatoes valued at £1 10s. 0d.

As a result of these changes in farming practices farmers were becoming wealthier, and many more now regarded themselves as yeomen rather than husbandmen. And it was the yeomen who owned the larger herds of cattle and flocks of sheep. In 1729 Robert Rimmer of Cross Slack had four calves, two drift heifers (cows not in calf and which gave little or no milk), two pinkt cows (probably cows that had had aborted calves), and one old cow with a total value of £26 5s. od. He also had sheep to the value of £10. In 1730 Lawrence Webster, of 'the Kiln' (Kilnhouse Farm), had four cows, four heifers, and four calves valued at £22 5s. od. in addition to fifty sheep valued at £12 10s. od.

The total value of Lawrence Webster's flock suggests that a sheep had not increased in value from 2s. 6d. in fifty or more years. Later inventories, however, indicate that the price, in spite of some fluctuations, was indeed rising and in the same year twenty sheep owned by Thomas Sanderson of North Houses were valued at £3 10s. od., or 3s. 6d. each; and in 1738 Richard Salthouse had sixty sheep valued at £9, or 3s. od. each.

With the exception of Lawrence Webster who had four mares and four colts with a total value of £20, all other farmers had between one and three horses. Typical was John Warbrick of Leach Lodge, with three mares valued at £10. Fifteen inventories mention a single swine all of which were probably reared for home consumption. Although directed more at residents in Lytham Town rather than the farmers of Heyhouses, the manorial court in 1739 felt it necessary to issue the following order:

We further order that all Persons within this Parish that keep any Swine that they immediately ring them sufficiently and keep them ringed … upon complaint to the Jury the Defaulter to forfeit 6s. 8d. to the Lord of the Manor [22]

An order of 1760, however, was almost certainly aimed at the cottagers of Heyhouses:

We order that no Person nor Persons shall keep any Cattle in the Lanes after the first of July next, or suffer or permit the same to Wander or stray therein in the Night time after the Sun is set, and in default thereof we amerce each such Person in the Sum 3s. 4d …[23]

Little notice seems to have been taken of it and almost one hundred years later the practice continued. In 1932 George Gillett, who was born in 1851 in a cottage (Greens) in Twiggy Lane, recalled that 'We kept a cow or two, running in the green lanes, and nobody said anything as long as you kept them out of folk's fields'.[24]

The increasing number of cattle owned by each farmer was becoming a matter of some concern. In addition to the two examples already given, John Gaulter of Commonside (Whiteside's Farm) had, in 1719, five kine, two bullocks, two heifers and two calves with a value of £25 0s. 0d. It was no doubt this increase in the number of cattle that led to the regulations relating to Lytham Common.

It would also seem that some farmers looked for alternative grazing sites and in July 1757 the manorial court found it necessary to issue an order concerning livestock on the moss:

> We order that no person or persons shall drive or put any Cattle to or upon Lytham Moss to graze or pasture upon the said Moss at any time after the 29th Instant and all Person or Persons so driving or putting any such Cattle on the sd Moss to pasture or suffering the same to pasture on the sd Moss we amerce them in 13s. 4d. Each [25]

Other farmers sought pasture beyond the parish of Lytham and at least two individuals drove their beast(s) some distance in order to take advantage of the valuable summer grazing afforded by Freckleton Marsh. In 1763 Nanny Wilson of Heyhouses leased one of seven cattle gates owned by James Coulborn, and ... Winstanley of 'Cominsid' (Commonside) leased a cattle gate from Mr Langton.[26]

However not all Heyhouses residents were able, or prepared, to lease or rent grazing land for their livestock. In October 1766 Thomas and William Wade, both described as labourers, were brought before the magistrates at Preston. The indictment against them was that in April that year they had depastured† four cows, to the value of £4, 'upon a certain Common called Layton Hays (Hawes) within the Parish of Bispham ... they nor either of them having any right to turn out or depasture any Cattle thereon for or by any reason or in any respect whatsoever'.

As a result of this trespass four of the freeholders of Layton Hawes attempted to drive the beasts to the open [cattle] pound at Layton whereupon 'the said Thomas Wade and William Wade by force and Armes ... unlawfully did rescue the said four cows out of their [the freeholders'] hands and custody ... and did cause the said cows to go at large without paying any money or recompense [to the freeholders].' At the magistrates court Thomas and William Wade were ordered to attend the next quarter sessions, and in the meantime 'to keep the Peace', failing which they were to be conveyed to the 'Common Gaol at Lancaster'.[27]

Farming in the nineteenth century

While the eighteenth century had witnessed a greater emphasis on pastoral farming the nineteenth century would bring even greater changes to farming practices.

In 1812 the Clifton estate carried out their major township survey. At about the same period the estate ended the practice of granting leases on the principal of 'three lives', which could result in a tenancy for sixty or more years, and began granting leases for an initial seven years only. It was an attempt by landowners to direct their tenants' farming practices. If during those seven years the tenant had not made a success of his holding, and thereby not contributed to the revenue of the estate, the lease need not be renewed. This change was paralleled by the comparable control of urban building in Lytham town.

One of the first of these new leases was for West End Farm. It was granted to John Westhead on 15 September 1818, and took effect from 2 February 1819, at an annual rent of £90. The acreage of the farm was then just over forty-four acres, of which there were thirteen acres of oats, two acres of barley and two and a half acres of wheat. The greater part was given over to pasture.[28]

In 1825 the lease granted to Robert Cookson of Heyhouses (Farm?) required him to:

(i) ditch 200 rods of ditching … And plant the whole length of the bank or cop belonging to the ditch with thorn quicksets … and fence and stake them behind …

(ii) cause to be eaten and consumed in the outbuildings belonging to the premises, All the hay, straw, potatoes, cabbages, turnips, carrots, and

Cops – thick walls of sand sods grown over with grass – were once a prominent feature of the Heyhouses landscape. In this view they enclose land adjacent to Cartmell's Farm on Heyhouses Lane.

all other fodder, grown or growing upon the premises or brought thereto ...

(iii) yearly spread upon some part of the meadow and pasture land ... all the compost, and manure arising therefrom ...

(iv) not push-plough, pare, or burn any part of the premises during the term; nor plough or otherwise break up ... into tillage ... meadows or pastures now green side up, nor plough above six acres summer works and clover included ...[29]

Cops, once a prominent feature of the Heyhouses landscape, had all but vanished by the early 1960s. In 1904 Catherine Jacson recalled a walk through Commonside taken in about 1834:

My mother and I were returning from Double Stanner inland. The way was then through a lane by Common-side bounded on each side by a 'Cop' – these cops, be it told for the benefit of the uninitiated, are thick walls of sand sods grown over with grass, and consolidated as far as sand may be. They are also rendered more effective, as a fence, by a dry ditch on each side, out of which, I presume, the sods are taken ...[30]

In 1932 George Gillet, then the tenant at Cross Slack Farm, recalled that:

Farming when I was a lad was a totally different matter from what it is now. Marton Moss [the term used for both Marton and Lytham Mosses] had not been drained, and horses could not be used for ploughing, as they would have sunk in too deep. So we had to use push-ploughs. These were like a spade with an additional blade, and they were attached to a long handle. These handles had leathers, making a broad belt, and they were pushed by the chest, a few feet at a time. The ploughing was done in the winter and there was a lot of peat turned up with ling on top. In March this peat was burnt and the ashes spread on the land to fertilise it. We grew a lot of corn, principally barley, because it was a quick crop.[31]

In spite of the changes introduced at the beginning of the century the Clifton estate was still not being farmed to its full potential. In 1835, when James Fair was appointed land agent for the Clifton family, the estate was described as having been 'long neglected owing to a non-resident landlord', and that 'west of Lytham was little else than a morass, in winter impassable, in summer yielding nothing but a sour and scanty herbage'.[32]

In a newspaper interview in 1887 his son, Thomas Fair, recalled that when his father first arrived he found:

... farming here at a very low ebb, the system of life-leasing having been almost universal throughout the district. This he was determined to alter. One of the first steps in the direction of improvement was the establishment in 1836 of an agricultural society at Lytham. The premiums given were co ... [?] to the tenants belonging to the estate. The result was very satisfactory. Each year the stock exhibited has gone on improving. After a short time some of the principal tenants joined together to purchase a bull from Northumberland for 100 guineas for the purposes of improving the breed of the county. The green crop system which before was scarcely known here was plentifully practised ...[33]

Prior to the arrival of James Fair the lessees had had to provide and maintain farm buildings for themselves which, according to Thomas Fair, were of 'a very inferior design, mud, clay and thatch'. A programme of improving these properties commenced as, in the words of Thomas Fair, 'you cannot expect to have good tenants unless you provide them with comfortable and convenient houses and buildings'. He added that 'up to 1886 the sum of £215,589 had been expended on buildings and repairs, about £12,000 on agricultural roads, and on drainage about £37,000'.[34]

This latter charge resulted in land which before had been useless for arable purposes becoming the most valuable farming land. In addition James Fair began to dispense with the traditional seven-year lease which, in the opinion of his son, 'could not have been granted to tenants either with advantage to themselves or their landlord'.

The most significant changes took place when James Fair 'got three or four substantial and intelligent farmers from Scotland to take on farms of about 250 acres each, on nineteen years lease'.[35] When James Fair died in 1871, the estate was described as 'instead of being a reproach to the agriculture of Lancashire', it had become 'the pride and boast of the county'.[36]

Based on the evidence of the census returns for the period 1841 to 1881, no Scottish farmer ever took out a lease for a farm in Heyhouses.

Farm Sale – Brook Farm. Evidence of the improved farming practices encouraged by James and Thomas Fair, in their roles as land agents to the Clifton family, is provided by this poster of the sale of farming stock of Frederick Porter and James Whiteside at Brook Farm in 1897.
BY COURTESY OF EDITH PORTER

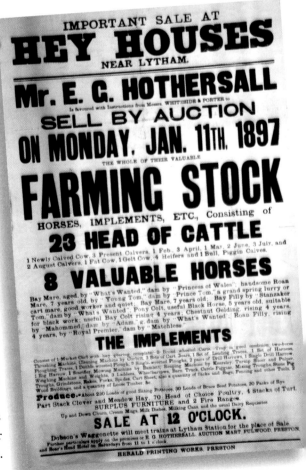

Nevertheless, the improved agricultural practices taking place elsewhere on the estate no doubt served as an example.

In 1852 Robert Ormond, then aged twenty-six, was granted an eleven-year lease for eighty-eight acres at Kilnhouse Farm. The yearly rental was £100, but out of this rent 'Mr' Clifton was prepared to allow £5 for two years 'if the husbandry and improvement of the tenant are satisfactory'.[37] In addition Robert Ormond was required to make into meadows the two Moss Fields; the Backside Field 'now an oat stubble' had to be green cropped 'then wheat or barley with a grass seed for a permanent Pasture'; and the remaining portion of the farm had to be managed under a six-course rotation.[38]

Farmhouses almost certainly rebuilt during the latter nineteenth and early twentieth centuries included Headroomgate Farm, Model Farm, West End Farm, and Kilnhouse Farm. By 1881 Robert Hargreaves of Headroomgate Farm farmed 180 acres that went northwards to the present Rodney Avenue, and southwards to the Parish Rooms. Thomas Swarbrick of Model Farm farmed 140 acres; Robert Hall, of West End Farm, had one hundred acres; and John Singleton of Kilnhouse Farm had eighty-eight acres, the same as Robert Ormond in 1852.

Other farmers included Edward Parkinson at Elmhurst Farm, John Hesketh at Moss Edge Farm, Alexander Moore at Leach Lodge Farm, Thomas Gillett at Cross Slack Farm and Thomas Jameson at North Houses.

Farming in the twentieth century

In spite of the ever-encroaching new town of St Anne's, it was not until after World War II that the irreversible decline of farming in Heyhouses commenced. A survey taken during the inter-war years concerning commutation of the tithe payments assessed the rental value of almost 1,500 acres of farmland at £2,892.[39]

Unfortunately there are few contemporary accounts of farming practices in Heyhouses for the years from 1920 to 1960. It would appear that most farms continued to combine arable and pastoral farming. Many farms had fields on the

moss where corn, potatoes and turnips were grown. In late summer Isaac Ball of Treales came and 'did the rounds' with his threshing machine, a time when each farmer helped his neighbour while their wives provided the food.[40]

At Elmhurst Farm there was a non-pedigree herd of between twenty-five and thirty milk cows which had been bought at market. The pasture field was to the rear of the farm, from the present Elmhurst Road to Poulton Avenue. Two horses were used for ploughing.[41]

When Edward Swann relinquished the tenancy of Headroomgate Farm in 1939, following the loss of much of his land for building purposes, the livestock was described as 'twenty-nine well-bred dairy cattle and young stock comprising ten new and recently calved cows and heifers. Five February and March calving calves. Heifer for close calving. Twinter [two winters], five spring and summer calving cows. Two coloury heifer stirks. Four wye piggin calves [female calves weaned out of a cow bucket made of wood], and well bred

In 1881 Headroomgate Farm, situated at the junction of Highbury Road (Twiggy Lane) and Leach Lane, was farmed by Robert Hargreaves and had the largest acreage of any farm in Heyhouses (180 acres). During the next half-century much of this land was taken for building, and in 1939 Edward Swann relinquished the tenancy following the loss of farmland northwards as far as Rodney Avenue. The last tenant was John Dockeray, and the farm was demolished in 1961.

BY COURTESY OF BRIAN SWANN

roan Shorthorn bull – six teeth – smittle and effective [good breeding stock].' In addition there were three horses, and nine pigs.

A wide range of farming implements was also offered for sale. Some of these items, such as a harrow or hay rake, would have been as familiar to the tenant at Headroomgate Farm in the 1730s as they were to the tenant of the 1930s. Other items, such as a potato digger or Massey Harris binder, were evidence of the vast changes in farming practices over those two centuries.[42]

Even as late as 1945 Heyhouses could still be described as a farming community. However if the establishment of St Anne's in 1875 had been the beginning of the end for Heyhouses, the years immediately following the end of the Second World War were its final days. The events leading to the effective disappearance of the Heyhouses farming community by the late 1950s and early 1960s will be told in Chapter 12.

CHAPTER EIGHT

Fishermen and innkeepers

Fishing

Because of lack of documentary evidence it is difficult to determine the extent to which fishing formed part of the economy of Heyhouses during the sixteenth and seventeenth centuries. As elsewhere on the coast of lowland Lancashire fishing had always been one of the principal occupations within the parish of Lytham, and catching on shore was the same method as that practised at North Meols and Birkdale. In 1517 the manorial court of Lytham Priory ordered that:

> All fishermen within the lordship of Lethum carrying their fish caught on the sea shore to the town of Lethum in winter-time, must sell them to the chapman licensed by the prior, penalty 2d.[1]

In 1615, nine years after the purchase of the estate by Cuthbert Clifton, the privileges of the lord of the manor were set out in detail by the manorial court:

> Mr Rogerley and his wyff in their time did usually take at footlynes and a boate; when fishe came in, ether by boat or footlynes and when they nedd [needed] they did take a milwyn [cod] for 1½d., a Raye or thornebegg for 1d. and at Christenmas a milwyn for 3d. and a Raye or Thornebegg for 1d ... And for a muskle boat 3s. 4d. a boate, for a baye Boate a share as they gott on their conscience, for a muskle skeare [bed] a porcion when stoare was to be sould to serve the house, for a skeare nett when they fall some 8d., some 4d., some 2d.[2]

It is probable, however, that fishing was more extensive than suggested, and in 1655 William Cookson had 'Sea geare' to the value of 12s. 0d.; in 1675 Robert Fletcher, the shoemaker, had 'one Breake and one ffishnet' to the value of 2s. 4d.; and in 1687 John Sanderson, of the Black Leach, had 'one half part of one fishing boat' valued at £1 0s. 0d.[3] The only entry in the church registers which refers specifically to a fisherman, with known association with Heyhouses, is that of Edward Bagot who, when he died in 1721, was described as 'Piscator Vetustissimus' (a very old fisherman).[4]

Despite their dwellings being situated almost on the coastline, there is no evidence that the tenants at Cross Slack combined fishing with agriculture. Their 'advantage' was ready access to the break up of a wrecked vessel. At the manorial court held in 1682 John Gaulter 'of the Cross Slack' together with William Salthouse, Richard Walsh and Thomas Fisher were each fined 3s. 4d. 'for takeinge up Wreck goods under a full Sea & offeringe to conceale them'. At the same court James Salthouse, Thomas Lawson and William Gaulter were each fined 1s. 0d. 'for Caryinge Roapes from the Vessele that was lost'.[5] A similar incident took place in 1705 when Thomas Webster, son of James Webster, senior, and James Colly, son of Thomas Colly 'of ye heyhouses' were each fined 6s. 8d. 'for taking up Wrack & Carring it away & concealinge it'.[6]

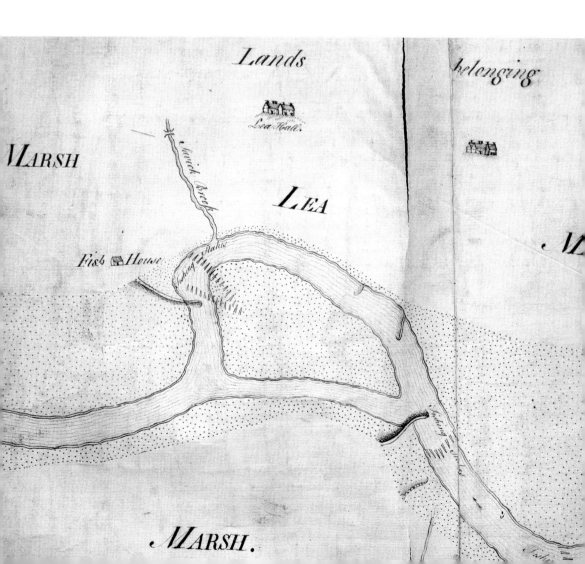

A life at sea, particularly for the young men of Lytham parish (including Heyhouses), must have always been an attraction, though the consequences of such a life for William Patrick were probably not what he expected. At the court of quarter sessions held in Preston at Easter 1685 his father, Thomas Patrick, presented the following petition to the magistrates:

Humbly Showeth That your poore petitioners sonne William Patrick labouringe in a Vessel called Samarritan belonginge to Liverpoole ... was upon the Seaventeenth Day of December last Saleinge from Droughader in ye Kingdom of Ireland taken by a Sally man of warr [Sallee Pirates who operated from the modern Sale, near Rabat, Morocco] where he now remains in Cruell Slavery & his usage and faire [food] is after a most barboruse manner that is one pinte of Water onlie in twenty-four hours Blacke barely breade ... and for every small faulte is most cruely beaten upon the soles of ye feet and belly ... foure hours rest in 24 ... six yards cheaned under ye Grounde and cannot be redeemed lesse than the sume of ffifty Pounds[7]

Although William Patrick appears to have come from Lytham 'Town' his plight would have been well known within Heyhouses. Although we do not know how long he spent as a prisoner of the Sallee pirates he must have been released, as on 17 November 1704 a son of a 'William Patrick, Saylor' was baptised at St Cuthbert's church.[8]

A more detailed account of fishing, and others aspects of coastal life during the late seventeenth and eighteenth centuries, is provided by the depositions of several Lytham men obtained in the case of John Clifton versus John Alexander, held at Lancaster assizes in 1824. The case of John Clifton was that he and his family had 'immemorially exercised the Manorial Rights particularly those of Anchorage, Wreck, Selling Stones and Gravel, and also of Setting Stake Nets for fishing'. During the trial a document entitled 'An ancient Document at Lytham Hall of the date 1696' was produced as evidence, to demonstrate how fishing had continued to be regulated since that date:

Every Fryday Morning all Fish that is taken with Nets called Trammells is due and belongs to ye Lord of Ye Manor, the Baliffe goes constantly to receive it & brings it to ye Hall unless it be notified to him before that no Netts are sett & hanging – if the Baliffe be come thither first he fishes the Netts himself but if the Fishermen be come before him they usually fishe theire Netts and keep what fish is gotten until the Baliffe have received it & taken thereout what he thinks fit for ye Lord of Ye Manor. If the Fishermen take theire Netts of upon Wednesday in the Evening they ought to acquainte the Baliffe therewith for in that case half of ye

A detail of a mid-eighteenth century plan of the river Ribble by Porter, showing the area around Lea, near Preston. Note the Fish House and the several ranks of fishing stakes in the river: such stakes were used to support nets to trap fish. Heyhouses fishermen would have used a similar method to catch fish along Lytham Sands, a practice regulated by the manorial court.

LRO, REPRODUCED BY KIND PERMISSION OF THE COUNTY ARCHIVIST, LANCASHIRE RECORD OFFICE

Fish is due to ye Lord, but if they take them of upon Thursday then all is due. If they sette theire Netts but upon Thursday Evening then half of ye Fish taken on Friday Morning is but due.[9]

Among the comments made by estate tenants at the time of the trial George Cartmell, born at Lytham in 1746, stated that he had lived in Lytham all his life and that he had held 'a tenement under Mr Clifton and also held one under his father, … that he had followed fishing and Farming for many years'. He added that he remembered the fishing rights being let by the then estate steward to 'Robert Cookson, the then Overseer of the Poor who let the privilege of Fishing to different Persons Inhabitants of Lytham who were to pay according to their ability, some 10s. 0d., some 5s. 0d., and others 2s. 6d.'[10]

John Parkinson, although born in Poulton in 1739, had lived in Lytham since a child. He recalled 'that Mr Clifton's family have collected wreck ever since witness could remember, if the fishermen found any on the sands they let Mr Clifton's Agent know, who fetched the wreck to Lytham Hall and paid them for their trouble, the wreck is kept by Mr Clifton for a year & a day and if not claimed in that time he sells it.' He added that he had often 'found dead bodies on the Sands and brought them up to Lytham Town and informed Mr Clifton's Steward who always ordered Coffins and paid for them, can remember (but it is long ago) when they buried dead bodies cast on shore without coffins but Mr Clifton's family always paid for bringing up the dead bodies for burial and coffins have now been found by the Clifton family for many years past.'[11]

Mellings Lane acquired its name from the Melling family, who came to live in the Lytham/Heyhouses area sometime in the late eighteenth century. By the late 1830s Henry Melling 'and others' were living in the cottages depicted here. In 1915 John Melling (see photograph opposite) recalled that during the violent storm of 8 January 1839 the thatch was stripped off the roof so that 'when we lay in bed we could see t'stars'.

BY COURTESY OF THE FAMILY OF THE LATE FRANK DEAN

John Whalley came to live in Lytham in about 1784 and 'kept the Bowling Green Public House'. He and James Slater also traded on the River Ribble, carrying stones and gravel to Preston and coals down the River Douglas to Lytham. John Whalley said that 'The Principal part of the stones were got in Lytham near a Place called Cross Slack and picked off the shore between high & low water mark whenever they could find them left bare by the sea.'[12]

The manorial court records confirm that strict control over fishing practices was enforced, as in 1758 when it was ordered that:

no person or persons shall set any Trammel Net or Nets to catch fish on Lytham Sands before any other Net or Nets that is already Set within the distance of 120 yards and that no person or persons shall set above two Nets in One Rank and also that no person or persons shall set any Net or Nets within the distance of 60 yards on the Scares or Gravel Beds and that no person or persons shall mark or stake any ground or let any stakes stand without being cover'd or nets hang'd thereon for above the time of two Tides in the spring Tides betwixt [the date of this court] and the first of May next whosoever is guilty of any of the above said Faults we amerce them in 13s. 4d. Each.[13]

By the middle of the nineteenth century a much clearer picture of the Heyhouses fishing community becomes possible. On the 1841 census twenty-two heads of household describe themselves as fishermen. Three fisherwomen, presumably the widows of fishermen, are also heads of households. Among these families was the Melling family, after whom Melling's Lane is named. In 1915 John Melling, then aged eighty-five, recalled fishing in the 1860s when:

Fish were far more numerous in the channel and boats from Banks, across the Estuary, came to the North Channel. Fluke were so plentiful that they could be got by wading with a drag net. Prices were vastly different, too, because there was no one to buy the fish except the farmers, and the fishermen were more numerous than now. Nice-sized plaice and flukes, half a century ago were sold at 2d. a pound, 'dabs' at threepence a score, nice cod, weighing 20lb, at 1s. 6d. each, and skate, of similar weight, at 1s. 4d. Of course there was no market and no railway. The fisherman's wife had to foot it to Blackpool – unless she possessed a donkey – and had to bring back the family's supplies. Shrimping was a great thing in those days, and a good source of livelihood …[14]

On the evidence of this account it would appear that by the mid-nineteenth century it was no longer a requirement that all the fish caught had to be brought to the estate bailiff or steward, nor does it appear that the manorial court exercised any influence over fishing practices. Nevertheless, if it was considered that any of the tenants were creating problems a letter to the estate steward was the usual course of action. The following example, which reinforces the observation made by John Melling some seventy years later, concerns the hawking of shrimps in Blackpool. In May 1845 the clerk of St John's Market, Blackpool wrote to James Fair:

At the request of the Shareholders I beg leave to write to you a few lines respecting people that comes here Hawking Shrimps etc from door to door. Your interference I feel confident would have the desired effect, the following are the Names – Grace Melling, Rebecca Melling,

Betty Melling, (the wife and children of James Melling of Commonside) John Carpenter, and Ann Johnson (the wife of Nicholas Johnson of Commonside). I understand there are a few besides the above names I have not got, they all I am told reside in the neighbourhood of Lytham.[15]

In a another interview, given in 1925, John Melling remembered 'finding a market for his fish at Blackpool and Lytham, and the scattered cottages and farmhouses'. He also recalled when there was very deep water at St Anne's but that 'largely through the Preston navigation works, the "run" of the tides has altered considerably', and he considered that fishing was then 'done'.[16] His son, Harry Melling, born 1867, also gave an extensive interview in 1932 recalling that he left the 'old' Heyhouses School in 1878 to go fishing:

We lived well over a mile from the sea (Mellings Lane), … and we had to go out at all times, according to the state of the tide. I am sure that, at times, when I was young, I must have been walking in my sleep. In bad weather we used to moor our boats at Lytham, at Granny's Dock, which is now Fairhaven Lake, and our boats were anchored where the refreshment house now stands.[17]

Echoing what his father had said seven years earlier he noted that 'The whole seashore was different from what it is today. The North Channel was a good channel and we never thought it would come to what it is now.'[18]

Trawl Boat Inn

Inns and innkeepers have always been subject to legislation, and from 1495 the law required every alehouse keeper to apply for a 'recognizance' supported by two sureties. Those responsible for order within the manor and parish likewise kept a close watch on matters relating to ale-houses. At the first manorial court held under the Clifton family in 1611 George Tinkler was appointed ale-founder, and at the same court William Jackson and Henry Walch were found guilty of 'playinge at the dyce in the Alehouse about an Eleven of the clocke in the night in November last past'. Their fine was described as 'quilibet', a set fine of 6d.[19] A statute of 1753 required the clerk of the peace to keep a register of all recognizances. A recognizance was granted annually and required that the innkeeper 'shall keep and maintain good order and rule and shall suffer no Disorder nor unlawful games to be used in his/her said house nor in any Outhouse Garden or backside thereunto belonging during the said term then this recognizance shall not be void'.

By the early nineteenth century any person who had not been licensed for the preceding year was also required 'to produce a certificate under the hands of the Minister and major part of the Churchwardens and overseers, or else three reputable and substantial householders of the place where he inhabiteth, setting forth that he is of good fame and sober life and conversation.' Evidence that the Church took an interest in the drinking habits of its parishioners is provided by an entry in the churchwardens' accounts of 4 December 1803 which noted that 'paid giving notice to Publicans to sell no liquor in Service time'.[20]

In view of the distance from Lytham town it is possible that an inn, though not necessarily on the same site, had existed at Heyhouses from shortly after the establishment of the seventeenth-century community. However, not until the early nineteenth century does it becomes possible to pinpoint the location of any particular inn. In 1806 Robert Cookson was licensed as an innkeeper.[21] On the Lytham survey of 1812 he is named as the lessee of a building which stood at the junction of the present-day Heyhouses Lane and North Houses Lane, and which later became known as the Trawl Boat. Included in the lease were several fields and it seems clear that the trade of innkeeping was combined with farming the land.

It was at this period of time that one writer recommended the way through the Heyhouses as an alternative route to Blackpool:

Pedestrians may visit Blackpool by other nearer routes, one by the common side, the other by the Hey-houses, either of these roads with a little attention and enquiry may be taken principally along field footpaths, which in summer is particularly desirable, as the dusty lanes are thereby avoided, and a much cooler and pleasing walk afforded.[22]

Trawl Boat Inn. In 1826 Thomas Greaves was licensed as the innkeeper of the 'Trall Boat'. The present building was erected in 1865/66, when James Houseman became the landlord. At that time John Talbot Clifton agreed to lay out 'a Bowling Green and Strawberry Gardens adjoining the House'. Following the death of James Houseman in 1875 his widow Mary continued to trade at the Trawl Boat until its closure in 1883. Mary Houseman is second from the left in the photograph. In 1967 the building was converted into a pair of semi-detached properties.

This route would have taken the traveller past the (yet to be named) Trawl Boat, but which was almost certainly the inn that was the butt of the oft-quoted comment 'You may trip to the Hay-houses and get bad ale', made in an 1821 description of Lytham by 'The Babbler'. The author did not name either the inn or the innkeeper but in 1826 Alice Greaves of 'North houses' took a lease on two properties one of which appears to have been that previously owned by Robert Cookson.[23] In the same year Thomas Greaves, her son, was licensed as the innkeeper of the 'Trall Boat'.[24]

Alice Greaves died in 1829; in her will she gave to Thomas Greaves 'all the stock and furniture of what nature or kind soever where I now live subject to a certain debt which I owe unto John Cookson's heirs late of Heyhouses ... of about ten pounds in interest.'[25] Her joint executrix and executor were her daughter Helen Rimmer and Robert Cookson of Heyhouses. If this was the same Robert Cookson who had been the former licensee it seems probable that some commercial connection had continued between himself and Alice Greaves.

When Thomas Greaves died in September 1833 his widow Ellen took over as innkeeper at the Trawl Boat. On the 1851 census Ellen, then aged fifty-three, was described as a public housekeeper. Her daughter Margaret aged seventeen, was the only other member of the family still living at the Trawl Boat and was working as an assistant to her mother.

Sometime between 1851 and 1856 Ellen Greaves appears to have retired as on 24 March, 1856, the lease for the Trawl Boat was granted to William Cartmell for seven years, at a rent of £59 16s. od. The lease required that the buildings be 'kept in good repair ... and to be left in tenantable repair at the end of the term. The tenant to do the alterations in the house should any be required'.[26]

Six years later, on 11 September 1862, Thomas Bennett of Bury Street, Preston, agreed to take the Trawl Boat for seven years at an annual rent of ninety pounds.[27] At this time the building was probably still a whitewashed cottage, but in about 1865 the decision was taken to rebuild the property. Following the rebuilding James Houseman became the new licensee, and under the terms of his lease he agreed:

> to take the Trawl Boat Inn and land now occupied by Mr Thomas Bennett, including a field now in the occupation of Edward Cross – altogether about fifteen acres – for a term of seven years from Candlemas and May 1866 at a rent of one hundred pounds a year payable in one entire sum on the 24th day of June in each year. Colonel Clifton to lay out and make a Bowling Green and Strawberry Gardens adjoining the House charging 5 per cent to the tenant upon the cost of the same. The whole of the land to be kept in grass excepting a small close on the Moss which may be in tillage. The House to be painted by Colonel Clifton and papers found for the rooms the tenant being at the expense of putting it in.[28]

By the 1871 census James Houseman is described as a publican and farmer of sixteen acres. When he died in 1875 his widow Mary, continued to trade at the Trawl Boat, and in 1881 was being assisted by her unmarried daughter Ellen, her married daughter Elizabeth Salthouse, and her son in law Christopher Salthouse.

The end of the Trawl Boat as a licensed house came in 1883. The full explanation as to the reason why the licence was allowed to lapse will probably never be known. The well-known and popular version is that Madeline Clifton (afterwards Lady Drummond) witnessed a brawl outside the Trawl Boat and as a result the licence was withdrawn. In reality the circumstances were probably as reported at the time:

> The End of the Trawl Boat Inn – For fifty years or more, a road-side inn 'The Trawl Boat' has stood on the north side of the road from Lytham to Blackpool, some two and a half miles from the former places, and has been a favourite 'calling place' especially in the summer time for many people travelling, on pleasure bent, betwixt Blackpool and Lytham. Last week saw its last days as a public house; the licence was allowed to lapse, and a fresh application has not been made. We believe that some time ago Mrs [Lady] Clifton suggested that this course should be adopted, and that a part of the premises should be utilised as a free reading room for

the residents in the Heyhouses district. The existence of the St Anne's Hotel at no great distance did away in a great measure with any necessity for the Trawl Boat to remain a public house, and it is now undergoing alterations necessary for its new life. The west end of the building will form a farm house, and at the east end is being arranged that part of the premises where Mrs [Lady] Clifton's excellent suggestion will be carried out ...[29]

Although the licence had not been renewed the Houseman family continued to occupy the west end of the premises as a farmhouse. Mary died in July 1884 at the age of seventy-five, and her daughter Ellen in 1895. Christopher Salthouse and his wife Elizabeth continued to serve food – it was said that her 'nine-penny dinners were delicious and generously heaped'[30] – until approximately 1897. At the same time the news room on the east side of the premises was also discontinued.[31]

During the first half of the twentieth century the former Trawl Boat was occupied principally by the Scott family and known as Trawl Boat Farm, but in 1967 was converted into a pair of semi-detached properties.

This Book was made by me William Silcock present
School Master of Lytham School for the entering of the Accompts
of the principall Moneys belonging to the said School of Lytham
March the 1ˢᵗ 1749

I have made it my Business to enquire, as much as possable I can how the
First Fund or Stock belonging to the said School was endowed
or given and by Whom

	£	s	d
1702 First Mr. Threlfall Clerk of Lytham gave	5	0	0
William Elston of Comon Side in Lytham Who died Buried March ye 17th gave 1704	3	3	0
John Shepherd of Mithop in Lytham Who died 1726 gave	10	0	0

This Money was put out to Interest and the Interest there from ar=
=rising was applied to some charitable Use within the Parish of
Lytham:-

In the year 1720 December there happened a great Inundation
of Salt Water, Which burst and break down the most part of the Sea
Cops in Lytham for which (amongst other Things) a Brief was grant
=ed and the Estimation or Value of the Damage of the said Cops
being entered into the Brief altogether in one Sum, and every per-
=sons respective Damage not being seperately valued; the Brief when
Collected could not be equally distributed to every person proportiona
=bly to his Damage; therefore they had a Consultation about it which
Way to dispose of it (being first some years in collecting) and they
agreed to put it to the above stock and Make a free School

CHAPTER 9

The Lytham Charities

The opening page
of Lytham Charities
Minute Book. In
1720, following the
devastation caused
by a great storm
that occurred
on the 18/19
December 1719,
the inhabitants of
Lytham requested
the magistrates at
Preston for the
grant of a Brief
or Royal Warrant
authorising
the collection
of charitable
donations. The
monies collected
were subsequently
added to other
monies donated
for charitable
purposes and
collectively they
became known
as the 'Lytham
Charities'. The year
'1702' appears to
be a later addition
to the document,
often leading to the
misunderstanding
that the first
donation took
place in that year.
DDX 103/28.
REPRODUCED BY
PERMISSION OF THE
COUNTY ARCHIVIST,
LANCASHIRE RECORD
OFFICE

The Rev. James Threlfall

The first contribution to the 'Lytham Charities' was made by the Rev. James Threlfall who had been appointed minister of St Cuthbert's in 1673/74. In his will dated 24 February 1691, in which he describes himself as a 'Clearke [in Holy Orders]' he made the following bequest:

> I give five pounds to buy Bibles with for ye poorest sort of people in Lytham parish & to be disposed of as my Loving wife Richard Shepard & John his brother Thomas Salthouse of Mithop Houses John Gualter of ye Towne & William Wade of Hey [?] shall think fittinge[1]

Rev. Threlfall died at Weeton in December 1693, where he was apparently combining his role as minister at Lytham with farming. It would appear that his request to buy bibles was not carried out, and the money was subsequentley included in what became known as the 'Ancient Charities'.

The Elston family

As we have already seen the Elston family had been resident in Heyhouses since 1616. In his will, dated 14 April 1682, Richard Elston referred specifically to the future education of his son William:

> Item I give & bequeath unto the said William my son a third part of the remainder of my said personal estate (that is to say of all cattle beasts corn hay husbandry gears & other goods whatever not before devized) … for & towards ye education & preferment of ye said William[2]

He also made various bequests to his wife Elizabeth, the daughter of the Rev. John Wilkinson, who, in his own will made in 1671, was described as 'Clarke [in Holy Orders]', and therefore possibly the then minister at St Cuthbert's.

Unfortunately there is nothing in his will that gives an indication as to where Richard resided. However assuming he was the same Richard who took out a lease in 1658 (the year his father died) then he was tenant at Heyhouses Farm.[3] His inventory, dated 20 February 1683, records items to the value of £127 14s. 8d. including:[4]

goods in the scoole house & the loft over it	£1 6s. 0d.
goods in the scoole more	£0 4s. 6d.

Whether the Elston family were providing education for their own children, or for the wider community is unclear but in either event it is the earliest recorded example of education in Heyhouses. There is no record of when the school was established but in his own will Thomas Elston, another son of Richard, describes himself as a schoolmaster. Among his bequests was the sum of £10 to the poor of Lytham. When Thomas died in December 1686 his inventory amounted to £93 0s. 6d.:[5]

in bills and bonds	£87 8s. 0d.
his books	£0 12s. 6d.
his suit of apparell and Trunk	£5 0s. 0d.

Although the death of Thomas Elston appears to have resulted in the temporary cessation of education in Heyhouses the involvement of the Elston family had not. Sometime prior to his death in 1702 William Elston of Commonside, almost certainly the son of the above-mentioned Richard, made a charitable gift of £3 3s. 0d., which was subsequently also included in the 'Ancient Charities'.[6] Even more significant, in relation to later bequests made to these charities, was the fact that Jennet, the daughter of William, married John Gaulter, whose own son was almost certainly William Gaulter the most substantial benefactor of the charities.

Lytham Charities

As a result of the devastation caused by the great storm of the 18/19 December, 1719, the inhabitants of Lytham, Warton and Westby cum Plumpton requested the magistrates at the quarter sessions, held at Preston on 12 January 1720, for the grant of a Brief or Royal Warrant authorising the collection of charitable donations. In the petition it was claimed that damage had been caused to the value of '£2055 and upwards'. It must therefore have been extremely disappointing that the Brief raised a sum of only £103. The events immediately following the receipt of this money were recorded by William Silcock, son of James Silcock the first schoolmaster of Lytham. In an account book noted

'This Book was made by me William Silcock present School Master of Lytham for the entering of the Accompt of the principal Moneys belonging to the said School of Lytham March 1 1749' he wrote:

> In the year 1719 December there happened a great inundation of Salt Water, which burst and breakdown the most part of the Sea Cops in Lytham for which (amongst other Things) a Brief was granted and the Estimation or Value of the Damage of the said Cops being entered into the brief altogether in one Sum, and every persons respective Damage not being seperately valued; the Brief when collected could not be equally distributed to every person proportionally to his Damage; therefore they had a Consultation about it which way to dispose of it (being first some years in collecting) and they agreed to put it to the above stock and Make a free school[7]

At some point during the 1720s the monies raised by the Brief, together with the £5 given by the Rev. James Threlfall and the £3 3s. 0d. given by William Elston, became known as the 'Ancient Charities'. Three further bequests were made between 1720 and 1748. John Shepherd, who died in 1726, gave £10 sometime between the years 1720 and 1726 – 'Shepherd's Charity'; John Harrison gave the residue of his personal estate (£60) in 1729 – 'Harrison's Charity'; and in 1748 William Gaulter, in addition to other gifts made in his lifetime, also gave the residue of his personal estate (£332 10s. 0d.) – 'Gaulter's Charity'. Collectively these four charities became known as the 'Lytham Charities'.

It is however the long-standing association between John Harrison and William Gaulter that is the most intriguing particularly with regard to the establishment of a school within Heyhouses. The first time the two men appear together is in the conveyance of a messuage and land in Heyhouses in 1706.

In a somewhat complicated lease the messuage was conveyed to William Gaulter of Great Eccleston, and three closes of land conveyed to John Harrison of Heyhouses.[8] One of the closes was 'the Sniddle' (which implies an area of coarse grass or rushes) and was located, perhaps significantly in view of later events, at the rear of what became 'old' Heyhouses School.

John Harrison died in February 1729. In his will he describes himself as a tailor, although he probably combined his trade with farming his land. The value of his inventory amounted to £121 3s. 4d. of which no less than £112 was recorded as 'debts owing to ye deceased'. He appears to have led a very frugal life as the next item in value was £2 8s. 0d. for 'five chairs and a box', while his 'wearing apparell' was valued at just £1. His executors were the Rev. Timothy Pollard (minister of Lytham, 1717–41), and Richard Salthouse. In his will he directed that:

all the rest residue and remainder of all my personal Estate ... I do hereby give and bequeath ... to and for such charitable use or uses as they the said [Rev.] Timothy Pollard and Richard Salthouse (Executors) shall think most proper for the use and benefit of ye said Township of Lytham and the inhabitants thereof[9]

Following this bequest a school, believed to have been built by Richard Salthouse, was opened in Lytham with James Silcock as the master. Richard Salthouse, whose estate included two tenements at Heyhouses, died in 1738. In 1742 his widow, Sarah, married the Rev. Robert Willacy (minister of Lytham 1742–58). There is no mention of a school at Heyhouses at this time and if this was so only those Heyhouses children sufficiently determined, or encouraged, will have made the journey to Lytham.

William Gaulter must have watched the progress of the school at Lytham with considerable interest. Although he was then living at Great Eccleston there is no doubt that he was a member of the Gaulter family of Heyhouses. Due to an absence of church registers for Lytham prior to 1679, it is difficult to compile a definitive Gaulter family history. However, by cross-matching information in Gaulter family wills and leases, a provisional picture begins to emerge.

The year of William's birth is unknown but when in 1696 Margaret Bennet left him her turf cart he was described as 'of Lytham, Taylor'. No reason for his later residence in Great Eccleston can be found, and on both the lease of 1706, and in his will dated 1745, he describes himself as a 'Taylor'. William Gaulter does not appear to have married and was still resident in Great Eccleston when he died on the 19 November, 1748. The inventory to his will provides some insight into his lifestyle:[10]

First in the Room over the house viz two feather Beds, a bedstead, Sheets and Bed Clothes & 2 Chests	£5	0s. 0d.
two pair of Sheets and linn Cloth	£0	12s. 0d.
Room over the Chamber Barrels etc	£0	8s. 0d.
In the Chamber one pair of Bed Stocks and a Chest	£0	8s. 6d.
In the house Meal Chist	£0	10s. 0d.
[In the house] Chares & Table	£0	8s. 0d.
Turves (Turf)	£0	8s. 0d.
In the Buttery Bottles & Cups with other Goods	£0	6s. 0d.
His Wearing Apparel	£4	10s. 0d.
Moneys in Cash and Securities	£588	13s. 6d.

William Gaulter must have been very astute to have amassed such a fortune. He may, however, have inherited some of his wealth as, in 1719, John Gaulter of

Commonside (Whiteside's Farm), probably his father, had bequeathed an estate in Warton, possibly the former Elston estate, to a son called William. In his own will William directed that £240, which he was owed by Richard Leckonby of Great Eccleston, was to be invested and the interest used to augment the salary of the schoolmaster at Copp. As has already been mentioned the residue of his personal estate, value £332 10s. 0d., he gave to his trustees upon trust to:

> invest and pay the yearly interest (less 20s. 0d.) unto the Schoolmaster of the School within the town of Lytham for the time being for ever in order for his better support and maintenance upon condition that such Schoolmaster should teach and instruct without any other gratuity or reward all such poor children within the Parish of Lytham as should be yearly appointed by the same trustees or their successors [11]

He further stipulated that in the event the school was without a master, or that the master refused to teach poor children, the monies were to be distributed 'amongst the poor inhabitants of such township where the poor were free to the said school'. His motive for such generosity, other than perhaps 'nostalgia' for his place of birth, may be explained by the fact that, in 1793, the Rev. Richard Pollard (the son of the Rev. Timothy Pollard), noted that 'William Silcock (the schoolmaster) was a relation [of William Gaulter]'.[12]

By 1754 the funds of the four charities comprising the Lytham Charities totalled £615. In the same year, because the Clifton estate declined to sell any freehold land in the parish of Lytham, the trustees decided to look further afield and purchased land in what became the very centre of Blackpool. In due course these investments were to provide a source of funding for schools in Lytham and St Anne's.

As we shall see, in the years since those early days, the trustees have had to face many challenges, and had to take decisions in response to events not necessarily of their choosing. Now (2007) the Lytham Charities continue to support King Edward VII and Queen Mary School, and also the two endowed, and original foundation schools – Lytham Church of England Primary School and Heyhouses Endowed Church of England Primary School.

CHAPTER TEN

'Old' Heyhouses school

The first direct mention of a school at Heyhouses occurs on 25 March 1780, when the account book of William Silcock notes that the trustees 'Pd to Mr [Rev. Richard] Pollard for Heyhouses School, out of Surplus gained £1 1s. od.' In March 1781 the same account book records 'Allowed to buy a Table for Heyhouses School 11s. 8d.', and in March the following year 'Allowed to finish the Table for Heyhouses School 7s. 10d.'[1]

There is no indication of where the school was, but on the Lytham survey of 1812 it is shown situated on Heyhouses Lane, facing down (what was to become) St Anne's Road, East.[2] This, of course, raises the interesting question of whether it was the same cottage and land, referred to in the previous chapter, that was conveyed to William Gaulter and John Harrison in 1706. If so, it is possible that it had been used for school purposes from soon after that date.

Returning to the events of the 1780s the entry in the account book for 25 March 1783 reads 'Allowed the Schoolmaster of Heyhouses School for loss (of revenue for that year) of Hanning Meadow 12s. od.' Hanning Meadow, situated in Freckleton and farmed by the owner of Marsh View Farm, had been purchased on 2 February 1760 by monies left by Elizabeth Leyland. Under the terms of her will, dated 13 October 1734, she gave £60 to be invested, and the yearly interest used 'for the purpose either of relieving the elderly Poor [of the Parish of Lytham] or for the benefit of School Learning or other Preferment of the Poor Children'.[3]

Elizabeth Leyland was the sister of Thomas Shepherd. If, as seems probable, this was the same Thomas who was the administrator of the will of John Shepherd (of Shepherd's Charity), then Elizabeth Leyland was the niece of John. Her gift was never amalgamated with the Lytham Charities but until 1859 a sum of £6 was received periodically from the trustees of the charity and applied towards Heyhouses School. Even so several Freckleton township books record 'Lytham Charities' as the owner of Hanning Meadow but in the 1910 township valuation the entry is specifically amended from Lytham Charities to read 'Leylands'.[4]

Writing in 1906, James Bowman, the editor of the St Anne's Express, said that for many years Hanning Meadow provided £3 10s. od. a year, of which £2

10*d*. 0*d*. was paid for educating poor children at 'Heyhouses School in Lytham' and the remainder given away to poor people. Prior to 1842 the annual rent of the meadow increased to £9 out of which £5 8*s*. 0*d*. was paid for several years for '… the instruction of eight or ten poor children. The children were instructed by a schoolmistress in reading, writing, knitting and sewing'.[5]

It is unclear whether the monies from the rent generated by the purchase of Hanning Meadow resulted in the establishment of a new school at Heyhouses prior to 1780, or whether it provided income for a school already in existence. Nor it is clear as to the reason for the loss of the monies in 1783, or whether the loss resulted in the temporary closure of the school. An entry in the accounts for the year 1805 may refer to Heyhouses school and, if so, then it would appear that the school had continued to function.

Hanning Meadow was sold on 20 November 1928 for £74 and the money invested. In May 1987 the charity was wound up and the balance transferred to the Lawrence Henry Clegg Charity for the Poor. Since 1928 the receipts of the investment have been distributed, in the form of Christmas food parcels, to deserving people within the ancient parish of Lytham.

Richard and Margaret Cookson

From 1813 there is a continuous history of the school. On 16 February that year Richard Cookson received £5 7*s*. 0*d*., and Margaret Cookson £3, 'for Mr Pollard's Charity'. At the same time Margaret Cookson had been given a further cash payment of £3: an annual payment that continued until 1831. On the 7 May 1816, when 'Mrs' Cookson received her £3, the entry is noted 'for wages Heyhouses School', and in 1822 her one years 'salary' was for 'Teaching 5 children at Heyhouses School'.[6]

Richard Cookson, the son of Thomas Cookson, was baptised at St Cuthbert's, Lytham, on 12 October 1777. On 21 February 1803 a Richard Cookson married Margaret Hull at St Cuthbert's. Although ten years older than her husband, she was presumably the same Mrs Margaret Cookson, schoolmistress, named in the accounts.

In 1824 Richard Cookson took out a lease for a messuage in Heyhouses and although the precise location of this building cannot be pinpointed it would seem to be that which was being used as the schoolhouse. Noted on the lease are the words 'Ground Rent for School at Heyhouses 5*s*. 0*d*.'; in addition the word 'Schoolmaster' is added after the name Richard Cookson.[7]

A Charity Commissioners' report of the time noted that 'children were selected by Mr Cookson, of Lytham, father of the parish clerk, under the directions of Thomas Birley of Kirkham, Esq, the sole trustee [of Leyland's Charity] who selected the poor to be relieved'.[8] In the trustees' account book for 1830 Richard Cookson is again described as 'Schoolmaster'.[9]

Situated on
Heyhouses Lane,
facing down the
present St Anne's
Road, East, 'old'
Heyhouses School
had a continuous
history from 1780
to 1880. The
building depicted
here was erected
in 1832/33, at a
cost of £140 3s.
3d., and extended
in 1863. The
school closed on
25 August 1880
and then became
a private dwelling.
The building was
demolished in 1959.
BY COURTESY OF THE
FAMILY OF THE LATE
FRANK DEAN

Richard Cookson died at Heyhouses and was buried on 18 May 1857. Margaret Cookson predeceased her husband and died on 24 May 1846 aged seventy-nine.

The school rebuilt

By an order of the quarter sessions, part of Heyhouses Lane was 'closed' in 1832.[10] Unfortunately the actual order does not appear to have survived but confirmation of the event is contained in the trustees account book where the entry, for 25 December 1833, reads 'By Cash paid Robert Bonny for Highway Rate for change of Rode [sic] 14s. 3d.'.[11] What exactly the change in the road layout had been is not clear but it did result in the rebuilding of the cottage/school on approximately the same site.

Money for the building came from subscriptions to the value of £35 10s. 0d., and the balance out of accumulated surplus charity money. A detailed breakdown of the building costs is recorded in the trustees account book for 25 June 1833 and totalled £140 3s. 3d. Altogether there are twenty-two separate payments including:[12]

By Cash paid Mr Pratt for Bricks as per Bill	£21 0s. 0d.
By Lime from Preston for the erection of Heyhouses School 75cwt at 8d. per	£2 10s. 0d.

Sometime after a new road from Lytham to Blackpool was made during the 1830s a series of mileposts were erected along the route. Of the four marked on the 1847 Ordnance Survey Map only two now survive, of which the one on Heyhouses Lane (opposite the Shell Service Station) is the most visible. Another survives by Bridge Road (Skew Bridge). Those mileposts which would have been near to the junction of Heyhouses Lane and Blackpool Road, and just north of Division Farm, are now lost.

By Cash paid Thos Catterall [the Contractor ?] as per Bill for Heyhouses School	£23 16s. 3d.
By Cash paid Thos Nickson for Carpenter Work at Said School as per Bill	£53 9s. 6½d.
By Cash paid Ellen Greavs [sic] for board and lodgings [the Trawlboat Inn] at said School	£1 10s. 0d.
By Cash paid William Whalley for a Cask to put into the ground to form a Well	£0 3s. 6d.

It was, no doubt, with some pride that the school trustees held a meeting on 26 March 1832 to draw up a set of rules and regulations for the new infants school (Appendix E). Although these new rules mention 'as well boys as girls' it would appear that few, if any, boys actually attended. In 1933 George Cartmell, who was born in 1843 at Division Farm, recalled that 'The only school in his boyhood was at Lytham and he attended this riding each day on a donkey'.[13]

The first mistress appointed to the newly rebuilt school was Miss Kellett. Her salary commenced at £21 per annum, with an additional £4 provided by Leylands Charity. She continued in post until 1839 by which time her salary had been increased by £5 a year. In 1839 she was succeeded by Miss Agnes Finch who was, as no doubt was her predecessor, only in her early twenties at the time of her appointment. Agnes Finch left the school in 1842 and was succeeded by Miss Beckett (1843–46) and Miss Musgrave (1846–49). This lack of continuity cannot have been to the advantage of the children, and at a meeting of the trustees, held on 25 March 1850, it was reported that 'the reports as to the several schools were submitted ... but that relating to the Heyhouses being unsatisfactory'.[14]

The response of the trustees was to appoint Mrs Isabella Kendall (sometimes spelt Kendal) as mistress. At the time of her appointment she was aged 49 and presumably had had previous teaching experience. In the census for 1851 her husband, Thomas Kendall, is also described as a schoolmaster, but there is no entry for him in the account book. In the trade directory published the same year he is described as 'Thos Kendall – Heyhouses Academy – Free'. It does therefore appear that he taught the boys on his own account.[15]

In 1852 the trustees made changes to the method by which the children were required to pay for their schooling:

> And it is resolved that £5 a year be paid to the Mistress of the Heyhouses School instead of the school pence heretofore received by her for her own benefit and that every child learning writing and accounts be required to pay in lieu of all such payments or having been previously made one penny per week to be accounted for and paid over by the Mistress to the Trustees she being required to forbid the attendance of any child whose payment shall be in arrears for two weeks until payment of such money. And that all copying books other books and writing materials shall be provided by and at the expence of the Trustees.

Such changes apparently did not have immediate effect, and in 1853 two of the trustees reported that 'they had on two occasions visited and examined the Heyhouses School – that the writing was very indifferent and the attendance of the children somewhat irregular and the discipline defective but that reading and spelling were good and the children repeated the catechism with correctness – It was recommended that attention be paid to Arithmetic.'

As it was not compulsory to attend school at this time it is perhaps not surprising that attendance was irregular. For such a scattered community the children would have had to trudge some distance across fields and along unmade lanes in order to reach the school. In the summer months family domestic requirements, particularly for boys, took precedence over schooling and in winter the children would have faced adverse weather conditions. During the winter months a fire was lit in the schoolhouse but, following a resolution passed by the trustees in 1855, the children had to provide their own fire money of sixpence per annum in addition to school pence.

In 1930 John Townsend, who was born in 1851 at 'a farm about three hundred yards from the old Heyhouses School', recalled that 'At the age on nine [he] started work on his father's farm, and when he was seven years old he stopped attending school in summer in order to help with the farming'. He also added that the master was Thomas Kendall and that 'every Sunday the schoolmaster and a number of scholars would start on their three mile walk to Lytham Parish Church, where the nearest Sunday school was held'.[16]

The school enlarged and school inspections

Beginning in 1862 regular inspections were conducted by Mr Charlton, a master at Kirkham grammar school. In his report of that year he must have expressed doubts about the school as the trustees 'with reference to the enlargement of the Heyhouses School … were requested to direct their attention to the report … with a view of putting the school into a better state of efficiency'.

At the trustees' meeting held on 25 March 1863 several important decisions were taken. The committee appointed the previous year reported 'the desirability of enlarging the school so as to make it at least double its present size'. As no conveyance of the school site had been made the trustees also decided to request John Talbot Clifton to grant such a conveyance. It was further resolved to dismiss the mistress, Mrs Kendall, and to obtain a master and mistress at salaries 'not exceeding £80 in the whole'.

At the time of her dismissal Mrs Kendall would have been in her early sixties and it appears that subscriptions were raised for the maintenance of both her and her husband. By 1870, apart from £3, the subscriptions were exhausted and the trustees resolved that 'two shillings a week be paid out of the Funds of the Charity towards the maintenance of Mr Kendall, who had survived his wife, and application be made to the Poor Law Guardians for a similar sum'. However, in 1878 three of the trustees reported that no such allowance had ever been paid 'but that Mr Kendall having recently died in a state of poverty they recommended that the trustees pay one half of the Bill of £9 15s. od. incurred by him for Medical attendance – (Mrs Clifton having agreed to pay the other half)'.

Following the dismissal of Mrs Kendall the trustees carried out their decision of March 1863 and by March 1864 Alexander Barnes had been appointed to the new post of master. At the same time Mrs Anderson replaced Mrs Kendall as the mistress. It was also reported that 'the Girls School[room] had been improved and rendered more airy and commodious and a new Boys School[room] [completed] at an expense including furniture of about £190'.

Mrs Anderson resigned as mistress in 1865 and was replaced by Miss Pownall. By this date the master had the use of a school house which stood adjacent to the school. In the same year Mr Barnes had his salary increased from £50 to £60 in consequence of his having given up the house in favour of Miss Pownall. Alexander Barnes resigned in November 1865 and was replaced by James Lomax. James Lomax appears to have been a sound choice and

within a year his annual salary had been increased 'in consideration of the very excellent report of Mr Charlton respecting the school'. In 1869 he was transferred to the school at Lytham, the only such transfer between the two schools. He was succeeded at Heyhouses by Thomas Corbishley.

In the same year, following a report by Mr Charlton the trustees resolved that 'no children be admitted into any of the schools until they know the Alphabet'. At the same meeting Mr Shepherd Birley, one of the trustees, reported that an examination by competent persons had found the Heyhouses schoolhouse damp and uninhabitable the walls being only nine inches thick. He further reported that the schoolroom was much too small for the purpose required, the size being only 22 feet by 18 feet. He also added that very great difficulty was being experienced in finding accommodation for the master and mistress there being no residences to be procured in the neighbourhood.

By April 1870 the mistress's house had been pulled down and John Talbot Clifton had expressed his readiness to build two new houses (now 29 and 31 Heyhouses Lane) as residences for the master and mistress of the school. In addition the schoolroom had been enlarged at a cost of £95 6s. 4d. and the following year the trustees purchased 'the Bell & Fittings lately belonging to the Market House, [Lytham]' for the use of the school.

Former School Houses. In 1869 it was reported that the schoolhouse occupied by the schoolmistress was damp and uninhabitable, the walls being only nine inches thick. By April 1870 the building had been pulled down and the present houses (29 & 31 Heyhouses Lane), one for the master and one for the mistress, built on the site.

Meanwhile there had been yet another change of master, with Richard Tuson serving from April 1870 until November 1871. It was during this period that Mr Charlton carried out one of his regular inspections of the school. His report appeared in the *Lytham Times* of 26 April 1871. Although lengthy, it makes interesting reading in that it captures a picture of education in rural Heyhouses that was about to vanish with the advent of the new town of St Anne's only four years into the future.

> The Girls School: 71 children attend this school: out of these 17 are learning the alphabet and know but little of it; 16 others are reading words of two or three letters, most of which they have to spell. Of the remainder the reading is good; writing good; spelling good; arithmetic moderate. The steadiness with which the church catechism was repeated and the intelligent answers given by the elder girls on this subject were very pleasing.
>
> They were tolerably familiar with a portion of Scripture history: had a fair knowledge of the early part of English history: and had decidedly more knowledge of English grammar and of geography than generally falls to the lot of girls. I fear there are more children in this school than can receive proper attention. It is impossible for one teacher to give such constant personal supervision as is required by the numerous little ones, and at the same time to give such advanced teaching as is required by the older girls. In such circumstances the little ones are the first to suffer; by degrees it becomes more and more difficult to keep the upper classes tolerably proficient, and the whole school gradually goes down.
>
> The Boys School: I found here 49 children present, out of a total of 52 on the register. The reading was very good; the writing very good (the copy books were uncommonly neat and clean); arithmetic good; spelling fair. The text of the church catechism was repeated with commendable accuracy, and its meaning had been carefully explained to the elder boys. The chief events connected with the early history of the Jews, and the events recorded in the Gospels were familiar to them; and they acquitted themselves very fairly in English grammar, and in a specially prepared period of English history; they had also studied with care the British possessions in all parts of the world, and considering the great extent and variety of these possessions they had as much useful knowledge of each as could be reasonably expected.

It is perhaps not surprising that under such teaching difficulties there was a regular change of masters and mistresses. Richard Tuson 'left his situation' in 1872 and was replaced by Joseph Porritt. Mr Porritt departed within twelve months of his appointment 'in consequence of illness' and in turn was replaced, in April 1873, by John Mattinson who himself resigned in June 1874 to be followed by Emmett Wright.

Some idea of the problems facing the teachers at Heyhouses can be discovered from entries in the school log books, begun by John Mattinson on 10 November 1873.[17] Although it was customary for incoming masters to make critical notes about the existing state of the school, in order to limit any subsequent blame on them by school inspectors, there seems little doubt that Emmett Wright inherited a difficult situation. On 20 July 1874 he wrote:

> This is my first day as Master of Heyhouses Boys School. Nine children were in attendance at the morning and seven during the afternoon assemblings of the School, all of which I found very deficient in the Simplest endiments [sic] of knowledge. So much so, that not more than one would be able to pass satisfactorily Standard 1 of the present Government Code.

Whilst attendance for boys increased in the winter months, from spring to autumn the domestic economy continued to take precedence. During autumn 1874 Emmett Wright recorded in the school log book the reasons behind some of the absences:

25 Sept. Nicholas Carpenter, John Webster, & William Hardman are invariably absent either the whole or part of every Friday from the most trivial of reasons, such as having to get blackberries etc.

28 Sept. Thomas Singleton was absent all day helping his father to get potatoes, he will be absent tomorrow for the same reason or course

1 Oct. John Barrow was absent today running errands and fetching turf in their cart

26 Oct. Re-admitted John Hesketh, Oliver Cartmell, Joseph Hardman, William Cross, Richard Pearson and Thomas Melling who have been away some months working

However, when it was known that Lady Clifton was due to pay a visit to the school it concentrated the minds of the parents, and on 5 October the same year Mr Wright wrote, 'the attendance of the children today has been very good. Her Ladyship The Hon. Eleanor Cecily Clifton paid her first visit to the Boys School since I became master.'

In December 1875 Emmett Wright was given three months' notice 'in consequence of the bad report of the present year added to the unsatisfactory report of the last year'. However, in spite his early dismissal, he must have retained some nostalgia for his time at Heyhouses and on 31 August 1916 he

Other than the school log books, for the period 1873–1880, the only known surviving item from the 'old' school is the school bell. The Bell is now in the ownership of Shirley Johnson.
PHOTOGRAPH: AUTHOR

made a visit to the 'new' school. An entry in the school log book noted that 'Mr Emmett Wright – master of this school over 40 years ago and now an old man of 74 visited the school this afternoon'.

The mistresses fared little better. Miss Pownall remained at the girls school only until 1870 when she was succeeded by Elizabeth Jane Carter. Although by 1872 Miss Carter appears to have had the help of an assistant or pupil teacher she was, nevertheless, in April 1873 asked to resign 'in consequence of the unsatisfactory reports in regard to the Heyhouses Girls School' and replaced by Miss Mary Ann Rathbone.

Such circumstances cannot have failed to concentrate the minds of the trustees. Their response in March 1876, was to appoint a master with drive and determination and in John Ratcliffe Banister they made an astute choice. Aged only twenty-eight at the time of his appointment, Mr Banister was to remain as master until 1890, overseeing the transfer from the 'old' school to the 'new' school. His wife, Mary Banister, took charge of the girls school. By the time of his appointment the foundation stone of St Anne's on the Sea had been laid and pupils from the new town were already attending.

A year earlier Mr Wright had recorded in the log book for 19 May 1876 'admitted Frank & Wilson Heap whose father has come to work as a Joiner at St Anne's from Rawtenstall'. Wilson Heap later recalled that, 'My brother, Frank, and I were sent off to school at the old Heyhouses School, at the top of St Annes Road East. In those days for two boys to set off to find the seat of learning was not so easy. The roads were not made and you had to get on what the farmers called the cops ... We arrived at the school ... and we signed the register. The school was mostly for the farmers sons and daughters, and we were something new to these boys and girls.'[18]

By late 1876, however, two letters had been published in the *Lytham Times* drawing attention to the need for school accommodation at St Anne's. The story of the building of the 'new' school will be told in Chapter 22. As far as the 'old' school was concerned 1877 was the beginning of the end of education within a tight-knit rural community that had spanned at least one hundred years.

Entries from the school log for 1879 provide a picture of the school in its final year. School holidays were Good Friday; a week at Easter; a week at Whitsuntide; Lytham Club Day; three weeks in July/August and two weeks at Christmas. Illness regularly affected attendance, as the following entries reveal:

31 Jan. This week I have received three Doctors Certificates of Sickness for children who are unable to come

21 Feb. Two children have died this week W. Houseman & W. Fisher. The attendance is very small

11 Mar.   The Cooksons have come back to school. They have brought
          a certificate from Dr Sharp stating there is no fear of contagion

Some idea of the condition of the school building in its final year can be gauged from an entry for 11 July 1879. On that day Mr Banister somewhat indignantly recorded that two of the trustees had 'complained insolently about the state of the school – the grass growing in the water spouts, etc. – of which I have nothing to do: in fact I had not noticed it. They spoke about the water being supplied in the school yard. During the play-time I got the children to pull up the grass in the yard & the [assistant?] teacher to clear the rain spouts. There were many nests under the slates.'

The last day at the school was 25 August 1880. The following day Mr Banister wrote in the school log book 'Yesterday Lady Clifton gave prizes & buns to the scholars previous to removing to the new schools. School work finished at ½ past 3 o'clock.'

There was some discussion as to the possibility of one portion of the old school being continued as an infant school for the younger children in the neighbourhood. However, it was decided that, in view of the fact that John Talbot Clifton had donated the land for the new school, the old school and the land be sold to him for £160 – being £100 for the buildings and £60 for the land. The exchange was completed on 20 December 1883 and the building was subsequently occupied as a private dwelling until its demolition in 1959.

The only known photograph of the 'old' school building, when in use as a private dwelling. In this photograph, taken in c.1915, Henry Pearson is standing next to his grandmother, Mary Ann Greaves.

CHAPTER ELEVEN

Religion in Heyhouses

Church of England

THE PARISH CHURCH OF ST CUTHBERT
Under the terms of the lease granted to Sir Thomas Dannett in 1539 he was
required to find 'one able and honest priest' to celebrate divine service and to
administer all sacraments to the parishioners at Lytham 'at all times requisite'.[1]
It would appear that throughout the 1540s Thomas Dannett endeavoured to
maintain this requirement. However in 1549, when he was forced to petition for
a reduction in his rent due to the 'rage of sand', the Court of Augmentations
and Revenues noted that in addition to loss of land the cost of the obligation
to keep a priest could no longer be recovered from the tithes of the parish.

Nevertheless, in spite of this observation it would appear that efforts were
made to ensure that spiritual needs of the parish were met, and between 1548
and 1562 Rev. George Lorrimer was the man charged with the requirement.[2]
Thereafter it is not until 1598 that there is any further documentary information
concerning parochial arrangements. In that year Sir Richard Molyneux leased
the manor of Lytham to Ellen and George Rogerley who were required 'to
maintain a sufficient minister or curate'.[3] A report compiled in 1604 containing
'certain brief observations truly gathered, partly by experience and partly
from others comprehending the whole estate of Lancashire clergy' described
Lytham as:

> an usurped impropriation, as it is supposed, possessed by one Mr Roger
> Ley [sic], gentleman, dwelling in the parsonage house; the stipendiary
> minister a bare reader and careless.[4]

In 1610, presumably as a result of the purchase of the manor by the Clifton
family, the Rev. Hugh Grimbalson was appointed. After this date there is an
almost continuous record of ministers serving St Cuthbert's. And it was at
St Cuthbert's that the men, women, and children of Heyhouses, who were

members of the Church of England, worshipped until the opening of the church of St Anne in 1873.

Sometime during the late sixteenth century the church may have been partially rebuilt and if so was the building described in 1764 as 'a low building, its walls being cobbles. The porch was built askew. The pulpit was against the south wall. The seats were of old oak.'[5] In the opinion of Fishwick it was not unlikely that at least portions of the church formed part of the building which existed in 1189.[6] Thornber provides additional information about the church noting that, 'To the east and west were the remains of thick walls, as if they might have been the ruins of some former and larger building'.[7]

It was almost certainly the church with a steeple depicted in the drawing of Lytham Hall made by an unknown 'artist' sometime in the seventeenth century. This assumption can be supported by the fact that when the rebuilding of the church was planned in the late 1760s part of the brief records 'but the same with the steeple thereunto belonging must be wholly taken down and rebuilt'.[8]

In 1642 the Rev. Robert Brodbelt was the minister and on the last day of February that year his name appears at the head of the Protestation Oath for the parish. This was the oath which, in May the previous year, had been taken by members of the House of Commons when they had sworn 'to live and die for the true Protestant religion, the liberties and rights of subjects and the priviledge of Parliament'. In Lytham the oath was taken by ninety-six men. Twenty-five other men, no doubt many of whom would have been Roman Catholic, were recorded as refusing to sign. Only two years earlier the Lay Subsidy Roll had recorded no fewer than one hundred and seven Lytham parishioners as 'recusants and non-communicants'.[9]

Throughout the second part of the seventeenth century the religious turmoil that so dominated the life of the nation can be seen in several events affecting the minister and parishioners at St Cuthbert's. In 1650 the Parliamentary Church Survey reported that:

Thomas Clifton, Esq, a papist delinquent, patron and impropriator of the whole tithes worth per annum twenty-nine pounds the minister being [the Rev.] Mr William Armistead who hath no allowance or salary, but only the sum of fifty pounds per annum allowed from the committee of plundered ministers.[10]

At an unspecified date, but between 1660 and 1680, a return of the church-wardens' visitations records that 'The church decently kept. A stone font standing towards the lower part of the church, a reading desk and pulpit. None in the parish do occupy themselves in servile works on Sundays or Holy days. All above sixteen come to the Lord's Supper.' The return also noted that thirty-nine individuals were presented 'for not resorting to church being popishly affected'.[11]

The reference to attendance at the Lord's Supper had particular relevance following the passing of the Test Act in 1673 which directed that all civil office holders receive sacraments according to the forms of the Church of England. As a consequence the Rev. William Woods – 'Minister of Litham' (a previously unrecorded minister) did, on 6 July 1673, at Preston parish church, 'immediately after divine Service and Sermon … receive the Sacrament of the Lords Supper according to the usage of the Church of England'.[12]

By the following year the Rev. Woods had been succeeded at Lytham by the Rev. James Threlfall. The earliest known registers of St Cuthbert commence in 1679 and from that date we can begin to identify the individuals from Heyhouses who were not only baptised, married and buried at St Cuthbert's, but who also played a prominent part in the daily life of the church.

Among the earliest recorded baptisms were James the son of James Webster of Cross Slack who was baptised on Christmas Day 1680, and Grace the daughter of Thomas Salthouse of the Heyhouses baptised on 5 June 1681. Early marriage entries do not specifically name the residence of the bride and groom, but Nicholas Sanderson, who married Elling Gualter on 30 January 1680, was almost certainly from North Houses. A year earlier on 6 September 1679 another Elling Gualter, a widow, had been buried.[13]

As is evident from the wording of their wills both Anglicans, and also the substantial Roman Catholic community, considered the right to burial in the churchyard as important. In 1676 George Bennet of the Heyhouses, and probably the same George Bennet who had signed the Protestation return in 1642, had stated that 'ffirst and principally I Comite my soule to god my maker Hopinge Through the merits deathe and passion of Jesus Christ our Saviour to bee one of the electe member that shall be saved and my body to Christian buriall especialy in ye parish Churchyard of Lytham att the discretion of my wife and Children'.[14]

During the three centuries that parishioners from Heyhouses were buried at St Cuthbert's it was the customary for the minister to conduct a funeral sermon. In 1675 Richard Salthouse instructed William Sanderson, his son in law and executor, that ten shillings 'be given to a minister to make a funerall sermond'.[15] As we have seen it was the same William Sanderson who, in 1710, instructed his executors to provide a penny dole to the poor on the day of his funeral.[16]

At the first manorial court held under the Clifton family in 1611, the churchwardens appointed were Thomas Harrison, Peter Windress, John …, and Richard Welch.[17] The right to appoint the churchwardens appears to have been according to the 'custom of the parish', and almost certainly had its origins in 'the four men' appointed at the monastic manorial court in the time of the Priory.

LETHAM HAILE·

Throughout the seventeenth century four men (of whom two were nominated by the Clifton family) were appointed annually to the office of churchwarden. In 1678 responsibility was shared between just three men – William Elston, George Salthouse, and Thomas Colly – all members of families which has a long standing association with Heyhouses. However this tradition was about to be challenged by the Rev. Peter Fisher (another previously unrecorded minister) who was appointed minister of Lytham on 21 August 1694. In 1697 his annual stipend was £20.[18] By 1705 he had become involved in a heated exchange with Thomas Clifton over the right of burial in the churchyard, dues belonging to the church, and the appointment of the churchwardens.

In response to the Rev. Fisher's complaints Thomas Clifton sought the advice of Nicholas Starkie, a leading Preston lawyer. The entry in the steward's accounts for 5/6 February 1706, and a letter written by Nicholas Starkie to the Rev. Fisher dated 25 February 1706, provide an intriguing picture of church life at Lytham at the beginning of the eighteenth century and are reproduced in full at Appendix F.[19] By 1709 the Rev. Fisher had been succeeded at St Cuthbert's by the Rev. Josiah Birchall.

As a result of this dispute it would seem that thereafter only two church-wardens, instead of four, were appointed. By the end of the eighteenth century there is some evidence that their election was determined by rotation of the various estates or locations within the parish. In 1778 it was Edward Bagot of Heyhouses; in 1779 Anthony Salthouse of North Houses; in 1782 James Newsham of Moss Edge; and in 1783 James Webster of Slated Barn.

The demands placed on the churchwardens must at times have seemed rather onerous. For some Heyhouses men each visit involved a journey of least three miles to a church that was in urgent need of repair or replacement. The Clifton family, however, despite their almost invariable devout Roman Catholicism, maintained their legal responsibilities towards its upkeep as the following entries from their stewards accounts reveal:[20]

30 October 1698   To Lawrence Butler (Lymer), in part forty
    shillings for beautyfying Lytham Church Chancel   £5 os. od.
19 May 1699
    Paid Lawrence Butler for plastering and whitening Lytham
    Chancel   10s. od.
    and more for pointing ye side walls, and part of ye ends   5s. 6d.,
    and for ye sizing   6d.

In 1763 the parishioners appealed to the magistrates at the quarter sessions for a 'brief' (i.e. licence) to empower them 'to collect alms and contributions' towards rebuilding the church. At the time it was stated that Robert Bailey, John Standish and William Roper, experienced workmen, had given an estimate to rebuild for 'the sum of £1,373 17s. 8d., exclusive of the old materials which sum the said Parishoners are unable to raise amongst themselves being mostly Tenants at Rack Rents and burdened with a numerous Poor and the said Parish being but very small'.[21] The church was rebuilt in 1770 on the same site. It was described as being 'built of rubble, rough cast and whitened, and certainly possessed both externally and internally no very extensive claims to architectural beauty'.[22] A year later a document entitled 'Lytham Church – The following copies are sent to Mr Clifton to enable him to state with precision the nature & value of the Living to any Gentleman to whom he may offer it' recorded that 'There are neither House, Glebe Land nor Tythes belonging to the Curacy of Lytham'.[23]

The document also describes the means by which the curate received payment for his services. Thirteen years later this amounted to £30 paid by four quarterly payments 'and also the sum of one pound ten shillings being wages due to the Clerk and the Lord of the Manor being patron of the Church provides six Gallons of Red port & Bread at Easter yearly and remainder the Church Wardens provides in respect of their share'.[24]

At the beginning of the nineteenth century the instrumental part of a church service was accompanied by means of a clarinet and a bass fiddle.[25] In addition to Holy Communion, and presumably Matins and Evensong, there were special services and proclamations to mark specific events in the life of the nation. In 1800 there was a proclamation 'recommending the greatest economy and frugality in the use of every species of grain'; in 1801 prayers and thanksgiving were said for the recovery from illness of King George III; and in 1802 a thanksgiving to mark the end of hostilities with France.

Unfortunately the late eighteenth- and early nineteenth-century churchwardens' accounts – an important source of information concerning church life at St Cuthbert's – now appear to be lost. In 1934 extracts from them were published in the church centenary brochure and the following entries provide a tantalising insight of church life at that time:[26]

1796, Aug 15th By Cash serving the Office [of Churchwarden]	£1 1s. 0d.
1796 By do for more trouble	£1 1s. 0d.
1796 Paid for Ale for Singers	£0 10s. 0d.
1803, May 20th Paid Musicioners two years reeds	£2 0s. 0d.

Lytham however was changing rapidly and the first half of the nineteenth century saw a transformation from a fishing village into a fashionable bathing place. The church of 1770 was very soon too small for new residents and visitors and in 1834 the present building was opened for divine service.

Although men such as Robert Ormond of Kilnhouse continued to serve in the office of churchwarden, the self-contained community of Heyhouses must have felt marginalised by the rapid changes taking place in Lytham, and appears to have begun to use the 'old' Heyhouses school as an alternative to attendance at St Cuthbert's.

Evidence that services were being held at the school, by at least the late 1860s, is confirmed by the report in the *Lytham Times* of 18 May 1870 that 'Mrs [Lady] Clifton has presented a new harmonium to the Heyhouses school in which divine worship is held every Sunday evening [at] 6.30 p.m. The new instrument was used for the first time on Sunday evening last.' The same newspaper provided further evidence when, on the occasion of the consecration of the new church of St Anne, it reported that:

> For a considerable time back divine service has been celebrated once each Sunday in the Heyhouses School, the duty being undertaken by the clergy of Lytham Parish Church – the service being in the afternoon in winter and the evening in summer.[27]

It was only a short-term arrangement, however, and 'the crowded state of the school during the service showed the want of better accommodation'.[28] In order to address this problem, a meeting presided over by the Rev. Richard Thistlethwaite who resided at Elmhurst Farm, was held at the school 'sometime in 1871'.[29] At the meeting 'it was proposed to build a new Church, and it was suggested that it be called the "Fair Memorial Church" in memory of the first Mr James Fair, and a proposition was actually passed to that effect'.[30]

At this time the birth of the new town of St Anne's was still four years away, and most of those present at the meeting no doubt assumed the new church was to be built near to the existing school. Indeed when the location of the new church was known it was considered by some of the older inhabitants to be 'much too far away', and 'it is said that a deputation of the tenantry waited upon the Lady of the Manor, but without success, to protest and to pray for the Church to be built nearer their homes'.[31] But, as we shall see in Chapter 21, it is clear that the new church was intended primarily for the benefit of the impending new town of St Anne's, rather than the existing Heyhouses community.

Even after the new church of St Anne (the earlier proposal that it be called the 'Fair Memorial Church' had been conveniently forgotten) had opened for worship, the farming community of Heyhouses continued to be hold services at the 'old' school and in 1875 it was reported that

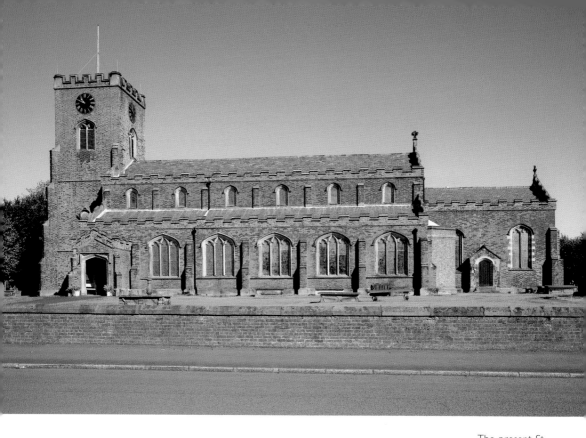

Many visitors, and possibly some residents in Lytham, may not be aware that there is divine service every Sunday evening at the Heyhouses School … The service was conducted by the Rev. H. B. Hawkins, vicar of Lytham … The musical portion of the service was taken by a good country choir, accompanied on the harmonium (the gift of Mrs [Lady] Clifton) … The congregation consisted, of course, almost entirely of farmers of the district, with their wives their families and their [farm] servants … Mrs Clifton and a few visitors were amongst the congregation.[32]

It would appear that sometime between 1876 and the closure of the 'old' school in 1880 even these services were discontinued, and for the parishioners of Heyhouses came the final break with the church of St Cuthbert, Lytham and a new beginning with the church of St Anne.

Roman Catholic Church

In the years immediately after the Reformation legislation, such as the Acts of Uniformity of 1552 and 1559, resulted in strict anti-Catholic laws. As elsewhere in south and west Lancashire many of the gentry, and their tenantry, refused to conform and became known as recusants or papists. The acquisition of the

The present St Cuthbert's church was built in 1834. It continued to be the parish church for Heyhouses, and in 1850 Robert Ormond of Kilnhouse Farm served as churchwarden. However as Lytham continued to expand the Heyhouses community had, by the late 1860s, begun to hold their own services in the 'old' school.

manor of Lytham in 1606 by Cuthbert Clifton, a staunch recusant, would have afforded some protection to those who wished to retain their Catholic faith.

In 1625 Sir Cuthbert Clifton (he was knighted in 1617) erected a mansion on part of the site of the former priory, incorporating a small portion of the old monastic buildings, and from that date there was a succession of priests acting as chaplains to the Clifton family. Lawrence Anderton was the first of the clergy and like all the priests that followed him was a member of the Society of Jesus (Jesuits). In 1773 the Society of Jesus was temporarily suppressed and the Lytham mission was taken by secular clergy.

Evidence of Catholics residing in Heyhouses in 1676 is provided by a list of inhabitants aged over sixteen years, compiled as part of a churchwardens' visitation in 1676. Out of a parish population of just over two hundred, some sixty-six men and women were described as 'popish recusants'. Presumably for 'political' reasons neither Sir Thomas Clifton nor his wife were listed among them.

Unfortunately, as there is no indication of places of residence within the parish, it is not possible to determine conclusively the number of recusants living at Heyhouses. However among those on the list, and known to be of Heyhouses at the time, were John Webster and his wife Jennet, James Fletcher and his wife, and George Fletcher and his wife.[33]

Two years later forty-seven Catholics, on this occasion headed by Sir Thomas Clifton, were recorded on a list of recusants. John and Jennet Webster were again named, as were William Snape and his wife Janett, Margaret Bennett a widow, and William Fletcher a shoemaker.[34]

On Tuesday 6 September 1687, during the reign of James II and a time of respite from persecution, Bishop Leyburn conducted a confirmation service at Lytham. Altogether 376 names are listed on the confirmation register, and those attending included families employed on the Clifton family estates at Lytham and Westby. Of known Heyhouses families there are entries for Elston, Salthouse, and Webster.[35]

In 1717, as a consequence of the Jacobite uprising of 1715, all Catholics were required to register their estates. A document known as the Lancashire Papists Estates provides a detailed account of the Lytham Catholic community at that time. Over one hundred individuals are named, either as lessees or occupiers of properties, together with the acreage of their estate and the rental. Once again many of the names are of those who were farming in Heyhouses, and would seem to suggest that a significant proportion of Heyhouses families adhered to the Catholic faith at that time

This community met for worship at Lytham Hall. Writing in 1877 of his parents' recollections (who were presumably recalling events remembered by their own parents) Richard Cookson in his 'Recollections of the Priests & Chapels at Lytham Hall and Lytham' wrote that:

The first priest of whom I know anything was the Rev. Mr Mansell, at his first coming (1743) he lived in the Hall & Divine Service was held in the servants Hall.[36]

In 1751 Thomas Clifton commenced the rebuilding of Lytham Hall, work that included incorporating 'the old chapel and chaplain's apartments in the new building'.[37] This particular part of the rebuilding would appear to have been completed in 1753 as in that year an entry in the accounts of Randolph Penswick, then steward to the Clifton family, notes that he 'paid Lancelot Butler – building of New Chapell';[38] it was also the year in which Rev. John Mansell began the existing baptismal register at Lytham.

During the period 1680 to 1770 it is estimated that the Catholic population of Lancashire increased by almost 60 per cent from 16–18,000 to 26,000, some 20 per cent of the county population. In order to determine exact numbers the House of Lords, in 1767, ordered a return to be made of 'papists' in every parish. In Lytham 373 persons were recorded and, considering that the total population in 1801 was still only 920, must have represented a significant proportion of the township. The other large Catholic population within the Fylde came from the Clifton family manorial village of Westby with Plumpton. Here 436 persons were recorded on the Return out of the total of 939 for all fifteen townships comprising the parish of Kirkham.

The return for Lytham is headed by Thomas Clifton and his wife Lady Jane Clifton, followed by seven other members of his family. The entry immediately following the family is that of John Mansal alias Talbut (sic) who was described as a Jesuit priest aged 58, having resided at Lytham for twenty-eight years. Forty-nine members of the Hall staff are recorded, including Ralph Watt who had succeeded Randolph Penswick as steward to the Clifton family in 1756. Mrs Penswick, the widow of Randolph, who although not entered on the return as a member of the Hall staff, is also recorded and had obviously remained at Lytham following the death of her husband.

Others who can be associated with Heyhouses, from evidence contained in their leases and later wills, included Richard Booth of Cross Slack, Roger Charnley of Charnley's House (Division Farm), Francis Gillett of 'Shoemakers Row' (Regent Avenue), John Newsham of Moss Edge Farm and James Webster of Kilnhouse.

In 1793 the number of Easter communicants recorded by Rev. Richard Pope was 250. In the same year Bishop William Gibson confirmed 75 members of the congregation. With such numbers the 1753 'new' chapel must have been becoming increasingly inadequate to meet the needs of the congregation. In 1800 a tithe-barn (the precise location of which is neither recorded nor known) just outside the park was fitted up as a chapel and the Rev. Pope went to live at the Woodlands (near the roundabout by Albany Road and Blackpool Road).

In the year of the Catholic Emancipation Act, 1829, the Rev. Joseph Walmsley was appointed to serve at Lytham. In his 'Recollections' the previously mentioned Richard Cookson wrote that soon after the arrival of the Rev. Walmsley, 'The old chapel was enlarged by adding the vestry & confessional (called the "Hearing Room") to it & making new vestries out of what was called the coal house'.[39]

The need for a new church to serve the increasing population, however, was pressing, and in 1839 St Peter's church in Clifton Street, Lytham was erected. No allowance, such as services held at farms within the district, appears to have been made for the Catholics living at Heyhouses and the new church thus presented a considerable extension to their journey to church.

There are no known accounts about church life for those Catholics living at Heyhouses during the nineteenth century, though an anecdotal story about Joseph Henry Melling (born 1880) may not be untypical. As a child he could recall walking with his parents Henry and Helen Melling, from their cottage in Heyhouses, to attend mass at St Peter's, taking with them a picnic to eat after the service.[40]

It must therefore have been of both comfort and some satisfaction to the Melling family and their fellow Catholics, when Our Lady, Star of the Sea was opened for worship in 1890.

Nonconformity

Other than the strong commitment to the Roman Catholic faith the extent to which nonconformity to the Church of England affected the community of Heyhouses appears to be negligible. There is, however, evidence that within the parish such dissent did take place.

In 1687 the constables of Lytham confirmed to the magistrates at Preston that in accordance with the ordinance granted the previous October, Thomas Crookall 'was sett in the stocks in the s[ai]d Town of Lytham for the space of two hours and afterwards whipped on his naked body till blood came, and then sett at liberty … for speaking Seditious words touching his Majesty.'[41]

The reason for Thomas's outburst is not known, but in view of the divisions within the country at that time, created by the religious policies of James II, it is reasonable to assume that his strongly held views were not unconnected.

In 1712 there was an attempt to establish a dissenting meeting place in Lytham. At Epiphany that year a James Salthouse submitted to the magistrates at Preston the following petition:

James Salthouse of Litham desires that his dwelling house in Litham may be recorded for a Meeting place for an assembly of persons dissenting from the Church of England persuant to an act of Parliament intitled an act for Exempting their Majesties Protestant Subjects dissenting from the Church of England from ye Pennaltys of Certaine Lawes — The places of such meeting are required to bee certified to the next Quarter Sessions where such meeting shall be held.[42]

The petition noted that 'Mr William Perkins Minister att Elswick desires to take ye oaths & ... the articles of his religion'. As the chapel at Elswick had been similarly licensed in 1672, 'to be a place for the use of such as do not conform to the Church of England, who are commonly called Congregational', it seems clear that the proposed meeting house at Lytham was also intended for members of that sect.[43] However we do not know whether the petition was successful; and it is not until 1792 that there is any definite evidence of a church other than the Church of England or Roman Catholic church holding services in Lytham.

In 1784 a small band of Methodists were meeting for worship in Preston but 'there was not a chapel, or a school, or a ministers house, or a circuit, or a

Gravestone of Thomas Gaulter, St Cuthbert's churchyard. There had always been a strong Christian ethos within the Gaulter family and when Thomas Gaulter died in 1767 the inscription on his gravestone recorded that 'Hee Charged his Childran to Love One Anothor and fear God and Keep his Commandments – and then He Died aged 62'. His grandson, also called Thomas, was subsequently one of the earliest members of the Freckleton Methodist community.

minister in the Fylde country'.[44] However in 1792 James Lyons, a preacher in the Blackburn circuit, persuaded James Marcer (Mercer) of Lytham to apply for a licence to the magistrates to open his cottage for meetings. The request, dated 27 December 1792, was signed by James Marcer, Thomas Marser, Thomas Gaulter, William Edmondson, John Marcer, and James Lyons and commenced:

> We the undersigned do certify that a House or meeting Situate in the South-side of Lytham, and in possession of Mr James Marser [*sic*] Fisherman's Row [Bath Street] ... is set apart by A society of Protestant Dissentors to Assemble in to hear Divine Worship ...[45]

Although it was the home of James Mercer in which the meetings were held it is the unrecorded role played by Thomas Gaulter that is the more intriguing. Thomas Gaulter was born in 1763 and on the death of his father, in 1796, became lessee of the farm situated in Commonside that later became known as Whitesides Farm. It would appear that the family, at some time during the late eighteenth century, sub-let the farm, of which they had been tenants since 1707, and moved to Lytham.

There had always been a strong Christian ethos within the Gaulter family and when the grandfather of Thomas Gaulter (also called Thomas) died in 1767 the inscription on his grave recorded that 'Hee Charged his Childran to Love One Anothor and fear God and Keep his Commandments – and then Hee Died aged 62'. Thomas Gaulter subsequently removed to Freckleton where in 1815 he and his wife Agnes (formerly Bryning) were among the earliest members of the Freckleton Methodist community, and where he contributed to the building of the first chapel.[46]

However, the man credited as being 'the key to the founding of Methodism in Lytham' was Moses Holden, and in 1811 he began his Fylde missionary work at Little Marton.[47] On his arrival at Lytham he recorded in his diary that 'I found a house licensed for preaching. I understood a Mr Lyons had got it licensed, and preached in it a long time before; but it had been given up'.[48]

A further entry in his diary records that 'they received me kindly and heard me gladly, but that was all'.[49] Indeed, it was not until the arrival of Thomas Crouch Hincksman and the building, in 1847, of the first Methodist chapel, embracing the house of James Mercer in Bath Street, that Methodism in Lytham become properly established.

A further indication that Methodism was not well established until the middle of the nineteenth century is supported by the evidence of the 1829 'Return of Sectarians'. In this return it was only the Scotch Baptists, other than the Roman Catholics, who were recorded as having a meeting place in Lytham. Their membership was recorded as fifty.[50] The Scotch Baptists appear to have become established in Lytham by 1802 as on 29 April that year a petition to the magistrates at Preston requested that the dwelling house of Richard Bryning be licensed 'as Meeting Place for Protestant Dissenters'.[51] As was the usual practice the petition does not specify the name of the sect concerned, but in light of subsequent events it seems reasonable to assume that it was indeed submitted by the Scotch Baptists.

A year later, on 19 April 1803, a further petition requested the magistrates to permit a dwelling house and warehouse in the possession of John Edmondson to be licensed as 'Meeting Places for Protestants dissenting from the Church of England to exercise their religious Worship in'.[52] This is presumably where Porter is describing when he tells us that at an unspecified date during the first two decades of the nineteenth century: 'A small [Scotch] Baptist chapel, having a school-room connected with it, also existed, standing on part of the ground now occupied by the premises of Mr Edmondson, draper.'[53] This site, in Clifton Square, is now (2007) occupied by the HSBC bank.

Additional evidence is provided by the reminiscences of John Bamber, who in 1902 recalled that 'My earliest recollection of Lytham is about the year 1827. My father was connected with the Scotch Baptists, and occasionally walked to Lytham [from Kirkham] to preach. I often came with him, and we met in a room behind Mr Edmonson's shop. The grandfather of the present Mr Edmonson was the pastor.'[54]

In 1840 John Edmondson (the son?) wrote to James Fair to enquire if Mr Clifton 'would permit a Dissenters Chapel to be built in the Village and if so – on what terms'.[55] It seems probable that this request was made on behalf of the Congregational church as the letter refers to Dr Thomas Raffles, the celebrated Congregational preacher at Liverpool. John Edmondson, however, does not initially appear to have been successful, and it was not until 1862 that the present Lytham United Reformed (Congregational) church was built.

As was suggested at the beginning of this part of the chapter there is no evidence that the Heyhouses community were influenced by any of the events just described. Apart from the role of Thomas Gaulter, in the early days of Methodism, their religious 'loyalties' appear entirely divided between the Church of England and the Roman Catholic church. Nevertheless, whenever they went into the 'village' they would have been aware of the events and debates taking place, and no doubt would have discussed the issues among themselves.

CHAPTER TWELVE

A vanished community

In the preceding chapters we have looked at the establishment and progress of the Heyhouses farming community through almost 350 years. Although it would be another ninety years before the community was finally to disappear, it must have been clear to Heyhouses residents of the early 1870s that, with the building of St Anne's parish church, the construction of Clifton Drive South, and the laying of the foundation stone of the new town of St Anne's, their lives were about to change dramatically.

When, in 1878, Lytham and St Anne's became separate local government authorities most of the Heyhouses district came within the authority of the St Anne's Local Board of Health. As the residents of Heyhouses would have regarded themselves as much Lytham born and bred as people born in Lytham town we can only wonder at their reaction to this change. It is probable that the comments of Jenny Whiteside of Whiteside's Farm were not untypical. In 1932 her grandson, Joseph Whiteside, recalled that his grandmother 'would not sell her milk to the new people whom she called "O'er yonners". I'll have now't to do with the o'er yonners, she would say, and daily rode past with her produce, leaving the new inhabitants to get their supply elsewhere.'[1]

Nevertheless, the new local board was to have an immediate impact on the lives of the residents of Heyhouses, which hitherto had been determined by the decisions of the Clifton estate. On 4 April 1881 Dr Dearden, the medical officer to the board, reported that in response to a ratepayer having made a representation to him concerning a cottage in North Houses Lane as being unfit for human habitation he had visited the cottage and noted the following:

> the dwelling is an oblong erection covered with thatch and divided internally into two compartments, both on the ground floor; the average height is somewhat short of eight feet, the length and breadth of each compartment being respectively 12 feet by 8 feet, ... There are the parents and four children housed here. Immediately adjoining and against the south end externally there is a sty for pigs, and, somewhat removed a hut for stalling a cow; the middens are closely adjacent. The health of the family is good, the pigs and cow included.[2]

On 22 July 1881, the Local Board wrote to Thomas Fair to inform him that Dr Dearden had reported that the water in the wells at eleven farms at Heyhouses was so polluted as to be 'injurious to health'.[3]

The board advised Fair that the tenants at the farms involved had already been requested to 'voluntarily close their wells and to obtain a supply of good water'. In addition they requested him to assist them 'by obtaining a supply of good water for Col. Clifton's tenants', and pointed out that, 'This week there have been four cases of Typhoid Fever all of whom were supplied with milk from Robert Hall, Farmer West End'.[4]

In August 1881 the board again wrote to Thomas Fair requesting him to close, within a month, all the wells previously reported by Dr Dearden. On this occasion they noted that although the well used by Thomas Gillett at Cross Slack 'was much better than the others' because it was 'necessary that all Milk Sellers should have good water' that 'Gillett's well with the others must be closed'.[5]

The initial response of Thomas Fair was to send two samples of the water to be tested at the Royal Infirmary School of Medicine, Liverpool. The resulting analysis confirmed the concerns of the Local Board. Sample one was described as containing 'so much impurity both of mineral and especially of animal origin as to be quite unfit for drinking or cooking purposes'. Sample two contained

Elijah Rawstrone, from Freckleton, travelled throughout the Fylde providing goods, including lamp oil, to the rural communities. Here he is standing (left) with his vehicle outside Fancy Lodge on Heyhouses Lane.

One of these cottages at the junction of North Houses Lane and Moss Hall Lane, and which continued to be occupied until at least the late 1940s, is probably the one condemned by the Medical Officer of Health in 1881 as being unfit for human habitation. In that year two adults and four children were housed there. Immediately adjoining, and against the south end, was a sty for pigs. Somewhat removed was a hut for stalling a cow, with the middens closely adjacent.

'such large quantities of impurities both of mineral and organic origin as to be quite unfit for domestic use'.[6]

At a meeting of the Local Board in September Thomas Fair reported that he had made arrangements with the Fylde Water Board for a supply of water to commence at Heyhouses and to go round by Hall's Farm (West End) and to Mr Hargreaves' (Headroomgate Farm). He added that 'Some farmers would not take the water at all, and the pipes had to be carted away again'.[7]

Although several of the leading Heyhouses farmers had, with the encouragement of Lady Clifton, managed to be elected to the Local Board, the Heyhouses community appears to have remained somewhat isolated from events in the new town. Social events continued to take place in the 'old' school until the opening of the present Heyhouses infants' school. Farm buildings also provided an alternative venue for social events such as the dances which took place in the barn of Leach Lodge Farm.[8]

In pagan European culture it was believed that the spirit of the 'corn' lived amongst the crop, and that when harvested it became homeless. Hollow shapes ('corn dollies') were fashioned from the last sheaf and brought indoors for the winter until ploughed into the first furrow of the new season. This ancient art of dolly-making continues to be practised. The extent to which it was practiced in Heyhouses, within the recent past, is unclear. However in the mid-twentieth century Bob Scott, the tenant at the Trawl Boat, taught himself the ancient art.
DDEY ACC 5582 BOX 8. REPRODUCED BY PERMISSION OF THE COUNTY ARCHIVIST, LANCASHIRE RECORD OFFICE

These events, however, were the swan-songs of a disappearing community. One of the first farms to be demolished was Whitesides, in 1897, to be replaced by the Victoria Hotel. Piped water finally came to Heyhouses in 1902 when a 5-inch main from Ballam was completed 'at a cost much below the engineer's estimate'. This it was claimed was due to 'a favourable contract for pipes, and to the exceptionally dry weather experienced during the progress of the work, particularly when crossing the moss land'.[9]

The first half of the twentieth century witnessed the demolition of several cottages, particularly along the former Commonside, as farmland gave way to urbanisation, while the cessation of the manorial court ended centuries of tradition. Farms and cottages along Heyhouses Lane, and at West End, survived the encroachment of the new town until after World War II, and as late as 1950 it was still possible to walk around Heyhouses and witness a scene much of which would have been recognised by previous generations.

During the 1950s and 1960s the pace of change accelerated and, as a result of the building of the main runway at Blackpool Airport in 1952/53, Division Farm, Leach Farm, and Moss Edge Farm were demolished. Leach Lodge Farm survived the loss of farming and effectively ended its days as a working farm. The 1960s saw the demolition of more farms, including Butcher's Farm (1960), Headroomgate Farm (1961), Brook Farm (1963) and Model Farm

As late as 1963 it was still possible to see cows being driven to and from pasture along modern roads within Heyhouses. The preferred dairy breed however had become the Friesian. In this photograph cattle are passing Kilnhouse Farm, the last tenants of which were the Whiteside family.

(1969). Heyhouses Farm survived until 1972 and Kilnhouse Farm until 1989. Now (2007), apart from Leach Lodge Farm, the only former farms to survive are Boardman's Farm, Church Farm House, Greaves' Farm (now known as Headroomgate Farm), the Elms, and West End Farm.

Although Heyhouses no longer exists as a distinct community it is still possible to travel along the same lanes and highways that the first pioneer families travelled almost 400 years ago. The records of the manorial court and the quarter sessions tell us of their life in the community and of their misdeeds and disputes. Their wills tell us of their achievements and of their concerns for the welfare of their surviving families. The roots of the community do indeed remain and the ancestors of many St Anne's residents are the men and women whose lives have been described in the foregoing chapters.

'Moonrise on Lytham Moss'. The Lytham St Anne's Art Society was founded in 1912. Among its earliest members was Walter Eastwood, whose work is included in the Fylde Borough Art Collection. The objective of the society was to stimulate 'an interest in all forms of Pictorial and Applied Art'. Thomas Battersby (1858–1942) was also a founder member and was the artist of this painting of 'Moonrise on Lytham Moss'.

Part II

St Anne's on the Sea

James Fair (*left*) and his son Thomas Fair (*below*). While still a boy James Fair was placed in the service of the earl of Derby and in 1830, at the age of 26, put in charge of the earl's Fylde estates. In arguably the most astute appointment ever made by the Clifton family Thomas Clifton appointed James Fair his land agent in 1835. It was to James Fair that John Talbot Clifton wrote in 1844 that he was 'delighted that a new village is about to be commenced to the westward'. Following his partial retirement in 1862, James's son Thomas became land agent to the Clifton family. Thomas was heavily involved in the establishment of St Anne's, though his over-riding commitment to the Clifton estate at times brought him into conflict with both the land and building company and the Local Board of Health. James died in 1871, aged 67, Thomas in 1914 aged 78.

CLIFTON CHRONICLE

CHAPTER THIRTEEN

Origins of the town

On becoming squire in 1832 Thomas Clifton began to initiate change, and the appointment of James Fair as land agent to the family in 1835 was part of that change. The general policy was to adopt efficient estate management methods and switch, whenever possible, from agriculture to urban development as a way of maximising revenue, while keeping tight control to ensure a high social 'tone' and thus high rents.

Under the guidance of James Fair, Thomas Clifton implemented this policy at (present-day) Lytham but appears to have been opposed to an extended development to the west of Lytham because the views from Lytham Hall might be obstructed. James Fair, however, appears to have readily gained the support of John Talbot Clifton, the eldest son of Thomas Clifton, for the development of the 'west end'. In a letter to James Fair, dated 16 May 1846, John Talbot Clifton commented that he was 'delighted that a new village is about to be commenced to the westward'.[1]

In 1850, the year before he succeeded his father as squire, John Talbot Clifton had written a further letter to James Fair expressing the view that 'land now is a very different article to what it used to be. It is a raw material from which, like the manufacturers, we are bound to get the greatest return.'[2] It was, however, to be another twenty-five years before his grandson, also called John Talbot Clifton, was to lay the foundation stone of St Anne's on the Sea.

In 1862 James Fair himself was succeeded as land agent by his son Thomas. Within a year of his appointment Thomas Fair was involved in an enterprise that was an essential stage towards the establishment of the new town. At Easter 1863 a single track railway, owned by the newly formed Blackpool and Lytham Railway Company and promoted by interests favourable to and under the influence of the Clifton family, began to operate trains between Lytham and Blackpool.

Although there were no cheap excursions, thereby helping to maintain the 'quality' of the traffic, the line carried over 35,000 passengers in the first three months of operation. By 1868 nine trains were operating every weekday in each direction.[3] On 3 October 1870 Thomas Fair met the directors of the railway company and 'pointed out where Mr Clifton would like a station between

Blackpool and Lytham'.[4] By the following year agreement had been reached and on 6 November 1871, Thomas Fair, in company with a Mr Eden, 'went over the B&L line and stopped to examine the site of the proposed (but then un-named) station'.[5]

Meanwhile, by an Act of Parliament in 1871, the Blackpool and Lytham Railway Company had been incorporated into the Preston and Wyre Railway. The same Act authorised a connecting line at Lytham, thereby making it possible to operate through trains from Preston to Blackpool. The Clifton family, with James and Thomas Fair the guiding lights, had provided substantial capital in the establishment of both companies, foreseeing both the expansion of Blackpool as a leading popular holiday resort and the opportunity of creating the new town of St Anne's along the route.

As we have already seen, a decision to build a new church had also been taken by this date, and on 4 June 1872 the foundation stone for a church dedicated to St Anne was laid by Lady Clifton, the dedication reputedly being in memory of her aunt Lady Anne Bentinck. The church was to provide the name of the new town.

A year later, on 4 August 1873, and two days before the consecration of the new church, Thomas Fair, together with Mr Henry Clifton, met the directors of the railway company and stopped 'to look at the site of the Station'. He later recorded, in abbreviated notes, that 'a discussion took place as to what the New place was to be called and I was desired by the Directors – after consulting Colonel & Lady Eleanor Cecily Clifton – to write and inform Mr Carr [of the railway company] what the name was to be'.[6]

The following day Thomas Fair wrote to Mr Carr 'informing him that the name was to be St Anne's [on the Sea]'. He added that 'Mr Carr afterwards sent me a proof of the Companys Time Table with the name of the New Station inserted'.[7] By January 1874 the company had 'fixed a platform at the point where the line intersects the high road at St Ann's [sic], so that passengers can now alight from the train with some degree of safety. The footpaths along the side of the road both to the church and to the shore have been asphalted ...'[8]

Although at the time it was claimed that the church had been built for the benefit of the parishioners within Heyhouses, it now seems obvious that its location was part of the grand plan for the establishment of a new town. On 13 August 1873 the *Lytham Times* reported that it was from the church that, 'a fine new road has been opened out and formed by the Lord of the Manor, at a very considerable cost direct to the shore. The Blackpool and Lytham Railway crosses this new road.'[9] A week later a further article implied that the building of the church was primarily related to the 'proposed establishment of a new seaside resort'. The inference that the commercial interests of the Clifton family came before the spiritual needs of the parishioners of Heyhouses was not well received, and the following week the newspaper carried the following short article:

> From the wording of a paragraph which we had last week in reference to St Anne's-on-the-Sea, some of our readers might be misled as to the intentions of the benevolent founder of the new church. The primary object of the Lady Eleanor Cecily Clifton, no doubt was to supply the want long felt in consequence of the limited accommodation afforded by the Heyhouses School, hitherto used for divine service on the Sundays, and then in selecting a site for this purpose, the requirements of a probable new town on the coast were not lost sight of.[10]

Construction of the above-mentioned new road through the sand hills had begun in 1872. Recalling the event in 1890 James Jackson, of the firm Jackson & Parkinson, Surveyors of Preston, said:

> [I] assisted Mr Fair 18 or 19 years ago in laying out the first Main Roads in connection with the then intended new town of St Anne's – viz the Drive from Ansdell to St Anne's (South Drive otherwise Clifton Drive, South) and thence in the direction of Blackpool to Stoney Hill – a distance in all of something near 4 miles – and also the road now called St Anne's Road running from the Shore across the Blackpool & Lytham Railway to Common Lane (Church Road) – and advised with him in fixing positions and gradients of these roads and of the drains which were laid thereunder and as to the number and positions of the Outfalls into the Sea.[11]

The Crescent, 1885. Construction of The Crescent had begun by the end of 1875, thereby eliminating the need for a level crossing by the present-day Whitesides Taxis booking office. In this photograph taken in 1885 the parish church, with its original small steeple, can just be made out in the distance, together with houses in St David's Road, South and St Anne's Road, East.

The expenses incurred in the making of these roads were entered in the Clifton estate account books.[12] The earliest entry is for 25 May 1872 when Richard Miller was paid £7 13s. 8d. for 'Levelling sand to New Church'. Following an advertisement in the *Lytham Times* on 19 October 1872 'for tenders' the contract for St Anne's Road (East/West) was given to William Moxham. From 1 January 1873 to 29 July 1874 he was paid a total of £1,509 8s. 3d., the final entry being noted, 'Balance of contracts forming & making St Annes Road & roads connected therewith ...'

Although it is less clear if they were involved in the making of the South Drive local Heyhouses men were certainly involved in the making of St Anne's Road. Robert Greaves recalled that he ploughed a road across a field between the parish church and what was to be the site of the St Anne's Hotel.[13] The following examples reveal that other Heyhouses men, whether as 'sub-contractors' or as part of their 'boon [manorial] services' also provided a wide range of services.

1 October 1873	Paid Thos Jameson for carting	£15 17s. 6d.
13 November 1873	Paid Richd Warbrick for carting	£8 4s. 0d.
15 September 1874	Paid Robt Smith for rubble	£22 11s. 8d.
12 November 1874	Paid James Houseman [Trawlboat Inn]	
	for dinners	£6 9s. 0d.

The account entitled 'New Road thro Sand Hills' records payments of £6,746 made between 5 November 1874 and 2 July 1877 and provides examples of the scale of the enterprise being undertaken.

16 April 1874	North of England Railway Carriage & Wagon Co.	
	6 new ballast wagons to carry rubble	£450 0s. 0d.
30 June 1875	Paid James Cookson	
	carting stones sand lime	£1 7s. 6d.
17 May 1877	Blackpool Corporation	
	for hire of Steam Roller	£24 0s. 0d.
24 October 1877	James Wilding (Superintendent of men)	
	Quarterly Salary	£25 0s. 0d.

Thus by 1874 Thomas Fair was able to put into effect his plans for the new town. However, due to prevailing economic circumstances the Clifton estate was unable to commit itself to heavy capital costs. Consequently Thomas Fair set out to attract major capital investment through a large building company which would also be responsible for the ongoing development of the town. He was also seeking additional income for the estate from future rents which new building land might generate. Finally he was anxious to maintain sufficient influence within the new town to protect the interests of the estate. It was to be a fractious relationship.

As early as December 1873 a building company had already written to Thomas Fair expressing an interest in taking out a lease on 2½ miles of coastline. Thomas Fair, in a reply to a Charles Evans, rejected the approach because the company also required the estate to contribute £20,000 towards road construction.[14] The company had in fact been farsighted in anticipating the problems of an initially small population maintaining a network of roads, a problem that was not resolved until the 'Roads Trial' of 1889.

However, as we shall see in the next chapter, a meeting held on 6 June 1874 was to produce a much different outcome and would see the beginnings of the new town. When, on 4 September 1874, Thomas Fair wrote to John Talbot Clifton advising him that the first leases for the new town had been granted he also noted that the expected rents 'will pay the interest on the cost of the new Roads'.[15]

During the next thirty years many problems had to be faced and overcome, but by the time Thomas Fair died in 1914 St Anne's was a well-established high-class residential and holiday resort, and the visionary ideas of father and son were recalled in the *St Anne's-on-the-Sea Express*:

> The town of St Anne's is an instance of the foresight and shrewdness of Mr Thomas Fair. The late Mr Fair's father was impressed with the suitability of the sandhills for a watering place, and when Mr Thomas Fair was appointed steward [land agent] he also possessed the same idea ...[16]

CHAPTER FOURTEEN

St Anne's Land and Building Company

The town of St Anne's on the Sea was planned, long before the days of town planning, by Mesrs Maxwell and Tuke, architects and agents to the St Anne's Land and Building Company. The original plan envisaged broad streets running at right angles and houses of the same type grouped together. A major problem with this original plan or design, however, was that it paid far too little attention to the unglamorous but essential aspects of the infrastructure, such as sewerage and drains. Neither the Land and Building Company nor the Clifton estate were prepared to spend money on such unprofitable, but absolutely vital, elements of the new town. It is extraordinary that in the 1870s, when industrial towns were spending vast sums on starting to provide modern and efficient sanitation to remedy the evils of public health, a high-class new town should have been contemplated, and partly built, without such amenities. In part, this was a result of there being three 'actors' – the Land and Building Company, the Clifton estate, and the Local Board of Health – but especially the result of the failure of the estate to take direct responsibility. That was a very serious weakness and as we shall see in the Chapters 16 and 17 brought the Local Board into constant conflict with both the company and estate.

The establishment of the Land and Building Company

The first meeting between the prospective company and Thomas Fair took place on 6 June 1874. Three days later Thomas Fair replied to Thomas Thomas, who was acting as company secretary:

Since you and Mr Hargreaves were here on Saturday I have carefully considered your proposals and I now enclose you a tracing showing a plot of Building Land with a frontage of about 500 yards to the sea & main carriage road, and also a frontage to St Annes Road, now formed – From the line of Garden wall, fronting the sea, to the Railway, is 550

This plan of St Anne's was prepared around the time of the granting of the first leases in 1874/75. It contains details of streets that were not subsequently laid out, particularly in the area in what became the junction of Clifton Drive, South, and St Thomas Road. It is also noteworthy that even at this early date there was a clear intention to develop the site of the later Hotel Majestic for commercial purposes.

yards or thereabouts, so that the total quantity will exceed 50 acres – I propose that another Road should be made parallel with, and 40 or 50 yards from, the Railway as shown on the tracing ...[1]

Other conditions then followed, together with the price of the land and the terms of the leases. Land prices were subsequently amended and fifty acres were offered at ⅘ths of a penny per square yard, and twenty acres at ⅝ths of a penny per square yard. Leases were to be granted for 999 years. Thomas Fair continued his letter in the following terms:

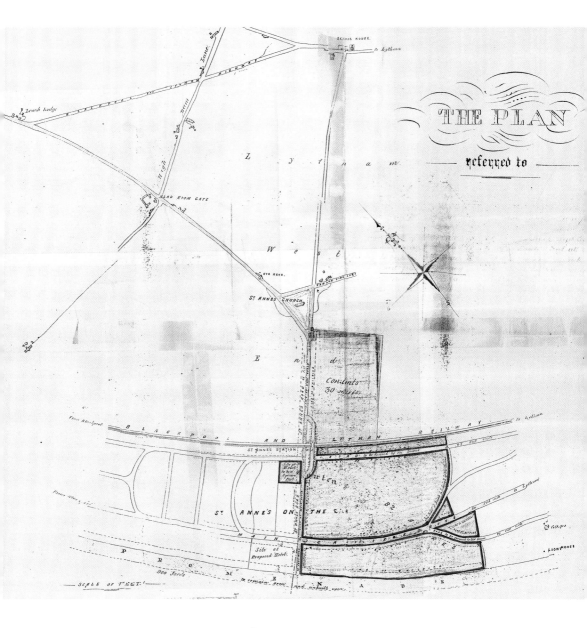

Detached or semi detached Houses only to be built on the plot fronting the Sea and no House to be built on such plot of a less annual value than £100 – No house to be built fronting St Annes Road [West] of a less annual value than £75 [2]

Thomas Fair concluded by requesting that 'If you are in a position to do so I shall be glad if you write to me at the United Hotel, Charles Street, St James', London, by Friday morning to say whether you take the Land on these

The original prospectus of the Land and Building Company issued in October 1874. By the time the first lease was granted on 14 December 1874 Henry Hardman Ashworth and John Warburton had been replaced by James Maxwell, an architect and surveyor, and Thomas Thomas, a cotton merchant.

DDCL UNCATALOGUED BOX 98. REPRODUCED BY PERMISSION OF THE COUNTY ARCHIVIST, LANCASHIRE RECORD OFFICE

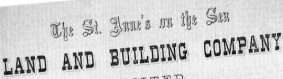

The St. Anne's on the Sea

LAND AND BUILDING COMPANY

LIMITED.

REGISTERED UNDER THE COMPANIES ACTS, 1862 AND 1867, by which the liability of the Shareholders is limited to the amount of their Shares.

CAPITAL, £50,000. in 10,000 Shares of £5. each.

Provisional Directors:—

JOSEPH WOOD WHITEHEAD, Esq., J.P., ALDER GRANGE, RAWTENSTALL.

JAMES TAYLOR, Esq., WARTH HOUSE, WATERFOOT.

HENRY HARDMAN ASHWORTH, Esq., LEA BANK, RAWTENSTALL.

JOHN WARBURTON, JUNIOR, Esq., GREENFIELD, HASLINGDEN, COTTON SPINNER.

THOMAS BARROWCLOUGH, Esq., BACUP, COTTON SPINNER.

JAMES CRABTREE, Esq., BACUP, COTTON SPINNER.

WILLIAM GREAVES, Esq., SPRING-FIELD HOUSE, BACUP, WARP SIZER.

ELIJAH HARGREAVES, Esq., RAWTENSTALL.

Bankers:—

THE LANCASHIRE & YORKSHIRE BANK, LIMITED: MANCHESTER AND ITS BRANCHES.

Solicitors:—

WOODCOCK AND SONS, SOLICITORS, HASLINGDEN.

Architects and Surveyors:—

MAXWELL AND TUKE, PEEL CHAMBERS, BURY.

Auditors:—

F. HUNTER, GREGORY, NUTTALL AND Co., PUBLIC ACCOUNTANTS, BACUP.

Secretary:—

THOMAS THOMAS, EAST VIEW, RAWTENSTALL.

An Agreement has been entered into with John Talbot Clifton Esquire, for a lease to certain gentlemen for 1100 years on very favorable terms of 80 acres of land at St. Anne's on the Sea, having a frontage to the Sea of more than half a mile, and to the main road leading from the Coast to St. Anne's Church, of more than half a mile, and adjoining the intended Railway Station at St. Anne's on the Sea, the lessors granting the lessees the right to a site for a brick croft, with liberty to get clay and make bricks, and the lessors binding themselves for a certain period to give the lessees the option to take land at a rent after the same rate as the 80 acres, for a Public Market, Town Hall and Public Baths and Wash-Houses, and also the exclusive right to take land for a site for Gasworks, with power to lay main and service pipes, and to use the land in front of the beach, as an approach to a pier.

St. Anne's on the Sea is situated on the West Coast between Blackpool and Lytham, about 2½ miles from the latter place on the main line of Railway from Preston through Lytham to Blackpool. The land agreed to be leased is part of the fine Estate belonging to John Talbot Clifton Esquire, and is most pleasantly situated on a light sandy soil with a splendid beach of hard dry sand and shingle, open to the full sweep of the Irish Sea, and from its position, combines the mildness of Lytham with the bracing atmosphere of Blackpool, the property inland being rich farming land, well wooded and laid out in parks.

Shareholders may pay in advance the whole or part of the amount uncalled on their Shares and will receive interest thereon at five per cent per annum.

Should no allotment or only a diminished allotment be made, the deposit will be returned in full to the Applicant, or the balance placed to his credit towards the amount due upon allotment.

somewhat as influenced by the greater or less ... enjoys a fine bracing air, and Lytham,— ... proposed new watering place, St. Anne's being ... anities of being built on virgin soil, and laid to drainage, sewerage &c.,—in the absence of ... ast of having the lowest rate of mortality in

... nor Cicely Clifton, at St. Anne's on the Sea, and

a road from Lytham through St. Anne's on the He has also made a main sewer at St. Anne's on Company will have the benefit of the whole of ... The whole of the land for a carriage drive ... p of land 60 yards wide co-extensive therewith ... benefit, are not included in the measurement,

... mpany, to supply Water at St. Anne's on the

Excursionists that a decided want is felt for a ... and commanding position on the coast as ... This want the Company will seek to supply. ... taken that no application shall be made for a ... y have obtained a license for the Hotel to be

been entered into between Mr. Clifton and the ... ss than a fixed rate, nor to allow buildings to

... ich the Company commences operations, the ... rman's huts or unhealthy dwellings to remove, ... o St. Anne's on the Sea one of the healthiest,

... the well-known salubrity of its climate, the ... it commands by means of the new Railway, ... nder it equally popular with many other of the ... tify this belief that the land will afford a fine

... eminary, as well as for other buildings have ... abt numerous other applications will be received.

... undertake to build for others, to advance money ... on the business of a land and building Society.

... e terms, that considerable profit will accrue to ... than land, and no investment which, under ... edly increases in value: land in Blackpool and ... ommanding a rental of no less than two shillings,

... le dividend will in a short time be paid to the ... best Dividend paying Companies in the District.

Mr. Clifton, and the Company has been formed ... h day of October, 1874, between Joseph Wood ... , William Greaves, Elijah Hargreaves, James ... , on behalf of the Company of the other part, ... resaid agreed to be leased by Mr. Clifton, with ... ay be inspected at the Offices of the Solicitors, ... n.

... that 5s. per share shall be paid on application, ... h case, 10s. per share, made at intervals of not ... call.

... obtained from the Provisional Directors, Bankers,

... been received, and applications for the remaining ... made upon the form enclosed and addressed to the

Joseph Wood Whitehead was the first chairman of the St Anne's on the Sea Land and Building Company. In the original prospectus for the company he was described as 'Occupation not stated' but in fact had been a cotton manufacturer at Higher Mills, Rawtenstall. He never lived at St Anne's and he died at his Rawtenstall home in 1879, aged fifty-six. His obituary in the *Bacup Times* of 3 May 1879 made no reference to his financial involvement at St Anne's.

terms'. He also added, presumably for his own benefit, the following notes to his copy of the letter: 'The Lessees are to build Houses to secure Ground Rents; Plans of all Buildings to be submitted and approved by Mr Clifton; The Lessees to build Hotel at Station at a cost not less than £3000.'[3]

During the summer of 1874 Messrs Woodcock & Sons of Haslingden, solicitors acting for the provisional company directors, corresponded with Messrs Wilson & Deacon of Preston, solicitors acting for the Clifton estate, concerning the requirements of the estate with regard to building leases and other legal matters. By 14 October 1874 the decision had been made and on that date, at the Queens Arms Hotel, Rawtenstall, eight men formed the St Anne's on the Sea Land and Building Company.

According to the prospectus issued by the company these provisional directors were:[4]

Joseph Wood Whitehead of Rawtenstall – Occupation not stated
James Taylor of Waterfoot – Occupation not stated
Henry Hardman Ashworth of Rawtenstall – Occupation not stated
John Warburton junr of Haslingden – Cotton Spinner
Thomas Barraclough of Bacup – Cotton Spinner
James Crabtree of Bacup – Cotton Spinner
William Greaves of Bacup – Warp Sizer
Elijah Hargreaves of Rawtenstall – Occupation not stated

As a a result of the affluence created by the industrial revolution there had been a Rossendale connection with the Fylde coast from the middle of the century, and the area offered many pleasant locations in which to build a prestigious holiday or retirement home. In addition, self-made entrepreneurs such as the eight directors of the Land and Building Company were men who were also seeking new investment opportunities. Thus St Anne's presented an ideal opportunity for the East Lancashire tradition of investing surplus capital in bricks and mortar.

Elijah Hargreaves

As we have seen in the previous chapter credit for the vision of a new town in the sand dunes must go to James and Thomas Fair. However, because of his perceived prominent role in the origins of St Anne's, it is appropriate to look at some aspects of the life of Elijah Hargreaves. He was born at Rawtenstall in 1831 and when aged between seven and eight years old started as a part-timer at Lower Mill, Rawtenstall, a company owned by Joseph Wood Whitehead, the first chairman of the Land and Building Company. Elijah Hargreaves progressed to become manager at Lower Mill and when the mill was gutted by fire he was reported to have been the last to leave the burning building by leaping from one of the windows.

It now seems probable that he acted as a 'front man' for the East Lancashire businessmen who formed the Land and Building Company, and that his role was to negotiate with Thomas Fair, on their behalf, the conditions and terms required by Clifton estate for the laying out of the new town.

In 1879 he moved to Bolton and became landlord at the Fleece Hotel, Bradshawgate. He interested himself in public affairs and was elected as a Liberal to the Bolton Town Council. He retired to St Anne's in 1900 and purchased 'The Elms' on St Andrew's Road, South, where he died in October 1904.[5] He was buried at the Zion Baptist Chapel, Cloughfold, Rossendale.

The first lease between the Clifton estate and the Land and Building Company. This comprehensive lease, dated 14 December 1874, covered every conceivable aspect with regard to the future development of the town.

The first lease

The first lease between the Land & Building Company and the Clifton Estate was for eighty-two acres of land, and was signed on 14 December 1874. The eight lessees were the original directors, with the exception of Henry Hardman Ashworth and John Warburton, who were replaced by James Maxwell of Bury – architect and surveyor, and Thomas Thomas of Rawtenstall – cotton merchant.[6]

The comprehensive lease covered every conceivable aspect with regard to the future development of the new town including:

the right of draining the said land into the existing drain, under or alongside St Anne's Road ... between the Railway from Lytham to Blackpool and the Sea, and the right of using for all reasonable purposes all the roads and drives ..., and all other public roads now made or which hereafter may be made by the lessors ...

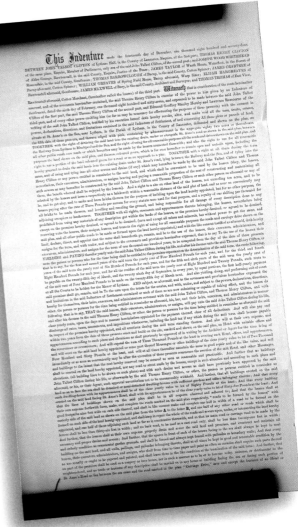

a right to drain the said lands into the existing drain … and of tying into the same, and using and tying into all sewers and drains (if any) which hereafter be made by the said John Talbot Clifton …

the right to a site on other land of the lessors, not exceeding ten acres, and to be selected by the lessors and lessees respectively as a brickcroft within a reasonable distance of the said plot of land, and as conveniently may be, to get clay, and to make and burn bricks thereon for the purpose of building upon the land hereby appointed, but for no other purpose …

Among the many other clauses in the lease there was a requirement to build an hotel and to 'erect Messuages or other buildings of the clear yearly value to let of Two Thousand Four Hundred and Sixty Pounds at the least'. There is also mention of a public market, town hall, public baths and wash-houses. Various rents are specifically itemised with the endorsement on the counterpart of the lease noting that 'twelve weeks rent shall always be paid in advance'. There was even a clause which required, in theory at least, that the lessees were to perform 'suit of court at all the Courts to be holden for the Manor of Lytham'.

The prospectus issued by the Land and Building Company announced that its capital was to be £50,000 divided into 10,000 shares of £5 each. The company was also covenanted to spend at least £70,000 on building and construction work with the stipulation that £50,000 should be expended in the first four years.

Foundation Day

The first contracts to be let were to Messrs Taylor and Duckworth for the laying out of the Promenade, and to Messrs Ogden, Hamilton, Roberts, Walmsley and others for the St Anne's Hotel. James Maxwell, of Messrs Maxwell and Tuke, architects and agents to the Land and Building Company, whose role in the history of St Anne's is described later in this chapter, recalled that:

On the 2nd of February 1875, the first workmen were set to work. The promenade was set out and the Hotel begun. The first batch of men left in despair and fresh ones had to be got. Then began to spring up wood huts some of which remain to this day [January 1878] as stables etc … A railway was laid down St Anne's Road [West] and joined to the permanent way, and in a short time the whole road was blocked with building materials …[7]

It was found impossible to keep the workmen without adequate housing. Accordingly Maxwell and Tuke began the erection of twelve houses in Common Lane. While these dwellings were under construction, a Mr Davenport put up 'a Log Store, a genuine American store' where 'tables that served for meals in the daytime served for the beds at night'. By spring 1875 the number of workmen numbered two hundred, and 'so arrangements were made whereby the railway ran a special train for the workmen night and morning between St Annes and Lytham, where plenty of lodgings could be had'.[8]

The foundation stone of the new town of St Anne's on the Sea was laid on Wednesday, 31 March 1875. The *Lytham Times* reported that:

> The day was remarkably fine, and a very large number of spectators, both by rail and road (special trains being run from Lytham and Blackpool), were attracted to the spot, so that when the proceedings took place, the formerly deserted scene was peopled by a crowd of at least two thousand persons who assembled round the site of the first new buildings to be erected in St Anne's.[9]

A temporary pavilion had been erected adjacent to the proposed new St Anne's Hotel, with a motto suspended over it – 'Welcome to St Anne's'. The foundation stone was the first of the basement course at the eastern angle of the new hotel which was being built from the designs of Maxwell and Tuke. The ceremony was performed by John Talbot Clifton, aged six and a half, the eldest son of Thomas Henry Clifton MP. He was presented with a trowel by Joseph Wood Whitehead bearing an inscription recording the event. In a bottle placed beneath the foundation stone were various items including a document which read:

> ... and is the first stone ever laid at the Town of St Anne's on the Sea and is intended to commemorate the foundation of what it is hoped under the blessing of almighty God may become one of the great Sanitariums [*sic*] of Lancashire.[10]

After the ceremony the invited guests proceeded to the Clifton Arms Hotel, Lytham, for what can only be described as a sumptuous luncheon, followed by speeches by various dignitaries. The same afternoon the directors of the Land and Building Company entertained the contractors, for works then in progress at St Anne's, to dinner at the Ship and Royal Hotel, Lytham. Mr Farington, on behalf of the company, informed those gathered that the directors had invited them so that they might become known to each other and that this first meeting would result in a good understanding among them all.

St Anne's Road, West (The Square) looking westward c.1886. The building centre right is now occupied by the Edinburgh Woollen Mill and was built by John Hindle in 1877. In 1932 J.H. Taylor recalled that the business part of the town in the late 1880s 'consisted of about a dozen shops in the main street, and the six old shops in Garden Street'.

The early years

Following the laying of the foundation stone the Land and Building Company set about the task of persuading builders to invest in the town, and individual investors to invest in the company. Typical of the former was an advertisement in the *Lytham Times* which read:

ST ANNE'S ON THE SEA LAND AND BUILDING COMPANY, LIMITED St Anne's on the Sea, situated between Blackpool and Lytham, possesses every advantage for Seaside Residences – good sea, fine sandy subsoil, dry climate, having a south-west aspect. Land to Let for Villas, Shops, Schools, and Cottages, on lease for 999 years, on most reasonable terms. A church is already built, several miles of roads laid out, and sewered. Upwards of one hundred villas and houses are now in the course of erection; also schools, hotel, and shops, covering more than an area of 30 acres – For plans, particulars, and conditions apply to Maxwell and Tuke, Architects to the Company, Bury.[11]

At the general meeting of the Land and Building Company, held at the Queens Hotel, Rawtenstall on 13 February 1875, John Woodcock of Messrs Woodcock & Sons, solicitors, announced that 4,160 shares representing a capital of £20,800 had been applied for.[12] Within just over a year of this meeting six subsidiary companies had been formed in order to further the objectives of the parent company:

St Anne's on the Sea Gas Light & Coke Co. Ltd
St Anne's on the Sea Public Accommodation Co. Ltd
St Anne's on the Sea Brick & Tile Co. Ltd
St Anne's on the Sea Hotel Co. Ltd
St Anne's on the Sea Gardens Co. Ltd
St Anne's on the Sea Pier & Improvements Co. Ltd.

As a result of the establishment of these subsidiary companies the directors decided that they would 'before long offer to the shareholders new shares in the Gas Company pro rata to their holding in the present [parent] company'.[13]

Indeed the initial confidence of the board of the Land and Building Company was such that in 1876 they had taken leases on a further 236 acres with the intention of developing one square mile of land from (what was to become) the Pier Head. A letter from Woodcock & Sons to Wilson & Deacon on 5 April 1876 refers to an additional six leases, and notes that 'as the lessees are entitled to possession or receipt of the rents of 200 acres from the 25th ult and the £10,000 is in the Bank the lessees will be entitled to the interest from it … It is very desirable for all parties to complete the leases as early as possible.'[14]

However, Thomas Fair was clearly unhappy with the quality of new buildings, and had initiated a review of building standards. On 7 March 1876 Messrs Aldridge & Deacon of Liverpool advised him that:

> In accordance with your request we have examined the Buildings in course of erection at St Annes on the Sea and we have to offer the following remarks concerning them. Speaking generally the houses fail in many respects to comply with any rules we are acquainted with that have been framed by competent authority for the purpose of regulating thickness of walls, strength of timbers and other details and we must also add that the workmanship in many points is most unsatisfactory.

After citing several examples of these poor standards Aldridge & Deacon were of the opinion that:

> The general conclusion we draw from our survey is that Mr Clifton's interest cannot be properly protected unless in all cases a code of building rules be strictly adhered to & for this purpose it is necessary that the Buildings be properly inspected from time to time.[15]

In spite of these initial concerns both Thomas Fair and the Land and Building Company came, in due course and in the light of financial reality, to share approximately the same ground on the matter of building controls.

In addition to the Land and Building Company the Lancashire Land Company also appears to have been involved in the erection of properties in the town during the late 1870s.

In October 1877 Maxwell and Tuke drew up a 'Measure Bill of Variation to Contract for the erection of Eight Dwelling Houses situate in St Annes Road [West], St Annes on the Sea done by Mr Jas. Roberts for the Lancashire Land Co'.[16] Nothing further is known about this company.

Board disputes

In November 1877 Maxwell and Tuke resigned as agents to the Land and Building Company. In their detailed letter of resignation Maxwell and Tuke noted their pleasure at the fact that 'the undertaking which at the first was looked upon with distrust by the investing public, has now become one of the most sought after of Local Public Charities'. They also admitted that during the past three years they had 'reaped a larger harvest in the sale of land than can in the ordinary course of events be expected to occur again in the Company's history'. But then came to the main point:

> but we feel that there has been so much discussion and suppressed dissatisfaction at the share of profits which we have been supposed to realize that we believe the best interests of the company will be secured by giving you the opportunity of making for the shareholders some new arrangement, which we hope will conduce even more to their interest, than the one we now conclude.[17]

The dispute continued into the following year when in April 1878, at the annual meeting of shareholders, an attempt to demand the appointment of a committee of enquiry into land leased to the directors, the architect, and the secretary was lost by 500 to 460 votes. At the same meeting James Maxwell failed to obtain a seat on the board.[18]

Feelings were obviously still strong when, at the shareholders' meeting held on 5 October 1878, James Hill, the chairman, questioned the remuneration Maxwell and Tuke had received while acting as architects and agents to the company. Ten days later Maxwell and Tuke issued a notice to the shareholders referring to the 'mendacity' of the chairman's remarks and pointing out that their 'pecuniary stake at St Anne's, is as far as we can ascertain, at least ten times as large as the Chairman's'.[19]

At the annual meeting the following year the company appointed a committee of enquiry to enquire into 'all disputes between the company and Messrs Maxwell and Tuke and to suggest to a future meeting of shareholders if practicable some arrangement whereby all such disputes may be settled and all questions between the company and the eight original lessees for ever set at rest.'[20]

James Maxwell

James Maxwell was born at Haslingden on 14 June 1838, the son of Thomas and Mary Maxwell. When aged fourteen or fifteen he was apprenticed to Thomas Holmes, a Bury architect. At twenty-one he set himself up as an architect and in 1865 took into his employment William Charles Tuke. Among many public buildings built to their design the most notable was Blackpool Tower.

On the evidence of a letter in the *Lytham Times*, he was a popular figure in St Anne's:

And then, how the happy smiling face of Mr Maxwell was looked for on the Saturday morning, for then as now, he was the man who was most respected by the people of anyone who came to visit here; and Mr Editor, I will close this little idea of change by saying long life to Mr Maxwell, and may he live to see greater changes even yet in St Anne's on the Sea.[21]

He can justifiably also be described as the town's first historian. A notice in the *St Annes Miscellany* for September 1877 informed its readers that:

The St Annes Miscellany for October will contain the first of a series of articles 'bringing down the History of St Annes on the Sea to the present time' kindly contributed by James Maxwell, Esq than whom (it is needless to say) no one can be more competent to write on this subject. We are sure these leaves of our infant history will be full of interesting details and well worth reading and preserving.[22]

It is therefore somewhat surprising that at the first elections for the Local Board in 1878 he failed to be elected by just three votes. The fact that this election took place only three months after his defeat at the annual meeting of the company shareholders may, of course, not be unconnected. However, in the board elections held in 1880 he topped the poll, and in 1883 was returned unopposed. Soon after his re-election he appears to have resigned from the board, probably in connection with the reluctance of his fellow board members to provide a modern drainage system for the town. By 1886 he had become reconciled with the Land and Building Company and was its vice-chairman. In 1888 he was elected as a Liberal for Bury Council, becoming an alderman three years later. He died at his home at Manchester Road, Bury, in September 1893. His obituary in the *Bury Times* recorded that:

Mr Maxwell was one of the eight persons who originally founded St Annes on the Sea after purchasing the land from the Clifton family; and eventually he came to own one-eighth of the original undertaking. As an architect and engineer he laid out the whole of the town, and during the first few years of the undertaking was the land agent. He himself or his firm prepared the plans for the hotel, the gasworks, and practically all the original houses, and they made the promenade and all the roads in the neighbourhood.[23]

Financial difficulties

The dispute between James Maxwell and the Land and Building Company took place during a period when the Company itself might have gone bankrupt. A table detailing expenditure spent since the formation of the company, totalling £62,077 4s. 4½d., was prepared for the March 1878 shareholders meeting and included the following items:[24]

By Promenade	£10,418 17s. 7d.
Formation of Streets as	£2,297 19s. 0d.
Purchase of Ground Rents	£10,000 0s. 0d.
Buildings	£35,619 12s. 2d.

In fact it was only the commitment of men such as Joseph Whitehead, the first chairman of the company, who tore up his personal guarantee of £10,000, and other directors that kept the company from bankruptcy.

Several of the associated companies also ran into difficulties and had to be rescued or supported by the parent company. Indeed between 1875 and 1889 no fewer than forty-five investors filed petitions for bankruptcy.[25] Some idea of the slump in the building trade can be gleaned from the account written by David Greaves in 1925, when he recalled how he came with his mother, in April 1877, to look for a house in Church Road, St Anne's:

> ... and we found plenty to be had, and empty. And what a state so many of these cottages then were in, – broken windows, rusty firegrates and boilers, were to be seen first in one and then another house. The reason for this was that there came a slump in the early building of St Anne's, and settlers had vacated their houses, having gone back to where-ever they had happened to come from. Hitherto the building of houses and property in St Anne's had been good for about three years[26]

At a meeting of the shareholders held in April 1880 it was reported that 'some conversation took place in reference to a change on the Board', many of the shareholders present believing that 'it would be beneficial to the interests of St Anne's'. It seemed to be generally understood, however, 'that so long as the shares of the Company remained in the present hands it would be a difficult matter to replace the old directors'.[27]

Although the 1881 census revealed that sixty-three properties in St Anne's were uninhabited the directors, at the 1882 meeting of shareholders, were of the opinion that 'property had seen its worst days'. However, in spite of this optimism no dividends on ordinary shares were paid from 1879 until 1892. In 1885 the balance sheet was 'far from satisfactory' and in the same year capital expenditure amounting to £41,232 10s. 0d. was written off. This was also the year that the pier was opened, an event which contributed to a recovery in the company's financial affairs.

Nevertheless in 1887 122 shareholders felt it necessary to petition John Talbot Clifton for a reduction in rents. In a detailed account of the financial history of the Land and Building Company, and pointing out that John Talbot Clifton was then receiving an annual rent of £2495 15s. 0d. increasing to £3395 15s. 0d. in 1896, they concluded by saying that:

> ... many of your petitioners are persons of small means and became shareholders ... as investors in the expectation that they would at least receive some interest for the money invested and it had been a great struggle on the part of many to pay calls on their shares and having

Financial Report of the Land and Building Company – 1885. In 1885 the balance sheet was 'far from satisfactory' and in the same year capital expenditure amounting to £41,232 10s. 0d. was written off. It was also the year the Pier was opened, an event which contributed to a recovery in the Company's financial affairs.

DIRECTORS' REPORT.

To the Shareholders.

Your Directors have to report an increasing activity in St. Anne's; and although the Balance Sheet presented is far from being satisfactory, still there are some features of hope to which your Directors desire to call your attention

During the Half-year, the Directors have let land to the extent of 31,988 yards, at an annual rent of £135 18s. 10½d.

All the property of the Company is now let, and there are no empty houses in St. Anne's, except the large new ones on the Promenade. There is a constant demand for houses at from £25 to £60 per annum; some have been built during the half-year; more are building; and plans are being prepared for others. *The demand for houses of this class is much beyond the supply.* Rents for convenient houses have considerably advanced, and property of the class referred to could now be built very cheaply, and to pay a fair return at the present rentals.

Your Directors would call the attention of the Shareholders to the fact, that in the erection of property lies the only hope of a dividend.

If the Shareholders would be at the trouble to analyze the Balance Sheet, they will find by dividing the Company into two parts, and separating the Land from the Building Account, that the capital invested in land, including Pier and Promenade. stands at £35,000; and that the nett income from the land at present, after deducting Ground Rents paid and the moiety of all expenses amounts to over £1,600 per annum, or more than 4½ per cent. on the capital invested.

On the other hand, the income from the Buildings looks very unsatisfactory this half-year; this arises from the fact that nearly £400 has been spent in repairs.

If Shareholders will take land from the Company and erect buildings thereon, they will be able to obtain a fair interest for their expenditure, and at the same time greatly help to develope the Company into a dividend paying concern.

On the other hand, those who are not disposed to take land, may find investments for money upon Mortgages at 4½ per cent., and thus enable others who are willing, to continue building operations.

Your Directors are strongly impressed, that if at the present moment active building operations by those already interested as Shareholders in the Company were begun, that the general public would immediately follow.

For the Directors,

WILLIAM H. NUTTER,

Secretary.

done so to lose all chance of any return is most disheartening especially in these cases where small investors have invested all they had on which ground your petitioners most earnestly appeal to you for favourable consideration of the matter.[28]

The first signature on the petition was that of William John Porritt, without whose commitment the Land and Building Company would probably not have survived. Of the other shareholders 100 came from various towns in East Lancashire, Manchester, Bolton and Burnley; fourteen came from St Anne's and two from Slaidburn; one each from Lytham, Preston and London; and two from Rio de Janeiro, Brazil.[29]

In 1891 James Hill wrote to Thomas Fair saying that he feared without William Porritt 'a collapse seems certain'. Mr Hill also urged Thomas Fair to forego 'for ever' the ground rents rather than see the enterprise 'drag on [in] such a miserable existence as it has done for the last 10 or 15 years'. Mr Hill concluded his letter by pointing out that 'Had I never known St Annes I should have been £5,000 richer'.[30]

In fact failed new resorts were far from unknown in the second half of the nineteenth century. Seascale in Cumberland and Ratchscar near Whitby are two examples. It was a very risky business.

William John Porritt

The name William John Porritt will forever be associated with the establishment of St Anne's as a successful new town. Born at Ramsbottom on 17 December 1828, the eldest son of Joseph and Sarah Porritt, he came from a family that had had long connections with the manufacture of woollens in north-east Lancashire, his grandfather having commenced in business in Bury in 1808. As a youth he worked at the family business as both a handloom weaver and also at wool sorting.

In 1866, together with his father he erected Sunnybank Mill at Helmshore, also acquiring Higher Mill in Helmshore in 1880. In addition he also owned three quarries in the Helmshore area. In religion he was an Independent (Congregational), and in politics a life-long radical – the *Rossendale Free Press* observing 'It would be strange if he were otherwise, for the Porritt family are noted locally as thorough Radicals and Nonconformists, and in this respect he has always been reliable'.[31]

William Porritt was present at the laying of the foundation stone at St Anne's, and 'since the establishment of St Anne's he has been wrapped up in its career'.[32] Soon after he became a director of the Land and Building Company and from 1881 to 1896 served as its chairman. He was co-opted onto the Local Board in 1879 but his first two attempts, in 1881 and again in 1882, to gain

William John Porritt. The man most associated with the establishment of St Anne's as a successful new town. It was however a more complex association than is sometimes realised, and his first two attempts to be elected to the Local Board were rejected by the electorate. C.G.D. Hoare, the headmaster of Lawrence House School, described William Porritt as 'a familiar figure walking about with his white umbrella ... and who had, under a somewhat gruff exterior, a very kindly heart'. At the time of his death in 1896 it was justifiably said that 'No man assisted more in the development of St Anne's.

re-election resulted in defeat. It was only when nominated in 1883, a year in which no election took place, that he regained his seat. Thereafter he served continuously until 1894, and was its chairman from 1891 to 1893.

He is probably best known for the development of the large area of land to the north of the pier, where he built the properties now known as the 'Porritt' houses. Although later estimates quote a figure of £250,000, at the time of his death, it was estimated he had erected property in St Anne's to the value of £100,000.[33] It was said that 'No man assisted more in the development of St Anne's ... No one could induce him to sell any of his houses, and there was always a long waiting list for tenancies.'[34]

William Porritt, and his wife Margaret, only resided at St Anne's for part of the year. They first occupied Fair View, South Drive, then removed to Stoneleigh, North Promenade. William Porritt was recalled as 'a familiar figure walking about with his white umbrella and an old favourite sheep dog, and who had, under a somewhat gruff exterior, a very kindly heart'.[35] He died at Helmshore on 30 October 1896 and was buried at Park Chapel, Ramsbottom.

On 28 July 1986 Fylde Borough Council designated the area of large Victorian houses, built by William Porritt, and situated around Ashton Gardens, as a Conservation Area. In their report the Council listed 'A number of architectural features [that] give the Porritt houses their particular character'. Under 'materials of construction' it was noted that 'The front elevations of Porritt houses are constructed of stone with the sides and rear of brick'. Often this brickwork incorporates patterns with courses of brick in different colours. The roofs of Porritt houses are typically blue-grey slate, often with different slates arranged in patterns. The roofs are then finished with ornamental red ridge tiles.

Success and prosperity

By the time of William Porritt's death the fortunes of the Land and Building Company were already improving. In 1896 the company handed over to the urban district council all the land lying between the roadway and sea wall on the South Promenade, together with the hulking, sea wall, shelters, and the company's rights in the land. These works, which up to that time had cost the company over £13,000, were handed over free of payment. Thus, one by one, the company's former financial involvement in the town, with the exception of the pier, steadily diminished, leaving it to concentrate on the leasing of land and the collection of ground rents.

Whereas in 1884 ordinary £5 shares in the company had to be written down to £2 10s. 0d. by 1892 a dividend of 1¼ per cent was paid. The dividend increased progressively, reaching 9 per cent in 1901, and from then until 1951, with the exception of the years 1923 to 1925, it was consistently between 9 per cent and 12 per cent. In 1923 the dividend paid was 14 per cent rising to 15 per cent the following year.

At the shareholders meeting held on 1 March 1924 the directors announced that 'the amount of Capital expenditure amounting to £41,232 10s. 0d. written off in 1885 has been re-instated and the premium on the shares formerly written off the Capital Account has been credited to the Profit and Loss Account'.[36]

At the annual meeting the following year it was announced that the share capital was £101,210 0s. 0d. Initially these financial adjustments resulted in a reduced dividend of 8 per cent in 1925, but from 1927 to 1951 it remained constant at 9 or 10 per cent. During the 1950s there was again some decrease but by 1962, when the company was purchased by Amalgamated Investment and Property Company, the dividend had again reached 10 per cent.

Amalgamated Investment and Property Company

In June 1962 the London-based Amalgamated Investment and Property Company sent a short announcement to the London Stock Exchange to the effect that they had made an offer to purchase the share capital of the St Anne's Land and Building Company. The purchase price was agreed at £240,000.

During the following twelve years the chairman of Amalgamated Property and Investment Co., Gabriel Harrison, took a keen interest in St Anne's, an interest which included the writing of his book *Rage of Sand*. After his death in 1974, the company was run by his son, but due to problems resulting from the earlier 1971 stock market crash the company subsequently went into receivership.

On 3 September 1979 Amalgamated Investment and Property ceased trading as a company. The last balance sheet showed properties, including those in St Anne's, with a book value of more than £200 million, but at the time of the stock exchange suspension, the shares were standing at just 16½p, making the whole company worth about £12 million.

St Anne's Land and Building Company (Successor Company)

During the period when Amalgamated Investment and Property was in receivership, and in order to collect ground rents in St Anne's on behalf of the receivers, the Webb family (of the Dalmeny Hotel) formed the Clifton Land and Building Company. In July 1977 the Clifton Land and Building Company bought the ground rents from the receiver and when the receivership ended was renamed the St Anne's Land and Building Company. Although this company has no connection with the original company, its name does provide a continuing link with the early pioneers of St Anne's.

The Crescent – c.1893. Among the commercial premises on the row of arcades are Redferns, the butchers; a small restaurant; Inghams, a confectioner and seller of 'fancy goods'; Pickups, a family grocers; and Walmsleys, outfitters and suppliers of mourning clothes.

CHAPTER FIFTEEN

Hotel, gardens and pier

St Anne's Hotel

The building of a major and quality hotel was seen as crucial in establishing the 'superior' tone of the seaside resort which the Clifton estate planned. It was no surprise therefore that when Thomas Fair replied to Thomas Thomas (*sic*) with his proposals for the development of St Anne's, he specifically raised the issue of forming a joint company in order to proceed with the erection of an hotel:

> The tracing shows the site of the proposed Hotel with one portion of which we are about to proceed forthwith at a cost of about £5000, and it has occurred to me that so far as the Hotel is concerned perhaps the Gentlemen with whom you are acting might feel disposed to join Mr Clifton & form a company. If so I would suggest a nominal capital of £15,000 (of which Mr Clifton will subscribe a third)[1]

Unless it was part of an agreement made with the railway company the previous year, this offer by the estate to subscribe a third of the capital necessary was probably a bait to attract outside investment in the proposed new hotel. Whatever the reason, by the time the first lease was drawn up between the Clifton estate and the Land and Building Company, enthusiasm had waned and the Land and Building were required:

> at their own expense, and within two years from the date of these presents erect and build on the site, marked ... on the said plan, an Hotel with suitable offices and appurtenances according to such plans and elevations as shall be previously be approved of in writing by the Architect or Agent ... And will expend the sum of Three Thousand Pounds at the least in erecting such Hotel, offices ...[2]

Having required the lessees to build an hotel the Clifton estate then added

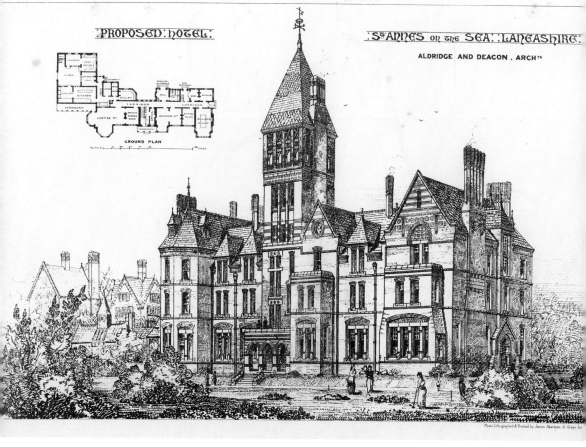

On 15 May 1874 – seven months before the first lease between the Clifton Estate and the Land and Building Company – The Buildings News published a drawing by Aldridge and Deacon (agents to the Clifton Estate) of a proposed hotel at St Anne's. It was this hotel which the Clifton Estate presumably wished to erect in partnership with a prospective building company. However when the first lease with the Land and Building Company was signed enthusiasm had waned and the Company were, at their own expense, required to erect the hotel depicted on page 168.

AUTHOR COLLECTION

another clause, which in effect meant that the future hotel had a monopoly of the licensed trade in the town for the next twenty-three years:

> the lessors will not within five years from the date of these presents within one mile of the land hereby appointed demise or let any land for the purpose of an Hotel or Public House, nor build or permit to be built an Hotel or Public House save and except the Hotel for which the lessors have already obtained plans ...[3]

High Victoriana: following the demolition of the St Anne's Hotel the St Anne's Tavern (now The Crescent) was erected on the site. The impressive 'Tiles Bar', a feature of the original St Anne's Hotel, survived the demolition of the hotel and was incorporated into the successor building.

Work on the erection of the hotel began in February 1875, and on 7 August 1875 James Maxwell, as manager of the Land and Building Company, announced by printed notice that he intended to apply to the magistrates for a licence for the hotel.[4] On 13 April 1876 the St Anne's on the Sea Hotel Company was formed, with a capital of £8,000 in £5 shares, 'for the purpose of acquiring the recently erected building ... known as the St Anne's Hotel'.[5]

In 1879 the Hotel Company was liquidated and the hotel, valued at £7,000, appears to have been sold at auction, to the parent Land and Building Company. Sometime after 1881 the lease was acquired by Arthur John Holloway, manager of the Clifton Arms Hotel, Blackpool. At the annual meeting of Land and Building shareholders in March 1883 the chairman was able to report that:

> During the last six months extensive alterations and improvements have been made in the Hotel, which is now in full working order, and will be found one of the most comfortable Hotels on the coast; the more this fact is spread, and the more chance of getting back the popularity once held by the Hotel ...[6]

Arthur Holloway died at Northampton in 1891. In his will he described himself as 'licensed victualler of St Anne's', and bequeathed all his 'real and personal estate ... particularly the benefit and lease of the said St Anne's

Construction work on the St Anne's Hotel began in February 1875. On 13 April 1876 the St Anne's on the Sea Hotel Company was formed 'for the purposes of acquiring the recently erected building'. In 1879 the hotel company was liquidated and by 1881 the lease had been acquired by Arthur John Holloway. Ownership subsequently passed to brewery companies and in 1985 the greater part of the building was demolished.
BY COURTESY OF TED LIGHTBOWN

Hotel which I now occupy … unto my dear wife Rose Jane Holloway'.[7] Rose continued to run the St Anne's Hotel with the help of her three daughters. At the same time she commenced building the Grand Hotel, which was completed in 1897. It would seem that she sold the lease of the St Anne's Hotel as, by 1904, the hotel was owned by Richard Seed & Co. of Radcliffe. In 1985 Whitbread plc, then owners, decided to demolish the building. The new building was originally renamed the St Anne's Tavern and subsequently The Crescent. The present owners are Greene King plc.

St George's Gardens

At the outset the necessity of landscaping the new town was addressed by the Land and Building Company. Not only would such a development create a green oasis within a vast expanse of sand but would also provide an area for popular Victorian leisure pursuits. When the Land and Building Company was formed, twelve acres of land in the centre of the estate, and known as 'The Oval', were allocated for development as a small home park or public garden.

On 8 October 1875 Maxwell and Tuke announced, by a preliminary notice, that The St Anne's on the Sea Public Accommodation Company was to be formed with the primary object of constructing a Public Garden, to be called St George's Gardens. Intended attractions included conservatories, music pavilion, archery, croquet, tennis, skating rink, reading and billiards room, aviaries, and flower and kitchen gardens. Significantly there was no provision for public dancing, 'or any amusement calculated to lower the status of the town'.[8]

At around the same period of time it would appear that a public gardens company – The St Anne's on the Sea Gardens Company – was also formed to manage the gardens. By August 1877 the gardens had been transformed 'under the experienced direction and management' of Mr Edward Thomas of Aughton, who was also responsible for the gardens on the esplanade. Instead of 'bleak barren sandhills' there was

> a flourishing garden with hills and dales, extensive masses of flowering plants, very tastefully grouped as to colour, bowling greens, archery ground, croquet grounds, a spacious conservatory, a handsome vinery, a well stocked kitchen garden …[9]

The Gardens Company was not to be a financial success and, in the early 1880s, together with the Public Accommodation Company, was taken over by the parent Land and Building Company.[10] The parent company managed them directly for several years before leasing them in 1886 to Robert Wild. Mr Wild was followed by John Ferguson, brother of Coun. Thomas Ferguson a former owner of the popular Cherry Tree Gardens, Blackpool. Such success was not to be repeated at St Anne's and eventually part of the Gardens was used as a nursery by William Cartmell of Messrs Cartmell and Sons.

In 1896 the Land and Building Company offered the Gardens to St Anne's Urban District Council, noting that they had spent £11,000 in laying them out. Following a suggestion by William Porritt, the Ratepayers Association urged the council to purchase the gardens for the town. The council declined, however, on the grounds that the ratepayers would probably object to an annual increase in the rates of 3*d*. in the £ which the purchase was estimated to cost.

The Porritt family themselves then purchased the Gardens, and proceeded to erect residential property bounded by the Gardens on two sides. The result was that St George's Square and Beach Road were formed on part of the former Gardens site, thereby reducing their size to approximately nine or ten acres. By 1913 it was recalled that 'the main portion of the Gardens had been running to waste, except for one or two portions used as playgrounds for private schools, and glass houses which were rented by Messrs Cartmell & Co'.[11]

In 1913, when St Anne's Urban District Council decided to request a further Improvement Bill, an informal conversation took place between Thomas Bradley (Clerk to the Council) and Oliver Porritt, the grandson of William Porritt. During that conversation Thomas Bradley suggested that William Porritt had originally purchased St George's Gardens with the intention of presenting them to the town. In due course Oliver Porritt agreed to sell, on condition that the council re-imbursed him fifteen years ground rent to the sum of £21,350.

The decision to proceed was a contentious one, as the council members were not unanimous. On 9 January 1914 a statutory meeting of ratepayers was held to decide whether to proceed with the Improvement Bill and to include a clause on the purchase of the gardens. On the same day the council announced that Mr Fred Harrison, of Lytham and St Anne's, had won a competition for a design of the layout of the gardens. The design included twelve tennis courts, two croquet lawns and bowling greens; the main entrance was to be from Clifton Drive through 'very handsome gates, and a pavilion in the English Renaissance style of architecture'.[12] The cost of the scheme was estimated to be £5,384.

Although at the ratepayers' meeting it was decided to proceed with the purchase, the vote, by a show of hands, had not been conclusive and a poll was demanded. The following week the council issued a public statement and requested that:

James Williamson was born in 1842 and created Lord Ashton in 1895. His benefactions to his native town of Lancaster were immense. He will forever be remembered in St Anne's for his generous contributions towards the purchases of Ashton Gardens and the War Memorial Hospital.
BY COURTESY OF FYLDE BOROUGH COUNCIL

St George's Gardens were renamed Ashton Gardens in honour of the generous gift made by Lord Ashton. The driveway leading from the entrance on Clifton Drive, North (once used as a builders' yard by the Porritt family) leads to the war memorial. In 2006 Fylde Borough Council was granted £1,475,000 from the Heritage Lottery Fund to revitalise the gardens.

We therefore ask you to support the Council in their endeavour to acquire St George's Gardens for the benefit of the town, as, in the opinion of the Council the property will prove to be an exceedingly valuable asset, situate as it is, in the very heart of the town, and would form an additional attraction to visitors and residents alike.[13]

It was at this point that events took a dramatic turn when Lord Ashton, the prosperous Lancaster linoleum manufacturer, who had begun to take an interest in the affairs of the town, intervened. A series of discreet contacts and meetings took place between Lord Ashton and Coun. J. H. Taylor, then chairman of the council. During these meetings Lord Ashton said that he was 'so charmed with the quiet attractiveness of St Anne's that his great desire was to contribute to the improvement and cultivation of the beauty of St Anne's'.[14]

The outcome was that Lord Ashton presented to the town the £21,350 necessary to purchase the gardens which, in recognition of his generous gift, were renamed Ashton Gardens. The gift also ensured that the St Anne's Improvement Bill went through the House of Commons unopposed.

The council subsequently spent £18,200 laying out the gardens to an amended design by Fred Harrision. They were officially opened on 1 July 1916, by Coun. Richard Leigh, Chairman of the Council. An additional £3,800 was spent in 1919.

St Anne's Pier

During the late nineteenth century it was the fashion for every seaside town to have a pier. It did not matter how short its length, or how dull and grey the sea, it was an amenity which visitors expected, and a stroll along the boards was part of the traditional holiday. On the evidence of the original lease granted to St Anne's Land and Building Company in 1874, it would appear that it was always the intention of the company to build a pier:

> And Further, that a strip of land ... shall for ever hereafter be left open and unbuilt along the sea coast to the distance of nine hundred yards from St Anne's Road ... save and except that a life boat house, pier, house, or other buildings of a similar description may be erected thereon.[15]

However it was not until 1877 that a subsidiary company was formed – the St Anne's on the Sea Pier and Improvements Company – with the stated objective 'to provide the town of St Anne's on the Sea with a Pier'. Due to the economic circumstances described in the previous chapter it was not until 1879 when 'civil engineers were reported clambering over the foreshore taking soundings and boreholes' that the decision was taken to proceed with the

construction of a pier, probably in the hope that it would stimulate renewed interest in the town.[16]

At the time the directors of the company were of the opinion that:

> The advantage to be derived from a pier at St Anne's is far beyond either Blackpool or Lytham ... If a Pier was erected here the sea at St Anne's would afford better boating and fishing than can be had at any seaport on the west coast, there being here a sheet of water a mile wide at low tide perfectly calm when the sea at Blackpool is not suitable for boating at all. The Pier would also enable the boats to run in all weathers between Liverpool, Fleetwood, Barrow, Southport, and St Anne's, a thing impossible to be done in the open sea at Blackpool and only when the tide serves at Lytham.[17]

Construction began in 1880 to a design by Mr A. Dowson CE, and took five years to complete at a cost of £18,000. The pier was officially opened on 15 June 1885 by Col. Fred Stanley, MP, and was described by the *Lytham Times* as:

> 350 yards in length inclusive, is spacious and of graceful light appearance, though built of sufficient strength to withstand the heavy seas which

St Anne's Pier, c.1893. St Anne's Pier was opened on 15 June 1885 by Col. Fred Stanley, MP. It was described as being spacious and of light appearance, 'though built of sufficient strength to withstand the heavy seas which occasionally break on the St Anne's shore'. The opening of the pier was arguably the catalyst for the rejuvenation of the fledgling town.
COURTESY OF TED LIGHTBOWN

occasionally break on the St Anne's shore. The Pier head is commodious, and a neat iron and glass band pavilion has been constructed, whilst round the sides of the Pier head are seats for visitors.[18]

The same edition of the newspaper opened its report in fulsome praise of the vision and commitment of the directors of the company in remaining faithful to the establishment of the town. The report vividly describes the new sense of optimism that must have been felt by many of those present on that memorable day:

> Mr Porritt, the Chairman of the St Anne's Land and Building Company, and his co-directors must be warmly congratulated upon the complete success of their efforts to make last Monday the red letter day in the history of the town. On Monday, the first great event in the annals of St Anne's took place. The Pier was opened to the public; an event that, judging from present prospects, will be followed by others of still greater promise and of more auspicious omen. That pretty little place, once a place of barrenness, has had her troubles, but is pluckily showing again to the front and challenging more pretentious places for public favour. Who would have thought, five years ago, when St Anne's was voted on all sides to be a lamentable mistake – a brick and mortar desert of uninhabited houses – that on a bright and breezy summer morning of

The pier in 1963. In 1901 it was decided to widen and enlarge the entire pier. The most notable addition was the Moorish Pavilion. In 1970 the Moorish Pavilion became the 'Sultan's Palace', but in 1974 the whole was destroyed by fire. A further extension to the pier took place in June 1910 with the opening of the Floral Hall. In 1966 the Floral Hall became the Tyrolean Bar, but it too was destroyed by fire, in 1982.

St Anne's Promenade in 2007, looking northwards towards the pier. Although during the late twentieth century both the Moorish Pavilion and the Floral Hall were destroyed by fire, the pier continues to welcome residents and visitors, and contains restaurants, shops and amusement areas.

Monday last she would come out in gala dress and be able to truly boast that in the whole town there was not a house to be let ... and gather together more than 4,000 people to look upon the result of well directed effort and applaud.[19]

The opening ceremonies included a procession of dignitaries, members of the Local Board, the lifeboat on its carriage drawn by six horses, the Order of Mechanics and schoolchildren who, headed by the band of the Preston Militia, walked from the railway station to the pier. The St Anne's Band, then only five weeks old, 'also made itself heard'. The opening ceremony included a ceremonial launch of the lifeboat, the soon to be fated *Laura Janet*. Afterwards, 200 invited guests attended a luncheon in a specially erected marquee in St George's Gardens, with food provided by A. J. Holloway of the St Anne's Hotel.

Within ten years the pier had become an established part of the social life of the town, and was described in 1895 in the following terms:

St Anne's in August ... People go on the Pier and watch the daring bathers getting wet. Visitors and their children go out in small boats – something which very few residents avail themselves! A passenger steamer called at the Pier one evening – a sight few cared to miss. In the evenings everyone goes to the Pier and listens to St Anne's Prize Band or entertained by white performers in peculiar dress made of white material with very large black spots on it. There is bycycling on the shore, fishing from the end of the Pier.[20]

An entrance pavilion was added in 1899 and in January 1901 the directors decided to widen and enlarge the entire pier. The engineers and architects were Messrs Garlick & Sykes of Blackpool and Preston. The extensions took three years to complete and were opened on 2 April 1904. The most notable addition was the 'Moorish Pavilion', with an auditorium measuring 84ft × 56ft, and seating accommodation for 920 persons. The *St Anne's on the Sea Express* noted that 'Viewed from any point the pavilion is a monument to skilful design and consummate taste'.[21] The total expenditure was estimated at £30,000.

Further extensions took place with the opening of the Floral Hall in June 1910 to a design by Coun. A. England. Built exclusively of steel and plate glass with seating accommodation for 500 persons, it was the venue for concerts and other entertainments. The first orchestra was that of Miss Kate Erl and her ladies' orchestra. In later years orchestral concerts were conducted under the leadership of William Rees and Lionel Johns. Celebrity artists have included Gracie Fields and George Formby. A more detailed account of recollections of the pier can be found in *Years of Piers*.[22]

The first sign of changing social attitudes came in 1954 when an £8,000 amusement arcade was added to the pier entrance. When the Amalgamated Investment and Property Company bought the Land and Building Company they began a programme of refurbishment. In 1966 the Floral Hall was turned into a Tyrolean Beer Garden, and in 1970 the Moorish Pavilion became the Sultan's Palace. These changes resulted in the pier being 'at its peak, with a quarter of a million adults and 100,000 children going through the turnstiles each year'.[23]

On 7 June 1974, as part of the town's centenary celebrations, a concert was held at the pier attended by HRH Princess Anne, but on 20 July 1974 the Moorish Pavilion was destroyed by fire. Following the collapse of the Amalgamated Investment and Property Company, the pier was bought by the Webb family (of the Dalmeny Hotel) on 6 December 1976. Although the former Floral Hall was also destroyed by fire in 1982 the Pier continues to welcome both resident and visitor. Seawards from the Victorian Pier Head there are restaurants, shops and amusement areas; at the western end verandahs overlook the beach.

CHAPTER SIXTEEN

Establishment of the Local Board of Health

Early in 1877 the directors of the St Anne's Land and Building Company, in conjunction with Thomas Fair acting on behalf of the Clifton estate, arranged for Thomas Woodcock, solicitor to the Land and Building Company, to attend a meeting of the Lytham Improvement Commissioners (the 'local government' authority for the parish of Lytham) to discuss the creation of a St Anne's local board of health. As a result of this meeting of 2 April 1877, the Lytham Commissioners resolved to set up a special committee, which included Thomas Fair, to agree the boundaries of the proposed St Anne's district and prepare a petition to be presented to the Local Government Board.[1]

Accordingly on 19 April 1877 a delegation, which included William Porritt, James Maxwell and Thomas Woodcock; an un-named representative of the Lancashire Land Company, and Thomas Fair for the Clifton estate, presented a petition to the Local Government Board together with a plan showing the proposed boundaries. Although the petition stated that it had been signed by 'one tenth of the Ratepayers' (a requirement of the 1872 Public Health Act) the delegation does not appear to have included anyone who subsequently became a member of the Ratepayers' Association. The petitioners opening statement read:

> In the opinion of your Petitioners it is desirable that the Public Health Act 1875 should be adopted within a district to comprise Saint Anne's on the Sea for the following reasons ...

Among the reasons given was that the town 'had been laid out as a health resort for the inhabitants of Lancashire'; the streets had been laid out and the line of buildings prescribed 'to secure the greatest amount of ventilation in and about the houses'; that a system of main drainage should be completed before the streets were completed; that the lighting of the district with gas should take place 'as early as possible'; that the management of the highways should be vested in the Surveyor of Highways.[2] Drainage was a principal concern, and the petitioners implied they were keen to undertake the work themselves rather than it be carried out by the existing Rural Sanitary Authority. They 'thought it inadvisable to deal with sewage in cesspools to any great extent', and pointed out that 'the cost of dealing with excreta in the district at the present time amounts to over £6 per week':

> In the opinion of your petitioners it is of the highest importance that the management of a town should be under the control of one governing body that body being composed of individuals having an interest in its welfare and they also think a Board of gentlemen of this class can be formed if the Public Health Act be adopted in the district.[3]

Inquiry and dissent

As a result of this petition an inquiry took place at St Anne's, on 2 August, 1877, before Lt Col Ponsonby Cox RE, one of the Inspectors from the Local Government Board. The meeting was again attended by Thomas Fair, Thomas Woodcock and directors of the Land and Building Company, Mr Smythe of Oldham representing the Lancashire Land Company, Mr W. S. Hodgson, chairman of the Local Board of Guardians, and 'a large number of ratepayers', including John Allen.

At the conclusion of the meeting 'there was no reply' when the inspector asked if there was any opposition to the proposed new district. In reply to questions the promoters stated they had no objection to taking the whole or a detached portion of Little Marton, 'although only a part of it had been included in their scheme'. As a result of the inquiry the boundaries of the proposed new district were defined and preliminary matters arranged.[4]

Shortly after this meeting a ratepayers' association was formed, as in the words of John Allen their president, 'the Ratepayers are, or should be, anxious to have their affairs managed in the best and most economical manner'. On 17 October 1877, a meeting was held in the 'old' Heyhouses School with the object of bringing together the farmers and other ratepayers of St Anne's. There was 'a large muster of the former class present', and it was evident from their manner and the interest they took in the proceedings, 'that they intend[ed] to be something more than mere spectators in the management of the affairs of the New District'. And on the suggestion of the chairman of the meeting, four farmers were added to the committee of the Ratepayers' Association.[5]

A week later an order was issued by the Local Government Board. Thomas Fair, acting as summoning officer for the ratepayers, then arranged for a meeting to be held in order to give the ratepayers the opportunity 'of passing or rejecting a resolution for the adoption of the Public Health Act, and for

An account of the inquiry, held in 1877, as reported by the *St Anne's Miscellany and Advertiser*.

fixing the number of members to be elected as the Local Board for the said district'.[6]

The meeting was held in the Billiards Room of the St Anne's Hotel on Saturday 17 November 1877 at 4 p.m. Among those attending were nine directors of the Land and Building Company; the chairman of the Lancashire Land Company; Rev. W. G. Terry, vicar of St Anne's; James Maxwell and forty two named ratepayers. Thomas Fair was chairman and Thomas Woodcock acted as clerk. It was a somewhat acrimonious meeting, with Thomas Fair and Thomas Woodcock clearly keen to have the resolution passed without dissent. And there would appear to be little doubt that the events of the past few months were no more than a ploy by the Clifton estate and the St Anne's Land and Building Company so that they could avoid or evade their responsibilities regarding expensive but non-remunerative infrastructure.

Opposition was led by John Allen, who pointed out that the when boundaries were defined at the meeting in August the ratepayers 'knew little or nothing of the district to be included, and as they should have to pay the piper for all, it was nothing but due that they should know something more about the boundaries than they did'. He was supported by Dr Howard who said 'he had never seen the petition until the time of the inquiry [in August]', and Mr Sugden who said that 'he had never been called upon to sign the requisition'.[7] James Maxwell said he was sorry that 'the ratepayers had got the impression they had. There had been no attempt to treat them in a fatherly manner'.[8]

The meeting ended 'on the hint of the Chairman' with a motion that those present accept the boundaries as laid out in the order of the Local Government Board. Just fifteen voted in favour and four against. Thomas Fair concluded by saying that 'if he had known there would have been any difficulty about the boundaries, he would not have felt himself justified in taking the chair. He hoped that the matter would be settled to the satisfaction of all.'[9]

In its report the *Lytham Times* reminded its readers that the proposed boundaries had been fully set out in the original petition 'so that there was ample opportunity for the ratepayers to have inquired into the matter' but added that at the time 'the only objection taken to the proposed boundaries was that they were not large enough'.[10]

Sixty-two ratepayers presented a new petition to the Local Government Board requesting a further inquiry, the essence of which was contained in the opening sentence of the second paragraph:

The bulk, if not the whole of your petitioners, and the Ratepayers generally, were in entire ignorance of the character of the district and its boundary at the time of your Inspector's visit in August last, and were therefore not in a position to take any action with regard to it, had they even known the importance of the matter.[11]

The inquiry was held on 21 March 1878 at the St Anne's Hotel, with Cox again acting as inspector. The ratepayers requested that certain areas of the proposed district, as settled on by the order of 24 October 1877, be excluded. They also asked that 'the whole of the roads, bounding the district, be divided equally between the authorities of St Anne's, and the adjoining townships or districts'. They pointed out that there were only some 200 ratepayers in the proposed St Anne's district compared with over 1,000 in Lytham, and as there were some five miles or more of road bounding the district, added that, 'the care of this large extent of road (over 20 miles) together with the cost of constructing the necessary and most expensive sanitary works, will place upon so small a body of ratepayers a burden too great for them to bear, and will act most prejudicially against the present and future welfare of the place.'[12]

It was not only the ratepayers of St Anne's that were to be affected by the proposed new district. Some 388 acres of Little Marton, part of the Clifton estate, were also to be included. Mr Bradley, the surveyor of the highways for Little Marton, claimed that the reason why the maintenance of Division Lane had lately become so expensive was that it had been used for hauling bricks from the Land and Building Company brick croft at Westby to St Anne's. However his statement was contradicted as it was shown that a greater number of carts passed to Lytham than to St Anne's itself.

The petition failed and the Local Government Board confirmed the order to set up the St Anne's Local Board of Health. The boundary of the new district was therefore defined as:

> So much of the Parish of Lytham and the Township of Marton as is comprised within an imaginary line commencing on the coast line at the point where the continuation of Fold Lane [Squires Gate Lane] would intersect the same, thence following Fold Lane as far as the Half Way House, thence for a further distance of seventy yards along Fold Lane in an easterly direction beyond the Half Way House, thence in a southerly direction in a direct line seventy yards distant from and to the east of Middle Lane [whose route was across the present Blackpool Airport] as far as a point seventy yards north of the township boundary line between Little Marton and Lytham: thence in an easterly direction, seventy yards distant to the north and following such boundary line to Moss Edge Farm: thence further following such boundary line of the Township of Westby with Plumpton: thence following the township boundary line between Lytham and Westby with Plumpton, as far as the road leading to Moss Hall Bridge, thence along and including such road past the west of North Houses to Hey Houses Lane thence across Hey Houses Lane along and including the road [Smithy Lane] leading to Common Side [Church Road], thence in a direct line in continuation of such road to the coast line, thence in a northerly direction along the coast line to the point of commencement.

For the next twelve years there was a constant battle between the ratepayers, the Land and Building Company, and Thomas Fair on behalf of the Clifton estate. The Land and Building Company wanted the Local Board to levy a sufficient rate necessary to aid development of the town as envisaged by the proposed boundaries, while Thomas Fair held to the view that the onus was on the Land and Building Company to finance major improvement works such as road maintenance and drainage.

CHAPTER SEVENTEEN

Local Board of Health,
1878–1894

It had been decided at the meeting held on 17 November 1877 that the number of councilmen, or commissioners, constituting the Local Board would be twelve. On 15 May 1878 a meeting of the Ratepayers' Association was held in an attempt to select candidates for election to the board. Debate was intense, passionate, and inconclusive. John Allen read out the list of proposed candidates observing that, 'he might state that the voting power was pretty equally divided between the farmers and the St Anne's people. Every interest should be represented; therefore, the names had been divided betwixt the farmers and the dwellers of St Anne's.'[1]

John Heap was of the opinion that Thomas Fair 'had more interest in St Anne's than any one else, and that his name ought to be accepted'. Mr J. Kane commented that 'the men who had spent most money ought to be elected'. The meeting ended with the motion 'That we [the Ratepayers Association] meet again next week, and vote by ballot as to the twelve members [to be nominated]'.[2] At the meeting the following week over two hundred persons were present. It proved to be of 'a somewhat unruly character' and amid scenes of confusion twenty-five candidates were nominated. Eventually when it was realised that the 'intention of the meeting could not be carried out, so far as the voting was concerned, the Chairman declared the proceedings closed'.[3]

The election for the first St Anne's on the Sea Local Board of Health took place in late June 1878, with twenty-one candidates. On Friday 28 June Thomas Fair, who did not stand for election but acted as summoning officer, went to the St Anne's Hotel to collect the twenty or thirty votes of ratepayers who lived outside the district. The following day the voting papers of the resident ratepayers were collected, and on Monday 1 July 1878 all the votes were counted and the following men elected.[4]

John Ogden	St Anne's Road	Confectioner, builder and contractor	210 votes
James Astley	Green Hill House [Blackburn ?]	Gentleman	207 "
Robert Hargreaves	Headroomgate	Farmer	160 "
William Pomfret	St Anne's Road	Gentleman	156 "
John Allen	Kilgrimol [School]	Schoolmaster	145 "
John Singleton	Heyhouses	Farmer	145 "
William H. Howarth	The Drive	Accountant	144 "
Thomas Swarbrick	Heyhouses	Farmer	143 "
William Cross	Heyhouses	Farmer	143 "
James Parkinson	Moss Hall	Farmer	142 "
Hanson Hamilton	North Promenade	Builder	136 "
John Marks	St George's Avenue	Builder	136 "

The election for the first Local Board of Health took place in late June 1878. The number of votes counted for each candidate was entered by hand on the right-hand side of this page of the board's minute book.

MBLS 4/1. REPRODUCED BY PERMISSION OF THE COUNTY ARCHIVIST, LANCASHIRE RECORD OFFICE

Thomas Fair must have been pleased with the outcome of the election in that five members were among the leading tenant farmers in Heyhouses. Robert Hargreaves was tenant at Headroomgate Farm, John Singleton at Kilnhouse Farm, Thomas Swarbrick at Model Farm, William Cross at Heyhouses Farm, and James Parkinson was at Moss Hall Farm. The other seven men came from a varied range of backgrounds and places, but none was as colourful and passionate as John Allen.

Among the defeated candidates was James Lomax, who had been the only ratepayer to oppose the petition requesting a review of the proposed boundaries, and James Maxwell who had resigned as agent to the Land and Building Company in November the previous year. Not a single director of the Land and Building Company stood for election.

The *Lytham Times* reported that 'the St Annettites [*sic*] went seriously to their work, and did it in most quakerlike and commendable fashion … On Monday the official counting of the votes took place in the new Billiard Room of the St Anne's Hotel before T. Fair Esq … By the time the state of poll was declared a few people were waiting outside the Hotel to hear from the first who came from the room where the votes were counted, and having heard it, lounged contentedly away.'[5]

At the conclusion of matters Thomas Fair observed that he 'both hoped and thought that the gentlemen who had been elected would so manage the affairs of St Anne's as to make it what it undoubtedly ought to be, one of the best and most successful of watering places'.[6]

All this would suggest that the election had been a low-key affair without much animosity. In fact, if the observations of 'San Tanner' published in the *St Anne's Miscellany* can be regarded as objective, the election had been full of cut and thrust. Having observed that now the election was over he trusted that 'it will be practicable to hold public ratepayers meetings … which may be convened for purposes other than protesting or petitioning (from both of which the Gods deliver us)'. He then continued:

> Possibly too, the contemptibly bitter and nasty spirit which has been abroad of late in St Anne's will pass away, and give place to better and more honourable feeling. The election has been warmly, – it is a pity we cannot add, fairly – contested. The splenetic temper which betrayed itself in some of the pamphlets circulated, … – the foul, scurrilous language employed – is so utterly contemptible that I need make only a passing allusion to them.[7]

1878–1880

The first meeting of the St Anne's on the Sea Local Board of Health was held at 4.30 p.m. on Saturday 6 July 1878, in the New Billiard Room of the St Anne's Hotel. James Astley was unanimously elected chairman of the board, and Thomas Woodcock was requested to act as clerk 'until the Board has got into working order'. The surveyor of the highways for Little Marton presented a statement of work done within the district since May, and was asked to continue to repair the highways until 'the Board themselves are in a position themselves to undertake the same'. A committee was appointed to deal with the sanitary arrangements and another appointed 'to look out for suitable premises for the transaction of the business of the Board'.[8]

At the board meeting the following Saturday John Allen reported that 'a house situate in the Drive belonging to Mr John Shackleton Slater' was considered to be the most suitable for the meetings of the Board, and that the rent asked was £40 per annum. It was agreed to take the property on a three-year lease. The property, known as Matlock House and numbered 300 Clifton Drive, South, is now 'the Clifton Drive Surgery'.

The board also resolved to place advertisements in the Lytham, Blackpool, and Preston newspapers in order to advertise for a person willing to undertake the duties of clerk collector and inspector of nuisances. Applications had to be in the candidate's own handwriting and 'accompanied by recent testimonials'.

Matlock House, Clifton Drive, South. The first meeting of the St Anne's Local Board of Health was held on 6 July 1878 in the New Billiard Room of the St Anne's Hotel. At a board meeting the following week John Allen reported that Matlock House was considered to be the most suitable building for meetings of the board. Matlock House (300 Clifton Drive, South) is now 'The Clifton Drive Surgery'.

In addition, the board wrote to the Preston Banking Company enquiring the terms on which the bank would perform the duties of treasurer.

By July three applications had been received for the post of clerk – Thomas Salthouse of Lytham, George Kay of St Anne's, and Clement Jones of Aberdovey. Clement Jones was appointed. He cannot have been impressed with St Anne's, however, as within a week he resigned, requesting the board 'to make him some allowance on account of railway fare and other expenses incurred in applying for the office'. He was replaced in September by William A. Lloyd who remained as clerk to the board until 1884.

Due to the reluctance of both the Land Company and Clifton estate to commit themselves to any expense with regard to the infrastructure of the new town, it was inevitable that early board meetings were dominated by two topics – the need for a modern drainage system, and the maintenance of the moss roads. The attitude of the board members on these matters must have made both the directors of the Land and Building Company, and Thomas Fair, regret their decision not to stand for election themselves in 1878.

The opportunity to remedy this situation came in 1879 when William Howarth left St Anne's. He was replaced by William Porritt, who was co-opted onto the board in August. William Porritt was obviously not impressed by what he found as by 13 October he was writing to Thomas Fair:

I attended a meeting of the Highways Committee at St Anne's on Saturday last. Of course my motion was lost. In fact with the present construction of the Board with such a Chairman [James Astley] it is next to useless & waste of time, he is very antagonistic & defiant to the harmonious working as will only lead to peaceful solutions. Excuse me saying that if your qualification is right to a seat on the Board that on behalf of Mr Clifton's interest it is absolutely imperative that you fill the vacancy at least for a time – they seem to be under the impression that me being connected with the Land Company & on friendly terms with you that I am a partizan of Mr Clifton's. Of course I am in all that I conceive to be right. Because I don't fall in with them in browbeating and blackguarding the representations of the Estate they point their remarks at me, they are not law abiding & don't know how to ask for a favour & presume they have rights when they have none & talk like men who have no land & don't care for the rights of those that have. We must get it [the Board] into shape as nicely as we can but it must be got into shape or the Town will be thrown back.[9]

William Porritt very quickly achieved his objective as on 5 November Thomas Fair was co-opted onto the board in place of John Marks who had died in May. By this time one other significant change in its composition had also taken place. In March that year John Allen had resigned over the matter of who was responsible for the maintenance of the roads within the district, and been replaced by John Greenhalgh. Not one of the replacement members therefore had stood for election in June 1878, and all had been co-opted onto the Board by the vote of existing members.

In the 1880 elections the three members, or their replacements, who had polled the least number of votes in 1878 were required to stand for re-election, namely Hanson Hamilton, James Parkinson and Thomas Fair. In addition John Ogden and William Cross did not offer themselves for re-election. Thomas Fair and Hanson Hamilton were re-elected, but James Parkinson failed by just one vote. The three new members were James Maxwell, who topped the poll with 177 votes, James Pye and Joseph Ellerbeck.

The *Lytham Times* reported that the election had cost the ratepayers 'about one-tenth what the last election cost', adding that the only persons deserving credit for this were James Astley, the chairman, and W. A. Lloyd, the clerk to the board. The report concluded by saying that 'altogether the election passed off very creditably', but that 'there were many bad votes'.[10]

At the first meeting of the new board on 17 April 1880 the question of the 'bad votes' was raised by William Porritt who said he was of the opinion that the election 'had not been conducted in conformity with the Public Health Act'. He further stated that a Mr Parkinson (presumably James Parkinson who had lost his seat by one vote) had, together with other persons, been misinformed about voting procedures. In reply James Astley as returning officer, and W. A. Lloyd as clerk, both expressed views that the election had been carried out according to the Act. Whatever the legality of the matter the dispute would

Born in Bolton in 1861 Thomas Bradley was appointed clerk to the Local Board of Health in March 1887 while he was still only 26. It Thomas Bradley who oversaw the Urban District Council Improvement Acts of 1896 and 1914, and guided events leading eventually to the merger of St Anne's with Lytham in 1922. At that time he was described as 'the power behind the throne'. When he retired as town clerk of Lytham St Anne's, he had served the town for forty years. He died in October 1936.
SOUVENIR – CHARTER DAY 1922

also appear to have been another personality clash between William Porritt and James Astley. It was probably one of the factors that contributed to James Astley being replaced as chairman of the board by John Greenhalgh. Both men had been proposed for the post, but James Astley withdrew in favour of John Greenhalgh without a vote being taken.

Thereafter he appears to have taken little interest in board meetings, and on 6 December 1880 the board minutes record that 'Seat caused by Mr Astley's non-attendance to continue vacant until next election'. Thus within two years only five members of the first elected board remained, while the new chairman had not at that time even had to stand for election.

1881–1894

From 1878 until 1894 some thirty-six men served for varying lengths of service, and only in 1883 and 1889 were elections uncontested. At the election of 1881 William Porritt lost his seat on the board and was not able to influence

(directly) events again for another two years. Had Robert Hargreaves not lost his seat, by just twenty-two votes, at the 1891 election he would have served throughout the entire period of the board. He was re-elected in 1892.

Only five men served as chairman of the Local Board (Appendix G). Robert Knowles, who had been elected to the board in 1887, became chairman in 1893 and remained in office until the transfer of authority to the urban district council. In January 1894 the board moved into new office accommodation in Park Road.

It was, however, the appointment of Thomas Bradley as clerk to the board, in March 1887, that was, arguably, the most astute appointment. His background influence on the development of the town was profound, and his remarkable tenure extended from the early days of the town to the incorporation of the Borough of Lytham St Anne's. He remained clerk until his retirement in 1927. In 1935 he recalled that in 1887:

> The Local Board had borrowed no money. They believed in the proverb, 'He that goes-a-borrowing goes a-sorrowing', and the chief concern of the members was to keep down the rates at 2s. 6d. ... The streets were wastes of sand and, in wet weather, quagmires. The esplanade was a howling wilderness.[11]

His description of how elections to the Local Board were conducted is most revealing and perhaps partly explains how the Board came to delay implementing necessities such as the drainage scheme. In spite of the Ballot Act of 1832 and the Representation of the Peoples Act of 1885 a system operated whereby certain electors, who were perhaps resistant to a particular scheme, could exercise considerable influence on the outcome of an election:

> The method of election was the open, cumulative system which preceded the ballot. A list of candidates was left at the home of each elector by a policeman, and initials were placed opposite the names of those you wished to vote for. The papers were collected by the police and conveyed to the Local Board office, where the counting took place. It was customary for the candidates to be present to make notes of broken promises! Under such a system, as might be expected, in a village [*sic*] where everybody knew everybody, a considerable number of papers were returned blank. Votes were granted according to a scale. Property rated at less than £50 was allowed one vote; up to £100 two votes; up to £150 three votes; up to £200 four votes; and so on, the maximum being six. Bricks had votes, not heads.[12]

Road maintenance and the Roads Trial of 1889/90

As we saw earlier the question of who was responsible for the network of roads within the new district preoccupied the minds of all those who served on the board from 1878 to 1891. The argument of the ratepayers was that they had known little of what had been agreed originally regarding the boundaries of the district, as shown by their petition and the subsequent inquiry, held on 21 March 1878.

In October 1878 the board took legal opinion concerning these highways. They were advised by Mr Morgan, solicitor of Blackpool, 'that with respect to roads used prior to [the Highways Act] 1835 the Board would have great difficulty in getting rid of having to repair them. With respect to roads made since 1835 they ought to have been adopted at the Parish Meetings or some other action taken before the JPs.'

The roads in dispute were the moss roads which, to the ratepayers of St Anne's in the 1870s, had little relevance to the new town they were endeavouring to establish. Their sentiments had been expressed by James Astley when he said 'that it ought to be known that the great grievance of St Anne's was, that it was saddled with all these roads, many of them Moss Roads which had never been made'.[13]

In December 1878 a deputation from the board met with Thomas Fair, who was reported to have been willing 'to relieve the Board of the repair of Coppin

Lane [?], Sluice Lane, and the two lanes that run parallel with Wilding's Lane subject to the condition that the Board should give an undertaking that the rates for the land on the Moss should not be more than 9d. in the pound.' James Astley observed at the time 'that owing to that gentleman's [Thomas Fair] disinclination to make any concession it was not likely that any compromise could have been affected'.[14]

On 5 February the next year the board resolved 'that owing to the evident impossibility of dealing satisfactorily with the Roads and Sewage of so large a district' to petition for a reduction in the area of the district. In reply the Local Government Board said that 'as at present advised, they can hold out no prospect that they would be willing to acquiesce in the present proposal of the [St Anne's] Local Board'.[15]

During the following ten years the question of responsibility simmered until March 1889, when, at a special meeting of the board, it was resolved:

> That this Board having made an inspection of the roads within the district, and having discovered that several of such roads have for some time past been occasionally repaired at the expense of the Board, in ignorance of liability of such repairs, hereby resolves and directs that all repairs of the Board to roads situated north-west of the Lytham and Blackpool Road (Heyhouses Lane) excepting one half of the boundary roads (if highways) shall henceforth be discontinued.[16]

In addition it was also resolved:

> That the Board discontinues the repair of the road from the smithy at the Trawl Boat to Commonside Road (the entire length of the present Smithy Lane).[17]

The roads in question were Moss Hall Lane, North Houses Lane, Ballam Lane, Anuses (Anna's) Lane, Division Lane, Wilding's Lane, Sluice Lane, Kilnhouse Lane, Moss Edge Lane, Headroomgate Road, Smithy Lane and Melling's Lane. By their action the board was attempting to pass responsibility for the repair of these roads either to the farmers themselves or the Clifton estate, and it brought the inevitable legal proceedings against them.

A total of twelve summons under the Highway Act, of 1835, were issued by the police against the board, and on 2 December 1889 the board, represented by their solicitors Messrs Holden and Holden of Bolton, appeared at the Blackpool petty sessional court, where the magistrates directed indictments to be preferred against them at the next quarter sessions to be held at Preston.[18]

Before the matter reached the quarter sessions the solicitors acting for the Clifton estate, who were the real prosecutors, gave notice that they had abandoned the procedure by indictment at the quarter sessions, and intended to proceed under a more recent Act of Parliament through the county council. A committee appointed by the county council visited St Anne's and inspected the roads in question. After listening to the views of both the board and the Clifton estate, during which it became evident that there was no reasonable terms for a compromise, indictments were preferred to be heard at the Liverpool assizes.

Both sides then began to prepare their case. As part of this process, Thomas Fair prepared a list of roads existing in 1843.[19] The board, however, were at some disadvantage in as much as the majority of those who knew most about the lanes were also tenants of the Clifton estate. In the end it did not matter, as a compromise was finally reached. Each party had to pay their own costs, and half costs of the juries.

The local board agreed to take over responsibility for Division Lane, Wilding's Lane and North Houses Lane. They also accepted responsibility for Headroomgate Road subject to the Clifton estate making the road to a uniform width of forty-five feet, and constructing a nine-inch earthenware sewer.

It was accepted that Moss Hall Lane, Ballam Lane, Anuses Lane, Sluice Lane, Kilnhouse Lane, Moss Edge Lane, Smithy Lane and Melling's Lane were not the responsibility of the board. Kilnhouse Lane and Smithy Lane were subsequently adopted by successor local government authorities. Interestingly, Melling's Lane remains unmade to the present day.

The present-day unmade condition of Mellings Lane is a direct result of the 1889/90 'Roads Trial', when it was accepted that the lane was not the responsibility of the Local Board.

In his account of the 'Roads Trial' Robert Knowles concluded:

> The struggle which has lasted so long has finally been settled. The Local
> Board know their position. The long felt grievance by the Ratepayers is at
> an end, and they have got what they tried for 12 years ago, at a moderate
> cost of £683 … I venture to say there is not a Ratepayer in St Annes
> today [who] would make an exchange back again.[20]

Sanitation

In contrast to the board's arguably justified stance in the matter of the moss
roads, their attitude to the provision of a modern drainage and sewerage system
is, perhaps, more debateable.

In 1875 a five-inch water main was laid from Starr Hills to St Anne's by the
Fylde Waterworks Company. However, by the following year it was considered
that this would soon be too small for the supply required, and in September
1876 the directors of the company informed the stockholders that:

> An additional supply of water being required for Lytham and St Anne's
> on the Sea the Directors have entered into a contract for a direct line
> of pipes from the Weeton Reservoir to the latter place, which will be
> available by extension for giving increased supply to South Shore.[21]

The new properties about to be erected in St Anne's were destined, therefore,
to have piped water – essential for flushing toilets – but as yet no drains had
been provided to take away the sewage. Even three years later the only existing
drain was the surface drain made by the Clifton estate, which ran from the
railway station into the sea, and an open ditch which drained the northern part
of the town into the surrounding watercourses.

This was the situation which confronted the members of the first St Anne's
local board. The petition for the establishment of the Board had included the
clause 'that a system of main drainage should be completed before the streets
were completed'. The sentiment had also been expressed that such work be
carried out by the Local Board which, under the Public Health Acts of 1872
and 1875, was also the urban sanitary district and obliged to take action on
sewerage matters.

At the first meeting of the board a committee was appointed 'to wait upon'
Mr Farrar of Lytham with a view to learning the terms on which he would visit
St Anne's and inspect the sanitary conditions; furnish a report; and advise the
board of the best means of dealing with the sanitary arrangements.

On 17 August 1878 the board received a deputation from the Land and
Building Company who were 'anxious to remove all causes of complaint'

concerning sewage in Common Lane (Church Road). As a result of this meeting the company agreed 'to arrange with Mr Fair for the use of the sewer in Common Lane to enable them to do away with the Cesspools there'. The company also suggested the formation of a permanent committee – with two representatives each, from the board and the company, and two other property owners – 'to discuss questions which might arise from time to time'. The proposal, however, was rejected by the board.

On 16 October the same year the Nuisance and Lighting Committee resolved to obtain estimates for the emptying and carting away of the contents of the ashpits and privies. However, on 25 October, after John Williams, the only person to have expressed an interest in the task, informed the board 'that as he had not a proper cart for the purpose he was not prepared to give an estimate', the committee decided that:

> the owners of Cottages and the occupiers of the better houses be seen as to what they are willing to give per time for the proper emptying and cleaning of their Closets and Ashpits, and that the Land Company be asked if they will provide a place for the Ashes and useless rubbish.[22]

At the May 1880 meeting of the Local Board, it was proposed by Thomas Fair and seconded by James Astley that the 'Sewerage Committee be empowered to consider a Scheme for sewering the whole district'. This was rejected and no further attempt was made until October 1882.

On 28 October 1882 the Local Board resolved 'that the Board undertake the duty of emptying all properly constructed Ashpits and Common Privies'. On the same day following a meeting, possibly public, of 'several owners of property', Thomas Fair, who had by then resigned from the Local Board, was asked to write, in his capacity as land agent to the Clifton estate, to the Local Government Board to request that an inquiry be held at St Anne's 'with a view to the furtherance of an efficient drainage scheme which may from time to time be carried out as circumstances may require'.[23]

The request provided an opportunity for Thomas Fair, in conjunction with the Land and Building Company, to try and force the hand of the Local Board into financing a modern drainage scheme. Although in January 1883 the Local Board had accepted the tender of Mr Ashworth for emptying ashpits 'for the sum of twenty-five pounds' there was an extensive correspondence between Thomas Fair, the Local Government Board, and the Local Board throughout January and February 1883.

In effect the hand of the Local Board had been forced. On 6 February 1883 Thomas Fair wrote to the Local Government Board to inform them that he now understood that the Local Board had decided to offer a premium of £25 for competitive plans for a sewerage scheme. In response the Local Government

Board informed the Local Board that 'they propose to defer for the present holding an inquiry with respect to the alleged default of the St Anne's on the Sea Local Board, in providing their district with sufficient sewers'.[24]

The sequence of events revealed the complete breakdown of any form of co-operation between the Local Board, the Land and Building Company, and the Clifton estate. The events as seen by the Local Board were expressed by Joseph Ellerbeck at a meeting of the board in February 1883, when he pointed out who was at the meeting of 28 October the previous year:

> There was Mr Fair himself who called the meeting, there was the Chairman of the Land and Building Company, two members of the Local Board, four property owners, and one ratepayer, and that constituted the great meeting of property owners, who met to condemn the Local Board for not doing its duty.[25]

Joseph Ellerbeck also questioned the contribution of the Clifton estate and the Land and Building Company:

> It was said that the greatest landlord had made a main sewer, but where was it? And what had the Land and Building Company done? They had spent £466 on their own 390 acres, but it was only on their own property … They [the Board] had no money to spend on sewers. If they spent the money on sewers instead of having a highway rate, it would not do the farmers much good.[26]

Conversely, in a letter to Thomas Fair in May 1883, James Maxwell complained that there was no private capital available and the Local Board was totally unresponsive to the idea of improvement work. He continued:

> I have been struggling for months to get a sewerage scheme but I am simply single-handed not only against the Board but the whole community of farmers and nothing but a generous proposal from the estate can help much.[27]

By September 1883 complaints had been received as to the manner in which Mr Ashworth was carrying out his work. The Local Board therefore resolved that he be given notice that unless he did the work in a more satisfactory manner 'the Board would engage other men and deduct the cost from the Account of the Contract'.

In January 1884 thirty-four ashpits, forty-eight earth closets, and twenty privies were emptied, and in February ten ashpits, sixty earth closets, and ten privies. In May complaints were again being received as to the cleaning out of ashpits, and in November Mr Ashworth left the district, leaving the Local Board with the problem of finding a replacement.

Three applications were received for the work, and in January 1885 the contract was awarded to William Cookson at the increased tender of £36. The work of emptying the various ashpits, earth closets, and privies was carried out during the night and, although the Local Board referred to William Cookson as 'the Contractor for Scavenging' he would almost certainly have been known to the residents as the 'night-soil man'. In May 1887 the clerk to the board was directed 'to write to Mr Cookson on the importance of his nightsoil cart being cleared out of the town earlier in the morning'.

In July 1885, following a recommendation by the Medical Officer of Health, the Local Board agreed that the ashpits in Church Road should be lime-washed but rejected that the order be extended to the whole of St Anne's. The Church Road sewer was itself a source of contention. In June 1886 letters were received from Thomas Fair and the Land and Building Company, declining to be responsible for the sewer. The Board replied by pointing out that under the Public Health Act of 1875 the sewers belonged to the Authority making them, and as the Local Board had not made the sewer they would like to know when it had been transferred to them.

However, after taking legal advice, the hand of the Local Board was again forced, and in March 1887 they instructed the clerk to 'see Mr Robert Greaves and authorise him to clean out Church Road Sewer from the Old Vicarage [131 Church Road] to the Land and Building Company's shop, formerly used as a Co-operative stores [junction of St Alban's Road]'.[28]

It has sometimes been assumed that the farmers on the Local Board were responsible for the lack of commitment in creating a modern drainage system, it being of no advantage to the rural community at Heyhouses. However, in October 1885, when the Sanitary and Lighting Committee of the Local Board agreed, by three votes to two to 'ask for powers to borrow money to carry out such parts of a scheme as are required' one of the two Board members to vote against the motion was none other than William Porritt.[29]

By 1890 the population of St Anne's was approaching 2,588 (census 1891) and it was apparent that a decision had to be made if the town was to grow and prosper. In February 1890, in response to a letter from the Local Government Board, the Local Board replied that plans for a scheme were already under consideration but 'as the question is such an important one they do not care to be unduly harassed and hurried in the matter'.[30] The Local Government Board responded by saying that following a formal complaint by Thomas Fair that the Local Board were in default in providing their district with sufficient sewers, they intended to hold a local inquiry at St Anne's.

Events then moved more rapidly than at any time in the previous twelve years. In October 1890 the Sanitary Committee recommended that the board

The cutting of St Anne's main drainage 1892. Throughout the 1880s the Local Board of Health prevaricated over the decision to build a modern drainage system. After fourteen years of acrimonious debate the cutting of the first sod for the main drainage scheme took place on 18 August 1892. Following the event a fete was held whilst 150 invited guests attended a banquet at the St Anne's Hotel. All expenses were met by William Porritt.

adopt the scheme proposed by Mr Bancroft, of Manchester, and that application be made to the Local Government Board for sanction to borrow money to carry out the portion of the scheme from Church Road, along St Anne's Road (East and West) to the sea.

In July 1891 the Local Government Board suggested that the Local Board reconsider the scheme and carry the outfall sewer further westwards. After Thomas Fair had indicated that Mr Clifton was prepared 'to bear one half of the interest money on the additional outlay providing the outfall was carried to such a point as would meet with his approval' the Board agreed to a total outlay of £7,865 17s. 9d.[31] Inevitably, however, costs increased as the work progressed and the final investment came to £9,780.

The cutting of the first sod for the main drainage scheme took place on 18 August 1892. The *St Anne's Parish Church Magazine* described the day's events in some detail:

18 August was a General Holiday in St Anne's on the cutting of the first sod of the new Drainage Scheme by Mr Porritt, chairman of the Local Board. By his generosity a fete was held – procession of ½ mile with banners and flags etc followed by the lifeboat, fire brigade, lurry with golf club makers, Local Board, guests etc plus 200 children. Children had tea

Silver and ebony spade and wheelbarrow used by William Porritt at the cutting of St Anne's main drainage scheme. Shortly after the purchase of the Land & Building Company by Amalgamated Investment Company the items were presented to Gabriel Harrison (centre) by Graham Woodcock of the Land and Building Company. Their present whereabouts are unknown.

RAGE OF SAND. REPRODUCED BY PERMISSION OF THE COUNTY ARCHIVIST, LANCASHIRE RECORD OFFICE

and games in St Georges Gardens – Mr Porritt's generosity. Banquet for 150 invited guests at the [St Anne's] Hotel. The old folk, 200, had tea in the Church Schools before a concert where every one received ¼lb of tea and some tobacco. All expenses met by Mr Porritt.[32]

In many respects it was extraordinary that such celebrations should be held for an event which had been so long delayed. William Porritt was presented with an illuminated address which acknowledged his endeavours to promote 'a thoroughly, efficient and practical scheme'. In his reply he noted that he was ever mindful of the trust confided in him by the ratepayers of St Anne's, and he had always put forth his best efforts 'in caring for ... the well-being, comfort, and happiness of the inhabitants of this rising town'.[33]

Perhaps it was an attempt to justify his decision in 1885, when he had voted against the motion to borrow money to carry out parts of the scheme, that he added '... thus the Board have in my opinion wisely deferred involving the ratepayers in an unjustifiable outlay'.[34] It was probably not what many St Anne's residents had thought in 1885 when the board declined to implement the decision of the sanitary committee.

Other board services

Although the two dominant matters that exercised the minds of the Local Board members from 1878 to 1892 were the moss roads and the need for a modern drainage system, they were also actively involved in other aspects of town life, as the following few extracts from the board minutes reveal:

13 May 1879   That steps be at once taken for lighting the District. That for the present 25 lamps be fixed at the places indicated on the plan prepared. That Mr Stanworth, the Gas Manager, to meet ... and be prepared to submit estimates for supplying Gas Lighting and Cleaning

7 July 1884   That the Post Office Authority be petitioned ... to put down two Pillar Letter – Boxes within the District, one at the crossing of St Anne's Road, with the Drive, and the other near to St Anne's Church.

19 Aug 1885   That [Underwood] Bennett light clean and extinguish all lamps now in use, and any that may be erected during the present lighting season – and find oil matches and material for cleaning – The Board to find lamp for lighting, and small ladder – for the sum of 12s. 0d. per week from 15 August 1885.

26 June 1893   That the Clerk ... write to the Land and Building Company re the annoyance caused by the keeping of hens in St Andrew's Road, South, and also to the Pot Auctions which have recently been going on in the District and ask if they will be good enough to have the same suppressed.

The end of an era

The Local Government Act of 1894 transferred the civil functions of the Local Board to an urban district council. By this date decisions determining future development of the town were under the increasing control of the property owners and ratepayers. And, perhaps more importantly, there was a lessening of the influences of Thomas Fair on behalf of the Clifton estate, and the Land and Building Company. The town's rateable value had increased from £8,409 in 1878 to £21,000 by 1893.

The general rate of 2s. 6d. in the pound was exactly the same in 1893 as it had been in 1878 though this is somewhat misleading as in 1879 it had dropped to just 10d. in the pound, and from 1881 to 1891 had remained constant at 1s. 6d. The town also had a modern drainage system. The last meeting of the St Anne's on the Sea Local Board took place on 6 April 1894.

CHAPTER EIGHTEEN

Urban District Council, 1894–1922

Elections took place for the first St Anne's Urban District Council in December 1894. There were twenty-two candidates for the twelve seats. In the elections all the former members of the old Local Board, with the exception of William Porritt, stood for election. The Ratepayers' Association ran six candidates. Polling took place at the council offices in Park Road and it was reported that 'Vehicles were conspicuous by their absence' but 'Feeling ran high and there were instances of mural literature being defaced'.[1]

The twelve successful candidates were R.H.Irving; Dr Staley; W.H.Nutter; George Benner; William Cross; Thomas Bilsborough; William Henry Hughes; John Allen; Matthew Fox; Robert Hargreaves; Robert Knowles; and John

Park Road Offices of St Anne's Urban District Council. New office accommodation in Park Road was acquired in January 1894 shortly before local government in St Anne's passed from a local board of health to an urban district council. The council chamber and offices were situated on the second floor (over the clock). The District Club was situated on the top storey. The original premises were erected by Richard Wade. The redeveloped site is now occupied by the Abbey.

Yorke. At the inaugural meeting of the council Robert Knowles was elected chairman. The general rate was agreed at 2s. 6d. in the pound.

Chairmen of St Anne's Urban District Council

Only thirteen of those councillors elected during the years 1894 to 1922 were chosen to serve as chairman of the council (see Appendix G). Not one had been born within the ancient parish of Lytham. J. H. Taylor could recall that his 'earliest acquaintance with St Anne's dated back to about 1875', but the only 'local' man was John Whiteside who had been born at Westby. Six of the thirteen had been born elsewhere in Lancashire, mainly in Manchester and East Lancashire, while others came from as far afield as Cumberland, Lincolnshire, Yorkshire and South Wales. Seven had been, or were, associated with commerce, particularly the cotton industry, and at least three had served as councillors elsewhere in Lancashire. John Dent Harker, an architect, was responsible for the design of several buildings in both St Anne's and Blackpool; and R. H. Irving had established St Anne's Collegiate School.

Party politics do not appear to have played any significant role, although both Sam Hodgkinson and Charles Critchley stood as Liberal candidates in

Robert Knowles. Only thirteen of those councillors elected during the years 1894 to 1922 were chosen to serve as chairman of the Urban District Council. Robert Knowles was the last chairman of the Local Board of Health, and the first chairman of the Urban District Council. In 1891 he wrote an account of the St Anne's 'Roads Trial'. (See also photograph p. 190.)
BY COURTESY OF FYLDE BOROUGH COUNCIL

local parliamentary elections. A chain of office, the gift of Richard Whitaker, chairman of the Land and Building Company, was first worn by George Walters Spring in 1904.

Plan of St Anne's, c.1900. Compared with the plan of 1874/75 (see also photograph p. 147) the infant modern town is instantly recognisable on this plan of 1900. By this date the Clifton estate was seeking developers not only for St Anne's but also for Ansdell, Fairhaven and Stonyhill.

Rise of the modern town

The population increased from 2,588 in 1891 to 6,807 in 1901, and to 9,837 in 1911. By 1921 it was over 11,000. On the 1891 census there were dwellings in twenty-nine roads, streets and lanes, including nine in the Heyhouses area. By 1901 at least another thirty roads had residences. One example of this

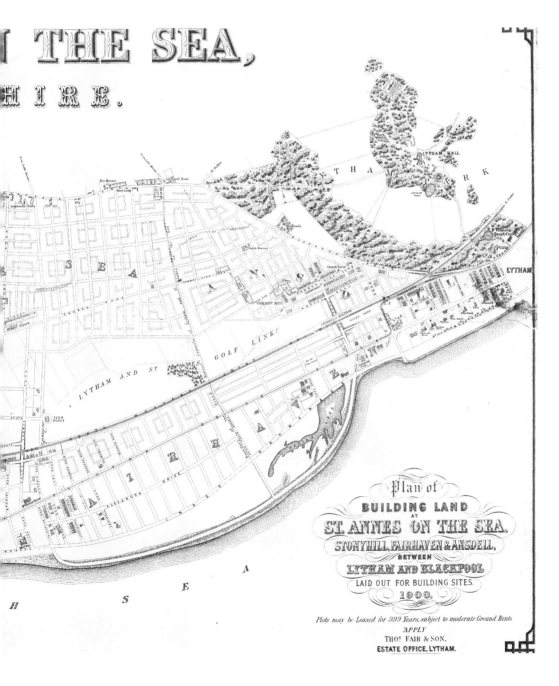

Plan of
BUILDING LAND
AT
St. ANNES ON THE SEA,
STONYHILL, FAIRHAVEN & ANSDELL,
BETWEEN
LYTHAM AND BLACKPOOL
LAID OUT FOR BUILDING SITES.
1900.

Plots may be Leased for 999 Years, subject to moderate Ground Rents.
APPLY
THOS FAIR & SON.
ESTATE OFFICE, LYTHAM.

expansion is the work carried out by the council in Headroomgate Road. It will be recalled that as a result of the 1889/90 'Roads Trial' the Clifton estate had made improvements to the road. During the years 1903 to 1905 the council spent almost £1,700 on further improvements. By 1908 completion of the Leach Lane improvement had cost a further £600.

In 1892 Thomas Riley of Fleetwood took out a lease on 264 acres of land, with the intention of developing the area now known as Fairhaven, a part of which came within the St Anne's boundary. On a plan prepared in 1893 the proposed estate extended from the present Fairhaven Hotel to St Thomas' church, and included a marine drive extending for one and a half miles, together with pleasure grounds and gardens. Following the death of his eldest son, however, Thomas Riley sold out to the Fairhaven Estate Company which, during the twentieth century, developed the area. In December 1980 the company was purchased at public auction by the Webb family.

In 1896 (the year the town was divided into electoral wards) the first

A plan of the Fairhaven estate as proposed by Thomas Riley in 1893. Had the full plan been implemented the area would have appeared greatly different from that of the present day. It also seems to have been the intention to extend the naming of the roads to places connected with the journeys of St Paul.
BY COURTESY OF ST ANNE'S LIBRARY

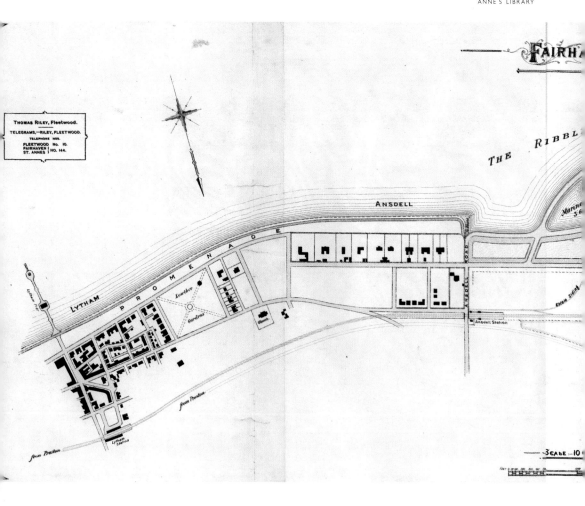

Improvement Bill was promoted by the urban district council, the chief object being to lay out the Esplanade from the Pier to Eastbank Road. Sanction to carry this work at a cost of £4,600 was granted in 1896 and 1898.[2] Between 1903 and 1915 additional sums totalling £9,374 completed the work as far as Fairhaven Road. Although it failed to purchase the gas works in 1898 the council obtained an Electric Lighting Order and the electricity works were established in 1901. Other civic amenities included the construction of a refuse destructor and a public abattoir in 1899.

The foreshore rights were purchased from the Duchy of Lancaster in 1899 for £350. Three years earlier St Anne's Council had expressed concerns when Preston Corporation sought powers to make training walls in the Ribble estuary, which it was feared would be injurious to the interests of St Anne's as a seaside resort. In 1905, when Preston Corporation sought further powers, St Anne's Council obtained a protective clause that dredgings should be dumped ten miles to the seawards.

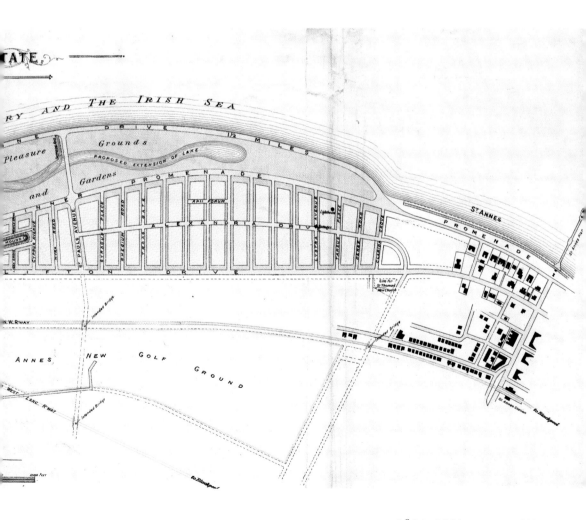

Removing sandhills at Fairhaven. There is no known photograph of the removal of the sand-dunes preparatory to the building of South Drive or St Anne's Road in the early 1870s. However at Fairhaven in 1893 Thomas Riley imported impressive earth-moving machines, nicknamed 'American Devils', to level the dunes.

The expansion of the town also placed demands on the existing sewerage arrangements. In 1892 the then Local Board had borrowed £9,780 to commence the laying of the main arterial sewer, and between 1894 and 1914 a further £22,850 was spent on sewering other areas of the town. Even at this period the existing sewers were becoming inadequate to cope with the increasing population and in 1911 the council invited competitive designs for further works. Although in July 1914 sanction to borrow £39,100 was granted, the government almost immediately imposed restrictions upon the borrowing of money by local authorities, and it was left to the successor borough council to deal with the problem.

The Public Offices

There was also the inevitable increase in the staff required to administer the town's affairs. Even by 1899 the offices in Park Road must have been rather cramped as council employees by then numbered between fifty and sixty. In August of that year Thomas Bradley reported to the General Purposes Committee of the council that a sub-committee had considered the plans of the suite of offices in the newly opened Public Hall but had 'decided not to recommend the council to take same, but to proceed with new offices on the land leased for the purpose on the South Drive'.[3]

The architect appointed was Thomas Muirhead, a local resident who also designed the St Anne's Parish Rooms and the Thursby Home. The building contractor was a Mr Woodcock, who from November 1900 to April 1902 received £3,080 in payment for building work. Other local contractors included George Rushfirth of St Alban's Road – Builders & Contractors, and Gill & Read of St Anne's Road West – Ironmongers.[4] The total cost of erection, including later additions, amounted to £6,707 14s. 8d.[5]

The formal opening took place on 22 January 1902 by Coun. Louis Stott, chairman of the council. In declaring the building open Coun. Stott looked back to the establishment of the Local Board in 1878 and the progress made since that time. He concluded by saying that 'great credit was due to past councillors for the position the town occupied today'.[6]

The Public Offices situated on Clifton Drive, South were opened as purpose-built offices for the Urban District Council on 22 January 1902 and are still in use by the successor authority Fylde Borough Council. The Public Offices are arguably the most important historical building in St Anne's as they represent a visible and enduring statement of civic pride evident in St Anne's at the beginning of the twentieth century.

St Anne's Library

By the end of the nineteenth century at least three circulating libraries existed in St Anne's. In 1897 Louis Stott unsuccessfully attempted to obtain funds to erect a public library to mark Queen Victoria's Diamond Jubilee. The following year he was elected to the council, and when chairman (1901–03), resumed his campaign for a library as, in his view, there was nowhere suitable for local fishermen and workmen to go when inclement weather prevented them from working.

In an effort to raise the required money Coun. Stott wrote to Andrew Carnegie, the American philanthropist who was well known for funding public libraries and church organs, asking for financial assistance. By June 1903 Carnegie had agreed to provide £3,500 for the building. The land at the corner of Clifton Drive South and Links Road was given by the Land and Building Company. The architect was John Dent Harker. Coun. Stott laid the foundation stone on 13 August 1904 and St Anne's Library was officially opened by Coun.

In 1897 Louis Stott unsuccessfully attempted to obtain funds to erect a public library. The following year he was elected to the Council and when Chairman (1901–03) resumed his campaign. By June 1903 Andrew Carnegie had agreed to provide £3,500 for the building which was opened in January 1906. The architect was John Dent Harker who himself was Chairman of the Council in 1900/01.

G. W. Spring, chairman of the council, on 10 January 1906. In the previous July Mr T. P. Thompson had been appointed librarian, at a salary of £60, but resigned less than a month after the library was opened, to be replaced by Miss Bertha Barrow. Opening hours for the lending department was until 8.00 p.m., while the reading room was open until 9.30 p.m. The council added 1d. in the pound to the rates for the upkeep of the library.

Parks and gardens

Hope Street Recreation Ground. In 1898 John Talbot Clifton 'desirous of commemorating the sixtieth year of the reign of Queen Victoria (1897)' granted a piece of land for a Recreation Ground.

St George's Gardens (Ashton Gardens) remained the only recreational area for the town until 1898. In that year John Talbot Clifton 'desirous of commemorating the sixtieth year of the Reign of Her Gracious Majesty Queen Victoria [1897] in some manner which may prove a benefit to the above named district has promised to grant a piece of land for the purpose of a Recreation Ground …'.[7] The offer was accepted by the council, and in the same year they provided facilities at Hope Street Recreation Ground, spending £290 on an iron fence

and gymnastic apparatus. Nine years later they spent a further £1,432 in laying out a bowling green and tennis courts and also erecting a pavilion.

In 1900 the only other area, apart from the Esplanade, that had been laid out by the council were the planted slopes near the railway station which became known as 'the Plantation'. The opportunity for further council involvement came in June 1902 when Thomas Fair, on behalf of the Clifton estate, wrote to the chairman of the council:

> I am instructed by Mr Clifton to inform you that it is his desire to mark the Coronation of King Edward VII by presenting to you and the Council on behalf of St Anne's a plot of land being about 9 statute acres in extent subject to the same being laid out and made into a Public Park for the use and enjoyment of the inhabitants of St Anne's.[8]

The site of this proposed park was on the north-west side of St Anne's Road East, facing across to the present-day Clarendon Road and Shepherd Road. There were conditions to the gift, however, and the Clifton estate required the council to enclose the park with fences, to make footpaths and to erect shelters. No games were to be permitted and the park was to be named Clifton Park.

The offer provoked immediate debate and as early as August 1902 the *Lytham Times* was predicting that, despite the offer of an additional four acres, the gift would be refused. Indeed, exactly twelve months later the council wrote to the Clifton estate saying they felt that 'taking into consideration the heavy expenditure which has been incurred on public works ... they are unable at the present to ask the Ratepayers to accept the responsibility of carrying out the conditions which Mr Clifton attached to the gift of land'.[9]

The new century

During the opening years of the twentieth century St Anne's continued to prosper, but between 1908 and 1912 there was a slump. In 1910 the general rate, which had been maintained at an average of 4s. 0d. in the pound, was increased to 4s. 8d. Although by 1912 the rate had been reduced the town had come to a standstill, with a reduction in rateable value for the first time since 1879. In the same year (1912) it was estimated that there were nearly 600 empty houses in the town – nearly one-third of all properties.

With the need to secure the town's future a second improvement bill was submitted to parliament to enable the council to acquire St George's Gardens and other properties, and to confer further powers upon the council in regard to the supply of gas and electricity.

Despite a petition against the Bill by the Clifton estate it was passed by parliament on 7 August 1914, thereby removing the last vestiges of estate

St Anne's Road West (The Square) 1910. Thirty-five years after the laying of the town's foundation stone 'The Square' was beginning to take on an appearance that was to be recognisable until the re-development of the early twenty-first century.
BY COURTESY OF ST ANNE'S LIBRARY

St. Anne's Road, West. St. Anne's-on-the-Sea.

An electric tramcar, originally owned by the Blackpool, St Anne's, and Lytham Tramways Company, which had operated between Lytham and Blackpool since 1903. In 1920 St Anne's Urban District Council purchased the company for £144,936. Following amalgamation the tramcar fleet was operated by Lytham St Anne's Corporation.

control over the town's affairs. Subsequent council spending included £140,000 on the purchase of the tramways from the Blackpool, St Anne's and Lytham Tramways Company; £93,000 on electricity works; and £80,000 on the purchase of the gas works from the St Anne's on Sea Gas Company. One of the last major commitments of the council was to spend over £12,000 on the open-air sea water baths in 1916.

Former tramway shelter. The Blackpool, St Anne's, and Lytham Tramways began to run gas trams between Blackpool and Lytham in 1896. These were replaced by electric trams in 1903. The former company shelter, at the junction of Clifton Drive, North, and St Anne's Road, West, is now an Information Bureau.

The end of an era

Although by 1922 the general rate had risen to 7s. 2d. in the pound the town had become a popular, if somewhat refined, holiday resort and, around this time, began to be known as the 'Opal of the West'. It is not certain who invented this term – the most probable candidate is James Bowman, then editor of the *Lytham St Anne's Express*. In the 1927 *Lytham St Anne's Express Yearbook* the town is described as the 'Opal of the Western Coast'. This undoubted progress, however, had not been without much debate. As we shall see in the next chapter, there had been two occasions when amalgamation with Blackpool was a serious possibility, before the decision was taken to amalgamate instead with Lytham, and to create the borough that was to take the name Lytham St Anne's.

The last meeting of the St Anne's on the Sea Urban District Council took place on 6 November 1922. In his valedictory chairman's speech Coun. Critchley thanked the members present for their past work and expressed the opinion that 'the reputation which the town now enjoyed had been made during the last eight years'.[10]

CHAPTER NINETEEN

Amalgamation

Proposed amalgamation with Blackpool, 1900

The St Anne's Urban District Council had only been established some six years before there was a proposal to amalgamate St Anne's with Bispham, Cleveleys, Poulton and Blackpool. In October 1900 the local press were invited to a meeting at Blackpool town hall, to hear about the scheme proposed by Blackpool's mayor, Dr Kingsbury. A report of the meeting in the *Lytham Times* considered that 'the possibilities of the scheme are tremendous, and whilst there may be some drawbacks, it seems to us that the places proposed to be received into the family circle will have much more to gain than lose.'[1]

Had the proposal proceeded the unified area would have become a county borough, independent of Lancashire County Council. A proportion of the St Anne's councillors would have become aldermen and once in so many years have had the right to nominate the mayor. Other advantages, it was argued, was that St Anne's would be able to borrow money at the same low rate as Blackpool. In administration there would be only one official such as town clerk, or surveyor, while at the same time St Anne's residents would be entitled to all the benefits of Blackpool's institutions such as hospital and free library.

The same newspaper report sought to reassure the residents of St Anne's that there was no intention to destroy the town's individuality, and reported that the 'present specially residential and scholastic features would be retained'. Adding that 'St Anne's would be a kind of "west end" to Blackpool, just as the north end of Blackpool has always been a select and quiet neighbourhood'.[2]

A week later the *Lytham Times* reported that the scheme had been discussed by members of the St Anne's council, and unanimously accepted by them. It was further reported that Blackpool had accepted twenty proposals made by St Anne's. Although St Anne's Council had the power to assent it was decided to put the matter before the ratepayers. The views of the Clifton estate were also of considerable interest and influence. Thomas Fair declined to enter into the discussion until he had seen the scheme but, on the general principle of union, he objected strongly 'to St Anne's being swallowed up, root and branch, by Blackpool'.[3]

When confronted with the possibility of amalgamation, not all the ratepayers were as enthusiastic as the council members. On 10 November there was a ratepayers' meeting in opposition to the idea and three days later St Anne's tradesmen likewise voiced their own opposition. On 14 November the St Anne's council decided to postpone the question for twelve months. The reasons given were a minor disagreement over the rate – St Anne's wanted 3s. 10d. whereas Blackpool reinserted the original clause for 4s. 0d. – and an unresolved matter concerning trams or omnibuses on the promenade.

Proposed amalgamation with Blackpool, 1916

In June 1916 the subject of amalgamation with Blackpool, which was now a county borough, again became the subject of heated debate. The chief proponent was Coun. Charles Critchley, who in 1913 had succeeded John Talbot Clifton as county councillor for Lytham and St Anne's. In 1914 he was invited to join St Anne's council at a time when it was described as a 'Council

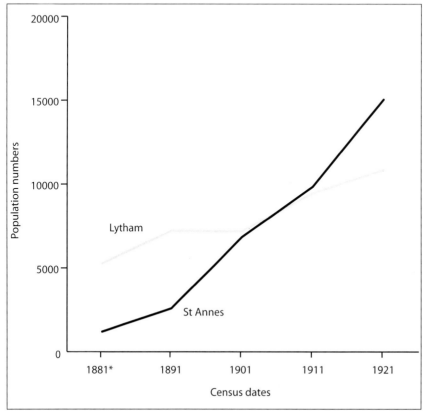

A comparison of population increase in St Anne's and Lytham covering the decennial census returns of 1881–1921. There was no separate figure for St Anne's in 1881 and the number shown here is that which is generally accepted as the population at that time. A corresponding number has been deleted for Lytham.

ST ANNE'S ON THE SEA

of intellect'. By 1916 he was chairman of the finance committee and renowned for his detailed calculations justifying an amalgamation. He argued that if St Anne's had accepted Blackpool's offer in 1900 the ratepayers collectively would have saved more than £100,000 in rates.

As in 1900, promises were given that the unique character of St Anne's would be preserved. Assurances were sought that certain projects, including the construction of a marine lake, the laying out of the foreshore between the pier and the baths, and alterations in the layout of St Anne's Road, West, would be carried out. It was also claimed that if Blackpool extended their boundary to include St Anne's then St Anne's rate would be set at an inclusive rate of 8*d*. in the pound more than the Blackpool rate for ten years, after which the rate would be the same for both. In effect this meant that St Anne's rate would have immediately fallen by 1*s*. 6*d*. to 5*s*. 8*d*. in the pound.

By July 1916 two opposing camps had been established. On 19 July a public meeting against the proposal was held in the Parish Rooms. Mr G. W. Parkes presided over a very large attendance amongst whom were Messrs H. A. Pickup, S. L. Stott JP, C. G. D. Hoare, G. Walmsley JP, H. Cooper, J. R. Taylor, Rev. C. H. Ellison, and Coun. J. H. Taylor. Thomas Bradley, secretary of the committee, read out a letter from Sir Charles Macara in which Sir Charles, whilst accepting 'there appears to be certain advantages by amalgamation' concluded by saying 'I hear that even with all the undertakings which may be given, it may be impossible to prevent its [St Anne's] present character being adversely affected. Personally, I should prefer to see it continuing to prosper on its present lines.'[4]

Contributors to the discussion included Louis Stott (not then a member of St Anne's council), and Coun. J. H. Taylor who described Coun. Critchley as 'an amalgamationist first and foremost and the principal point he had at heart was amalgamation. He was not concerned with the 1*s*. 6*d*. [rate] except as an argument.' Financial matters inevitably dominated the meeting, but it was also felt that with only eight members out of sixty on an amalgamated council 'St Anne's would be more or less a petty cash committee and the rest would naturally exploit St Anne's for the benefit of the rest of the district'.

The consensus of the meeting was summarised by Louis Stott, who proposed the following resolution:

> That this meeting of the ratepayers of the Urban District Council of St Anne's on the Sea condemns the proposals for the amalgamation of St Anne's and Blackpool as outlined in the statement published by the Council and contained in published correspondence with Blackpool, and records its conviction that a policy of amalgamation is not in the best interests of St Anne's, and hereby pledges itself to resist that policy by every legitimate means.[5]

Charles Frederick Critchley was Charter Mayor of Lytham St Anne's. He was born in Accrington in 1858 and began his working life in the telegraph office of the local railway before deciding to work in the cotton industry. By various stages he ultimately became managing director of Moorbrook Mill, Preston. In 1913 he was elected to represent Lytham and St Anne's on the Lancashire County Council and the following year he joined the St Anne's Urban District Council. During 1916 he was the leading proponent for amalgamation with Blackpool. Following his death in 1935 a tribute in the Lytham St Anne's Express considered that he would 'go down in local history as one of the outstanding characters of Lytham St Anne's.

The following Monday, 24 July, the Amalgamation Association held their meeting in the Parish Rooms. Mr James Prestwich presided and supporters included by Couns. C. F. Critchley, J. W. Hallam, and G. R. Eyre, Messrs G. Thompson, W. Heap, F. Heap, and H. Nickson.[6] The meeting was dominated by Coun. Critchley's criticism of his opponents' financial arguments. His comments did not go unchallenged, and throughout the meeting there was a continuing and, at times, highly personalised clash of opinion with Louis Stott. At one stage uproar ensued and when order had been restored Coun. Critchley commented that 'I think the best thing will be for Mr Stott and myself to start at four o'clock some day and have a public discussion.'[7]

During the following weeks both sides wrote letters to the *St Anne's Express* – which had always been in favour of amalgamation – and produced pamphlets in favour of their particular argument. In view of such entrenched opinions it was perhaps inevitable that, following a deputation to the Local Government Board, the council agreed to postpone amalgamation until after the war.

It is notable that throughout the debate most arguments were financial or related to infrastructure, and not (as would later be the case) that the perceived character and reputation of Blackpool would make it an unsuitable partner for St Anne's. Lytham was largely ignored in all this.

Amalgamation, 1918–1922

The question of amalgamation was reopened in November 1918 when Blackpool, subject to the removal of certain restrictions imposed by the Treasury, promised to complete the marine lake, and also made commitments with regard to the rates. An editorial in the *St Anne's Express* was supportive of amalgamation, stating:

> Time will have an interesting tale to tell of the Amalgamation problem; how men of vision counselled amalgamation with the County Borough of Blackpool and so obtained relief from the annual tribute imposed by an alien authority (Lancashire County Council). The record will tell how other men, lacking prevision, opposed any change in the existing form of government but lived long enough to regret their hasty action.

The editorial also predicted that 'opposition to amalgamation with Blackpool would collapse' and that:

> the people will be glad in years to come that they took the right course when St Annes and Lytham shared the fortune of their big brother, Blackpool, and the League of Fylde Coast Health Resorts became a reality.[8]

Negotiations with Blackpool continued but ultimately foundered on the relatively minor matter of funding a ladies' orchestra at St Anne's. Blackpool were reluctant to provide such funding, arguing that other parts of an enlarged borough could make similar requests. After breaking off negotiations in May 1919, St Anne's council, having regard to all the circumstances, finally decided against amalgamation with Blackpool in May 1920.

During this period, however, other events that were to shape the future of the town had been taking place. In 1918 a committee of residents had presented a petition to the Privy Council requesting a charter of incorporation (conferring borough status), expressing the belief that it would be 'to the great advantage of the town by giving it a higher and more efficient form of local government'. However, in view of the modest size of the town's population, this course of action was unlikely succeed. It was almost certainly as a result of this potential rebuttal that, in February 1919, Lancashire County Council wrote to St Anne's council suggesting a merger with Lytham council.

By this date the climate of opinion in central government was moving towards a simplification of the structure of local government, by amalgamating smaller units, so the timing was just right. Although it could be described as a marriage of convenience, there were, in reality, sound arguments for such an amalgamation. St Anne's had its own electricity works and tramway system which linked both towns; Lytham had its own gasworks whereas St Anne's was still to purchase the St Anne's on Sea Gas Company; and King Edward VII School and St Anne's Technical College served both towns.

On 31 March and 1 April 1921 a Privy Council inquiry was held, at the Ansdell Institute, into the application of St Anne's Urban District Council for a charter of incorporation and the application of Lytham Urban District Council to be included in the charter, by amalgamation with St Anne's. Those represented at the inquiry were both councils; the St Anne's Incorporation Committee; the Lytham Anti-Amalgamation Committee; Lancashire County Council; the St Anne's Land and Building Company; and the Clifton estate.

At the outset the Privy Council commissioner said that the charter would not be granted to St Anne's alone, so that the only question was whether the charter should be granted to the two places. The inquiry was wide-ranging, and the *St Anne's Express* reported the proceedings in detail. Subjects discussed included the development of St Anne's; the question of rates; the accounts of both councils; trading undertakings; a borough court; county council support for the scheme; and opposition to amalgamation. One of the many contributors to the debates was William Whinnerah, on behalf of the Clifton estate, who agreed that as Lytham and St Anne's had the same interests it would be a decided advantage for them to amalgamate. In his opinion 'it would help in the development of the district'.[9]

The application for a charter was duly granted, whereupon Coun. Critchley was appointed Charter Mayor, and Thomas Bradley appointed Charter Town Clerk. In late March 1922 both men went to London to receive the charter of incorporation. They returned to St Anne's with the charter on Friday 31 March 1922, when members of both councils met at the St Anne's 'town hall' (the Public Offices). The *St Anne's Express* reported the event including the tribute to Thomas Bradley, described as 'the power behind the throne' for his 'persistent endeavours and his tactful handling' during the negotiations leading to the granting of the charter.[10]

Charter Day, 1922

Charter Day was held on Monday the 1 May 1922. According to the *St Anne's Express*, 'elaborate arrangements were made to celebrate the event, and great care was taken to ensure that the ceremonies should be impressed on the minds of the children of the two towns'. The newspaper added that '... unfortunately the weather was most adverse, and almost all day there was a heavy downpour – so heavy that the only surprise was to see so many people assemble at Lytham and again at St Anne's to hear the reading of the Charter'.[11]

Ceremonies commenced shortly after 9 a.m. when members and officials of St Anne's council motored to Lytham, where they were met by members of the Lytham council and Mr and Mrs J. T. Clifton and their son Harry. Proceeding to the Lytham/Warton boundary Coun. Critchley, on behalf of St Anne's council, handed over the charter to the Deputy Charter Mayor, Coun. T. Horatio Wood of Lytham Council.

The motorcade then re-formed to travel to the St Anne's/Blackpool boundary, stopping at the Lytham council offices where the charter, in spite of the heavy rain, was read to 'a fairly large crowd including the schoolchildren'. At the Blackpool boundary the charter was returned by Coun. Wood to Coun. Critchley. Coming back along Clifton Drive [North] the party was met at Beach Road by the St Anne's band which led the procession to The Square 'where a large body of ex-servicemen were lined up in addition to the school-children and the general public'.

The charter was then read out by Thomas Bradley after which Coun. Critchley proposed the loyal toast. In a short speech he also said that they were delighted to have the presence of Mr Clifton with them as fifty years previously he was – 'the man who had laid the foundation stone of St Anne's'.

The reading of the Charter at St Anne's 1 May 1922. The choice of location would appear to have been deliberate. Coun. J.H. Taylor had been a leading member of St Anne's UDC since 1910, and Chairman of the Council 1913–1915.

SOUVENIR BOOK – CHARTER DAY 1922

Charter Day
Monday May 1st 1922.

This Certificate is to commemorate the granting by His Majesty King George V of a Charter dated the 28th day of March 1922 amalgamating and incorporating the Urban Districts of Lytham and St.Annes on the Sea into a Municipal Corporation to be named the Borough of Lytham St.Annes.

C.F. Critchley. Charter Mayor.
J. .... Deputy Charter Mayor.
.... Charter Town Clerk.
.... Deputy Charter Town Clerk.

Certificate presented to schoolchildren to commemorate Charter Day. On Charter Day all elementary schoolchildren in the new borough were presented with a souvenir certificate. The certificate illustrated here was presented to Edith Gregson, a pupil at Heyhouses School.
BY COURTESY OF JACKIE ROBERTS

After the reading of the charter a luncheon was served at the Grand Hotel to about 120 guests, following which various speeches were made as to the future success of the new borough.

Although it was undoubtedly the coming together of two quite distinct communities, even today it is often forgotten that amalgamation was, in effect, the restoration of what had been the ancient parish of Lytham. On Charter Day these sentiments were fully expressed by Coun. Wood who, when responding to the toast 'The Lancashire County Council', referred to the fact that the two places had been described as bride and bridegroom:

> He did not know whether it was quite correct, because really it was the making-up after a split. The geographical area was just simply restored to what it was before 1878. Still there were points of resemblance to a marriage, and the first similarity in relation to marriage was that there was a diversity of opinion, (Laughter).

He concluded by saying that:

> The new Borough started with greater and grander possibilities than some of the older ones ever knew. They had splendid possibilities and they needed co-operation. He hoped the good wishes of those present for the success and development of the new Borough would be realised.[12]

The area of the new Borough was 11,697 acres, of which 5,902 was foreshore. According to the 1921 census the population was 15,041 at St Anne's and 10,830 at Lytham. The rateable value exceeded £225,000.

The very first permanent building in St Anne's was Alpha House. It was also the first Post Office with Clement Rawstron the first postmaster. When he first came to St Anne's in 1875 Clement Rawstron lodged with the Heap family at Pine Cottage (see photograph p. 254) before occupying Alpha House where he resided until his death in 1916.

Alpha House datestone, now incorporated into the premises of Thomsons, opticians.

In 1901 J. R. Taylor opened a store within the newly erected Century Buildings. J.R. Taylor was elected to the Lytham St Anne's Borough Council in 1922, and was Mayor in 1943/44.

CHAPTER TWENTY

Town life in St Anne's, 1875–1922

Expansion of the town

In 1935 James Bowman, editor of the *Lytham St Anne's Express*, wrote an article entitled 'A Review of the Pioneer Builders of St Anne's'.[1] Among those he named was John Heap who built the first four houses, including Alpha House (now Thomson's opticians), in St Andrew's Road, South. Alpha House became the first post office and was occupied by Clement Rawstron, the postmaster.

Other early builders include Hanson Hamilton, who built the first house on North Promenade; John Hindle, who built the first shop on the west side of Garden Street (now Edinburgh Woollen Mill); and James Lord, who built a portion of West Crescent and also houses in Park Road. Hydro Terrace in St Anne's Road, West (now forming part of Booth's and W. H. Smith's) was built by Stephen England for Messrs Maxwell and Tuke. Some of the materials used in the construction of this latter property were acquired from the Manchester Queen Victoria 1887 Jubilee Exhibition. The Century Buildings (J. R. Taylor Ltd) were designed by Messrs England, Winstanley and England in 1901.

By the end of 1875 the railway station had been built and construction of the railway bridge (The Crescent), which eliminated the need for the level crossing in St Anne's Road West, had begun. John Cookson was the first station master, and Jacob Miller was the company's authorised station attendant for passengers' luggage. During the following fifty years various additions were made to the station, but in March 1925 a new station was opened. This was demolished in 1985 and replaced by the present booking office.

The Local Board established the St Anne's Fire Brigade in August 1887. By January 1888 a hose cart and appliances had been acquired and stored in the rear of the Local Board offices at Matlock House, Clifton Drive, South. The first superintendent was J. E. Pennington who held the post for almost forty years. A fire station was erected in St Andrew's Road, North, in 1902

Club carriage interior. In 1895 a meeting, initiated by seventeen businessmen who travelled daily between the Fylde coast and Manchester, resulted in the establishment of the Lytham, St Anne's and Blackpool Travelling Club. Those who belonged to 'the Club' travelled in their own specially adapted carriage. Membership was confined to a limited number of first-class season-ticket holders, who paid an additional fee for the privilege.

BY COURTESY OF THE NATIONAL RAILWAY MUSEUM

Club carriage – exterior. An exterior view of the Club Train taken prior to World War I. On the left of the photograph is Richard Almond who was employed by the Lancashire & Yorkshire Railway as a club car attendant and ticket collector.

BY COURTESY OF ROY POTTER

to be replaced by the present station in 1985. The first police station serving St Anne's was located at 10–12 Park Road. The present police station, at the junction of St Andrew's Road, North and St George's Road, was built in 1901 by John Whiteside.

Health

At their first meeting in July 1878, the St Anne's Local Board had made temporary arrangements with Dr Poutney to act as the Medical Officer of Health. This arrangement only lasted until February 1879 when Dr Wartenberg of Blackpool was appointed, at an annual salary of £30. In March 1879 he reported to a meeting of the Local Board that several cases of scarlatina had occurred in Common Lane (Church Road) due to the 'indiscriminate visiting which went on between one family where the disease was and others'.[2]

However, it was the potential health problems associated with impure drinking water, a problem not confined just to Heyhouses, which exercised the thoughts and concerns of the Local Board during the early years of the town. At their meeting, in March 1879, discussion among the board members revealed that some residents in Common Lane were supplied by Fylde Waterworks Company but others were supplied from pumps. The board therefore agreed to write to Dr Wartenberg requesting him 'to obtain samples of the water in the wells near Common Lane'.[3]

In July 1879 Dr Wartenberg was able to report that, although in the previous six months there had been five deaths from scarlatina and one from typhoid, 'the Sanitary Conditions of St Anne's was very good'.[4] This assessment was confirmed by Dr Dearden, who had succeeded Dr Wartenberg at the beginning of 1881. In April that year Dr Dearden reported to the Board that 'The Health of your district is excellent'.[5]

It is actually quite remarkable that the relatively poor sanitary conditions which prevailed until the 1890s did not have a more detrimental effect upon the inhabitants of St Anne's, as it would appear that it was more a matter of chance that an epidemic (or major outbreak of disease) did not happen. If it had, the effect on the reputation of the growing town and its establishment as a premier health resort could have been devastating.

Nevertheless by February 1883 it is clear that Dr Dearden had become exasperated with the way in which the board was prevaricating over providing an adequate drainage system. At an acrimonious meeting of the board Dr Dearden's report of the death, due to typhoid fever, of William Butler Harrison, the coxswain of the St Anne's lifeboat, was challenged and the meeting was terminated by the chairman just as Dr Dearden was about to speak.

It would appear that as a result of this disagreement Dr Dearden resigned and Dr Wartenburg resumed his former office. In his report for 1884 Dr

Wartenberg 'was able to give such a satisfactory Report of the health of the District … which was considered would compare most favourably with any health resort or Watering Place in England'.[6]

In certain circumstances it was not always within the control of the Local Board to protect its own residents. In 1888 there was a serious outbreak of smallpox in Preston, and Thomas Bradley, as clerk to the Local Board, was instructed to write to the Local Government Board and request them 'to confer temporary powers with a view to not allowing passengers to land on our coast line from Preston during the present grave epidemic of Small Pox in that town …' In addition the Local Board had notices printed desiring 'the Lodging-House Keepers of St Anne's to be careful whom they take in'.[7]

Of particular concern during this potential threat was the absence of any hospital in the town, let alone one for infectious diseases. Thomas Bradley was therefore requested to write to Thomas Fair to ask him if the Clifton estate 'would consent in the event of an outbreak of Small Pox to the Board erecting a temporary Hospital Tent away in the Sandhills'.[8] Although there were attempts to provide a site for an infectious hospital during the 1890s no such facility was ever built.

Appendix referred to on page 57

LOCAL BOARD
OF
ST. ANNE'S-ON-THE-SEA

CAUTION.

In view of the very grave Epidemic of **Small Pox**, now unfortunately raging in Preston, this Board most urgently desires the Lodging-House Keepers of St. Anne's to be careful whom they take in. As a preventative the Medical Officer for this Board recommends Vaccination.

By Order of the Board,

THOS. BRADLEY,
CLERK.

Printed at the Times Office, Church Street, Blackpool.

In December 1892 the St Anne's Nurse and Sick Aid Society was established. At the inaugural meeting Rev. Terry explained that St Anne's was no longer able to receive the assistance of the Lytham nurse, as Lytham itself now required her full services. Dr Booth testified to 'the great need there was for the help of a trained nurse in many cases among the poor, to assist in the nursing and to see that the orders of the doctor were properly carried out'.[9]

By 1898 five physician/surgeons, including Dr Booth, were in practice in St Anne's, but there was no general hospital in the town and residents had to rely entirely upon the Cottage Hospital at Lytham. In 1908, as a result of representations by Dr Booth, who was then the Medical Officer of Health, John

Talbot Clifton indicated he would be prepared to offer a site for a cottage hospital.

A site on the corner of Headroomgate Road and Highbury Road was subsequently offered, and at a meeting of St Anne's Sick-Aid and Nursing Society held in April 1916, the Rev. H. E. Butler, vicar of St Anne's, made a strong plea for the cottage hospital to be built in commemoration of 'those who had fallen in the war'.[10]

Sums of money began to accumulate, and on 30 April 1919 a lease was drawn up between John Talbot Clifton and the 'Trustees for the time being of the St Anne's on the Sea Cottage Hospital' for the erection of a hospital on the site originally offered.[11] The project was not pursued 'for the simple and satisfactory reason that a better scheme presented itself'.[12] The story of that hospital will be told in the next chapter.

The holiday industry and retail trades

By the 1890s, and particularly following the implementation of the main drainage scheme in 1892, St Anne's had become recognised as a leading health resort. In 1893 Dr David Little, senior surgeon at the Manchester Royal Eye Hospital wrote:

> I entertain a high opinion of St Anne's on the Sea as a health resort. It has a pure bracing, and invigorating air and good sanitation. It is particularly well adapted for children. I speak from a lengthened personal experience in case of my own family, and have no hesitation in recommending its claims as a place of health.[13]

During the late nineteenth century most holidaymakers obtained their accommodation at the many lodging-houses in the town. In 1898 *Barrett's Directory* listed no fewer than 133 lodging-house keepers located around the Promenade, St Andrew's Road and in St Alban's Road. The weekly lists of visitors printed in the *St Anne's on the Sea Express* reveal that in addition to those from inland Lancashire towns others came from Yorkshire and the Midlands.

The first licensed building to be erected in St Anne's had been the St Anne's Hotel. Although Howarth's Temperance and Commercial Hotel, on Clifton Drive, South, also provided accommodation in the late 1870s it was to be another twenty-two years before another licensed hotel, intended primarily to cater for visitors, was built in the town.

At the Blackpool Brewster Sessions held on 23 August 1897 Rose Holloway, widow of A. J. Holloway, the former proprietor of the St Anne's Hotel, was granted an application in respect of a new hotel then being built on

The Grand Hotel. In 1897 Rose Holloway, widow of A.J. Holloway, the former proprietor of the St Anne's Hotel, was granted an application in respect of a new hotel then being built on South Promenade. The Grand Hotel remained in the ownership of the Holloway family until 1950.

South Promenade.[14] This hotel, the Grand, remained in the ownership of the Holloway family until May 1950. By the late 1890s other smaller hotels, including the Southdown Hydro (later to become the town hall) began to cater for the increasing number of visitors.

The early twentieth century witnessed a rapid expansion in building and in 1908 Oliver Porritt, the grandson of William Porritt, commissioned the architects J. D. & S. J. Mould of Bury to design the Imperial Hydro, later to be known as the Majestic. The original prospectus described the scheme as 'the erection of a palatial hydro hotel in the Renaissance style'.[15] This impressive building enjoyed its heyday during the 1920s and 1930s. During World War II the building was requisitioned by government departments, and although re-opening as a hotel after the war, its popularity waned and in 1975 it was demolished to be replaced by luxury apartments.

Away from the main tourism area there was no licensed premises until three applications were made at the Blackpool Brewster Sessions, for hotels within a few yards of each other. Thomas Tattersall applied to build an hotel

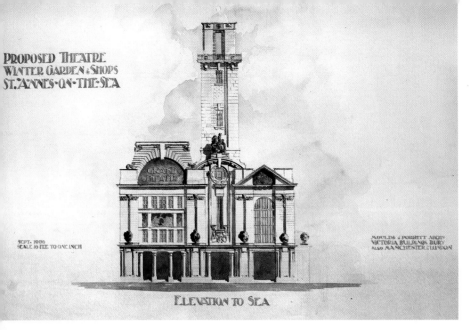

PROPOSED THEATRE
WINTER GARDEN & SHOPS
ST. ANNES-ON-THE-SEA

GRAND THEATRE

SEPT. 1906
SCALE 16 FEET TO ONE INCH

MOULDS & PORRITT ARCHTS
VICTORIA BUILDINGS BURY
ALSO MANCHESTER & LONDON

ELEVATION TO SEA

Winter Gardens
and Theatre,
architects'
drawings. Although
the precise site
was not indicated
it was almost
certainly where the
Hotel Majestic was
subsequently built.

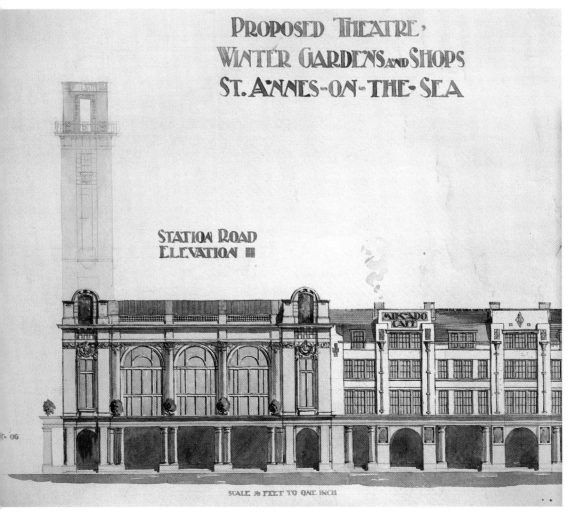

PROPOSED THEATRE,
WINTER GARDENS AND SHOPS
ST. ANNES-ON-THE-SEA

STATION ROAD
ELEVATION

MIKADO CAFE

SCALE 16 FEET TO ONE INCH

at the 'junction of St Anne's Road East and Church Road'. William Whitehead applied for provisional permission to build 'at the corner of Church Road', and the third application was from Frank Redfern also for the 'Church Road corner'.[16]

Witnesses for and against each application were questioned in detail but, after some deliberation by the magistrates, the only application granted was that to Thomas Tattersall who had in fact already entered into a contract with the Clifton estate to take the plot of land for the purpose of building a hotel.

One of the arguments used to convince the magistrates that his was the best site was 'one advantage of the present plans was that there was only one door, and that was in such a position that a policeman standing at the corner of Church Road and St Alban's Road could see all who passed in and out'.[17] The architect was John Dent Harker, and the Victoria Hotel, as the new hotel was subsequently named, opened in 1898.

In order to supply the needs of both residents and holidaymakers traders of various kinds very quickly established themselves in the town. In 1935 James Bowman wrote a complementary article to that already mentioned, entitled 'The Trading Community of Other Days', in which he recalled the tradespeople of the late nineteenth and early twentieth centuries.[18]

Of those early traders George Rhodes & Son, butchers (1877), Worthington & Co., boot dealers (1879), J. H. Taylor & Son, chemists (1880), Walmsley & Son, drapers, dressmakers and milliners (1883), F. & J. Redfern, butchers

Victoria Hotel c.1897. In 1897 three applications were made to the Blackpool Brewster Sessions to erect licensed premises within a few yards of each other. The successful applicant was Thomas Tattersall who subsequently built the Victoria Hotel. One of the considerations in favour of the site was that 'a policeman standing at the corner of Church Road and St Albans Road could see all who passed in and out'.
BY COURTESY OF ROBERT HALEY

(1888), and Mrs Lambert, West Crescent Post Office (1895) were still trading in the town in 1935.

One firm not mentioned in the article was that of Whitesides, which had been founded in 1880 by Thomas Whiteside (of Whiteside's Farm). Starting with 'one cart and a grey horse from his father's farm he quickly built it up to a large scale cab, haulage and removals business'.[19] During the twentieth century the firm continued to expand its travel and transport (Whiteside's Taxis) business, and now (2007) continues to have a prominent presence in the town.

On 8 October 1894 the traders formed themselves into an association, and in addition to securing early closing and a half-day holiday (Wednesday), gave support to other public improvements in the town. In 1896 the traders' association requested residents of St Anne's 'to do their shopping earlier so that shops may be closed at 7 p.m.' The purpose of this was to provide the assistants with the opportunity of attending technical and other classes 'which now they are unable to do since they cannot leave their shops till 9 p.m.'[20]

In the years immediately after World War I there was a demand for additional shops. On 3 February 1920 the Land and Building Company wrote to the Clifton estate suggesting that as Wood Street 'would be an attractive and beneficial feature of the town':

James Bowman was born at Fleetwood in 1865. He became editor of the St Anne's on the Sea Express in 1904, and subsequently, until 1935, of the *Lytham St Anne's Express*. The meticulous recording of events during his editorship, combined with his own recollections, continue to provide a rich source of information relating to the early days of St Anne's. He died at St Anne's in 1941.

BY COURTESY OF DOROTHY CSESZNYAK

R.F. Tomlinson purchased his business on the Crescent from H. Rothwell in 1930. On their billheads both men described themselves as 'Butcher and Pork Specialist'. This photograph, taken sometime in the 1930s, reveals the extent to which retailers in the town 'dressed' their premises at Christmas. The property is now 'Genesis', the bathroom specialists.

PHOTOGRAPH: AUTHOR

the time has now arrived when the temporary understanding between you and ourselves which restricts the property in Wood Street to dwelling-houses should be reconsidered with a view to allowing the lessees to convert such property into shops should they so desire[21]

Golf

The definitive history of the first golf club, now the Royal Lytham and St Anne's, has already been published.[22] It is therefore necessary only to provide a brief overview of the history of this prestigious club. In February 1886 a circular letter was sent to local gentry proposing the formation of 'The Lytham and St Anne's Golf Club'. Although signed by J. T. and J. S. Fair, it was actually prompted by Alexander Doleman – 'The Father of Fylde Golf' – who had tried, unsuccessfully, to interest Blackpool in the game.

The club was founded on 16 March 1886 and established its headquarters at the St Anne's Hotel, where the billiards room became known as the 'Golf Room'. By 1889 the men's course extended northwards from the St Anne's Hotel to the present St Anne's Old Links, and eastwards to the area of present-day Mayfield Road/St Leonard's Road. The ladies' course was east of the men's, bounded by Headroomgate Road and Highbury Road.

In its early days the club attracted both new residents and visitors to the town. However, the detrimental effects on children's education whenever a major tournament took place were not appreciated by the headmaster at Heyhouses School. An entry in the Heyhouses School log book for 1 February

The Royal Lytham and St Anne's Golf Club was founded on 16 March 1886 and established its headquarters at the St Anne's Hotel where the billiards room became known as the 'Golf Room'. The Club moved to the present course in 1897, the formal opening of the Clubhouse taking place on 7 March 1898.

1888 records that 'This afternoon Robert & Arthur Cartmell, Henry & Fred Hodge were absent from school, carrying Golf sticks. Arthur Cartmell is only nine years old.' In November 1888 a further entry notes that the school attendance officer was resolved 'to put an end to the employment of school children by members of the Golf Club'. It also noted that, 'the committee of the Golf Club seem to have done their best to prevent their [the children's] employment, but some of the members treat the matter very indifferently'. The school staff, however, appear to have become resigned to the situation and on 3 October 1890 the log book notes that 'the school was closed on Thursday on account of the Annual Golf Competition'.

It must have been particularly frustrating to the staff knowing that it was Rev. Terry, their own vicar (and vice-president of the Lytham and St Anne's Golf Club), who usually 'requested' the closure of the school. Even after his death in 1899 the school managers at Heyhouses continued to sanction the closure of the school for certain events, and the practice only seems to have ceased at the outbreak of World War I.

The club moved to the present course in 1897, the formal opening of the clubhouse by the Marquis of Lorne taking place on 7 March 1898. In May 1926 King George V granted the club permission to use the 'Royal' prefix, and in June the same year the Open Championship was first held at the course.

The Old Links Golf Club was established in June 1901 and played over part of the original Lytham and St Anne's course. On 5 May 1902 the club was formally opened by the captain T. W. Markland who, prior to the ceremony, was presented with a silver-mounted club by George Lowe. On 10 June 1905

The St Anne's Old Links Golf Club was established in 1901. The original Clubhouse is now the Royal British Legion Club in Mayfield Road. The present Clubhouse was opened on 22 April 1911.

the Old Links clubhouse in Mayfield Road (now the Royal British Legion Club) was opened by Thomas Fair, to a design by Messrs England and Winstanley of St Anne's.

In 1906 the club changed its title to 'The St Anne's Old Links Golf Club'. In 1909 a lease was secured on land embracing much of the former hamlet of Cross Slack, and subsequently developed into the present course. The new clubhouse, to a design by Messrs Stirrup, Cooper and Slater of Manchester and Blackburn, was opened on 22 April 1911.[23]

Lifeboat disaster

The late eighteenth and nineteenth centuries witnessed a considerable increase in shipping activity at both Liverpool and Preston. Vessels entering Preston had to negotiate the deadly sandbanks of the Ribble estuary and in adverse weather conditions many foundered. In an effort to guide vessels using the estuary the Ribble Navigation Company, in February 1848, erected a lighthouse on the Double Stanner. In January 1863, following several days of severe weather, the foundations of the Lighthouse were undermined and the building fell.

The *Laura Janet* being launched on 15 June 1885, to take part in the opening ceremonies of the pier. Posing for the photographer at East Bank Slade, the *Laura Janet* was the St Anne's lifeboat from which all thirteen crew were drowned when attempting the rescue of the *Mexico*.

The following year the Navigation Company erected a wooden lighthouse on the top of a sandhill which stood between Riley Avenue and Lightburne Avenue. The last keeper of this lighthouse, which was not demolished until 1901, was Josiah Cartmell the uncle of Robert Cartmell who became the manager of the St Anne's Land and Building Company.

Lytham acquired its first lifeboat in 1851. Thirty years later, following somewhat protracted negotiations, a lifeboat house in Eastbank Road (Linrone Funeral Home) was built at St Anne's. The naming ceremony of the *Laura Janet*, the first St Anne's lifeboat, performed by Mrs Chadwick, the wife of James Chadwick the donor of the St Anne's station, was on 24 September 1881.

The definitive history of the St Anne's lifeboat station from 1881 to 1925 has already been published, but no history of St Anne's would be complete without some mention of the dreadful fate which befell the crew of the *Laura Janet* when attempting to rescue the crew of the barque *Mexico* on the night of 9 December 1886.[24] It was the Lytham lifeboat which completed the rescue, returning to Lytham in the early hours of 10 December. The *Laura Janet* was found later the same day, upturned on the shore near Southport. All the St Anne's crew had been drowned. The Southport lifeboat was also lost, although two of her sixteen crew survived. The bodies of twelve members of the St Anne's boat

were brought home on the afternoon train – the last body was not found until March 1887. On 14 December funeral services took place at St Anne's parish church, St Cuthbert's, Lytham, and Layton Cemetery. The loss of life remains the greatest tragedy in the history of the RLNI.

On 23 May 1888 the lifeboat monument on South Promenade, built in memory of the lost crew, was unveiled by John Talbot Clifton, and bears the names of all thirteen crew members of the *Laura Janet*. The statue 'was based on a portrait of Thomas Harrison, the assistant coxswain of the *Nora Royds* [the successor lifeboat to the *Laura Janet*], his left hand rests on a life-buoy and his weather beaten and bearded features are said to be in the likeness of William Johnson of Commonside, coxswain of the *Laura Janet*'.[25]

Following the *Laura Janet* disaster Sir Charles W. Macara. Bt, who came to reside at North Promenade in 1885 and whose concern for the welfare of St Anne's lifeboatmen remained paramount until his death in 1929, was responsible for establishing 'Lifeboat Saturday'. The first event, held to raise funds for the National Lifeboat

Institution (later the RNLI), was held in Manchester in October 1891 and included the St Anne's lifeboat the *Nora Royds*. Within two years it had become a nationwide event.

The Militia

The militia was a system of voluntary enlistment for a period of six years which included measures to train the force in conjunction with regular troops, and during the 1880s the militia encampment was an annual event at St Anne's. At the first such encampment, in 1879, the *Lytham Times* reported that 'Yesterday the officers and men of the 3rd Royal Lancashire Militia mustered at the Militia Barracks, Preston, for their annual training, which will this year be spent under canvas at St Anne's, where they will be encamped for 20 days'. The campsite, provided by Robert Hargreaves of Headroomgate Farm, was described as 'a spacious field near St Anne's church'.[26] It was anticipated that approximately 1,000 men would be present.

On 23 May 1888 the lifeboat monument on South Promenade, in memory of the crew of the *Laura Janet*, was unveiled by John Talbot Clifton.

Opinion was divided as to how desirable it was to have regular militia encampments in the town. Events such as those which occurred on Saturday 24 June 1882, when a hundred militiamen travelled to Kirkham and created what was described in the *Preston Guardian* as a riot, supported such reservations. The commotion at Kirkham continued until midnight when the police, assisted by some civilians, were able to regain control. On the following Monday those convicted of riotous conduct were sentenced to three months' imprisonment with hard labour.[27]

In July 1882 over 1,000 men from the East Lancashire Regiment of Rifle Volunteers, comprising six companies from Blackburn, two from Darwen and two from Clitheroe, were encamped. By August these had been replaced by men from the 3rd Battalion Lancashire Fusiliers, and in the words of the unnamed writer of a letter to the *Blackpool Times* in August 1882 'and from about 2nd of May down to the present time there has hardly been a day in which one or the other (volunteer or militia) have not been present'. His detailed letter concluded by trusting that 'St Anne's will get rid of this drawback to its prosperity, and that its deliverance will not long be delayed'.[28]

The same edition of the newspaper also reported that Dr Dearden, at a meeting of the Local Board, called attention to the bad sanitary arrangements on the field where the militia were encamped. He noted that there had been three previous deaths on the same field, and in each instance the sanitary arrangements, for almost 1,200 men 'had been so bad that a great and dangerous nuisance has existed'. John Greenhalgh, the chairman of the board, commented that in his opinion, 'Militia and similar bodies of men were a perfect nuisance to the district, and also very injurious to the prosperity of the place'.[29]

The events of 1882 would appear to have focused the minds of those responsible for organising the campsite and for discipline among the men. In 1885 a petition in favour of a militia encampment was signed by 88 residents, including the Rev. Terry and Dr Wartenberg, noting that 'we only state the truth when we say it gives us pleasure to notice year by year the continual improvement in the behaviour of the Men'.[30]

By 1887 the *Lytham, St Anne's & Kirkham Sun* was able to report that the band of the 3rd and 4th Battalions of the North Lancashire Regiment, under the direction of Mr Norwood, was playing at certain times in St George's Gardens.[31] A particularly vivid description of the militia encampment was penned by Harry Cooper in 1932 when recalling events of 1886:

There was then a huge field stretching away without cops or hedges from the Parish Rooms to Headroomgate Farm … This huge field was known as the 'Camp Field' … The left handed side of Oxford Road was the cook-house area – open fires and ovens stretching as far as Mayfield Road. As a kiddy I used to distribute reading matter to these men in their bell-tents and chat delightedly with the redcoats as they polished brass buttons and pipe-clayed belts, and on a Sunday listened with awe to a military service or stood by as the bands played outside the officer's marquee during dinner. When the tide served whole battalions marched to the sea for a dip, and what a blinding dust their tramping feet raised.[32]

World War I

As in every other town and village throughout the United Kingdom the outbreak of World War I, in August 1914, meant that St Anne's would have to bear the loss of men killed in action, and also accept a considerable change in community life.

Among the first victims of the war were the Belgian refugees who at the outset were forced to flee their homes. During September and October 1914 nearly 200,000 men, women and children, sailed into English ports. These refugees were then dispersed across England, with large numbers being sent to Blackpool and the Fylde. By early October 1914 the first refugees had arrived at St Anne's.[33]

The Church of Our Lady, Star of the Sea provided accommodation for twenty refugees at Holly Nook, Queens Road, and a similar number were maintained by St Thomas' church in Orchard Road, All Saints' Road, and Lightburne Avenue. By March 1915 St Thomas' had raised over £530 and spent £370 in expenditure on Belgian refugees' homes.[34]

In addition to accommodation provided by the churches, 85 children were housed at the children's camp on Clifton Drive, North. The Heyhouses school log book for 23 October 1914 records that the vicar visited the school concerning admittance of Belgian children. Four days later the log book of Our Lady, Star of the Sea school likewise noted that Belgian children were to be admitted as ordinary scholars.

By May 1915 most refugees had left the district, as shown by the entry in Our Lady log book for 20 May: 'All the Belgian children from the Camp leave the district today – leaving three only attending school'. It was perhaps these same children who on 17 March 1919 were the 'Belgian children [who] left for their own country'.

Between February and August 1915 St Anne's became a training ground for men of the Royal Field Artillery, who were billeted in fields by Headroomgate Road. As in the days of the militia encampments the attraction of watching men undergoing military training proved a distraction for the young. On 14 May 1915 George Sanderson wrote in the Heyhouses School log book: 'For the past two months scholars have arrived late, morning and afternoon – due to troops in billets. There are 3,500 in the town this week – belonging the Royal Field Artillery.'

In September 1915 the King's Military Convalescent Hospital at Squire's Gate opened, with accommodation for 2,000 wounded soldiers. And in May 1916 Chaseside Convalescent Hospital, St George's Square, provided accommodation for thirty soldiers. The Imperial Hydro (Hotel Majestic) was also requisitioned and became the Imperial Convalescent Hospital for wounded officers. Throughout the war local tradesmen contributed to the war effort, while schoolchildren were constantly reminded of the progress of the war, and of the need to support the troops. On 22 May 1916 pupils at St Thomas' school sent their second parcel to wounded soldiers in France, and also 'adopted' Pte Rowley Good, a former St Anne's policeman and then a prisoner of war, by sending him a fortnightly parcel to the value of 5s. 0d. At St Anne's council school a war loan savings association was commenced in December 1916. And on 22 February 1918 several scholars were absent from Heyhouses School 'viewing the Tank "Julian" at Blackpool'.

Although no longer a resident of St Anne's at the time of his death, Lieutenant Hardy Parsons, a former pupil of King Edward VII school, and whose father had been minister of the Drive Methodist church, was awarded a posthumous Victoria Cross for his heroism at the Battle of Cambrai in 1917. Another former pupil of the school, whose name appears on the St Anne's war memorial, is that of Burton Critchley, the son of Charles Critchley the Charter Mayor of Lytham St Anne's. A total of thirty-seven former King Edward VII pupils died in the war.

It is this appalling loss of life for which the war continues to be remembered.

Prior to the erection of the War Memorial in Ashton Gardens a memorial was erected in Church Road by St Anne's parish church, and dedicated to parishioners who had been killed in World War I. A similar memorial was erected in Curzon Road (then Clifton Street) by the Boy Scouts of the parish church. Both memorials were unveiled in 1920.

On 12 October 1924 the St Anne's war memorial was unveiled, witnessed by a crowd of 15,000. Designed by Sir Walter Marsden, MC, the cost of £10,000 was met by Lord Ashton. The names of 170 men from St Anne's are inscribed on the Roll of Honour. Among them is the name of R. Greaves. In the Heyhouses school log book for 2 October 1915 there is an entry, 'Robert Greaves an old scholar of this school has been awarded the Military Medal'.

Social activities

In June 1880 the *Lytham Times* published a letter from 'A Lover of Change' who, amongst other observations, recalled the establishment of the first club in St Anne's:

> And next the Club. What a change here, when Ogden, Thomas, Hill, Farrar, Lomax, Moore, and one or two others, met in that brick hut, close to where the [St Anne's] Hotel stands, and decided to see what the directors [of the Land & Building Company] would do. But no, the directors would do nothing, and so the Club collapsed, but only for a time; Peter Moore was not asleep, and so, soon after, a [new] Club was formed ...[35]

The first public building in St Anne's was the St George's Assembly Rooms, located at the St George's Road entrance of St George's (Ashton) Gardens, and opened in about late 1879. In 1935 the *Lytham St Anne's Express* recorded that 'Fifty years ago the Institute (Assembly Rooms) served a dual purpose,

a concert and meeting hall during the week and Congregational services on Sundays. The early residents spent many pleasant hours at tea parties, concerts, lectures and prize distributions.'[36]

In 1888 Charles Tuke (of Maxwell & Tuke) invited several leading members of the community to a meeting where he outlined a scheme for the establishment of a young men's institute. The outcome of this meeting was that on 13 March 1890 W. H. Nutter, acting on behalf of the Land and Building Company, allowed the Assembly Rooms to be used as an institute. The St Anne's Institute, open to residents and visitors alike for a small fee, was both non-sectarian and non-political. A statement of accounts, sometime prior to 1893, reveals that expenditure in furnishing the building amounted to £132 18s. 1d., including a billiard table at a cost of £51 16s. 9d.

In 1915 the secretary of the Institute was given notice to terminate the tenancy of the building, and at the same meeting instructions were given to remove the building to within Ashton Gardens. In January 1916 it was resolved that the material from the original Institute be 'utilised as far as possible' in the construction of the 'Games Pavilion', later to be renamed the Ashton Institute.[37]

The various churches also provided a focus for social activities, including annual Sunday School and choir outings. In 1893 the choir of St Anne's parish church went by train to Chatsworth House, Derbyshire, departing at 5 a.m. and not returning until 11 p.m. Other organisations in the town also held annual events, and from the late 1890s, usually in May or June, school log books regularly had entries 'school closed for two days due to Tradesmen's Holiday'.

As we have seen, the cutting of the first sod for the main drainage was accompanied by a procession of schoolchildren and local organisations. A similar event was held to celebrate the 1897 diamond jubilee of Queen Victoria. The procession was headed by the police, firemen, and (unnamed) band. Following were the Sunday school children and children from the Ormerod Convalescent Home. After some speeches at the pier entrance the procession proceeded to the sports field in Glen Eldon Road. This event appears to have been the catalyst for the subsequent annual St Anne's Gala, held from 1898.

By the late 1890s social life in St Anne's was described in the following terms:

As a winter residence St Anne's ... is anything but a dull place. Social gatherings and concerts are numerous. In summer Concerts are given, besides the music supplied by the Pier Orchestra from the Bandstand, and by the St Annes Prize Band.[38]

However, the town still did not have a public venue for large-scale

THE GLEANERS

WHILE THE EARTH REMAINETH SEED TIME AND HARVEST SHALL NOT CEASE

An undated photograph taken at an early war memorial fete day parade.

entertainments, as opposed to the recreation and social events provided by the St Anne's Institute. With the intention of redressing this deficiency St Anne's Public Hall and Assembly Rooms were erected, by the St Anne's Public Hall Company, on the corner of Garden Street and St George's Road, and opened by Mr Fred Hilton, the managing director of the company, on 14 March 1900.

Built at a cost of approximately £11,000, to a design by John Dent Harker, the Public Hall had a seating capacity of 800. It was licensed for dramatic and musical 'representations', had excellent dressing rooms and scenery, and its stage measured 40 foot by 26 foot. It was here, beginning in 1901, that a series of winter lectures known as the St Anne's Lectures were held. These continued until 1910 and 'were able to attract to St Anne's ... some of the most notable men and women in the country's literary and scientific life'.[39]

However, due to competition from the Pier Pavilion, built four years later, the Public Hall failed to attract sufficient custom. In 1906 the Hall was taken over by Thomas Bannister and in 1910 renamed as the Public Hall Picturedrome. It was resold in 1921 when the St Anne's Palace Cinema and Cafe Company was formed. Nine years previously, in 1912, a second cinema, the Empire de Luxe Picturedrome, designed by Arnold England and built by John Heap and Sons, had also opened in St George's Road.

Thus by the early 1920s, through a combination of public, private and religious activities, St Anne's provided a wide range of entertainment facilities to resident and visitor alike.

Two photographs on 14 March 1900 showing the opening of the St Anne's Public Hall and Assembly Rooms, situated at the junction of Garden Street and St Georges Road. They were opened by Fred Hilton, the managing director of the company.

In 1906 the Public Hall was taken over by Thomas Bannister and renamed the Public Hall Picturedrome. It was resold in 1921 and in 1925 bought by the Blackpool Tower Company and became the Palace Cinema and Restaurant. It continued as a cinema until 1959 when it was sold to Lytham St Anne's Freemasons. The lower storey is now the St Anne's Market and St George's Emporium.

CHAPTER TWENTY-ONE

Religion in St Anne's

It will not be possible here to provide a detailed history of every church or religious community within St Anne's. Indeed, most have already published their own detailed histories, providing information not only about the building but also of the many individuals who have taken an active role in the life of their community. This chapter therefore focuses on the events leading to the establishment of each community, noting the role of any individuals whose contributions played a significant part in that establishment.

Church of England

PARISH CHURCH OF ST ANNE

As we saw in Chapter 11 the decision to build the new church of St Anne had been taken four years before the establishment of the new town, in 1871. Lady Eleanor Cecily Clifton provided the money for the building at her own cost, while the land, 2½ acres in extent, was donated by John Talbot Clifton. Although the land was owned by the Clifton family it was occupied by John Whiteside as the tenant farmer. In 1899 Thomas Fair recalled the events of 1871/72 that led to 'agreement' being reached between landowner and tenant:

St Anne's parish church shortly after it was built, c.1877. The laying of the foundation stone took place in June 1872, and the building was consecrated in August 1873. The architects were the famous Lancashire firm of Paley & Austin, to a design better known as the Queen Anne period. The building costs amounted to £4,229. The lych-gate originally opened onto Church Road (that is nearest to the Heyhouses community), but in c.1886 it was removed to face towards the new expanding town.
BY COURTESY OF THE VICAR AND CHURCHWARDENS OF ST ANNE'S PARISH CHURCH

It was then proposed to build a new church, the late Lady Eleanor Cecily Clifton undertaking to build the edifice. Partly at the speaker's (Thomas Fair) suggestion the site was fixed along the old highway to Blackpool, but very strong objection was taken to the selection by one old farmer, whose family were still on the property. Eventually the farmer and his friends were brought before the late Lady Cecily, and his statement was 'I suppose there will be a burial ground, and if we are buried there we shall be scrat up by the rabbits'. That was his strongest objection.[1]

The laying of the foundation stone by Lady Clifton took place at 6.30 p.m. on 4 June 1872. The trowel used was the same as that used for the laying of the foundation stone of St Cuthbert's, Lytham, in 1834. The principal guests included Rev. H. B. Hawkins, vicar of Lytham, Rev. R. Thistlethwaite, Rev. S. A. Thompson Yates and Thomas Fair. Following the formal speeches a supper in commemoration of the event then took place at the 'old' school where 'a party of eighty, consisting of the farmers of the neighbourhood and their wives sat down to a repast remarkable for the profusion, the rarity, and the excellence of the viands'.[2]

Over the next twelve months the church was constructed to a design by Messrs Paley & Austin of Lancaster, in the 'Geometrical Period of English Architecture' but better known as the Queen Anne period. The sole main contractor was Mr G. Smith, joiner, of Great Marton; the sub-contractors were James Cardwell – brickwork and excavation; Joseph Fielding – masonry; George Seed – slating; and James Walmsley – plumbing and glazing. The clerk of works was Mr Holmes. The building costs amounted to £4,229.

On Wednesday 6 August 1873 Dr Fraser, the Bishop of Manchester, dedicated the church to St Anne, and on the Saturday following a large party

The Heritage Mural, St Anne's parish church, is a celebration of the history of the community of St Anne's. Made to a design by Betty Mansfield and Helen Thornber it measures 18 ft × 6 ft 5 ins, and contains over two million stitches. It took from 1989 to 1996 to complete and involved 28 members of the congregation.

BY COURTESY OF THE VICAR AND CHURCHWARDENS OF ST ANNE'S PARISH CHURCH

of farmers and other residents of Heyhouses were entertained to dinner in the 'old' school. 'The invited guests consisted chiefly of those farmers who by "boon" [manorial] carting had assisted in conveying materials to the site of the new church'.[3] These materials were presumably the bricks supplied by the Clifton estate from their kiln on Marton Moss, when 'every able-bodied man [tenant] … put in one day, or two half days work with horse and cart'.[4] Among those attending the dinner there must have been mixed feelings knowing that there were major changes about to take place within their community.

Although St Anne's now had a church with 300 sittings, of which 150 were free, it served only as a chapel of ease to St Cuthbert's, Lytham. In September 1873 Rev. A. W. Booker was appointed to take charge of the district, to be succeeded by Rev. William Gregory Terry, who first officiated as curate in charge, on 6 May 1877. Two months later, on 26 July 1877, he became the first vicar of the newly constituted parish.

At the annual vestry meetings of the parish two churchwardens were appointed. During the late nineteenth century these meetings were usually reported in the local newspaper. In 1879 William Pomfret was appointed vicar's warden, and Robert Hargreaves appointed people's warden. It is probable however that both men had already been appointed to their respective offices two years earlier when the parish had been established.

It is interesting to compare the backgrounds of these two men representing as they did the 'new' St Anne's and the 'old' Heyhouses. William Pomfret was one of the earliest residents of St Anne's and had been born in Blackburn in 1820. He built 'the Willows' opposite the church, and came fourth in the elections for the first St Anne's Local Board in 1878. He served as churchwarden until 1881/82 and died in 1897.

Robert Hargreaves was born in Grindleton in 1840 and married the daughter

Following the addition of the tower in 1890 further additions and alterations, made at various stages during the late nineteenth and early twentieth centuries, transformed the parish church to the substantial building of today.

of the then vicar of that parish. He came to live in Heyhouses in 1878 when he became the tenant of Headroomgate Farm, then one of the largest farms on the Clifton estate. As we saw in Chapter 17 his public service extended from election to the first Local Board in 1878 until he retired from the successor Urban District Council in 1900. He served as churchwarden, first as people's warden and then as vicar's warden from 1877 to 1886.

During the 1880s church membership steadily increased and various improvements to the church were made. At the evening service on Easter Sunday 1880 the church was lit by gas for the first time. The *Lytham Times* reported that 'the church was very well attended. The choir sang their services very creditably, but it would be as well if the congregation were allowed to join in the singing of the psalms and canticles. The appearance of the choir also would be much improved if in surplices.'[5]

A harmonium provided the music until Lady Clifton gave a new organ in 1886. The opening service for the new organ, placed in the old vestry on the south, was held on Easter Tuesday 1886. At the same time the dedication of the enlargement of the church with the north aisle, north bay, and new vestry also took place. These additions cost just about half of the original cost of the church. This event was marked at the morning service by invited members of the various lodges of Freemasons in the district, being met at the lych-gate by the churchwardens and escorted to their seats in full masonic attire.

In 1890 the tower, to a design by R. K. Freeman was added at a cost of £1,261, money which had been raised by the parishioners. At the same time Lady Clifton paid for the bells, pealed for the first time on 5 January 1891. The removal of the original steeple in about 1898, and further additions and alterations made at various stages during the late nineteenth and first half of the twentieth centuries, completed the transformation from a church with plain nave and steeple to the substantial building of today. The original vicarage was built in 1881, and Thomas Muirhead was the architect for the Parish Rooms, the foundation stone of which was laid on 9 July 1910.

PARISH CHURCH OF ST THOMAS

By 1892 it was becoming obvious that, as a result of the impending development proposed by the Fairhaven Estate Company, there was a need for another church to serve the southern part of the town. Consequently a mission church, constructed of wood and corrugated iron, was erected on the site of the present St Anne's synagogue. The building, with accommodation for 340 people, was dedicated to St Thomas and opened on 8 October 1893. A curate in charge was appointed but served only one year; from then until 1898 the services were conducted by clergy from St Anne's parish church. At Easter 1898 Rev. C. H. Ellison was appointed curate in charge.

During the same year revised plans, by Austin & Paley, for a new church to

A photograph of St Thomas' Church taken sometime between 1900 and 1905. Originally a chapel of ease to the Parish Church the first stage of the building was consecrated in June 1900, and in 1902 the Rev C.H.Ellison was inducted as vicar of the new parish.

be built on land given by John Talbot Clifton were considered and decided on. A subscription list was opened headed by Mr R. S. Boddington (of Boddington's brewery) with a donation of £500, and on 12 April 1899 the foundation stone of the church was laid, by Mr O. L. Leigh Clare, MP.

The initial contract for £5,000 was for the erection of chancel, south chapel, organ chamber, vestries, two and a half bays of the nave and the north and south aisles, with a temporary porch.[6] The efforts to raise money were so successful, however, that four bays of the nave were subsequently built.

This first stage of the building was consecrated on 22 June 1900. The mission church then closed but was re-opened in 1902 by St Anne's parish church, and became known as St Mary's church. It finally closed in 1928. On 12 August 1902 the parish of St Thomas was formed and on 21 November the same year Rev. Charles H. Ellison was inducted as the vicar. The first churchwardens were Mr R. S. Boddington and Mr J. E. Pennington. In 1904 construction of the west end and the tower was begun and, in November 1905, dedicated by the bishop of Manchester, thus completing the church as it now stands.

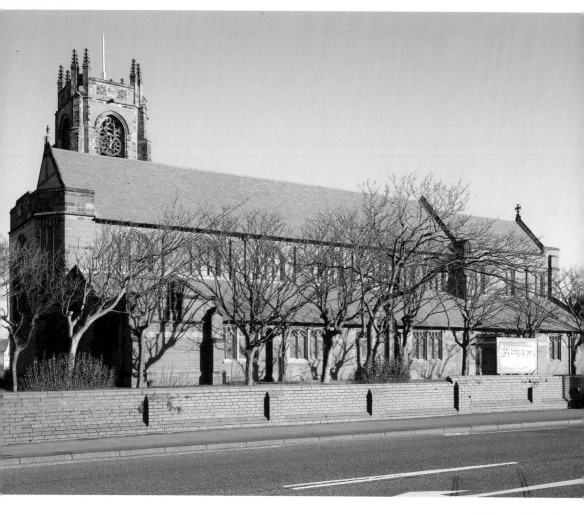

St Thomas' church, 2007. In 1904 construction of the tower commenced, followed by the dedication in 1905, thus completing the church as it now stands.

Parish church of St Margaret of Antioch

Just as expansion of the southern part of St Anne's had resulted in the erection of the church of St Thomas so the expansion, during the 1920s, of the northern part of the town resulted in the building of the church of St Margaret. The foundation of a semi-permanent church was laid on 20 December 1924 by the bishop of Whalley, and dedicated on 1 April 1925. It was built of wood and asbestos upon a brick foundation on land given by the Clifton estate. The architect was Ernest Hill of St Anne's, and the contractors were Messrs Ginger & Co. of Manchester.

On 13 August 1959 the foundation stone of the present church was laid, and on 10 February 1966 the building, to a design by Mr W. H. Ingham, was consecrated by the bishop of Blackburn. Five days earlier St Margaret's had been created a separate parish with the Rev. Peter Aspden as the first vicar.

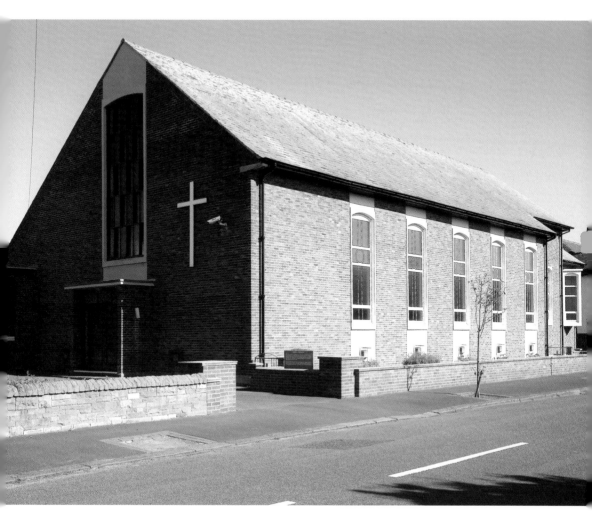

St Margaret's
church. Built
to serve the
expanding
northerly part of
the town, a semi-
permanent church
was dedicated in
1925. The present
building was
consecrated in
February 1966.

Roman Catholic Church

OUR LADY, STAR OF THE SEA

In the original plan for the creation St Anne's two acres of land had been
set aside by John Talbot Clifton for a Roman Catholic church, school, and
presbytery at the corner of Beach Road and North Promenade. However, it was
not until the late 1880s that Canon James Taylor, rector of St Peter's, Lytham,
decided that the increase in the population of St Anne's justified the erection
of a church in the town.

In 1887 Canon Taylor had attended the funeral of Flora, Duchess of Norfolk,
at Arundel and while there he appears to have received the support for a new
church from both the Duke of Norfolk and Lord Donington, the brother of the
late John Talbot Clifton and father of the late Duchess of Norfolk. The Duke of

Our Lady, Star of the Sea RC Church. In the original plan for St Anne's two acres of land had been set aside for a church at the corner of Beach Road and North Promenade. However Canon Taylor considered that the site had many disadvantages and negotiated a transfer for a site at the junction of St Anne's Road, East and St David's Road, South. The first stage of the building was opened in June 1890 and the building as seen today was completed in 1927.

Norfolk agreed to pay for the erection of the church, provided that the names of his late wife and John Talbot Clifton were suitably commemorated.

Canon Taylor therefore instructed Messrs Pugin & Pugin to prepare plans for a church. He considered, however, that the original site had many disadvantages to it. Consequently on 1 March 1888, by arrangement with the Clifton estate, the site of the present church was purchased from the Land and Building Company by Madeline Clifton, daughter in law of John Talbot Clifton, for £600 and 'demised' to the then bishop of the diocese at a peppercorn rent for 999 years.

The church was built in the Early English style of architecture and could seat 280, which was considered 'sufficient for the wants of the Catholics in the district at this time'.[7] The foundation stone was laid on 21 October 1888 and the solemn opening took place on 15 June 1890, in the presence of Dr O'Reilly the Roman Catholic bishop of Liverpool. There was a large congregation which included the Duke of Norfolk and 'many of the gentry resident in the neighbourhood'. The church was named Our Lady, Star of the Sea, in recognition of the fact that the late Duchess of Norfolk's steam yacht had sailed under the protection of Mary, Star of the Sea.

By June 1890 William Eaves, the contractor, was claiming he had spent £7,867 in building costs. At this first stage, however, the nave consisted of only four bays and a 'dull grey temporary wall' and a porch completing the west end of the building. Outside, a temporary bell tower and weather vane in the shape of the Duchess of Norfolk's steam yacht, were built. Rev. A. J. Bradley was appointed the first parish priest in April 1890, but, as we shall see, he resigned in September the same year to be succeeded by the Very Rev. Dr J. Lennon.

In 1911 it was decided to complete the church to the original design, but due to World War I, it was not until 16 October 1925 that the foundation stone was laid by Dr Pearson the Roman Catholic bishop of Lancaster, who also formally opened the completed extension on 3 June 1927. The alterations cost £9,500 and involved 'taking down the brick work at the west end of the church and widening the existing structure on either side of the nave which was then extended to the building line in St David's Road, South'.[8] Plans for a tower, however, were abandoned. The contractor was parishioner John Whiteside of St Anne's.

The actual consecration of the church took place on 30 September 1947 and from then until 1974 there were no major alterations to the church fabric. In 1974 liturgical changes necessitated a reorganisation of the sanctuary, but the exterior is the building as it was completed in 1927.

St Alban's

In 1962 there was a proposal to build a chapel of ease to the church of Our Lady, Star of the Sea. The project however was not followed through as the bishop decided to appoint a priest to be in charge of a new parish. The first Mass was celebrated by Rev. John McGough on 29 September 1963 in the Queensway Hotel, and on that first day 272 people were present.

St Alban's RC Church. In 1964 the former Cross Lane Farm was bought and converted into a small chapel. The new church was built on adjacent land and completed in April 1965. The cost was about £18,000.

In January 1964 the former Cross Lane Farm on Kilnhouse Lane was bought, and converted into a small chapel for about twenty people, where a daily Mass started on 2 March 1964. By this date plans had already been drawn up to build a permanent church/hall on the site and work began in the middle of 1964. The architect was Edward Livesey of Harry Walters and Livesey, the building contractor was Thomas Waldron, and the cost was about £18,000.

The new church was completed by April 1965. On 2 May 1965 the last Mass was said in the Queensway Hotel. The same evening, after the blessing of the new church the first Mass was celebrated by Dr Foley, bishop of Lancaster.[9]

Pine Cottage and St Anne's Meeting Room

The first meetings of the Baptist, Congregational, and Methodist churches in St Anne's were in the home of John Heap who, in 1875, had erected Pine Cottage, the first rented house in St Anne's, close to the present Hove Road and Springfield Road. His son, Wilson Heap, recalled in 1936 that:

> As St Anne's grew father was pleased to open his house for nonconformist residents going over the railway lines for worship. Maxwell and Tuke, who were responsible for the lay-out of our beautiful town together with their wives worshipped in that log cabin.[10]

In February 1876 a room above a stable in Back St Anne's Road, West (later owned by Whiteside's garages) was opened as a meeting room for the three communities. An account of the opening of this room is contained in the records of the Congregational church:

Heap family cottage. The first rated house in St Anne's, called Pine Cottage, was erected by John Heap in 1875, close to the present Hove Road and Springfield Road. In his first day at the 'old' Heyhouses School Wilson Heap, the son of John Heap, recalled that he and his brother Frank were 'something new' to the farmers sons and daughters.
COPYRIGHT UNKNOWN

In the month of February 1876, a meeting Room was opened at St Anne's on the Sea, for the use of Nonconformists generally, but managed by a Committee of Independents & Baptists, and supported by voluntary offerings. All sects of Nonconformists used the Room until about August 1877 when the Wesleyan Methodists, having erected a School Chapel on 'the Clifton Drive' separated themselves and became a distinct interest.[11]

The directors of the Land and Building Company each gave 10s. 0d. towards the cost of furnishing the room. On hot summer days the congregation were said to be subjected to 'the odours which permeated the apartment'. Following the separation of the Wesleyan Methodists, the Baptist and Congregational communities decided, in August 1877, to continue worship at the meeting room.

This arrangement, including the operations of a Sabbath School, continued until August 1880 when the Congregational community began to worship in the St George's Assembly Rooms. At this time the existing Baptist community 'not being strong enough to have a place of their own were then disbanded' and it was not until 1883 that they reformed and rented a meeting place of their own.[12]

Wesleyan Methodist Church

THE DRIVE

The first nonconformist community to build a permanent church in St Anne's were the Wesleyan Methodists. At a meeting held at Lytham on 3 November

The first non-conformist community to build a permanent church were the Drive Wesleyan Methodists. On 2 April 1877 the corner stone of a chapel was laid by John Warburton of the Land and Building Company. This original '(Sunday) School/chapel' still stands though it is now hidden by the later lecture hall. It is however one of the few surviving buildings in St Anne's designed by James Maxwell.

1876, it was decided that as a result of the donation by John Warburton, one of the directors of the Land and Building Company, of a plot of land on Clifton Drive, South, 'That in the opinion of this meeting the time has now arrived when the erection of a Sunday school chapel should be proceeded with'.[13] At the same meeting James Maxwell was appointed architect and on 3 February 1877 the building contract was given to Mr Roberts of Rawtenstall. On 2 April 1877 the cornerstone of the new building was laid by by John Warburton.

It would appear that the building was always intended as the first stage towards erecting a more substantial one. In reporting the laying of the foundation stone the *Lytham Times* noted that 'the new building will be a neat brick structure, with stone dressings, designed to become an adjunct to the intended handsome stone-built chapel in the Italian style of architecture'.[14] This theme was continued by the same newspaper when, on the occasion of the opening of the school chapel on 16 August 1877, it noted that the building would eventually 'be the school attached to a larger chapel hereafter to be built adjacent to it'.[15]

Drive Methodist Church. The foundation stone of the present church, on Clifton Drive, South was laid in August 1891. The architects were Walker and Collinson (see also photograph p. 260). At the time it was reported that W.H. Hincksman had given 'not far short of one-fourth of the total cost' of £4,400.

The foundation stone of the present church was laid on 29 August 1891 by Rev. C. H. Kelly, and the church opened on 13 October 1892. The architects were Messrs Walker and Collinson of Bradford and the cost of the building was £4,400. At the time W. H. Hincksman, the leading Methodist in Lytham, was reported to have given 'not far short of one-fourth the total cost of the building'.[16] The church was further enlarged in 1911 to provide accommodation for 750. The original school-chapel still stands though it is hidden by the later lecture hall.

CHURCH ROAD

The first attempts to establish the Methodist cause in the Church Road area were undertaken, not by the Wesleyan community, but by the United Methodist Free Churches. In November 1876 the *Lytham Times* reported that:

> On Sunday 19 November inst Ebenezer Chapel, situate in Church Road, St Anne's (in connection with the United Methodist Free Churches) was opened for divine service ... Collections were made in aid of the Chapel fund ... amounting to about £4 ... Mr Wilkinson, and other gentleman subscribed £10 10s. towards the funds of the chapel, and £10 was promised towards securing a piece of land in case a new chapel should require to be built.[17]

It is unclear from the wording of this report as to the location of the chapel. Nor is there is any known description of the building. It is, however, possible that it was the building known as the 'Band Room' which was closed by the United Methodist Free Churches following the depression in the building trade of the late 1870s.

Sometime prior to 1881 a small number of Wesleyan Methodists began holding meetings in the Church Road area. In 1905 John Roberts recalled the events of those early days 'from the cottage where Mr Boswell had his shop [in Church Road], then kept by Mr [James] Jackson as the Rochdale Children's Home, to the bakehouse down the side street near the church; then to the room above, and [then] the new Mission Room'.[18]

It would seem that prior to building the new Mission Church a room, probably the former 'Band Room' of the United Methodist Free Churches, was acquired. In 1886 the *Blackpool Times* reported that 'The Wesleyans at St Annes are just now extending their borders, they having opened a mission-room in Church Road'.[19]

On Saturday 21 July 1888 the foundation stones of a new Wesleyan Methodist Mission Hall were laid. The *Lytham Times* noted that 'it seems that a good deal of the work in connection with the new building is being done by members whose hands and sinews are their capital'.[20] Before the end of August the

Church Road Methodist Chapel. The first attempts to establish the Methodist cause in the Church Road area was undertaken by the United Free Methodist Churches. Sometime prior to 1881 a small number of Wesleyan Methodists began to meet locally and in 1888 erection of a Mission Hall was begun. This building now forms part of the Church Road Centre.

Church Road Methodist Church. Foundation stones of the present church were laid in 1904. Built to a design by H & W Wade, of St Anne's and Blackpool, the church was opened on 8 June 1905 by John Roberts who said that 'he was pleased to be there as a working man to represent the labour party of that church, the working men and women of that congregation'.

building was roofed and the opening ceremony, performed by Rev. Charles Garrett of the Liverpool Mission, took place on 3 October 1888. After the ceremony and first service 'a large number of the congregation assembled at the old Mission Hall, and partook of tea ...'[21]

By 1902 'the question of the urgent need for increased Church accommodation in this neighbourhood' was considered at a meeting of the trustees.[22] On 26 November the same year the trustees agreed to accept an offer from the firm of Messrs Maxwell & Tuke for a proposed site of the new church. Tenders for designing the church were invited from fifteen firms, the plans of Messrs H. & W. Wade of St Anne's and Blackpool being accepted. The style adopted was late Gothic, with an octagonal tower seventy-five feet high. The contractors were Messrs S. Butterworth & Sons of Blackpool and the cost £5,500.

Foundation stones were laid on 16 April 1904, including one by Mrs Jackson the widow of James Jackson. The church was formally opened on 8 June 1905 by John Roberts, who said 'he was pleased to be there as a working man to represent the labour party of that church, the working men and women of that congregation ...'[23] The story of the church during the twentieth century is one of active involvement in the local community and in 1957 a new Sunday School extension was opened, followed in 1975 by the day care unit of the new Church Road Centre.

Congregational (United Reformed) Church

The Congregational Church opened a mission room on 9 September 1880, in the St George's Assembly Rooms which, as we have seen, stood at the St George's Road entrance to St George's Gardens (Ashton Gardens). Rev. James Wayman conducted the opening service, and 'close upon 100 persons were present.[24]

In 1886 William Porritt built St George's Hall. The following year he executed a deed vesting the hall in the trustees of the Congregational Church, in effect letting the hall to the church members at a nominal rent. The hall was purchased by the church in 1913.

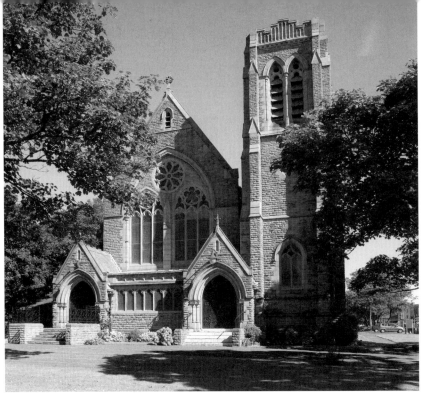

United Reformed Church (formerly Congregational Church). William Porritt laid the foundation stone of the present church in May 1894. The architects were Walker and Collinson (see also the photograph on page 256, and their original design included a spire. The completed church opened for worship on 19 March 1896.

In February 1883, on the suggestion of William Porritt, a leading member of the church, members decided on the provision of a new chapel. William Porritt offered £500 in money and land, provided that the chapel was built of stone.[25] This proposal was not pursued, however, and services continued at the Assembly Rooms, until William Porritt himself built the present St George's Hall in 1886.

On 5 September 1886 the Congregationalists held their first service in the new hall, the Rev. James Wayman conducting the morning service.[26] At a meeting of the church trustees held on 29 September 1887 the Rev. Wayman explained that William Porritt had executed a deed, vesting the hall in the trustees and 'that the intended effect of such deed was not to alter the present occupancy of the building by the Church, on Sundays and Thursday evenings, but that they should be considered tenants of the trustees instead of Mr Porritt'.[27] In reality William Porritt was letting the hall to the Congregational Church at a nominal rent.

In January 1892 a subscription list was opened 'for the augmentation of the new Chapel Building fund', and exactly a year later the church trustees recommended that 'the time had come when steps should be taken to secure a New Church'.[28] By this date £1,100 was already in hand and it was suggested that, in due course, about £4,500 be expended on a new church. It was also decided to request William Porritt to 'transfer the site for the new Church from the plot of land adjoining St George's Gardens to a plot fronting to the Drive and St George's Road'.[29]

In February 1893 Messrs Walker & Collinson of Bradford, who had been the architects for The Drive Methodist church, were appointed as architects for the new church, and in April that year William Porritt offered an interest-free loan of £2,000. In September 1893 the architects were requested to reconsider their plans, in as much as the tenders were in excess of the amount contemplated. This was done to the satisfaction of the trustees and in February 1894 the tender for the stonework, except the spire, was given to Messrs T. J. Foster of Ramsbottom at £3,780.

William Porritt laid the foundation stone on Whit Monday, 14 May 1894, and the present church was opened for worship on 19 March 1896 at a service conducted by Rev. W. Elstub. Even though lack of funds meant that the spire was never built, the final cost amounted to £7,575. In September 1906 Oliver Porritt 'wrote off' £500 of the loan given by his grandfather in 1893 and the outstanding £1,500 was paid off in September 1908.

In 1913 St George's Hall was purchased from the Porritt family for £600. In February 1914 there was a scheme for the extension of the hall. Prepared by local architect Walter Wade the plans included a second storey comprising four class rooms.[30] Presumably due to the outbreak of World War I these plans were never implemented.

In 1972, following the union of the Congregational Church of England and Wales with the Presbyterian Church of England and Wales, the church became known as the United Reformed Church.

Baptist church

As we have seen earlier the Baptist community had disbanded in 1880, and although some members had moved to other churches others continued to

Baptist chapel. From March 1884 until late 1886 Baptist services were held in a room over a shop on West Crescent. The foundation stone of the first Baptist chapel was laid on 18 September 1886. The chapel, in St Andrew's Road, South, was built by John Heap in just thirteen weeks at a cost of about £800, and was opened on Christmas Day 1886. The building is now Sanders of St Anne's.

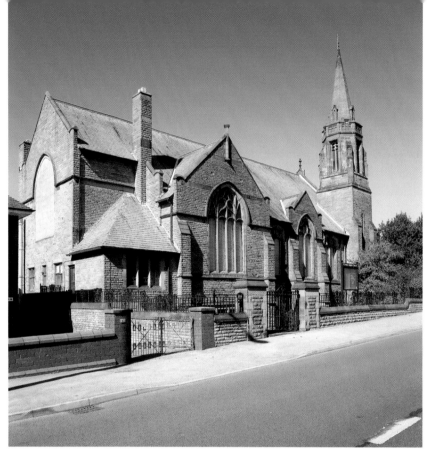

During the 1890s a scheme was adopted for the erection of the present Baptist church at the junction of St Andrew's Road, South and St Thomas' Road. The opening ceremony on 23 April 1910 took place 'in a severe gale of wind and fierce sandstorm'.

hold meetings in various homes within the town. In November 1883, at the home of John Heap, Rev. Samuel Pilling of Blackpool introduced Rev. Edwin Brown to members of the church. On 10 December a meeting was held at the home of William Walker when it was decided to take, 'at half a crown a week', a room over a shop on West Crescent, known as the Assembly Room, belonging to James Lord.[31]

The first service, presided over by Alderman Hargreaves of Bacup, took place on Sunday 6 January 1884. The room, however, was 'so inconveniently situated – being the top room of a building three stories high – that many people have been deterred from attending worship on account of the number of steps …'[32] And it was up these steps that every Saturday night that 'Mr H. W. Heap carried the harmonium on his back, … played the instrument, and carried it home at six o'clock on Monday morning'.[33]

The church proper was formed on 31 March 1884 by Rev. Charles Williams. Rev. Edwin Brown was formally appointed pastor, and John Heap and Joseph White appointed as deacons. Early on the morning of Friday 4 July 1884, in what was described as 'a very interesting ceremony', Rev. Brown baptised five church members in the sea beside St Anne's pier.[34]

By late 1885 a plot of land in St Andrew's Road, South (now Sanders of St Anne's) had been purchased for the purpose of building a permanent chapel. The foundation stones were laid on 18 September 1886, the first one by Mrs Porritt, the wife of William Porritt, and the second by Alderman Hargreaves of Bacup. The chapel was built by John Heap in just thirteen weeks at a cost of about £800, and opened on Christmas Day 1886.

Rev. Brown resigned in 1894 and was succeeded by Rev. J. W. Varley, during whose pastorate a scheme was adopted for the erection of a new church. Richard Whitaker, then chairman of the Land and Building Company, offered the present site at the junction of St Andrew's Road South and St Thomas' Road, promising to buy out the ground rent on condition that £3,000 was raised before any building commenced. These conditions had been fulfilled by the end of 1908 and on 24 July 1909 foundation stones were laid by no fewer than fourteen individuals.

The architect for the new church was C. W. Matley of the firm Messrs Smith & Matley of Manchester, and the contractors were Messrs Joseph Fielding & Company. The style of architecture was late Gothic and the building costs were about £6,000. The opening ceremony, performed by Mrs Walker the widow of William Walker, took place 'in a severe gale of wind and fierce sandstorm' on 23 April 1910.[35]

Particular and Strict Baptists

Sometime during the late 1880s and early 1890s there appears to have been two Baptist communities in the town. In addition to marking the site of the chapel in St Andrew's Road, South, the Ordnance Survey map of 1893 also notes a Particular Baptist Ebenezer chapel near the junction of St Patrick's Road, South, and St Anne's Road, East. In 1932 this was recalled as being 'a Baptist "tin-tab" chapel'.[36] Due to an absence of any known documentary evidence it is unclear when the community was first established or for how long it existed. However in about 1890 the Particular and Strict Baptists began to meet at Ansdell. The meeting place was almost certainly Common Side Farm, the home of Robert and Alice Rossall (James Fairclough, the father of Alice Rossall, was responsible, to some degree, for establishing the Strict Baptist Church in Blackpool). In 1898 a chapel was erected in Pollux Gate, Fairhaven and opened by Hugh Gruber of Manchester who preached at the opening services. The chapel closed in 1956.[37]

Primitive Methodist Church

It was at the Primitive Methodist Conference held in 1907, at Liverpool, that the decision was taken to form a society in St Anne's. The conference was reminded by one of its leading ministers that, 'if you intend to build in St Anne's it's no use thinking in terms of a Tin Tabernacle; St Anne's is a very beautiful place with beautiful churches and Primitive Methodism must have a beautiful Church also.'[38]

The same conference appointed Rev. George Bicheno as the minister to be responsible for establishing the Primitive Methodist cause in St Anne's, and on Sunday 26 July 1908, at 7 a.m., he commenced his work by holding a prayer meeting in the Public Hall. Two further services were held in the morning and afternoon, and by the end of the day nine people had expressed their intention to join the new church.

In September 1908 an upper room was taken in the Assembly Rooms within the Century Building at 4 Garden Street (6 and 8 Garden Street were already occupied by J. R. Taylor). This room was renamed the Primitive Methodist Church Hall and was formally opened by Mrs Barkby, daughter of Sir William Hartley, General Missionary Secretary of Conference, on 17 September 1908.

By March 1909 agreement had been reached with the Land and Building Company for the site of a new church, at the corner of Links Road and Clifton Drive, South. The proposed site however brought immediate objections from the Clifton estate, and James S. Fair (who had by this time succeeded his father as land agent to the Cliftons) wrote to William Nutter of the Land and Building Company in the following terms:

> I noticed some little time ago that a Board has been erected on the land at the corner of Links Road fronting to Clifton Drive, intimating that a Primitive Methodist Church is to be built there and it occurred to me that the locality is not at all suitable for another place of worship owing to the close proximity of St Thomas' Church ...[39]

James Fair continued by asking the Land and Building Company to arrange for another site. He added that, in justice to Rev. Ellison (vicar of St Thomas'), objections to another church being built on the proposed site were 'no way due to any unfriendly feeling to the Primitive Methodists', but were based entirely upon the the annoyance which he (Rev. Ellison) believed would arise to persons worshipping at churches so closely adjoining. The outcome of a protracted correspondence was that a plot was reserved at the corner of Kings Road and Clifton Drive, South, providing it was on equal conditions.

In July 1909 it was reported that the room in the Assembly Rooms had become too small for the growing congregation and that the last five Sunday evening services had been held, by the generosity of the Congregational Church, in St George's Hall.[40] A month earlier arrangements had been concluded between the St Anne's Liberal Club (the prospective purchasers) and the Baptist Church trustees for the Primitive Methodists to take over, for

Primitive Methodist church. It was at the Primitive Methodist Conference of 1907 that the decision was taken to form a society at St Anne's. Conference however was reminded that 'if you intend to build in St Anne's its no use thinking in terms of a Tin Tabernacle'. The stone-laying ceremony of the church took place in August 1910, and a year later the completed building, in Kings Road, was opened by Sir William Hartley (of Hartley's Jam, Colne). The church closed in December 1968 and the site is now occupied by Clifton Lodge luxury flats.

BY COURTESY OF
ROBERT HALEY

the following twelve months, the chapel, in St Andrew's Road, South, about to be vacated by the Baptists.

By this time, however, the design for a new church had been put out to competition and in March 1910 that of Messrs T. E. Davidson of Newcastle was chosen, the estimated cost being about £5000 of which Sir William Hartley promised £600. The stone-laying ceremony took place on 1 August 1910. No fewer than fifty-four stones were laid, the first by Miss Hartley, another daughter of Sir William Hartley. Sir William himself opened the new church on 7 August 1911.

In 1932, as a result of the Uniting Methodist Conference of that year, the Drive Wesleyan Methodist church and the Kings Road Primitive Methodist church were brought together. However, it was not until 1967, when the Primitive Methodist church faced potential repair costs of £2,000, that amalgamation of the two churches was discussed. The outcome was the closure of the Primitive Methodist church and the last service was conducted there on 29 December 1968. The site is now occupied by a block of flats.

Ansdell Unitarian church

The first meeting of Unitarians from St Anne's, Ansdell and Lytham was held, largely through the efforts of Mr C. C. (later Sir Cuthbert) Grundy, in a private house, at 3 Pollux Gate, Lake Road, Fairhaven, in February 1905. After about

six months a decision was taken to build a temporary church, with the intention of erecting a permanent church within five years. The £400 necessary for the erection of the temporary church, at the junction of Kingsway and Channing Road, was quickly raised and the church opened, practically free of debt, on 14 April 1906. A description of the building appeared in the *Lytham Times*:

> The Church is of corrugated iron lined with pitch pine, and has been erected by the Portable Building Co. Manchester, from plans drawn by the hon, architect, Mr S. Thomas. The church is 50ft. long and 25ft. wide, … the walls are stained green, the rest being varnished. The rostrum is at the south end, and at the foot there is a piano and American organ. Though there are only a hundred chairs at present, there is room for two hundred.[41]

Although Rev. Richard J. Hall was appointed as the first resident pastor in July 1908 it was to be another twenty-two years before the temporary church was replaced by the present building. The architect for the new church was Samuel Thomas (presumably the same man who had drawn the plans for the original church), and the opening, by Sir Cuthbert Grundy, took place on 19 July 1930. Built of Ravenhead rustic brick, with stone facings and slated roof, the church measured 68 feet by 27 feet, with a tower 35 feet high. The building costs amounted to £3,500. Centenary celebrations took place in 2006.

St Anne's Hebrew Congregation

A Jewish community had existed in Manchester from the early eighteenth century and was of European significance in the late nineteenth/early twentieth centuries. With the migration to Manchester in the 1910s, of very poor

Jewish migrants from eastern Europe, St Anne's became a classic location for the older, more settled Jewish mercantile families. The establishment of the Jewish community in St Anne's commenced in the early years of the twentieth century.[42] One of the earliest members was Joseph Hamwee who, in about 1920, began to hold summer services in his home, 'Winsleigh', 5 Clifton Drive, North (now the Manhattan Hotel).[43] These meetings eventually became the nucleus of the St Anne's Hebrew Congregation. Although a permanent congregation was not formed until about 1927, partly because many members continued to reside in Manchester for business reasons, each August saw a packed room with visitors from both Manchester and Leeds.

The first synagogue in St Anne's, obtained through the efforts of Mr S. Abouhab, was in the Union Bank Chambers, Park Road. The honorary secretary was Gerald Bright (better known as Geraldo the band leader). The next location was at 14 Orchard Road. During 1940 there was an influx of the Jewish community into St Anne's, principally from Manchester, and as a result it was decided to open a permanent synagogue as soon as possible. The former St Mary's Mission Church in Orchard Road was purchased, and within six weeks had been made suitable for worship. The consecration, on 22 September 1940, was conducted by Rabbi Dr S. M. Lehmann of Liverpool, Rev. D. Garb of Blackpool, and the Revs S. Evans and A. C. Jaffe of St Anne's.[44] During the next twenty years the congregation became firmly established in the town. On 13 September 1959 the foundation stone of the present synagogue was laid by Philip Lewis, chairman of the building committee and past president of the congregation.[45]

The new synagogue, built at a cost of £50,000 on a site adjacent to the original synagogue, was opened on 21 June 1964 by Philip Lewis and Harry Satinoff and consecrated by Dr Israel Brodie, the Chief Rabbi for Great Britain and the Commonwealth.[46]

St Anne's synagogue. The establishment of the Jewish community in St Anne's commenced in the early part of the last century. The first services were held in the home of Joseph Hamwee on Clifton Drive, North, now the Manhattan Hotel. The present synagogue, in Orchard Road, was opened in June 1964, and consecrated by Dr Israel Brodie, the Chief Rabbi for Great Britain and the Commonwealth. The architect was A. Maxwell-Caplin.

CHAPTER TWENTY-TWO

Education in St Anne's

The history of education in St Anne's could form the subject of a book in itself. In order to provide an overview, this chapter focuses on the establishment and progress of just some of the institutions which have provided education to many thousands of St Anne's children since 1875.

Heyhouses Endowed School (Church of England)

In 1876 the only non-private school for the children of the new town of St Anne's, and the farming community of Heyhouses, was 'old' Heyhouses School. In November that year the question of a school for the children of the new residents was raised in a letter to the *Lytham Times*. It was signed 'A Father' and read:

> Dear Sir, – I want to draw attention to the want of School Accommodation for St Anne's. We all know it is a new place; but there are now over 90 houses at present occupied, and the children from these houses are compelled to walk a mile or stay at home and nurse one another; thereby losing all chances of Education. What are the Board of Guardians for the Fylde District doing in this matter? It rests with them till such times as there are School Boards elected, which I presume will not be yet awhile. Hoping that some pen more able than mine may be take this question up ...[1]

The following week a correspondent calling himself 'G' endorsed these comments, asking 'What is there to prevent the school-house being removed from the place where it is comparatively only little required to the district where the want of means of education at moderate cost is now so urgently felt?' 'G' concluded his letter by trusting that the vicar of St Anne's (Rev. Terry) would 'take some steps to remedy the present educational deficiency'.[2]

Reacting to such public comments (and no doubt aware that since the Education Act of 1870 elementary schooling had been compulsory; that the provision of schools was no longer optional; and that the possibility of central government imposing a school board to promote facilities was a real one) Thomas Fair, at a meeting of the Lytham Charities trustees on 9 April 1877, brought forward 'the desirableness of removing the Heyhouses School to St Anne's'. The trustees indicated their willingness to proceed with the matter 'so soon as a feasible scheme is proposed'. A year later, on 25 April 1878, the trustees resolved that they would be willing 'to entertain the subject if new Schools were erected at St Anne's free of cost to the Trustees'.

Another year was to pass before, on 6 May 1879, the committee appointed by the trustees met at the St Anne's Hotel and resolved 'that in the event of new Schools being built at St Anne's in all respects satisfactory to the Trustees, and handed over to them free of expense the Committee will recommend the Trustees to accept such Schools and take the management thereof'.[3]

By June 1879 plans prepared by Messrs Maxwell and Tuke had been approved subject to the approval of their own architect. The following month they submitted four plans to Messrs Longworth and Gardner of Preston and resolved to carry out the chosen plan themselves 'in consideration of receiving a contribution of not less than £1,000 from the St Anne's New School Committee'.[4]

By December 1879 this amount had been raised by means of £500 by subscription, including two donations of £50 and £70 from Lady Clifton, and £500 given by John Talbot Clifton who also gave the land which was valued at £800.[5] The foundation stone of the new school (now part of Heyhouses Infants' School) was laid by Lady Clifton on 4 December 1879. The school was described as comprising a mixed department for 65 boys and 65 girls, and an infant department for 70 children. There was a porch and cloak rooms, with extensive playgrounds and offices (toilets). The schoolrooms had open roofs and were warmed by open fireplaces, having stone chimney-pieces.[6]

The contractors were Richard Warbrick for brickwork; Richard Hacking for masonry; Thomas Walker for slating, flagging and plastering; J. F. Lomax for plumbing, glazing, painting and gas fitting; Rawstron and Fielding for carpentry and joinery; and Robert Greaves for forming the grounds. By April 1881 the total costs amounted to £1,327 5s. 9d., an amount which included £10 3s. 1d. for grates and fire guards, £4 6s. 6d. for flagstaff and flag, and £5 6s. 0d. for the silver trowel used by Lady Clifton when laying the foundation stone.[7]

The first day at the new school was Thursday 26 August 1880, a fact noted by Mr Banister in the log book:

> Today is our first day at new school. The desks are more suitably arranged than the old school allowed. The 1st standard is brought into my room, as the infants will now in all probability become pretty numerous. I have taken charge of them ... Rev. Terry called this morning. This afternoon Lady Clifton again called with Mrs Terry and gave presents to the children in memory of the opening of new schools.[8]

Heyhouses (Infants') School. The design for the original school (now part of the infants' school) was by Maxwell and Tuke. The foundation stone was laid, by Lady Clifton, on 4 December 1879. The contractors for various stages of the work included Richard Warbrick, Richard Hacking, and Robert Greaves. The school opened on 26 August 1880.

As predicted by Mr Banister, there was a significant increase in the number of pupils attending, and by December there were 138 pupils on the register. This fact was also noted by the inspector in the government report of March 1881:

> The school has been supplied with excellent new buildings, which are well fitted and supplied with apparatus. Attendance is increasing ... I recommend the employment of an Assistant Teacher in the principal room. Discipline is good ...

Discipline was, indeed, a feature of Mr Banister's headship. In October 1881 he required pupils who 'are wrong with their sums' to stay behind after school had been dismissed only allowing them to go home 'when they are right'. It was not only the pupils who often received short shrift if Mr Banister thought it necessary. In January 1882 he noted in the log book that 'A gentleman – a ventriloquist – came at noon today to solicit entertainment this afternoon. I gave him no encouragement.' However if considered beneficial to the pupils, visitors were welcomed. In October 1882 Mr Banister recorded that 'This morning a blind man visited the school, and I allowed the children to witness his reading from a book, and calculation of sums of the various standards. The children gave him their half-pence.'

In spite of his attempts to ensure that all pupils made regular attendance the social and economic forces which so dominated habits at the old school, continued. On 28 April 1882 Mr Banister noted that 'attendance is somewhat less owing to many children being engaged in the fields, and other in home duties'. On 14 July the same year attendance was again 'very faulty' and although Mr Banister gave Mr Fletcher, the attendance officer, the registers, he was clearly not optimistic of the outcome commenting that 'as to the good he does is not worth the time spent on writing out a list'.

By 1885 a total of 198 pupils – 61 boys, 48 girls and 89 infants – were on the school register. In 1889 the government report considered discipline and tone in the mixed school was 'highly satisfactory' and the infant school 'as a whole exceedingly satisfactory'. Mr Banister, however, was not satisfied: in the school log for 5 September 1889 he recorded, 'The absence of children is proving a great obstacle to progress. There are children absent several times in the week, who have no right to be absent once, and yet there seems no preventing it. I am trying what the effect of caning will have upon it.'

Possibly in frustration at what he saw as lack of progress, Mr Banister resigned as headmaster on 12 September 1890. A week later he was succeeded by George Sanderson, a former pupil of Heyhouses School who had been appointed a pupil teacher at the 'old' school in August 1876 before leaving in December 1880 to enter training college. At the time of his appointment to Heyhouses his annual salary of £100 was supplemented by half of the 'school pence', ten per cent of the government grant, and £10 a year towards the rent of a house.[9]

Until the passing of the Elementary Education Act of 1891, school pence formed a substantial contribution towards the running costs of endowed free schools. In 1885 income at Heyhouses had comprised £59 19s. od. in school pence and £130 9s. 6d. received from government grants. Under the Act a fee grant was made to schools which enabled the Heyhouses school managers, in August of that year, to abolish the school pence. At the suggestion of the vicar, all children were encouraged to deposit the 2d. previously paid every week in school pence into the Penny Bank.[10]

By this date the population of St Anne's had increased to 2,588, and although the great majority of pupils lived in the fast developing town there are suggestions that a division remained between them and the older community of Heyhouses. The school log for 17 October 1890 had noted that due to wet and stormy weather 'the country children' had not attended very well. On 27 January 1891 Mr Sanderson on leaving school 'found a quarrel was going on in the roadway between boys of Church Road and [Heyhouses] West End and that stone throwing was being indulged in'. The following morning he punished 'three of the ringleaders'.

Until the opening of the Roman Catholic primary school in 1896 Heyhouses Endowed was the only free primary school in the town. It is not surprising therefore that the government report for 1893 considered that 'the accommodation afforded by the School is far from adequate for the needs of the district'. In response the school managers agreed to a considerable enlargement, and by late 1894 extensions had been completed at a cost of £1,303 4s. 3d.[11] That such extensions were required can be seen from the fact that by January 1896 133 boys, and 112 girls were on the mixed school register, and 121 infants on the infant school register. Teaching staff had also increased, and in 1899 the mixed school was served by George Sanderson and two assistant masters, while at the infants' school Miss Annie Tebay had three assistant teachers and one pupil teacher.

Contrary to the image of St Anne's being a prosperous new town, entries in the school log book suggest that daily life for some children was far from comfortable. An entry for 15 February 1895 records that 'Two ladies called on Monday to inform me that a Soup Kitchen would be opened on that day – and desired me to acquaint the poorest children. An increasing number of scholars attend the Kitchen at noon each day.'

Ill-health also continued to affect attendance, with regular outbreaks of measles, whooping cough, and smallpox, which on occasions resulted in the school being closed for up to a month. More personal cases included an 'apparently neglected' female pupil who, in December 1896, was sent home because her head 'was so filthy [with] vermin and sores'.

By the beginning of the twentieth century, however, the children enjoyed longer holidays than had their parents and were also given a holiday on special occasions such as the coronation of Edward VII in 1902, or the visit of

'Baby' Class – Heyhouses School 1912. Annie Tebay was headmistress of the Infants Department at Heyhouses School from 1878 to 1920. For most of that period she was assisted by her sister Isabella Tebay who is pictured here with the 'Baby' Class. Second left on the back row is Harry Youles who, in 1960, was the publisher (Weaver & Youles) of a previous history of the town – *Sand Grown* by Kathleen Eyre.
COURTESY OF PETER YOULES

Field-Marshal Lord Roberts to St Anne's in July 1903. Attendance continued to increase and in June 1905 the Board of Education ordered that average attendance, at the mixed school, must be reduced to 273, and that grants only on this number would be paid.

It must therefore have been of some relief to George Sanderson and his teaching staff when, in July the same year, St Thomas' Church of England school was opened. However it was not until a public enquiry, held in 1908, into the educational needs of St Anne's, that the problem began to be resolved. One outcome of this was the opening of the new girls' department in May 1909 at a cost of £1,650.

During the Great War school hours were adjusted to comply with the lighting restriction order. In October 1916 several boys were absent gathering the potato crop, whilst in October the following year the demand for labour was so great 'that boys are leaving at the earliest possible time'. Also in 1917 a war savings committee was formed. It was not possible to celebrate Armistice Day in 1918 because the school was closed from the 4th to 29th of November on the orders of the Medical Officer of Health.

The school log of 16 June 1919 notes the achievement of Captain John Alcock, a pupil from 1900 to 1905, who together with Lieutenant Arthur Whitten-Brown, made the first non-stop aerial crossing of the Atlantic. They took off from near St John's, Newfoundland, on 14 June 1919, and landed the following day at Clifden, Ireland. The time for the crossing was 16 hours, 27 minutes. Both men were knighted by George V for their pioneering achievement. Sir John Alcock was tragically killed in a flying accident in Normandy in December 1919, aged just twenty-seven. On 13 June 2003 a plaque commemorating the crossing was unveiled at Heyhouses Infants School.

George Sanderson had resigned as headmaster on 31 August 1919 and was succeeded by James Hardman, who remained until his death in 1929. Samuel Hazeldine was headmaster from 1930 until 1932, when he in turn was succeeded by Thomas Chadwick, who remained at Heyhouses until 1945.

During the inter-war years entries in the school log book become much less detailed. It is clear, however, that in addition to maintaining the required educational standards there were also regular social and sporting activities. In 1931 the former boys' and girls' departments were merged to become a mixed department. During World War II events included an Army Display, an Air Force Display, a Warship Week, an Aid to Russia Week and an Aid to China Week.

F. S. Owen was headmaster from 1946 until 1948, and F. Gander from 1949 to 1952. It was under the headship of J. Noel Jones, from 1953 to 1975, however, that the most major changes for almost a hundred years were to take place. The HM inspectors' report for April 1955 noted that during the previous eight years the number of pupils at the junior school aged between seven and fourteen,

had increased by 100 to 342. Although some of the accommodation problems were to be eased in September 1955, by transferring pupils aged eleven to the present Lytham St Anne's High School, the need for a new junior school was pressing.

In May 1957 the Ministry of Education approved £10,000 for the first phase of a new junior school to be built on Clarendon Road, North. The architects were Messrs Lamb and Walton, and the tender to carry out the building work was won by Messrs Gregson of Marton. The foundation stone was laid on 18 June 1958 and the first pupils occupied the premises on 12 November the same year. The second phase was occupied by staff and pupils on 12 September 1961, and the third phase opened on 17 May 1965 when the original 'new' school then became the infants' school. Noel Jones retired in 1975 and was succeeded by Malcolm Ardern until 1993 when the present headteacher, Clive E. Barnes, was appointed.

In 2005 the *Lytham St Anne's Express* reported that 460 children were being taught on two sites – 200 infants in seven classes at the 'new' school of 1880, and 260 juniors in eight classes at the 1960s buildings on Clarendon Road, North.[12]

St Thomas Church of England school

Although the datestone on the original building is 1902, it was not until 17 July 1905 that St Thomas' school was opened. The school was divided into two portions by a sliding screen, one half being used for the older pupils and the other for the infants. Fifteen pupils were admitted on the first morning, followed by a further eight in the afternoon.[13]

The first headmistress appointed was Miss Ebba Karstens. By April 1906 the number on the school roll had reached 100, although this number was much reduced in 1910 when 'a great many' went to the newly opened St Anne's council school. By 1913, however, numbers had recovered and extensions were required to the school buildings. The location of the school adjacent to the railway line must have presented its own problems, and in July 1919 several boys found crossing the railway lines 'were punished accordingly'. In 1917 Miss Karstens resigned, and from then until the present time there have been eight other headteachers. During this period the school has continued to expand and in 1956 a new extension was opened by the bishop of Blackburn followed, in 1968, with the opening of the new infants' school.

Our Lady, Star of the Sea (Roman Catholic)

The first attempt to provide a school for the children of Roman Catholic families was made by Rev. A. J. Bradley, who had been appointed the first parish priest of the newly opened church in April 1890. His intention was to purchase an 'Iron Room' and erect it, with 'petties' (toilets) alongside, on the site of the present church car park. However, both the bishop of the diocese and Canon Taylor, who wrote 'It will disfigure the House and the Church which has cost me thousands', were opposed to the idea. The Rev. Bradley was ordered to demolish buildings then erected, but rather than do so he resigned in September 1890.[14]

On an episcopal visit in 1892 it was pointed out that the Church of Our Lady, Star of the Sea, was the only Catholic church on the Fylde coast without a school. Therefore Dr Lennon, who had succeeded Rev. Bradley, began to seek financial assistance. His efforts were successful when in August 1894 Charles Gillow (of Messrs Waring & Gillow), and his brother the Rev. George Gillow provided most of the money for a new school. Canon Taylor also contributed a further £500. John Whiteside was contracted to build the school in St Alban's Road (now Ormerod Home Trust) for £1,120.

By August 1896 Miss Jane Roberts had been appointed headmistress, and the school, which appears to have been divided into a mixed school and an infants' school, opened on 14 September the same year. In March 1897 the report of the government inspector noted that 'The Mistress seems to have made a very satisfactory start with this School.' In September the same year, however, Jane Roberts resigned and between then and 1902 no fewer than four other headmistresses served at the school.

Apart from the addition of certain religious festivals most absences at the school in the years leading up to World War I were not dissimilar to those already described at Heyhouses Endowed School:

8 December 1901   School opened this afternoon at 1 o'clock to allow country children to get home before a storm comes in.

25 June 1902   School closed this afternoon until Monday for Coronation festivities.

16 September 1904   School closed by order of the Medical Officer of Health on account of a severe outbreak of measles.[15]

Throughout the first decade of the twentieth century the number of pupils continued to increase and two new classrooms, for use as a new infants' school, were opened on 9 March 1909. On the same day the school log book records the number of 'mixed' pupils as 138, and the infants as 80.

No further additions were made to the building, but by 1949 it was obvious that the school was inadequate for the increasing number of pupils. In 1957 two acres of land were purchased in Kenilworth Road, and in 1966 the first phase of the present school was begun. In October 1975 the erection of two more classrooms was started, and in September 1983 a third phase was completed.

The St Anne's education question

Members of the nonconformist churches had always had concerns about sending their children to what they considered denominational schools, which in effect meant Heyhouses School. As early as 24 May 1897, at a meeting held at the Drive Methodist church, a committee representing several nonconformist churches had been appointed to look into 'the desirability of providing Day School accommodation for the Nonconformist children of St Anne's'. However at a further meeting held on 31 July the same year it was decided that, in reality, there was 'no probability' of such a movement being successful.[16]

At the same period both the nonconformist churches and the Roman Catholic Church 'were anxious to establish' whether the Lytham Charities were undenominational 'in order to forward their claims to the equality of their Schools with the Church of England Schools as regards distribution of income'.

At a public inquiry held at Lytham on 16 November 1898, the Assistant Charity Commissioner, whilst admitting that the trust was undenominational, made it clear that the Charity Commissioners would 'continue to support the view of the Trustees that the schools of the Foundation should have first priority'.[17] This discontent, particularly among the nonconformist churches, was increased following the passing of the 1902 Education Act which integrated denominational schools into the state system and legislated that they were to be supported by taxation. Because the Church of England had the large majority of denominational schools the nonconformists argued that it was unjust that they should pay for a religious education with which they disagreed.

A movement called the National Passive Resistance Movement was established and, in February 1905, the distrained articles of an un-named passive resister, to the value of £34 16s. 7d., were sold by auction at the corner of Garden Street. The purchaser however was 'acting on behalf of the gentleman involved in the serious matter of distraint'. Several nonconformist ministers were also present including Rev. W. Elstub (minister of St Anne's Congregational Church) who stated that 'we are here to renew our vigorous protest against an iniquitous Act under which this sale takes place'. After the sale a protest meeting was held in St George's Hall.[18]

The 1902 Education Act had given powers to county councils to provide elementary schools within their authority. However, in April 1907, notice was issued of the intention to enlarge Heyhouses Endowed School by providing additional accommodation for about 200 children. And in June 1907 a similar notice was issued of the intention to enlarge the Roman Catholic school by providing additional accommodation for 80 children. Appeals against both these proposals were sent to the Board of Education by members of the nonconformist churches in St Anne's, and throughout 1907 the columns of the St Anne's Express were regularly filled with correspondence concerning the need for a council school in the town.

Because of this strong diversity of opinion the Board of Education held a public inquiry into the educational needs of St Anne's, on 6 March 1908. During that day the schools at Heyhouses, Our Lady, Star of the Sea, and St Thomas' were inspected. The inquiry was held in the Public Hall and attended by about 300 people. It lasted from 3 p.m. to 5 p.m., and from 6 p.m. to 8 p.m. On 27 April 1908, the Board of Education wrote to Lancashire County Council:

> The Board have decided that the enlargement of the Heyhouses Endowed School by 150 places, and of the Roman Catholic School by 80 places, and the erection of a Council School for 300 children are necessary within the meaning of Section 9 of the Education Act, 1902.[19]

Throughout late 1908 and early 1909 a debate dubbed the 'Battle of the Sites' focused on where to build the new council school. Three sites were considered, and in March 1909 it was decided to erect the school in Alexandra Road (now Hove Road – Alexandra Road originally continued to the junction of St David's Road, South) and Sydney Street. Mr H. Littler, the county architect, designed the building, which was constructed at a cost of £4,847.

COUNCIL. SCHOOL.
ST. ANNES. ON. THE SEA.

St Anne's council school

The St Anne's council school opened on 29 August 1910, and was described as 'lofty, airy, excellently ventilated, with the classrooms so arranged that most of them will be flooded with sunlight'. There were separate entrances for the boys, girls, and infants.[20] The first headmaster was John. E. Fallowfield BA who since 1901 had been the first assistant master at Revoe council school, Blackpool. Miss Lilian Longworth was appointed headmistress of the infants' school.

The school log books covering the years 1910 to 1981 provide a detailed account of school life which, apart from less emphasis on attendance at church services, was not dissimilar to life at other elementary schools within the town. In February 1911 the report by the Inspector of Schools noted that 'This School … has made a promising start. The Headmaster rightly taking account of the natural capacity of the children has provided a full and varied Curriculum …'[21] Pupils were always kept informed of events of local and national importance, and during both world wars took part in activities to support the war effort.

Mr A. E. Briggs, who succeeded Mr Fallowfield as headmaster in 1936, inherited the problem of overcrowding which had been present almost since the opening of the school. In 1937 the Inspector of Schools noted that 'In assessing the work of the school it is necessary to make allowance for the crowded conditions under which it is carried on. The Hall has been temporarily recognised as a class-space since 1924 and continuance of abnormal conditions adversely affects the work and welfare of both children and teachers …'[22]

In 1945 the boys', girls' and infants' departments were amalgamated and

St Anne's council school. As a result of the implications of the 1902 Education Act the first decade of the twentieth century witnessed a series of debates in St Anne's as to the future of education in the town. One outcome was the opening of St Anne's council school, in Sydney Street, in 1910. The first headmaster was John E. Fallowfield, who remained in post until 1936.
BY COURTESY OF ROBERT HALEY

the school became known as St Anne's County Primary School. Some 348 children, aged from four to eleven were attending by 1955, and it was obvious that the school was inadequate for such numbers. To relieve the pressure Mayfield County Primary School was opened in 1962, to be followed in 1972 by Clifton County Primary School. St Anne's County Primary School itself finally closed in July 1981.

King Edward VII School and Queen Mary School

In November 1884 the trustees of Lytham Charities appointed a committee to look into the feasibility of establishing a grammar school in the parish of Lytham. The following February the trustees decided against pursuing the idea on the grounds that a grammar school for one hundred boys, with an endowment of about £1,000 a year, already existed at Kirkham. But as Kirkham Grammar then had only forty-four pupils, of whom only six came from the parish of Lytham, they considered that:

> The Establishment of a Grammar School at Lytham would injure Kirkham and those who know the two places will easily form an opinion of the prospects there would be of obtaining sufficient scholars to make such a School a success, in fact there can be little doubt of its entire failure.[23]

By 1901 however a different attitude towards secondary education began to prevail and, following the sale of land to Blackpool Corporation, the trustees

decided 'that it is desirable to erect … within Lytham … a good secondary school for boys …' The history of that school – King Edward VII School – which opened on 25 September 1908 has been recently published.[24]

However it was not until 23 September 1930, following the sale of further land in Blackpool, that a girls' school – Queen Mary School – was opened by the Earl of Derby on a site adjacent to King Edward VII School. By the late 1990s the school fees of half of all pupils at both schools were being paid under the Assisted Places Scheme. In 1999, as a consequence of the abolition of this scheme, there was a halving of pupil numbers and the school governors were forced into selling Queen Mary School. The last pupils left at the end of summer term, 1999, and the school officially closed on 31 August 1999. From 1 September 1999 Queen Mary School was merged with King Edward VII School and became known as King Edward VII and Queen Mary School.

St Anne's Technical School (College for Further Education)

At the same time that the trustees of Lytham Charities were building King Edward VII School, Lancashire County Council were completing their plans

Queen Mary School. In 1901 the Board of Education advised the trustees of the Lytham Charities that 'some money should be set aside for girls' secondary education'. However it was not until 23 September 1930 that Queen Mary School was opened on a site adjacent to King Edward VII School. On 1 September 1999, following a merger of the two schools, King Edward VII School became known as King Edward VII & Queen Mary School.

for the opening of St Anne's Technical School, on Clifton Drive, South. Built to a design by Mr H. Littler, the county architect, the new school was opened on 30 September 1907 and provided courses in cookery, woodwork and elementary science. The first principal was local councillor Robert Hugh Irving, formerly principal of the Collegiate School for Boys (now the site of the St Ives Hotel). By 1932 examination results for students included passes in shorthand, senior electrical engineering, building construction, and mathematics and geometry.

In 1949 the Technical School, or the College for Further Education as it had then become known, was still the only school, apart from King Edward VII School and Queen Mary School, providing any secondary education in St Anne's and Lytham. In the same year pupils aged fourteen and fifteen, from no fewer than eight elementary schools in St Anne's, Lytham, and the adjacent Fylde villages, were accommodated with the seniors of St Anne's council school at the college. In 1951 further accommodation was provided at Ansdell Institute and it was not until 1955 that a purpose built secondary school was opened. In 2003/04 the College for Further Education was converted into luxury flats.

Lytham St Anne's High Technology College

Ansdell County Secondary Modern School (as the present college was then known) was opened on 8 September 1955 by Sir David Eccles, the Minister of

St Anne's Technical School. The need for extending opportunities in secondary education was another factor in the education debate, and in 1907 St Anne's Technical School, later renamed the College for Further Education, was opened in Clifton Drive, South. In 2003/04 the College was converted into luxury flats.

Education. Built at a cost of £142,000 the original building was intended to be a short-term solution to the overcrowding at other schools in the town, a situation described, at the time, as 'the bugbear of education since the war'.

The first headmaster of the non-denominational mixed school was Mr A. H. Hall, BA. There were nine classrooms with accommodation for 400 to 450 pupils aged from eleven to fifteen years. The teaching staff numbered sixteen. Subsequently enlarged, the school was renamed Lytham St Anne's High School, and in 1999 became known as Lytham St Anne's High Technology College. It is currently (2007) the largest secondary school in Lancashire, with around 1,840 pupils.

Private schools

The story of education in St Anne's would not be complete without reference to some of the private boarding schools which have flourished in the town. One of the earliest was Montauban School for Boys (now Seafarers Restaurant) established in 1875 by the Misses Surr. In the same year John Allen opened Kilgrimol School where, on census day 1881, there were seventeen boy pupils aged between eight and fifteen years. In 1892 James F. Davenport entered into a partnership with John Allen, who sadly took his own life in 1904. The school continued to function until the late 1920s. In 1931 the premises became the St Anne's District Club.

In 1890 J.R. Banister resigned as headmaster of Heyhouses School and established St Anne's Grammar School for Boys. The building later became the Sandown Hotel, and in 1959 the headquarters of the Football League. The modern luxury apartments which now occupy the site are named after Alan Hardaker, the former secretary of the Football League.
BY COURTESY OF TED LIGHTBOWN

District Club (formerly Kilgrimol School). The story of education in St Anne's would not be complete without reference to the many private boarding schools. In 1875 John Allen opened Kilgrimol School, and in 1892 he entered into a partnership with James Davenport. The school functioned until the late 1920s. Since 1931 the building has been the headquarters of the District Club.

St Anne's College Grammar School was opened on its present site at Clifton Drive, South in 1902 by the Misses Oldfield. In that year it was reported that 'special attention has been given to the ventilation of all the apartments and to the sanitary arrangements'.

In addition to the academic subjects, both schools appear to have been involved in the social life of the infant town. In 1882 it was reported that 'Guy Fawkes Day' was celebrated with some enthusiasm and that the bonfire built by the boys of Montauban 'continued burning through the night and far into the following day', whilst at Kilgrimol 'some 400 or 500 people were present'.[25]

When John Ratcliffe Banister resigned as headmaster of Heyhouses Endowed School in 1890, he established St Annes Grammar School for Boys on Clifton Drive South, where subjects included Latin, French and sciences. The building later became the Sandown Hotel, and in 1959 the headquarters of the Football League. The site is now occupied by luxury apartments called Hardaker Court, named after Alan Hardaker the former secretary of the Football League.

The leading girls' school was the St Anne's High School for Girls. Established in Lytham in the early 1870s, by Miss Elizabeth Hall and Miss Catherine Sharpe, they removed to St Annes Road, West in 1875. On census day 1881 there were sixteen girl pupils aged between eleven and seventeen attending. The school later relocated to North Promenade and these latter premises, which later became the Princes Hotel, are now occupied by the Ormerod Trust.

On the occasion of the death of Miss Hall the *St Anne's Express* noted that 'her sympathetic nature, her cheerful disposition, and her inherent goodness endeared her to everyone who were brought into contact with her'.[26]

In 1898 *Barretts Directory* listed eighteen private academies and schools, including Lawrence House School which opened in 1895 under the headship of C. G. D. Hoare. Originally located in Clifton Drive, North, and then Clifton Drive, South, it moved in 1905 to premises in Links Gate, overlooking the Royal Lytham and St Anne's Golf Club, where it remained until its closure in 1993. The oldest surviving private school is St Anne's College Grammar School which has been situated on its present site in Clifton Drive, South since 1898.

CHAPTER TWENTY-THREE

St Anne's, 1922–2007

The 1922 borough elections

Elections took place for the new Lytham St Anne's Borough Council on
1 November 1922, when twenty-seven candidates stood for eighteen seats.
Four councillors at St Anne's, who had previously been members of the
urban district council, failed to gain election to the borough council: Coun.
J. W. Hallam, of the Parks Committee; Coun. A. E. Lee, of the Tramways
Committee; Coun. A. Rawstron, of the Sanitary Committee; and Coun.
J. H. Taylor, of the Finance Committee. In the opinion of Coun. Taylor he
and his colleagues had been defeated because:

> In the course of negotiations for amalgamation with Lytham certain
> conferences had to be held in camera before it was wise to divulge the
> nature of them to the public ... But these circumstances, supplemented
> by the perennial grizzle about rates, assessments and officials' salaries
> ... made a grand stick to beat the candidates standing for re-election
> ... Glib orators used it to such effect, joyfully holding up the 'old gang'
> to the derision and contumely of the community ... It was my belief,
> shared by many of my colleagues, that if sufficient new candidates had
> been nominated for all the vacancies not one of us would have been
> returned.[1]

The electors, however, had expressed their wishes and the successful candidates
were J. C. Martin, J. Harwood, and J. Watts in East Ward; J. R. Taylor,
J. Hallam, F. H. Hill in North West Ward; and A. England, R. Leigh,
G. R. Eyre in South Ward. Of the new councillors Coun. England had
previously served on the urban district council from 1906 to 1912; Coun.
Harwood had campaigned on the slogan 'keep a safeguard on the ratepayer's
money'; Coun. Martin was chairman of the St Anne's Ratepayers' and Citizens'
Association; and Coun. J. R. Taylor, who in 1901 had established the company
which continues to trade under his name.

Lytham St Anne's Town Hall. The Southdown Hydro Hotel was built by the Porritt family in 1896. In June 1925 it was purchased by Lytham St Anne's Corporation and converted into the new town hall. Now (2007) its future is a source of considerable debate.

At the first meeting of the new council on 9 November 1922, Charles Critchley who, due to his role as Charter Mayor had not stood in the election, was created an alderman and confirmed as mayor of the new borough. He was, however, well aware of the strength of feelings among St Anne's ratepayers, and his valedictory speech to the St Anne's Urban District Council had included the observation that 'my position [as Charter Mayor] imposed upon me a silence which I have scrupulously kept, but under which I chafed'. He added that 'I am told that if I had come before the electors I should have been relegated to the same obscurity as you [the defeated candidates].'[2]

The first resolution to be submitted to the borough council was to invite Lord Ashton to become the first freeman of Lytham St Anne's. Coun. Leigh and Coun. Hallam were created aldermen. They were replaced, as councillors, by W. Hope and S. Smith. In the years between 1922 and 1974 forty-six men and four women served as mayor of Lytham St Anne's, of whom nine were also honoured as freemen (Appendix G). The only other freeman was John Talbot Clifton who was granted the honour on 26 January 1925.

Municipal progress and inter-war expansion, 1922–1939

The years 1922 to 1939 were years when the new borough continued to expand, the council being responsible for a wide range of services including electricity, gas, roads, sewers, refuse collection, parks, swimming baths, and transport. The scheme promoted in 1920 by the former St Anne's Urban District Council, 'for the housing of the working classes' in the area between Heeley Road and Cross Street, was also begun.[3] In June 1925 the former Southdown Hydro was purchased for £14,263 and during the following eighteen months was converted into the new town hall. A particularly detailed description of the interior of the building was published in 1936.[4]

Progress was not always readily achieved, however, and on several occasions there were sharp disagreements between St Anne's and the Lytham councillors. In 1932 attempts to unify the council were made when it was decided that instead of rotating the mayoralty between the two towns it would be offered each year to whomever was considered best for the office. In 1939 Lytham and Ansdell Citizens' Association, St Anne's Ratepayers' and Citizens' Association, amalgamated, to become the Lytham St Anne's Citizens' Association.

Of all the municipal events during the pre-war years it was perhaps the controversy over 'Battle of the Trams' that caught the imagination of the

On 6 August 1923 the borough council began to operate a bus service on routes not served by the trams. The first route went from St Anne's Pier to Clifton Square, Lytham via Church Road, Commonside, Seafield Road, and West Beach. The service was every half hour, and there were four 1d stages. The first bus had a Guy chassis with Blackburn Aero bodywork seating twenty passengers.
COPYRIGHT UNKNOWN

Tramcars were
withdrawn
between Lytham
and St Anne's in
1936, and between
St Anne's and
Blackpool in 1937.
The replacement
buses included the
well-known Leyland
Titan "gearless"
double-deck one
of which, no 45,
photographed
here in 1963, has
recently been
restored.
COURTESY OF PETER
FITTON

public. As early as 1879 the former St Anne's Local Board had approved an application by the Blackpool, St Anne's and Lytham Tramways 'to construct, maintain, and work the Tramways ... in the district of St Anne's on the Sea'.[5] The application does not appear to have been pursued, and it was not until 1896 that gas trams began to run between Blackpool and Lytham, to be later replaced by electric trams in 1903. In 1920 the Blackpool, St Anne's, and Lytham Tramways Company was purchased by St Anne's Urban District Council.[6]

On 6 August 1923 the borough council began to operate a bus service between St Anne's Pier and Lytham Square via Church Road. A Leach Lane service commenced on 6 October 1923.

The tramways themselves began to lose money and by 1935 most of the aldermen and St Anne's councillors wanted to sell out to Blackpool Corporation. The man who defeated this proposal was Coun. J. W. Horsfall who, within seven months of joining the council in March 1935, 'won the main battle', persuading the council to vote in favour of retaining the transport undertaking under municipal control.[7] A bus service replaced the trams between Lytham and St Anne's on 15 December 1936, and between St Anne's and Blackpool on 28 April 1937.

Another outcome of the amalgamation was the need to rename roads and streets which had the same names in both St Anne's and Lytham. For example Clifton Street became Curzon Road, while Nelson Street became Holmefield Road. Although the number of houses in St Anne's increased from 2,350 in 1918 to 4,000 by 1930, the St Anne's architect Walter Wade, whose father had erected property in St Anne's Road West, Park Road, and Oxford Road, regretted that in his opinion, 'we cannot admit many of these houses as being of the type and character that we should desire for during the boom of the building speculative builders entered the town, and I am afraid they have left considerable legacies behind them'.[8]

Walter Wade gave no indication as to the properties he had in mind, and in fact much of St Anne's appears to have been developed by local residents or well-established building companies. By 1935 Messrs Arnold Ingham and Son had developed the Headroomgate district, and P. S. Uttley was 'changing the appearance of the open country of Leach Lane'.[9] In November the same year Coright & Sons Ltd built three dwelling houses in Highbury Road, and in February 1936 W. D. Ratcliffe erected seven dwelling houses in Parkside Road/Curzon Road.[10]

Leach Lane. During the 1930s the town continued to expand. Typical of local builders at the time was P. S. Uttley who was reported to be 'changing the appearance of the open country of Leach Lane'. This photograph depicts some of those properties, and also others built earlier in the century.

St Anne's War Memorial Hospital

At a town's meeting, held in the Ashton Pavilion on 11 Febrary 1920, it was agreed to support the erection of a cottage hospital, in memory of those who died in World War I, on the site offered by John Talbot Clifton. By March of that year over £8,000 had been raised by subscription, and on 28 March Coun. Leigh announced that Lord Ashton had made a gift of £10,000.

However, when Banastre Holme, St Anne's Road, East, the home of the late Thomas Bannister, came onto the market the trustees of the hospital fund decided that its conversion presented a better option than building a new hospital. A deed of assignment was made between Martha Bannister, the widow of Thomas Bannister, and the trustees of the King Edward VII Cottage Hospital (later renamed the St Anne's War Memorial Hospital) on 29 September 1920. The amount agreed was £10,000.

During 1921 Lord Ashton contributed a further £5,000. By May 1922 the building and furnishing fund had reached £26,609. Alterations and extensions included an operating theatre, enlargement of the kitchen, new lavatories, several baths, and an up-to-date electrical installation. The building contained

The property that was later to become St Anne's War Memorial Hospital was built in 1900 as the private residence of Thomas Bannister, and named by him as Banastre Holme. Purchased in 1920 by the trustees of the King Edward VII Cottage Hospital, and aided financially by Lord Ashton, the War Memorial Hospital opened in 1922. It was closed in 1988 and the building demolished in 1996.

BY COURTESY OF ROBERT HALEY

six wards – two large public wards, and four smaller wards for private patients.

The St Anne's War Memorial Hospital was formally opened by the Earl of Derby on Charter Day 1922. On the same day a telegram from Lord Ashton was read in which he announced that he was donating a further £5,000 to the endowment of the hospital. From 1922 to 1948 the hospital was run as a voluntary institution and, in order to provide continuous funding, an annual hospital fete day was held from 1920 to 1945, raising a total of £45,000. In spite of this voluntary fundraising, income was sometimes insufficient to meet expenditure, as shown in 1946/47, when there was a shortfall of £5,300. On 5 July 1948, following the introduction of the National Health Service, the hospital passed into the control of the Blackpool and Fylde Hospital Management Committee. In 1988, against much local opposition, it was decided to close the hospital. Final closure came in 1991 and the hospital building itself was demolished in 1996.

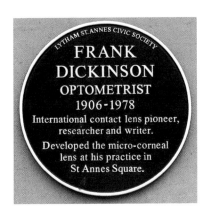

Frank Dickinson began his study of contact lenses in 1935. By the time of his death he was recognised as a top international contact lens specialist. This blue plaque, in St Anne's Road, West, was unveiled by his son and daughter on 15 July 2006.

World War II

As at the outbreak of World War I so in World War II evacuees were quickly sent to St Anne's. As early as 18 September 1939 an entry in St Thomas' school log book notes that 'a great number of people came to the school during the day to enrol the names of private evacuees'. During the period of the so-called 'phoney war' life appears to have continued almost as normal, and on 30 April/1 May 1940 schools were closed for Tradesman's Holiday.

Nonetheless, by early 1940, the borough council had signed contracts for the erection of an Air Raid Precautions (ARP) shelter at Cloverley College on St Anne's Road, East. The contract was awarded to John Heap and Sons and, in October 1941, the same company also carried out work at the first aid post in St Andrew's Road, North. In November the same year they converted the basements at the Lindum Hotel, York House, and the Sunningdale Hotel into refuges.[11]

Air raid shelters were erected throughout the town, and in the Leach Lane area, in addition to a shelter at the corner of Leach Lane and Dawson Road, there were shelters at the end of Chatham, Clive, Collingwood, and Rodney Avenues. Almost inevitably, shelters were also sometimes put to other 'uses'. On 31 July 1943 the headmaster of St Thomas' School wrote in the school log book that he had fallen over a 'portable lavatory placed in the dark passages of the A.R.P. Shelter', adding that 'The shelters are not fit to be used due to their misuse in the evenings.'

The grim reality of war first came to St Anne's on 1 October 1940, when ten high explosive and about thirty incendiary bombs were dropped on the town. 202 and 204 Church Road were severely damaged and there were two huge craters in the playing fields of Lawrence House School. The attack resulted in eleven casualties, including one fatality.

Throughout the war nearby Squires Gate airport was the base for various RAF units, and between September 1940 and October 1945 over 3,000 Vickers-Armstrong Wellington bombers were constructed at the factory there. This important military presence resulted in Squires Gate airport being bombed on several occasions.[12]

Although men and women from St Anne's served in all the theatres of war a particular impact was felt in February 1942 when, following the fall of Singapore, many Lytham and St Anne's men of the Blackpool Regiment were captured by the Japanese. On a lighter vein the entry of the United States of

America into the war would appear to have been the reason for the headmaster of Heyhouses School attending a course at Manchester University on 'American History'.

During World War II the people of Lytham St Anne's contributed £6 million pounds towards the war effort. Of this £2,884,932 was raised by War Weapons, Warships, Wings for Victory, Salute the Soldier, and Thanksgiving Weeks. Other wartime events included raising £5,000 during Aid to Russia Week, and £6,300 for a Spitfire. During Warship Week the borough 'adopted' the warship HMS *Queenborough*. After the war the names of 128 local men who had lost their lives in the war were added to the St Anne's war memorial.

Social life

It is only necessary to read any edition of the *Lytham St Anne's Express* to appreciate the extent of social activities that have been, and continue to be, a regular feature of life in St Anne's. During the past eighty years many clubs, societies and organisations have flourished and been superseded due to changing attitudes and interests. Churches, too, have continued to provide a social focal point for their congregations.

In the 1920s War Memorial Fete Day dances were usually held on the evening of the fete, as in 1928 when a 'Grand Carnival Dance' was held at the Hotel Majestic from 7.30p.m. to 11.30p.m. Prices were 8s. 6d. for Dinner and Dance, 5s. 0d. for Dance only. Dances were also regularly held in the Refreshment Marquee in Ashton Gardens, The Parish Rooms, The Westmorland Hotel, and Sharp's Cafe (the upper storey of Woolworth's).

The impressive ballroom of the Hotel Majestic was a particular attraction and the venue for dinner dances of many of the local organisations. From 1924 to 1929 three-times-weekly radio shows featuring Geraldo and his orchestra were also broadcast from the hotel.

Cinemas enjoyed their heyday during the years 1910 to 1960. As we saw in Chapter 20 the former Public Hall had become a cinema in 1911. In 1925 the building was bought by the Blackpool Tower Company for £40,000 and became the Palace cinema and restaurant. It continued as a cinema until 1959 when it was sold to Lytham St Anne's Freemasons. The lower storey is now the St Anne's Market. The upper storey is occupied by the Freemasons.

The Empire de Luxe Picturedrome continued as a cinema, latterly under the name The Plaza, until 1988. The ground floor had been in use as a bingo hall since 1984 and in 1989 the upper floor became a casino. Sold for re-development in 2001 the building was demolished in 2005.

In 1922 there were plans to build yet a third cinema in St Anne's. A company called the Princess Super Cinema Co. Ltd was formed with the intention of erecting a massive, 1,600-seat 'Super Cinema, Cafe, Grill-room etc' on a site in

St Andrew's Road, North, adjacent to the police station. The chairman of the directors was Joe Entwistle, then described as a cotton manufacturer but later as a well-established local estate agent. Mr R. P. Cottrill was the managing director. Among the special features were 'a spacious Entrance Hall with magnificent Elizabethan Staircase'. It was also intended that the 'Luncheon Room, Cafe and Roof Gardens' were to be 'patronised independently of the Cinema'. However, presumably due to lack of public subscription towards the purchase of shares, the cinema was never built.[13]

The ending of World War I had seen the return to civilian life of many ex-servicemen. To provide a venue for their social events an army hut was erected on Alexandra Road, at the junction with Nelson Street (Holmefield Road). First registered in 1922 by 1929 the club had progressed to a new spacious headquarters on the same site at a cost of £4,000. This building was opened on 2 October 1929 by Admiral of the Fleet Earl Jellicoe. At that time the club also served as an ex-servicemen's club and a Royal British Legion. In 1964 the building was extended further when a second storey was added for use as a concert room. The Royal British Legion meanwhile (1947) had acquired the

The YMCA has served the youth of the town since 1922 when a wooden building was erected in St Albans Road. New headquarters were opened in 1968, and a further rebuild and extensions were completed in 1999.

original clubhouse of the St Anne's Old Links Golf Club, in Mayfield Road, as their own headquarters.

Prior to 1920 there was no organisation devoted to the young people of the town. In that year Charles Critchley (then chairman of the Urban District Council), F. S. Airey, C. G. D. Hoare (headmaster of Lawrence House School), and G. W. Parkes met two organisers from the YMCA, the outcome of which was the launch of an appeal to raise funds to build the St Anne's YMCA Lad's Club. A public meeting was held in the Ashton Pavilion in January 1921, attended by HRH Princess Marie Louise.

By 1922 the wooden building, which served as the local headquarters for over forty years, was erected in St Alban's Road. Opened in December 1922 by HRH Princess Helena Victoria, the building originally consisted of a main hall, one committee room, an office, and a canteen. In 1948 the Mellor Annexe – a wooden building at the then Squires Gate army camp – was transferred to provide additional facilities.

During the early 1960s there was a determined effort to raise funds for a new, larger, building and by 1965 the first phase had been completed – the year in which girls were also admitted to membership. The new headquarters were opened on 13 March 1968, by HRH the Duchess of Kent. A further rebuild, and extensions adding yet more facilities, was completed in 1999.

Throughout the last eighty years the St Anne's YMCA has made a major contribution to both the sporting and social life of the community. It has also been most fortunate in the local men and woman of the town who have given many years of voluntary service to ensure its continued success.[14]

While organisations such as the ex-servicemen and YMCA have progressed from wooden buildings to substantial modern headquarters, no such progress has been made in providing an art gallery for the impressive collection of over two hundred paintings and objects d'art owned by Fylde Borough Council. The collection includes twenty-eight paintings by Richard Ansdell (who lived at Starr Hills, Ansdell); five paintings by Sir Edward Landseer; and four paintings by local artist Walter Eastwood.

The first donation – 'The Herd Lassie' by Ansdell – was made by Major John Booth (of Booth's grocers) followed, in 1926, by 'Rabbiting on Lytham Sandhills' again by Ansdell, the gift of John Talbot Clifton. It is however the numerous donations – including 'The Vision of Catherine of Aragon' (also known as 'Queen Catherine's Dream') by Henry Fuseli – made by Alderman James Dawson for which the collection is mostly recognised. Throughout the second quarter of the twentieth century Alderman Dawson gave some fifty art items to Lytham St Anne's Corporation to mark specific events.[15]

In 1956 the borough council discussed the possibility of erecting an art gallery – the Dawson Art Gallery – on land to the rear of St Anne's Library but the matter was never pursued. However in 2007 when Booth's opened their new store in Lytham they included an art gallery within the building, thereby enabling the collection finally to be put on display.

The modern town, 1946–2007

Although monetary restrictions held back progress in municipal development during the immediate post-war period, it was clear that the problem of lack of affordable housing had to be resolved. Prefabricated houses were first erected at Spring Gardens (now Derwent Road) soon after the ending of the World War II, and during the late 1940s and early 1950s the area north of Blackpool Road became the site of a major development of council-built property.

Such was the demand for these properties that Lytham St Anne's Trades Council launched a petition against the 'unfair method of allocating council houses'. At a public meeting, the housing committee was asked to make known the principles on which tenants were selected for the homes, and a second public meeting asked for a housing manger and a new housing committee. As a result of this pressure a housing manager was appointed in 1952 and a points system for allocating houses introduced.

During the 1950s and 1960s land throughout the town was taken for private housing developments. Additional housing was also provided by the War Memorial Homes, erected as a memorial to local men who lost their lives in World War II. Situated at the junction of Church Road and Smithy Lane, on land given by the Clifton estate, they were opened in September 1950 by the Earl of Derby. Extensions, costing £123,500, were opened in 1970. Further extensions are due to open in 2008.

One area of major development during the 1960s was that between Heyhouses Lane and Church Road. This area also housed the Government Buildings which had been built when various government departments were evacuated to the town at the outbreak of World War II.

When, in 1956, the Ministry of Agriculture, Fisheries and Food was relocated to Guildford, fears were expressed about the disruption this would cause to families who had settled in the town. As a result of representations to central government the Government Buildings became the location for the newly introduced Premium Savings Bonds, usually referred to as ERNIE. During the 1980 and 1990s the Department for National Savings progressively moved their offices to Marton, and the buildings occupied by other government departments.

In 1974, as a result of local government reorganisation, the borough of Lytham St Anne's was merged with Kirkham Urban District Council and Fylde Rural District Council to form Fylde District Council, later renamed Fylde Borough Council. The names of St Anne's councillors who have become mayor of Fylde Borough are listed in Appendix G.

St Anne's Road, West ('The Square') 2007. In contrast to the preceding photograph the first decade of this century has witnessed a regeneration project, backed by English Heritage and Fylde Borough Council, of St Anne's Road West ("The Square") and adjacent shopping area. The controversial "Domes" now being a major feature of the principal shopping area as St Anne's progresses into the twenty-first century.

The Bandstand, on South Promenade, erected in 1897, was a popular social venue. In summer 1909 St Anne's UDC made an agreement with Johann Beck of Manchester for him to act as bandmaster to the council for a period of ten weeks. One the seven requirements Johann Beck was required to undertake was to provide 'music of a thoroughly up to date character'. The Bandstand has recently been restored.

Many of the functions of the former councils were taken over by Lancashire County Council and this, combined with the privatisation of other services, has led to a decreasing role for borough councillors. Nevertheless, it is they who have ultimate responsibility for the future success and progress of St Anne's while, at the same time, safeguarding its heritage.

Although some early buildings have been lost, many others of architectural and historical importance survive. Since 1960 Lytham St Anne's Civic Society has campaigned vigorously to save various buildings and to encourage an interest in the historic character of the town.[16] The Public Offices on Clifton Drive, South are arguably the most important as they represent a visible and enduring statement of the civic pride evident in St Anne's at the beginning of the twentieth century.

In contrast the early years of the twenty-first century have seen concerns expressed about the individual identity of the town. In 2002, following a public meeting, various organisations came together and formed the St Anne's Town Council Steering Group. A petition was organised following which a submission for parishing – the first stage to town council status – was presented to central government.

On 29 July 2004 the Office of the Deputy Prime Minister signed an order creating the new parish of Saint Anne's on the Sea. The boundaries of the new parish are, with just minor variations, the same as those of the Local Board in 1878. Electoral wards wholly or partly in St Anne's, were each allocated one parish councillor, and elections in four wards took place on 25 May 2005. The parish council met for the first time on 7 June 2005, when Coun. Barbara Mackenzie was elected chairperson. At a meeting, held on 31 January 2006, the council members voted to change the name of the council to St Anne's on the Sea Town Council.

The creation of the new St Anne's on the Sea Town Council was just one further stage in the history of the area. It is a history which probably began, almost 5,000 years ago, with Neolithic people fashioning flint tools here by the sea; early written documents witness the granting of the first leases to tenants in Heyhouses in the early seventeenth century; and our picture of the past becomes ever clearer with the commencement of the new town of St Anne's on the Sea in 1875. During the past 130 years since the town was founded, it has continued to grow, expand and develop. Nevertheless it remains the quintessential coastal resort, the vision of which was so appealing to the early pioneers who were present at the laying of the town's foundation stone. And credit should be given to all those who, since 1875, have been responsible for the progress of St Anne's as it continues to evolve and change. Although the ever-present need to balance the expectations of residents while ensuring its continued prosperity as a seaside resort will, no doubt, continue to dominate events, the town can justifiably be proud to be known as the 'Opal of the West'.

Notes and references

Historical Societies, Record Offices etc

CS   Chetham Society
LPRS   Lancashire Parish Record Society
LRO   Lancashire Record Office
PRO   National Archives (formerly Public Record Office), London
RSLC   Record Society of Lancashire and Cheshire
THSLC   Transactions of the Historic Society of Lancashire and Cheshire

Newspapers

Lytham and Kirkham Times changed its title to *Lytham Times* on 25 May 1888. In these notes it is referred to as the *Lytham Times* irrespective of the date of publication.

St Anne's Express and District Advertiser was first published on 7 October 1898. From 8 January 1904 it was retitled as the *St Anne's on the Sea Express*. In these notes both newspapers are referred to as the *St Anne's Express*. The newspaper changed its title to the *Lytham St Anne's Express* on 24 September 1926.

Notes to Topography of Heyhouses

1. LRO, MBLS 3/1.
2. LRO, DDCL 2205.
3. LRO, DDCL 1731.
4. LRO, DDCL 1790.

Notes to Chapter 1: Early history

1. *The Wetlands of North Lancashire* (Lancaster University Archaeological Unit, 1995) pp. 90–1.
2. *Lytham St Anne's Express*, 26 June 1986.
3. Fishwick, H., *The History of the Parish of Lytham* in CS, n.s., vol. 60 (1907), p. 107 (hereafter Fishwick, *History of Lytham*).
4. *Lytham Times*, 25 March 1893.
5. Ashton, E., *Lytham* (Mather Bros (Printers) Ltd, 1946), p. 15 (hereafter Ashton, *Lytham*).
6. Higham, Dr M. C., 'Place Names and the Early History of the North West', Course Notes, Lancaster University, 1998.

Notes to Chapter 2: Lytham Priory and the origins of Heyhouses

1. For a more detailed account of the history of the Priory see Fishwick, *History of Lytham*, pp. 65–93; Although most are too fragile for examination, extracts of the priory manorial records have been published, LRO, Report for 1965 pp. 20–4; Lytham Priory *compoti* (accounts) 1346–1533, LRO, MF1/1.
2. Fishwick, *History of Lytham*, p. 3.
3. *The Victoria County History of Lancashire* (1906)
4. Fishwick, *History of Lytham*, p. 72–3.
5. I am indebted to Mr A. Piper of the University of Durham for this information.
6. Fishwick, H., *Pleadings and Depositions – Duchy Court of Lancaster*, in vol. ii, RSLC vol. 35 (1897), p. 16.
7. LRO, DDCL 685. This is a certified copy of the original *c.*1531/32 map in the National Archives. It

(hereafter *VCH*), vol. vii, *Lytham*, p. 215 n. 24.

was so certified by Ben Ayloffe on 15 March 1700.

8. LRO, DDCL Box 303. This also is a certified copy by Ben Ayloffe made on 15 March 1700. There is no apparent explanation on either this or the foregoing document as to the reason why they were copied in 1700.

9. Fishwick, H., *Pleadings and Depositions – Duchy Court of Lancaster*, in vol. i, RSLC vol. 32 (1896), p. 207.

10. Fishwick, H., *Pleadings and Depositions – Duchy Court of Lancaster*, in vol. ii, RSLC vol. 35 (1897), p. 19.

11. LRO, DDEY acc 5582, Box 17. Transcript of document in Clifton Papers, author unknown.

12. Ibid.

13. Ashton, *Lytham*, p. 27. Original source not stated.

14. Fishwick, *History of Lytham*, p. 16.

15. LRO, DDCL 2139.

16. Oldfield, F., 'The Mosses and Marshes of North Lancashire' (unpublished dissertation, Liverpool University, 1956).

Notes to Chapter 3: Community life in the seventeenth century

1. J. Kennedy (with an historical introduction by Dr Alan Crosby), *The Clifton Chronicle* (Carnegie Publishing, 1990).

2. LRO, DDCL 2161.

3. LRO, DDCL 686.

4. LRO, DDCL 687.

5. LRO, DDCL 2162.

6. LRO, DDCL 688.

7. LRO, DDCL 689.

8. LRO, DDCL 691.

9. LRO, DDCL 762.

10. LRO, DDCL 2228.

11. LRO, DDCL 1899.

12. LRO, DDCL 2163–2165.

13. LRO, DDCL 1662.

14. LRO, DDCL 2169.

15. LRO, DDCL 2177–2207.

16. LRO, DDCL 2187.

17. LRO, DDCL 2170.

18. LRO, DDCL 2168.

19. LRO, DDCL 2171.

20. LRO, DDCL 2197.

21. LRO, DDCL 2185.

22. LRO, DDCL 1723.

23. LRO, DDCL 1673.

24. R. Sharpe France, *Lancashire Papists' Estates, 1717–1788*, vol. ii, 1717, in RSLC, vol. 108 (1960), p. 73.

25. R. F. Taylor, *The St Annes Hoard*, in THSLC, vol. 118 (1966) (hereafter Taylor, *The St Annes Hoard*).

26. Taylor, *The St Annes Hoard*, p. 39.

27. *Lancashire Evening Post*, 25 August 1962. Article by Kathleen Eyre.

28. LRO, QSP 358/2.

29. LRO, QSP 497/9.

30. LRO, WRW(A), 1658–1700.

31. P. Laslett, *The World We Have Lost* (3rd edn, Methuen, 1983), p. 43 (hereafter Laslett, *The World We Have Lost*).

32. Laslett, *The World We Have Lost*, p. 44.

33. D. G. Hey, *An English Rural Community: Myddle under the Tudors and Stuarts* (Leicester University Press, 1974), p. 56.

Notes to Chapter 4: The community in the eighteenth and nineteenth centuries

1. LRO, DDCL 522.

2. LRO, DRB 1/128.

3. LRO, DDCL 1831.

4. LRO, DDCL 1848.

5. LRO, DDCL 1887.

6. LRO, WRW(A) 1728.

7. LRO, WRW(A) 1789.

8. LRO, DDCL 1910.

9. LRO, WRW(A) 1750/1.

10. LRO, DDCL 1941.

11. LRO, WRW(A) 1776.

12. LRO, DDCL acc 1325, box 26.

13. LRO, DDCL 1945.

14. LRO, WRW(A) 1760.

15. Ibid.

16. Lytham Heritage Group Archives.

17. LRO, WRW (A) 1701–1776.

18. LRO, DDCL 2050.

19. *Lytham Times*, 28 April 1880.

20. National Archives PL26. I am indebted to Dr M. Duggan for advising me about these documents.

21. Brierley, H., *The Registers of the Parish Church of Lytham*, in LPRS, vol. 33 (1908), p. 52 (hereafter LPRS, vol. 33).

22. LRO, 1742/QI/08.

23. Fishwick, *History of Lytham*, p. 36

24. LRO, 1742/QI/09.

25. LRO, QSB 241/4.
26. LRO, DDCL 1188/29.
27. LRO, DDCL 1193/1.
28. *Lytham Times*, 23 February 1876.
29. LPRS, vol. 33, pp. 47–51.
30. LRO, DDPr 25/6.
31. LRO, WRW(A) 1849.

32. LRO, RCLy 2/1.
33. J. Porter, *History of the Fylde* (W. Porter & Sons, Fleetwood and Blackpool, 1876), p. 103 (hereafter Porter, *The History of the Fylde*).
34. Ibid, p. 103.
35. *Lytham Times*, 26 May 1880.

Notes to Chapter 5: The manorial court

1. LRO, DDCL 1141. All subsequent information relating to the court of 1611 is taken from this source.
2. Ibid. All subsequent information relating to the courts of 1639 to 1712 is taken from this source.
3. LRO, DDCL 1129.
4. Ibid.
5. LRO, DDCL 1121.
6. LRO, DDCL 1124.
7. LRO, DDCL 1125.
8. LRO, DDCL 1118.
9. LRO, DDCL 1115.
10. LRO, DDCL 1121.
11. LRO, QSP 1170/15.
12. I am indebted to Mr W. A. Darbyshire for providing me with a copy of this Act of Parliament.
13. *Lytham Standard*, 8 January 1915. 'Oldest Fylde Fisherman' – John Melling.

14. LRO, DDCL 2176.
15. LRO, DDCL 1126.
16. LRO, DDCL 2134.
17. *Lytham St Anne's Express*, 18 November 1932. 'In the Days of my Youth' – Joseph Whiteside.
18. LRO, DDCL 1128.
19. LRO, DDEY acc 5582, box 23.
20. LRO, DDCL acc 2164, box 4.
21. LRO, DDCL acc 2831, box 8.
22. *Lytham Times*, 23 June 1880.
23. LRO, DDCL, uncatalogued box 311.
24. Ibid.
25. Ibid.
26. I am indebted to Mr B. Turner for this information.
27. LRO, DDCL acc 1325, box 1.
28. Ibid.

Notes to Chapter 6: The poor

1. LRO, QSB1/189/40.
2. LRO, DDCL 1141.
3. LRO, QSP 134/8.
4. LRO, DDCL 1141.
5. LRO, QSP 130/4.
6. LRO, QSP 146/3.
7. LRO, QSP 150/4.
8. LRO, WRW(A) 1675.
9. LRO, DDCL 1141.
10. Ibid.
11. Ibid.
12. Cunliffe Shaw, R., *The Clifton Papers* (hereafter Cunliffe Shaw, Clifton Papers) (The Guardian Press, 1935), pp. 115, 119 ,144, 147.

13. LRO, WRW(A) 1684/5.
14. LRO, WRW(A) 1710.
15. LRO, WRW(A) 1743.
16. LRO, WRW(A) 1745.
17. LRO, WRW(A) 1778.
18. LRO, PR 827/156.
19. LRO, PR 2646.
20. *Lytham Times*, 26 May 1880. *Lytham Past and Present*, no. iv – Scrutator.
21. Binns, *Notes on the Agriculture of Lancashire* (Dobson & Sons, Preston, 1851), p. 123.
22. LRO, DDCL, uncatalogued box 289.
23. LRO, DDCL 1208.

Notes to Chapter 7: Agriculture

1. LRO, DDCL 2183.
2. LRO, DDCL 2204.
3. LRO, Various Wills under reference WRW(A) 1630–1699.
4. LRO, DDCL 2139.

5. Cunliffe Shaw, Clifton Papers, p. 134/140.
6. Beaumont, W., *A Discourse of the Warr in Lancashire*, in CS, OS, vol. 62 (1864) p. 53.
7. LRO, DDCL 2215.
8. LRO, DDCL 2220.

9. LRO, DDCL 1115.
10. LRO, DDCL 1120.
11. LRO, DDCL 387.
12. Ibid
13. LRO, DDCL 1122.
14. LRO, DDCL 1124.
15. LRO, DDCL 1125.
16. LRO, DDCL 485.
17. LRO, DDCL, uncatalogued box 99.
18. LRO, DDCL, uncatalogued box 314.
19. LRO, Various wills under reference WRW(A) 1701–1773.
20. Holt, J., *General View of the Agriculture of Lancashire* (Augustus M. Kelley, New York, 1969; reprint of 1795 edn), p. 51.
21. Cunliffe Shaw, *The Clifton Papers*, p. 152.
22. LRO, DDCL 1115.
23. LRO, DDCL 1125.
24. *Lytham St Anne's Express*, 22 July 1932.
25. LRO, DDCL 1122.
26. LRO, PR 5010/12.

27. LRO, QSP 1900/12.
28. LRO, DDCL 2069.
29. LRO, DDCL 2107.
30. C.J. (Mrs Catherine Jacson), *Neptune the Wise* (George Bell & Sons, 1904) pp. 4–5. I am indebted to Mrs S. Allen for drawing my attention to this publication.
31. *Lytham St Anne's Express*, 22 July 1932. 'In the Days of my Youth' – George Gillett.
32. *Lancashire Advertiser*, 23 August 1871.
33. *The Visiter* [sic] (o/w Lytham, *St Anne's, Kirkham News*), 22 September 1887.
34. Ibid.
35. Ibid.
36. *Lytham Times*, 23 August 1871.
37. LRO, DDCL, box 314.
38. Ibid.
39. Lytham Heritage Group Archives.
40. Information courtesy of Mr H. Greaves.
41. Information courtesy of Mr J. Tomlinson.
42. Information courtesy of Mr B. Swann.

Notes to Chapter 8: Fishermen and innkeepers

1. LRO, *Two Centuries of Manorial Life in Lytham* (Report for 1965), p. 22.
2. Ibid, p. 23.
3. LRO, WRW(A) 1655/1675/1687.
4. LPRS, vol. 33, p. 46.
5. LRO, DDCL 1141.
6. Ibid.
7. LRO, QSP 597/9.
8. LPRS, vol. 33, p. 9.
9. LRO, DDEY acc 5582, box 32 (Transcript of document at the National Archives).
10. Ibid.
11. Ibid.
12. Ibid.
13. LRO, DDCL 1123.
14. *Lytham Standard*, 8 January 1915.
15. LRO, DDCL 1198/40.
16. *Blackpool Gazette and Herald*, March 1925.
17. *Lytham St Anne's Express*, 10 June 1932.

18. Ibid.
19. LRO, DDCL 1141.
20. Rosher, Rev. H. G., *Centenary of Lytham Parish Church, 1834–1934* (published by the church), p. 31 (hereafter Rosher, *Centenary of Lytham Parish Church*) (The present whereabouts of the accounts are unknown).
21. LRO, QSB/3.
22. A description of Lytham (1813).
23. LRO, DDCL 2134.
24. LRO, QSB/3.
25. LRO, WRW(A) 1829.
26. LRO, DDCL, uncatalogued box 314.
27. Ibid.
28. Ibid.
29. *Lytham Times*, 17 October 1883.
30. Eyre, K., *Fylde Folk – Moss or Sand* (published privately, 1973), p. 79.
31. *Lytham St Anne's Express*, 19 February 1932.

Notes to Chapter 9: The Lytham Charities

1. LRO, WRW(A) 1694.
2. LRO, WRW(A) 1683.
3. LRO, DDCL 1728.
4. LRO, WRW(A) 1683.
5. LRO, WRW(A) 1687.
6. Wright, G. L., *The History of the Lytham Charities* (The Guardian Press, Preston, 1950), p. 13

(hereafter Wright, *History of Lytham Charities*).
7. LRO, DDX 103/28.
8. LRO, DDCL 1835.
9. LRO, WRW(A) 1728/9.
10. LRO, DDX 103/28.
11. Ibid.
12. Ibid.

Notes to Chapter 10: 'Old' Heyhouses School

1. LRO, DDX 103/28.
2. LRO, DDCL 522.
3. LRO, WRW(A) 1734.
4. LRO, DVPr 1/7/4.
5. *St Anne's Express*, 7 November 1906.
6. LRO, DDX 103/28.
7. LRO, DDCL 2105.
8. Fishwick, *History of Lytham*, p. 107.
9. LRO, DDCL 533.
10. *St Anne's Express*, 7 November 1906.
11. LRO, DDX 103/28.
12. Ibid.
13. *Lytham St Annes Express*, 18 September 1933.
14. LRO, DDX 103/29. All subsequent references to

'Trustees account book' refer to this source.
15. *History, Topography, & Directory of Westmorland and the Hundreds of Lonsdale & Amounderness in Lancashire* (Mannex, 1851), p. 597.
16. *Lytham St Annes Express*, 29 August 1930.
17. I am indebted to Mr C. Barnes, the Headmaster of Heyhouses Junior School, for allowing me the free use of the School Log Books for the years 1873 to 1969 without which it would have been impossible to write the remainder of this chapter or to have obtained information that appears in other chapters of this book.
18. *Lytham St Anne's Express*, 10 July 1936.

Notes to Chapter 11: Religion in Heyhouses

1. Fishwick, *History of Lytham*, p. 9.
2. *VCH*, vol. vii, p. 218, Lytham Footnote 62.
3. LRO, DDCL 2139.
4. Fishwick, *History of Lytham*, p. 31.
5. Ibid., p. 36.
6. Ibid.
7. Thornber, W. *The History of Blackpool* (1837), p. 341; republished by Blackpool and Fylde Historical Society, 1985.
8. Fishwick, *History of Lytham*, p. 37.
9. Ibid p. 31.
10. Ibid p. 35.
11. Ibid.
12. LRO, QSJ/8/3/92.
13. LPRS vol. 33.
14. LRO, WRW(A) 1676.
15. LRO, WRW(A) 1675.
16. LRO, WRW(A) 1710.
17. LRO, DDCL 1141.
18. Cunliffe Shaw, The Clifton Papers, p. 114. Church Documents now in the custody of Lytham Heritage Group Archives.
19. Ibid.
20. Cunliffe Shaw, *The Clifton Papers*, p. 130 and 134.
21. LRO, QSP 1848/18.
22. Porter, *History of the Fylde*, p. 438.
23. Lytham Heritage Group Archives.
24. LRO, DDCL, uncatalogued box 99.
25. Porter, *History of the Fylde*, p. 438.
26. Rosher, *Centenary Lytham Parish Church*, p. 31.
27. *Lytham Times*, 13 August 1873.
28. Ibid.
29. *Lytham St Anne's Standard*, 3 July 1925, quoted in an article by W. Ward. The original source is not

given by Ward but the report would appear to be authentic.
30. Ibid.
31. Anon., *The Parish Church of St Anne – An Outline of its History* (published privately, 1937), p. 4.
32. *Lytham Times*, 1 June 1875.
33. Fishwick, *History of Lytham*, p. 23.
34. Gardner, G., *List of Recusants* (North West Catholic History Society, 1998).
35. Hilton, J. A., *Bishop Leyburn's Confirmation Register* (North West Catholic History Society, 1997).
36. LRO, RCLy 7/28.
37. Fishwick, *History of Lytham*, p. 50.
38. LRO, DDCL 411.
39. LRO, RCLy 7/28.
40. I am indebted to Mrs A. Mullineaux, the granddaughter of Joseph Henry Melling, for this information.
41. LRO, QSP 628/4.
42. LRO, QSP 1031/3.
43. Fishwick, H., *History of the Parish of St Michaels* in CS, n.s., vol. 25 (1891), p. 128.
44. Taylor, J., *Apostles of Fylde Methodism* (T. Woolmer, London, 1885), p. 131 (hereafter Taylor, *Apostles of Fylde Methodism*).
45. LRO, QSP 2316/6.
46. Shakeshaft, P., *History of Freckleton* (Carnegie Publishing 2001), pp. 82–3; Thomas Gaulter died in 1849 aged 85, not 1847 aged 82.
47. Dykes, Rev. E. W., *The Beginnings and Early Development of Lytham Methodism* (published privately, 2003), p. 10.
48. Taylor, *Apostles of Fylde Methodism*, p. 51.
49. Ibid.

50. LRO, QDV/9/36.
51. LRO, QSP 2465/14.
52. LRO, QSP 2481/13.

53. Porter, *History of the Fylde*, p. 439.
54. *Lytham Times*, 1 August 1902.
55. LRO, DDCL 1188/46.

Notes to Chapter 12: A vanished community

1. *Lytham St Anne's Express*, 18 November 1932.
2. *Lytham Times*, 6 April 1881.
3. LRO, DDCL, uncatalogued box 103.
4. Ibid.
5. Ibid.
6. Ibid.
7. *Lytham Times*, 7 September 1881.

8. Eyre, K., *Sand Grown* (Weaver & Youles Ltd, Lytham St Anne's, 1960), pp. 69–70. (hereafter Eyre, *Sand Grown*).
9. Arthur, C., *History of the Fylde* Waterworks 1861–1911. (Fylde Water Board, 1911), p. 260. [hereafter Arthur, *History of the Fylde* Waterworks].

Notes to Chapter 13: Origins of the town

1. LRO, DDCL 1200.
2. LRO, DDCL acc 1325, box 11.
3. Ramsbottom, M. and C. Pickup, *The Preston to Wyre Railway* (Hedgehog Historical Publications, 1996) un-numbered, p. 8.
4. LRO, DDCL acc 2831, box 7.
5. Ibid.
6. Ibid.
7. Ibid.

8. *Lytham Times*, 28 January 1874.
9. *Lytham Times*, 13 August 1873.
10. *Lytham Times*, 27 August 1873.
11. LRO, DDCL, uncatalogued box 97.
12. LRO, DDCL, uncatalogued box 124.
13. *St Anne's Express*, 31 March 1904.
14. LRO, DDCL acc 2831, Box 2.
15. Kennedy, J., *The Clifton Chronicle*, p. 104.
16. *St Anne's Express*, 13 March 1914.

Notes to Chapter 14: St Anne's Land and Building Company

1. LRO, DDCL Acc 2831 Box 7.
2. Ibid.
3. Ibid.
4. Harrison, G., *Rage of Sand* (Ernest Benn Ltd, London, 1971), pp. 54–55. (hereafter Harrison, *Rage of Sand*).
5. *St Anne's Express*, 14 October 1904.
6. LRO, DDCL, uncatalogued box 98.
7. *St Anne's Miscellany*, January 1878. [Copies of *St Anne's Miscellany* in LRO, DDEY acc 5582, box 18].
8. Ibid.
9. *Lytham Times*, 7 April 1875.
10. LRO, DDCL, uncatalogued box 98.
11. *Lytham Times*, 14 July 1875.
12. Harrison, *Rage of Sand*, p. 58.
13. Ibid, p. 60.
14. LRO, DDCL acc 2831, box 8.
15. LRO, DDCL, uncatalogued box 104.
16. I am indebted to Mr D. Thompson for providing the original document.
17. LRO, DDX 1970, acc 6479.
18. Harrison, *Rage of Sand*, p. 76.

19. LRO, DDCL, uncatalogued box 104.
20. Harrison, *Rage of Sand*, p. 76.
21. *Lytham Times*, 9 June 1880.
22. *St Annes Miscellany*, September 1877.
23. *Bury Times*, September 1893.
24. LRO, DDX 1848, Box 1.
25. *Preston Guardian*, 16 June 1894.
26. Greaves, D. W., *Chats concerning Heyhouses, Lytham & St Annes on the Sea since the days of 1870 AD* (published privately, 1925), p. 10.
27. *Lytham Times*, 7 April 1880.
28. LRO, DDCL, uncatalogued box 98.
29. Ibid.
30. LRO, DDCL, uncatalogued box 104.
31. *Rossendale Free Press*, 14 March 1890.
32. *Preston Guardian*, 31 October 1896.
33. Ibid.
34. *Lytham St Anne's Express*, 25 April 1930. 'From Sandhills to Village and Borough' by Walter Wade.
35. *Lytham St Anne's Express*, 9 September 1932. 'In the Days of my Youth' by C. G. D. Hoare.
36. LRO, DDX 1848, Box 1.

Notes to Chapter 15: Hotel, gardens and pier

1. LRO, DDCL acc 2831, box 7.
2. LRO, DDCL, uncatalogued box 9.
3. Ibid.
4. LRO, DDCL, uncatalogued box 101.
5. *Lytham Times*, 26 April 1876.
6. LRO, DDX 1848, box 1.
7. I am indebted to Mrs T. Adams for information about the Holloway family.
8. I am indebted to Mr R. Haley for a copy of the original notice.
9. *Lytham Times*, 8 August 1877.
10. Harrison, *Rage of Sand*, p. 77.
11. *Lytham St Anne's Express*, 6 June 1930. 'In the Days of my Youth' by J. H. Taylor.
12. *St Anne's Express*, 9 January 1914.
13. *St Anne's Express*, 16 January 1914.
14. *Lytham St Anne's Express*, 6 June 1930. 'In the Days of my Youth' by J. H. Taylor.
15. LRO, DDCL, uncatalogued box 98.
16. Harrison, *Rage of Sand*, p. 110.
17. Ibid, p. 109.
18. *Lytham Times*, 17 June 1885.
19. Ibid.
20. St Anne's Parish Church Magazine, September 1895.
21. *St Anne's Express*, 31 March 1904.
22. Cantrell, P., *Years of Piers* (Handbook Publishing, 1984).
23. Ibid, p. 9.

Notes to Chapter 16: Establishment of Local Board of Health

1. *Lytham Times*, 4 April 1877.
2. LRO, DDCL, uncatalogued box 97; *Lytham Times*, 18 April 1877.
3. LRO, DDCL, uncatalogued box 97.
4. *Lytham Times*, 8 August 1877.
5. *St Anne's Miscellany*, November 1877.
6. *Lytham Times*, 21 November 1877.
7. Ibid.
8. Ibid.
9. Ibid.
10. Ibid.
11. R. Knowles, *The Queen v. The Local Board of St Anne's on the Sea – Observations on the Recent Roads Trial* (Printed by J. Miller 14, Guildhall Street, Preston, 1891), p. 5. (hereafter referred to as Knowles, *The Roads Trial*).
12. *Lytham Times*, 27 March 1878.

Notes to Chapter 17: Local Board of Health, 1878–1894

1. *Lytham Times*, 22 May 1878.
2. Ibid.
3. *Lytham Times*, 29 May 1878.
4. *Lytham Times*, 3 July 1878.
5. Ibid.
6. Ibid.
7. *St Anne's Miscellany*, July 1878.
8. LRO, MBLS 4/1. All subsequent information in this chapter also taken from this source unless stated otherwise.
9. LRO, DDCL, uncatalogued box 104.
10. *Lytham Times*, 7 April 1880.
11. *Lytham St Anne's Express*, 29 March 1935.
12. Ibid.
13. Knowles, *The Roads Trial*, p. 8.
14. Ibid.
15. *Lytham Times*, 12 March 1879.
16. Knowles, *The Roads Trial*, p. 8.
17. Ibid.
18. LRO, QSP 4316/63–4316/74.
19. LRO, DDCL, uncatalogued box 97.
20. Knowles, *The Roads Trial*, p. 13.
21. Arthur, *History of the Fylde Waterworks, 1861–1911*, p. 77.
22. LRO, MBLs 5/7.
23. *Lytham Times*, 8 November 1882.
24. *Lytham Times*, 7 March 1883.
25. Ibid.
26. Ibid.
27. LRO, DDCL, uncatalogued box 103.
28. LRO, MBLS 5/8.
29. Ibid.
30. LRO, MBLS 5/9.
31. Ibid.
32. *St Anne's Parish Church Magazine*, September 1892.
33. *Lytham Times*, 20 August 1892.
34. Ibid.

Notes to Chapter 18: Urban District Council, 1894–1922

1. *Lytham Times*, 24 December 1894.
2. This and all subsequent financial information taken from the Borough of Lytham St Anne's – Abstract of Accounts 1935
3. LRO, MBLS 5/4.
4. LRO, MBLS 5/16.
5. *Barrett's Directory, Preston & Fylde*, 1904.
6. *Lytham Times*, 24 January 1902.
7. LRO, DDCL, uncatalogued box 315.
8. LRO, DDCL, uncatalogued box 97.
9. Ibid.
10. *St Anne's Express*, 10 November 1922.

Notes to Chapter 19: Amalgamation

1. *Lytham Times*, 26 October 1900.
2. Ibid.
3. *Lytham Times*, 2 November 1900.
4. *St Anne's Express*, 21 July 1916.
5. Ibid.
6. *St Anne's Express*, 28 July 1916.
7. Ibid.
8. *St Anne's Express*, 28 February 1919.
9. *St Anne's Express*, 1 April 1921.
10. *St Anne's Express*, 7 April 1922.
11. *St Anne's Express*, 5 May 1922.
12. Ibid.

Notes to Chapter 20: Town life in St Anne's, 1875–1922

1. *Lytham St Anne's Express*, 5 April 1935.
2. *Lytham Times*, 12 March 1879.
3. Ibid.
4. LRO, MBLS 4/1.
5. *Lytham Times*, 6 April 1881.
6. LRO, MBLS 4/1.
7. Ibid.
8. Ibid.
9. *St Anne's Parish Church Magazine*, January 1893.
10. *St Anne's Express*, 14 April 1916.
11. LRO, DDCL, uncatalogued box 309.
12. *St Anne's Express*, 5 May 1922.
13. *Pictorial Guide to St Anne's on the Sea* (No date but c. 1896. (hereafter *Pictorial Guide c. 1896*].
14. *The Visiter* [sic] *and Lytham, St Anne's and Kirkham News*, 26 August 1897.
15. *St Anne's Express*, 7 February 1908.
16. *The Visiter and Lytham, St Anne's and Kirkham News*, 26 August 1897.
17. Ibid.
18. *Lytham St Anne's Express*, 12 April 1935.
19. *Lytham St Anne's Express*, 17 January 1980.
20. *St Anne's Parish Church Magazine*, November 1896.
21. LRO, uncatalogued box 101.
22. E. A. Nickson, *The Lytham Century and Beyond – A History of Royal Lytham and St Anne's Golf Club* (published by the author 1999).
23. I am indebted to Mr T. Murphy for sharing his research into the history of the St Anne's Old Links Golf Club.
24. Mayes G. I. and J. E, *On a Broad Reach – The History of the St Anne's on the Sea Lifeboat Station, 1881–1925* (Bernard McCall, 2000).
25. Ibid. further reading; F. Kilroy, *The Wreck of the Mexico* (Lytham St Anne's Branch R.N.L.I., 1986). D. Forshaw, *On Those Infernal Ribble Banks* (Lytham St Anne's Branch R.N.L.I., 1992).
26. *Lytham Times*, 24 June 1879.
27. *Preston Guardian*, 30 June 1882.
28. *Blackpool Times and Fylde Observer*, 9 Aug. 1882.
29. Ibid.
30. LRO, DDCL, uncatalogued box 103.
31. *Lytham, St Annes and Kirkham Sun*, 18 June 1887.
32. *Lytham St Anne's Express*, 16 December 1932. 'In the Days of my Youth' – Harry Cooper.
33. *St Anne's Express*, 2 October 1914.
34. LRO, PR3226/1/14.
35. *Lytham Times*, 9 June 1880.
36. *Lytham St Anne's Express*, 13 September 1935.
37. Moor, F., *The Ashton Institute, An Outline History 1888 to 2005* (published privately 2005).
38. *Pictorial Guide*, c. 1896.
39. *Lytham St Anne's Express*, 23 December 1932. 'In the Days of my Youth' – Harry Cooper.

Notes to Chapter 21: Religion in St Anne's

1. *Lytham Times*, 15 April 1899.
2. *Lytham Times*, 5 June 1872.
3. *Lytham Times*, 13 August 1873.
4. Eyre, *Sand Grown*, p. 77.
5. *Lytham Times*, 31 March 1880.
6. *Lytham Times*, 15 April 1899.

7. *Lytham Times*, 19 September 1891.

8. Charles, L. R., *The Church of Our Lady, Star of the Sea – A Centenary History, 1890–1990* (published privately), p. 5. (hereafter Charles, *Our Lady, Star of the Sea – A Centenary History*). I am indebted to Mr Charles for allowing me to quote freely from his publication.

9. I am indebted to Mr M. Lord for providing all the foregoing information.

10. *Lytham St Anne's Express*, 10 July 1936.

11. Robinson, Rev. D. G., *St Anne's on the Sea United Reformed Church – Centenary Booklet 1880–1980* (published privately), opening page (hereafter Robinson, *United Reformed Church Centenary Booklet*).

12. *Lytham Times*, 22 September 1886.

13. *Lytham Times*, 4 April 1877.

14. Ibid.

15. *Lytham Times*, 22 August 1877.

16. *Lytham Times*, 15 October 1892.

17. *Lytham Times*, 29 November 1876.

18. *St Anne's Express*, 9 June 1905.

19. *Blackpool Times*, 3 December 1886.

20. *Lytham Times*, 27 July 1888.

21. *Lytham Times*, 5 October 1888.

22. LRO, MLy 5/1/1.

23. *St Anne's Express*, 9 June 1905.

24. *Lytham Times*, 15 September 1880.

25. Robinson, *United Reformed Church Centenary Booklet*, 'Some Milestones'.

26. *Lytham Times*, 8 September 1886.

27. Minute Book of St Anne's Congregational church 1886–1913. I am indebted to the present church officials for allowing me to quote from this book.

28. Ibid.

29. Ibid.

30. *St Anne's Express*, 20 February 1914.

31. *St Anne's Baptist Church Year Book*, 1959.

32. *Lytham Times*, 22 September 1886.

33. *St Anne's Baptist Church Year Book*, 1959.

34. *Blackpool and Fleetwood Gazette and News*, 11 July 1884.

35. *St Anne's Express*, 27 April 1910.

36. *Lytham St Anne's Express*, 16 December 1932. 'In the Days of my Youth' by Harry Cooper.

37. I am indebted to Mr D. Woodruff, Strict Baptist Historical Society Librarian for this information.

38. Chesworth, Rev. C.W., *King's Road Methodist Church* (published privately, 1958), p. 1.

39. LRO, DDCL, uncatalogued box 101.

40. *St Anne's Express*, 28 July 1909.

41. *Lytham Times*, 20 April 1906.

42. I am indebted to Mr L. Caro for providing me with much of the information for this part of the chapter.

43. *Lytham St Anne's Express*, 27 September 1940.

44. Ibid.

45. *Lytham St Anne's Express*, 17 September 1959.

46. *Lytham St Anne's Express*, 25 June 1964. Further reading: Anon., *The Parish Church of St Anne – An Outline of its History* (1937); Holliday, Evelyne, *The Parish Church of St Anne – A Century of Achievement* (1973); Cave, Rev. A. J., *A History and Description of St Thomas' Church* (1968); Charles, Les, *The Church of Our Lady, Star of the Sea – A Centenary History 1890–1990*; *Church Road Methodist Church – Centenary Booklet, 1888–1988*, in particular the article 'How an oak tree grew from a small acorn' by John Mayes; Robinson, Rev. D. G., *St Anne's on the Sea United Reformed Church – Centenary, 1880–1980*; Tongue, Rev. E. J., *St Anne's on the Sea Baptist Church – Jubilee Souvenir, 1884–1934*.

Notes to Chapter 22: Education in St Anne's

1. *Lytham Times*, 29 November 1876.

2. *Lytham Times*, 6 December 1876.

3. LRO, DDX 103/29.

4. Ibid.

5. *Lytham Times*, 10 December 1879.

6. Ibid.

7. LRO, DDX 103/29.

8. Heyhouses School Log Book.

9. LRO, DDX 103/29.

10. *St Anne's Parish Church Magazine*, September 1890.

11. LRO, DDX 103/29.

12. *Lytham St Anne's Express*, 17 November 2005.

13. I am indebted to Miss P. Johnson, former headteacher of St Thomas' School, for allowing me free use of the school log books.

14. Charles, *Our Lady, Star of the Sea – A Centenary History*, p. 12.

15. I am indebted to Miss J. Hornby, headteacher of Our Lady, Star of the Sea Junior School, for allowing free use of the school log books.

16. LRO, MLy 5/1.

17. Wright, *History of Lytham Charities*, p. 7.

18. *St Anne's Express*, 17 February 1905.

19. *St Anne's Express*, 13 May 1908.

20. *St Anne's Express*, 24 August 1910.

21. LRO, SMSN 1/2.

22. Ibid.

23. LRO, DDX 103/28.

24. Boddy, M., *King Edward VII School – The School by the Sea* (Scotforth Books, 2004).

25. *Lytham Times*, 8 November 1882.

26. *St Anne's Express*, 3 August 1910.

Notes to Chapter 23: St Anne's, 1922–2007

1. *Lytham St Anne's Express*, 3 June 1932. 'In the Days of my Youth' by J. H. Taylor.

2. *St Anne's Express*, 10 November 1922.

3. LRO, DDCL, uncatalogued box 315.

4. *Lytham St Anne's Express*, 14 August 1936.

5. LRO, MBLS 4/1.

6. For a comprehensive history of tramways in St Anne's see Abell, P. H., J. A. Garnham and I. McLoughlin, *The Tramways of Lytham St Annes* (The Oakwood Press).

7. *Lytham St Anne's Express*, 20 November 1958, 'Battle of the Trams Recalled' by T. Pomfret.

8. *Lytham St Anne's Express*, 25 April 1930.

9. *Lytham St Anne's Express*, 5 April 1935. 'A Review of the Pioneer Builders of St Anne's' by James Bowman.

10. LRO, DDCL, uncatalogued box 76.

11. Minute Book of John Heap & Sons Ltd. I am indebted to David and Elaine Cooper for allowing me access to these documents prior to their deposit at the Lancashire Record Office under reference LRO, DDX 2520.

12. For a detailed account of Squires Gate Airport during World War II see Ferguson, A. P., *Lancashire Airfields in the Second World War* (Countryside Books, 2004).

13. *St Anne's Express*, 10 March 1922. I am also indebted to Mr J. Harrison for providing me with details of his work on the history of Fylde cinemas.

14. For a detailed account of the history of St Anne's YMCA see articles written by Harry Youles and Ian Paterson, and published by the YMCA, on the occasion of its golden jubilee. I am indebted to Mr J. Cronin for providing me with copies of these articles.

15. I am indebted to Mrs M. Race for information about Fylde Borough Council art collection.

16. Coupe, M., J. Turner and K. Wayland, *The Listed Buildings of Lytham St Anne's* (Lytham St Anne's Civic Society, 2003).

Appendices

A. *Depositions concerning a case of infanticide, 1734*

The Information of Alice Rossall wife of James Rossall of Lytham ... Husbandman taken before Jonathan Cowburne one of the Coroners for the said County the 13th day of December 1734 touching the death of a Male Infant lying dead at Lytham aforesd

This Informant saith that she verily believes Alice Wade late of Lytham Singlewoman was on Tuesday the Twelfth day of November last Great with Child but did not then think she was near her time that on Wednesday following one Margaret English (Wife of Abraham English) now abroad told this Deponent the said Alice Wade was not with Child whereupon this Deponent on Thursday Morning following told the said Alice Wade twas well if she had not bore a Child and Shutt it, the said Alice replied, where should she have a Child, she had not and any body shou'd search her if they pleas'd. And this Deponent sent for one Alice Biggins widow a Midwife who together with this Deponent talk'd to the said Alice Wade about her having had a Child and for a good while she wou'd Confess nothing but at last told this Deponent and the said Margaret Biggins that she had parted with something but nothing that made any matter on. And this Deponent saith that she several times asked her what she had done with that she parted with but the said Alice Wade wou'd not acquaint her only told her she had put it in the Chamber Pot and thrown it out of the window, [Signed Ales Rossall]

The Information of James Rossall of Lytham ... Husbandman taken before Jonathan Cowburne one of the Coroners for the said County on ffriday the 13th of December 1734 touching the death of a Male Infant lying dead at Lytham aforesd

This Informant saith that he verily believes Alice Wade of Lytham Singlewoman was in the Month of November last Great with Child and lived in this Deponents House, this Deponent know not where she was delivered but saith that the said Alice Wade for three weeks or more before she was supposed to be delivered of her Child she used to lye in Bed for most part of her time. And further saith that he never saw the said Child 'till Richard Crookall one of the Constables for the Township of Lytham came to this Deponent's House on Wednesday last and Commanded this Depon't to Assist him in searching whereupon this Depon't took a Spade and by the direction of the said Crookall (who had some information from a little Boy) found a Male Child wrapt in a Blue Brat with a piece of blue Tape three times about its Neck and tied with a knott. [Signed James Rossall]

Lytham Parish Registers – Burials
  15 December 1734
  Alice Wade – Who Drowned Herself
  (Septentrionali Pte Templi – The Northern Part of the Churchyard)

B. *Copy of the Petition by the Sufferers from the Great Flood in the year 1719 to the Quarter Sessions for a Brief*

To the Worshipfull his Majesties Justices of the Peace for the County Palatine of Lancaster at the General Quarter Sessions of the Peace to be held at Preston in & for the said County on Thursday the 12th day of January 1720

The humble Peticion of Robert Bawbell, Richard Gerrard, Thomas Wilkinson, James Carter, Thomas Ball, Robert Bennet, Thomas Dewhurst, Robert Hardman, John Ball, John Heys and Richard Fisher, Inhabitants farmers and Tenants within the Townships of Lytham, Warton, and Westby cum Plumpton within the County Palatine abovesaid, Sufferers by a dreadful inundacion of the Sea.

Sheweth
  That upon Sunday & Monday the eighteenth & nineteenth days of December last past at the Change of the Moon & very height of the Spring Tyde there happened a violent Tempest of Wind which occasioned such an extraordinary & uncommon Flood that it break down & washed away the Banks Rampets & Sea Fences in the said Towns & overflowed the greatest

part of the Land lying there utterly destroying all their Lands & Grounds and washed down & carryed away above forty dwelling houses with the barns & outhouseing thereto belonging and all their Corn hay and household Goods and a great number of their Cattle, And your Peticioners being ready to make appear to your Worships not only by their own oaths but also by the oath of severall credible persons who have viewed the premisses that the damadges done to your Peticioners by the said Inundacion amounts to 2055 li (£) and upwards.

Your Peticioners humbly pray that your Worships will be pleased to grant your Peticioners a propper Certificate under your hands with a Due Representacion of their said Losses in order to obtain his Majesties most Gracious Letters Patents for the collecting and receiving the Charitable Contribucions of all such disposed Christians as shall be duly touched with a sence of human Misfortune & therefore be Ready and willing in some Measure to Contribute to such an unexampled Losse, And your poor Peticioners shall pray etc

> Robert Bawbell
> Richard Gerrard
> Thomas Ball
> Robert Bennet
> Robert Hardman
> Thomas Dewhurst
> John Heys
> Thomas Wilkinson
> James Carter
> John Ball
> Richard Fisher

C. *Watercourses: order issued by the Lytham manorial court, 5 October 1708*

Whereas much damage and loss in ye Sd Lordshipp has been heretofore Suffered and Sustained by water as well for want of ye watercourses being made of Sufficient breadth and depth as also for want of clensing and Scowring ye Same when need require as to us hath been evidently made apparent we therefore order all and every such pson and psons whatsoever who have any parts or Shares in ye Watercourses either on ye South or North Side of the Heyhouses that they make their sevral and respective parts or Shares therein of such depth and breadth as followeth (viz) from Leach Lane to ye west side of James Webster's low ground in the South heys to be made four foot broad in ye bottom and of sufficient depth according to ye Judgment and discretion of ye Overseers of ye Watercourses and Sea ditches and from ye West Side of James Webster's low ground to ye meeting of sd Watercourse being in the Pasture to be made six foot wide in ye bottom and of Sufficient depth as afforesd and that the Watercourses on ye North side of Heyhouses from ye head thereof all along to ye Sd meeting of ye Watercourses to be made six foot wide in ye bottom and of Sufficient depth as afforesd and the Sd Watercourses to be made and done afforesd on Such days and times as shall hereafter be appointed by ye Overseers which shall be sometime before the Twenty-fift Day of July next and at all times the [watercourses] to be so mentaned and kept on pane of ye Sume of Thirteen Shillings and four pence for every default made in ye premises

also we further order yt all ye Watercourses within the Said Lordshipp be well and sufficiently cleansed and Scoured at all times hereafter as often as need shall require upon sufficient notice given by ye Sd Overseers or any of them on ye like penaltie as afforesd and if ye sd Overseers for ye time being or their successors or any of them do or shall willfully neglect their office or duty in the premises they or any of them so failing in there duty as afforesd shall forfeit ye sum of Twenty Shillings for every Such default.

D. *Overseers of the poor – abstract of returns, 1804*

Total Money raised within the Year ending Easter 1803 by the Poor-Rates or any other Rate or Rates	£618 12s. 3d.
At what Rate in the Pound for that Year	£0 8s. 9d.
Total Money expended in that Year for the Maintenance and Relief of the Poor Out of House	£379 2s. 9d.
In the House	Nil
Expenditure in Suits of Law. Removal of Paupers, and Journies and expences of Overseers or other Offices	£55 15s. 3d.
Expenditure for any other Purpose, Church Rate, County Rate, Highways, Militia, etc.	£235 13s. 9d.
Total Expenditure of the Parish or Place within the year ending Easter 1803	£670 11s. 9d.
Money expended in purchasing Materials for employing the Poor	

Out of House/In the House	Nil /Nil
Money earned by the Labour of the Poor towards their Maintenance and accounted for to Parish or Place Out of House/In the House	Nil /Nil
No (Number) of Persons relieved from the Poor's Rate permanently, not including children of such Persons Out of House	30
In the House	Nil
No of Children of Persons relieved permanently Under 5 Years of Age	15
From 5 to 14 Years of Age	5
No of Persons relieved occasionally	30
No of Persons relieved who are above 60 Years of Age, or disabled from Labour by permanent illness, or other Infirmity	21
No of Persons relieved who were not Parishioners	15
No of Friendly Societies who hold their usual Meetings within the Parish or Place, if any	2
No of Members in the said Societies, including Members belonging to the Parish or Place, as well as those belonging to it	190
No of Children in any School of Industry in the Parish or Place	Nil

E. *Copy of the printed Regulations made by the Trustees in the year 1832 for the conduct of Heyhouses School*

AT A MEETING
OF THE
TRUSTEES OF THE SCHOOL
AT THE
HEY-HOUSES, IN LYTHAM
IN THE COUNTY OF LANCASTER
HELD THE 26th DAY OF MARCH, 1832,
THE FOLLOWING
RULES AND REGULATIONS WERE MADE:

1st.   That the Trustees shall, immediately after the vacations at Midsummer and Christmas in each Year, admit such and so many children into the School, (as well boys as girls) to be taught and instructed therein as they may think proper.

2nd.   That the Teacher shall instruct the children in reading the Scriptures, the Church Catechism, and such expositions as is by Law established, and knitting and sewing to the girls.

3rd.   That the Teacher shall instruct the Children every day in the week throughout the year, Saturdays, Sundays, and the times allowed for vacations excepted.

4th.   That no child shall be admitted into the School who hath not a perfect knowledge of its letters.

5th.   That the Parents of Children shall provide them with all Books requisite and necessary, and such as approved of by the Trustees or Teacher.

6th.   That all boys admitted to the School, shall be removed on their attaining to the age of 9 years.

7th.   That each child shall, on the first Monday in the month of October in every year, pay to the Teacher one shilling, or a compensation of equal value in lieu thereof, for fuel for the use of the School.

8th.   That each Child shall, on the first Monday of the several months of January and June, in every year, pay to the Teacher one Penny, for brooms or brushes for sweeping and cleansing the School-room.

9th.   That the following vacations be allowed in each year, viz – Good-Friday, Easter Monday and   Tuesday, Whit-Monday and Tuesday, and two whole weeks at Midsummer and Christmas.

J. WALKER, PRINTER, CHURCH-STREET, PRESTON

F. *Accounts and correspondence concerning Mr Clifton's rights to Lytham Church, 1706*

5/6 February 1706 – Stewards Account Book, Lytham Hall
Charges at Preston when I [Gilbert Heyes] went to Mr Starkie 3s. 2d.
Mr Starkie his fee about Lytham Sinecure 10s. 0d. more.
To Mr Shaw for searching [blank] at Chester (the diocese of which Lytham was then part) to see if there ever had been any induction and Institution of a Vicar at Lytham where it was proved there never had been any, Lytham being a sinecure 7s. 0d. Mr Shaw's fee 3s. 4d.   In all 10s. 4d.

25th February 1706 Lawyer's Starkie's oppinion about Mr Clifton's Rights to Lytham Church

For the Reverend Mr Fisher in Lytham

Sir

The designe of this is to preserve a good correspondence betwixt you & yr patrone Mr Clifton who has lately shewn me severll deeds relateing to ye Church of Lytham by wch I'me very well satisfied that the freehould both of ye Church and Churchyard is in him as Impropriator And that you have no collour [?] of pretence to give leave to any person liveing out of ye parish to bury there without Mr Clifton's pticular lysence or consent Nor ought you to oppose the buriall of any pson there who has Mr Clifton's lysence for that purpose And I'me satisfied by a certificate from ye register at Chester that neither you nor any of your predecessors had ever institution or induction to that Church nor have any further right there than barely a lysence from ye Bishop to officiate there as curate to Mr Clifton so can't in Strickness entitle yrselfe to any dues belonging to that Church otherwise than by Mr Clifton's connivance and prmision and being subject to an account to him for ye same Nor can you Inplifie [?] any further demands than what by contract or agreemt are due from him to you for Serveing that cure However I've requested Mr Clifton to be as Kind to you as formly he has been And think twill not be for yr interest to contend with him for small matters

If ye custome of ye Parish has formly been to elect foure Church Wardens And that Mr Clifton has Antiently had ye election of two of them And that twas for convenience sake the number is reduct to two then I think yt Mr Clifton ought to Nominate One and the parish another I should be glad to hear yt you had laid aside all thoughts of p'secucon of any of Mr Clifton's Servants for Marriage Dues that in Strickness of Law you've no collour [?] of pretence of title to …

Yr humble Servant
Nic[holas] Starkie
25 feb 1705/6

a true Coppy of a letter sent from Mr Starkie Genrll Attorney to Mr Fisher Curate of Lytham red and examined by – Gilbert Heyes [Steward to Thomas Clifton]

G. *Officer holders*

CHAIRMEN OF ST ANNE'S LOCAL BOARD OF HEALTH

1878–1880	James Astley
1880–1885	John Greenhalgh
1885–1891	Robert Hargreaves
1891–1893	William J. Porritt
1893–1894	Robert Knowles

CHAIRMEN OF ST ANNE'S URBAN DISTRICT COUNCIL

1894–1896	Robert Knowles
1896–1899	Richard Shepherd
1899–1900	Robert Hugh Irving
1900–1901	John Dent Harker
1901–1903	Sylvester Louis Stott
1903–1904	Thomas Ferguson
1904–1906	George Walters Spring
1906–1907	John Whiteside
1907–1910	William M.Thompson
1910–1912	Sam Hodgkinson
1912–1913	Thomas Ferguson
1913–1915	Joe Harry Taylor
1915–1920	Richard Leigh
1920–1922	Charles F.Critchley

MAYORS OF THE BOROUGH OF LYTHAM ST ANNE'S

1922–25	Charles F.Critchley * † F
1925–26	Edward R.Lightwood † F
1926–27	Arnold England * †
1927–28	William F.Holden † F
1928–29	Sydney Smith * F
1929–30	Arthur J. Price
1930–31	Wilfred Ingham *
1931–32	Harry Eastwood
1932–33	James H. Dawson F
1933–34	Charles D. Sharman
1934–35	William Hope * †
1935–36	Charles W. Urwin
1936–37	Charles H. Riley *
1937–38	Lady Edge F
1938–39	William Jowett *
1939–40	John Kay
1940–41	Jane Rossall F
1941–42	Lindsay Dobson *
1942–43	John W. Horsfall
1943–44	James R. Taylor *
1944–45	Frank W. Pickles F
1945–46	James Simpson
1946–47	Ernest Wren-Hilton * †
1947–49	John R. Butterfield F
1949–50	Thomas Banks *

1950–51	Ernest Kenyon *
1951–52	Charles S. Urwin
1952–53	Ernest Hoyle *
1953–54	Arthur F. Williamson *
1954	John A. Hinchcliffe
1954–55	Walter Dewhirst *
1955–56	John Faulkner
1956–57	William Crook *
1957–58	Isabella Coope
1958–59	G. Harold Smith *
1959–60	Traviss Carter *
1960–61	Norman G. Utley *
1961–62	Anthony E. Wilding
1962–63	Edward Crossley *
1963–64	John W. H. Lloyd
1964–65	Henry Nuttall *
1965–66	Doris E. Parfitt *
1966–67	Percy A. Nicoll *
1967–68	John M. Tavernor
1968–69	Ernest Porter *
1969–70	Wilfred Callon
1970–71	George R. Bowley
1971–72	Alfred W. Jealous *
1972–73	Jack Shepherd
1973–74	John E. Gouldbourn *

MAYORS OF THE BOROUGH OF FYLDE

1974–75	F. Ronald Jordan *
1975–76	Robert M. Joyce *
1976–77	Harry L. Cartmell *
1977–78	Harry Dobson *
1978–79	John Braithwaite
1979–80	Robert H. Fisher
1980–81	George Bradley
1981–82	David Howorth
1982–83	George Warbrick
1983–84	Eric G. Bamber
1984–85	Christine Hodgson
1985–86	Jack Payne
1986–87	Joan M. Mason *
1987–88	Richard Spencer
1988–89	John Tavernor

1989–90	Wilfred Callon
1990–91	M. Eileen Hall
1991–92	Louis Rigby
1992–93	J. Milton Lane *
1993–94	Jean Wilding-Walsh
1994–95	George Bamber
1995–96	George Caldwell *
1996–97	Alfred Jealous *
1997–98	Dawn S. Prestwich *
1998–99	Elizabeth Ann Smith *
1999–2000	Margaret Procopides *
2000–01	Paul Hayhurst
2001–02	Patricia Fieldhouse
2002–03	Hannah Cummings-Miller
2003–04	John Longstaff *
2004–05	Trevor Fiddler
2005–06	Ronald Wilson
2006–07	Harold Butler
2007–08	William J. Prestwich *

*   Denotes a councillor who represented an electoral ward wholly, or partly, in St Anne's.

†   Denotes those who were aldermen (as opposed to councillors) during their mayoralty.

F   Denotes an Honorary Freeman of Lytham St Anne's 1922–1974.

Bibliography

Primary sources

Heyhouses School Log Books.

Minute Book of John Heap & Sons Ltd.

Minute Book of St Anne's Congregational church 1886–1913.

Our Lady, Star of the Sea School Log Books.

St Anne's Baptist Church Year Book, 1959.

St Thomas' School Log Books.

Published secondary sources

Anonymous, *A Description of Lytham* (1813).

Anonymous, *The Parish Church of St Anne: An Outline of its History* (privately published, 1937).

Arthur, C., *History of the Fylde Waterworks 1861–1911* (Fylde Water Board, 1911).

Ashton, E., *Lytham* (Mather Bros Ltd, 1946).

Beaumont, W., "A Discourse of the Warr in Lancashire", *Chetham Society*, old series, vol. 62, 1864.

Binns, *Notes on the Agriculture of Lancashire* (Dobson & Sons, 1851).

Boddy, M., *King Edward VII School: The School by the Sea* (Scotforth Books, 2004).

Brierley, H., "The Registers of the Parish Church of Lytham", *Lancashire Parish Record Society*, vol. 33, 1908.

Cantrell, P., *Years of Piers* (Handbook Publishing, 1984).

Charles, L.R., *The Church of Our Lady, Star of the Sea: A Centenary History 1890–1990* (privately published, 1990?)

Chesworth, Rev. C.W., *King's Road Methodist Church* (privately published, 1958).

Coupe, M., Turner, J. and Wayland, K., *The Listed Buildings of Lytham St Anne's* (Lytham St Anne's Civic Society, 2003).

Cunliffe Shaw, R., *The Clifton Papers* (Guardian Press, 1935).

Dykes, Rev. E.W., *The Beginnings and Early Development of Lytham Methodism* (privately published, 2003).

Eyre, K., *Sand Grown* (Weaver & Youles Ltd, 1960).

—, *Fylde Folk: Moss or Sand* (privately published, 1973).

Fishwick, H., 'History of the Parish of St Michaels', *Chetham Society*, new series, vol. 25, 1891.

—, 'Pleadings and Depositions: Duchy Court of Lancaster, *Royal Society of Lancashire and Cheshire*, vol. 32, 1896 and vol. 35, 1897.

—, 'The History of the Parish of Lytham', *Chetham Society*, new series, vol. 60, 1907.

Forshaw, D., *On Those Infernal Ribble Banks* (Lytham St Anne's Branch RNLI, 1992).

Gardner, G., *List of Recusants* (North West Catholic History Society, 1998).

Greaves, D.W., *Chats concerning Heyhouses, Lytham & St Annes on the Sea since the days of 1870 AD* (privately published, 1925).

Harrison, G., *Rage of Sand*, (Ernest Benn Ltd 1971).

Hey, D.G., *An English Rural Community: Myddle under the Tudors and Stuarts* (Leicester University Press, 1974).

Higham, Dr M.C., 'Course Notes: Place Names and the Early History of the North West' (Lancaster University, 1998).

Hilton, J.A., *Bishop Leyburn's Confirmation Register* (North West Catholic History Society, 1997).

History, Topography, & Directory of Westmoreland and the Hundreds of Lonsdale & Amounderness in Lancashire (Mannex, 1851).

Holt, J., *General View of the Agriculture of Lancashire*, 1795 (reprint Augustus M. Kelley, 1969).

Jacson, Mrs Catherine, *Neptune the Wise* (George Bell & Sons, 1904).

Kennedy, J., *The Clifton Chronicle* (Carnegie Publishing, 1990).

Kilroy, F., *The Wreck of the Mexico* (Lytham St Anne's Branch RNLI, 1986).

Knowles, R., *The Queen v The Local Board of St Anne's on the Sea: Observations on the Recent Roads Trail* (J. Miller, 1891).

Laslett, P., *The World We Have Lost* (Methuen, 1983).

Mayes, G.I and Mayes J.E., *On a Broad Reach: The History of The St Anne's on the Sea Lifeboat Station 1881–1925* (Bernard McCall, 2000).

Moor, F., *The Ashton Institute: An Outline History 1888 to 2005*, (privately published, 2005).

Nickson, E.A., *The Lytham Century and Beyond: A History of Royal Lytham and St Anne's Golf Club* (published by author, 1999).

Oldfield, F., 'The Mosses and Marshes of North Lancashire' (Liverpool University dissertation, 1956).

Pictorial Guide to St Anne's on the Sea, c.1896.

Porter, J., *History of the Fylde* (W. Porter and Sons, 1876).

Ramsbottom, M. and Pickup, C., *The Preston to Wyre Railway* (Hedgehog Historical Publications, 1996).

Robinson, Rev. D.G., *St Anne's on the Sea United Reformed Church: Centenary Booklet 1880–1980* (privately published, 1980?).

Rosher, Rev. H.G., *Centenary of Lytham Parish Church 1834–1934* (published by church, 1934?).

Shakeshaft, P., *History of Freckleton*,(Carnegie Publishing, 2001).

Sharpe France, R., 'Lancashire Papists Estates 1717–1788, vol.ii 1717', *Royal Society of Lancashire and Cheshire*, vol. 108, 1960.

Taylor, J., *Apostles of Fylde Methodism* (T. Woolmer, 1885).

Taylor, R.F., 'The St Annes Hoard', *Transactions of the Historic Society of Lancashire and Cheshire*, vol. 118, 1966.

Thornber, W., *The History of Blackpool*, 1837, (reprint Blackpool and Fylde Historical Society, 1985).

The Victoria County History of Lancashire, 1906, vol. vii.

The Wetlands of North Lancashire. (Lancaster University Archaeological Unit, 1995).

'Two Centuries of Manorial Life in Lytham', Report 1965, Lancashire Record Office.

Wright, G.L., *The History of the Lytham Charities* (Guardian Press, Preston, 1950).

Newspapers and magazines

Barrett's Directory 1898, Preston and Fylde

Blackpool Gazette and Herald

Blackpool Times and Fylde Observer

Blackpool & Fleetwood Gazette & News

Bury Times

Lancashire Advertiser

Lancashire Evening Post

Lytham St Anne's Express, formerly *St Anne's Express*

Lytham, St Anne's and Kirkham News

Lytham, St Anne's and Kirkham Sun

Lytham Times, formerly *Lytham and Kirkham Times*

Lytham Standard

Preston Guardian

The Visiter [sic] and *Lytham St Anne's, Kirkham News*

Rossendale Free Press

'St Anne's Miscellany', Lancashire Record Office

St Anne's Parish Church Magazine

Index

Watson, Arthur 62
Watt, Ralph 128
Watts, J. 285
Wayman, Rev. James 259–60
Waynewright, William 26, 48
Webb, family 163, 176, 202
Webster, Ann 32
Webster, Elizabeth (1663) 24
Webster, Elizabeth (1674) 25
Webster, Elizabeth (1727) 36
Webster, Ellen 71
Webster, Ellin 25
Webster, family 17
Webster, James (1663) 24
Webster, James (1680) 54, 92, 121
Webster, James (b. 1680) 121
Webster, James (ob. 1751) 33
Webster, James (1778) 68, 128
Webster, James (ob. 1831) 34, 123
Webster, Jane 25
Webster, Jennet 127
Webster, John (ob. 1685) 26, 48, 127
Webster, John (1874) 116
Webster, Lawrence (ob. 1617) 15–16, 18, 46, 53, 73
Webster, Lawrence (ob. 1663) 22, 24–6, 74, 76
Webster, Lawrence (ob. 1691) 24, 76
Webster, Lawrence (ob. 1730) 37, 82
Webster, Lawrence (1737) 33
Webster, Lawrence (ob. 1745) 68
Webster, Margret (ob. 1674) 25
Webster, Margret (1674) 25
Webster, Margret (ob. 1727) 37, 39
Webster, Mary 34
Webster, Thomas (1646) 48
Webster, Thomas (ob. 1664) 74, 76

Webster, Thomas (1705) 92
Webster, Thomas (ob. 1748) 33
Webster, Thomas (ob. 1776) 33, 81
Webster, Thomas (1789) 32
Webster, William 77
West Crescent 220, 262
West End Farm xx, 35, 81, 84, 87, 134–5, 137
Westhead, George 42
Westhead, John 84
Westhead, Joseph 71
Whalley, John 95
Whalley, William 111
Whitaker, Richard 200, 263
Whinnerah, William 61, 216
White, Joseph 262
Whitehead, Anne 66
Whitehead, Christopher 65, 65–6
Whitehead, Joseph Wood *149*, 149–50, 152, 158
Whitehead, William 227
Whiteside, Jenny 133
Whiteside, John (1871) 244
Whiteside, John (early twentieth century) 199, 222, 253, 275
Whiteside, John (1924) 60
Whiteside, Joseph 55, 133
Whiteside, Mathew 24
Whiteside, Thomas (1842) 40
Whiteside, Thomas (1880) 228
Whiteside's Farm xx, 20, 36, 79, 82, 107, 131, 133, 136, 228
Whitten Brown, Lt Arthur 273
Wild, Robert 169
Wilding, James 144
Wilding's Farm xx
Wilding's Lane 189–90
Wilkin, widow 71
Wilkin(s), family 79
Wilkinson, Rev. John 103
Wilkinson, Mr 257

Willacy, Rev. Robert 106
Williams, John 192
Williams, Rev. Charles 262
Wilson, Nanny 83
Wilson & Deacon, Messrs 149, 155
Windress, Peter 121
Windress, Robert 77
Winstanley, Francis 81
Winstanley, James 81
Winstanley, Robert 67, 69
Winstanley, Thomas 50
Winstanley, William 79
Winstanley, —— 83
Wolf, John 49, 79
Wood, T. Horatio 217–18
Woodcock, John 154
Woodcock, Mr 205
Woodcock, Thomas 177–9, 184
Woodcock & Sons 149, 154–5
Woodlands, The 128
Wood Street 228, 230
Woods, Rev. William 121
World War I
    Belgian Refugees 237
    Convalescent Hospitals 237
    Royal Field Artillery 237
    Schools 237–9
World War II
    Air Raid Precautions 291
    Blackpool Regiment 292
    Bomb Damage 292, *292*
    Squires Gate Airport 292
    War Effort 293
Worthington & Co 227
Wright, Emmett 116–17

Yeat, Ann 34
Yeat, Francis 34
YMCA *294*, 295
Yorke, John 198–9